The 20th CENTURY

YEAR by YEAR

*The family guide to the people and events from
the first to the last day of the century*

General editors: Fiona Courtenay-Thompson and Kate Phelps

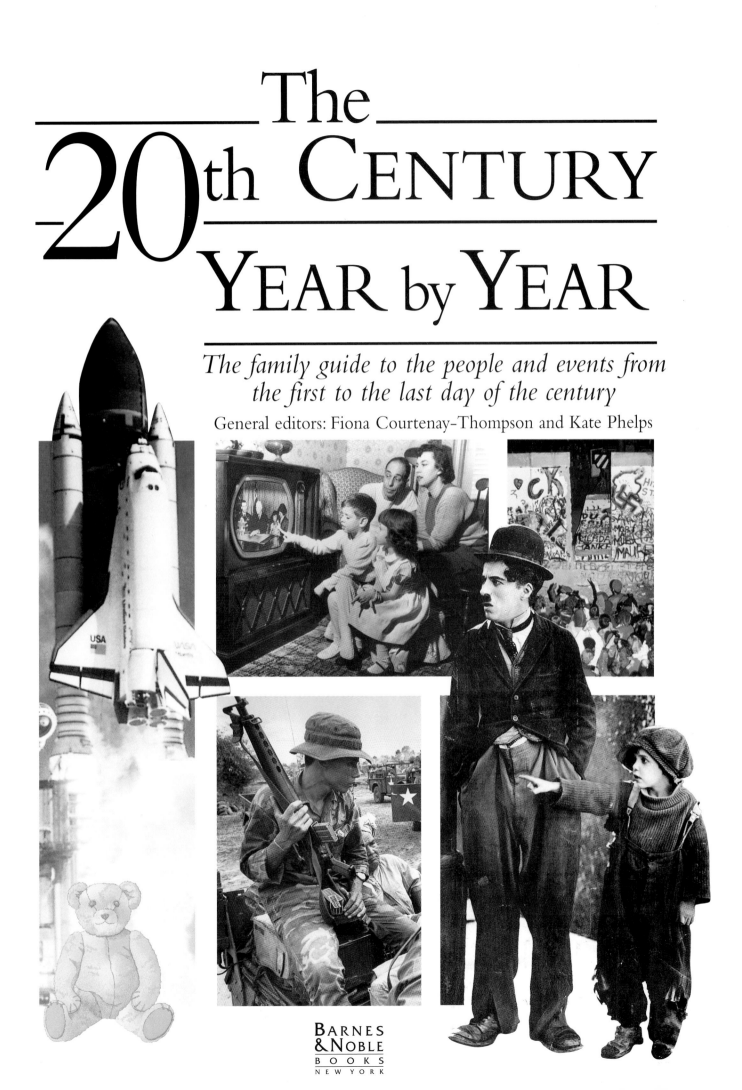

BARNES
&NOBLE
BOOKS
NEW YORK

A Marshall Edition
Conceived, edited, and designed by
Marshall Editions Ltd
The Orangery
161 New Bond Street
London W1Y 9PA

First published in the US in 1998 by
Barnes & Noble

10 9 8 7 6 5 4 3

ISBN 0-7607-2201-3

Originated in Singapore by HBM
Printed in Germany by Mohndruck
Graphische Betriebe GMBH

Authors: Charles Phillips, Neil Grant,
Margaret Mulvihill, David Gould,
Trevor Morris, Mark Barratt,
Reg Grant
Consultants: R.G. Grant (MA Oxon),
Roger Boulanger, Robert Stewart (MA,
D. Phil Oxon)
Senior Designer: Caroline Sangster
Designer: Siân Williams
Design Manager: Ralph Pitchford
Art Director: Simon Webb
Managing Editors: Kate Phelps, Fiona
Courtenay-Thompson
Editors: Claire Berridge, Jolika Feszt,
Margaret Mulvihill, Constance Novis,
John C. Miles
Editorial Director: Cynthia O'Brien
Indexer: Laura Hicks
Proofreader: Lindsay McTeague
Editorial Coordinator: Becca Clunes
Picture Research: Zilda Tandy
Research: Lynda Wargen, Angela Koo,
Michael Pitchford
Production: Janice Storr, James Bann,
Selby Sinton

CONTENTS

The Earth is very old—it formed about 4.6 billion years ago, but people have only existed on the planet for 2 million years. This fact hasn't stopped us, more than any other creature in the history of the planet, having a massive impact on the world. And the 20th century, a mere hundred years, has probably seen more changes than in the rest of the history of humankind. This fast-paced century has seen the Wright brothers' first flight, the appearance of moving pictures, the sinking of the *Titanic*, two world wars, the first radio and television broadcasts, the splitting of the atom, the assassination of a president, astronaut Neil Armstrong's first steps on the moon, the fall of the Soviet Empire, and the ever-increasing dominance of computers. The list goes on and on.

The 20th Century Year by Year, written in the style of a newspaper and illustrated with the best contemporary photographs, celebrates this dramatic century, decade by decade, year by year. It tells the story of the headline events and the people involved in them: politicians and movie stars, athletes and kings, hippies and punks, scientists and fashion designers—and also the millions who have found themselves caught up in the making of history. Scattered throughout the book are special pages on the trends, scientific breakthroughs, ideologies, and other topics of global significance that have characterized this century.

This chronicle allows you to revisit the 20th century in a spirit of wonder for its achievements, but with the benefit of hindsight to recognize its failures. So whether it is read for simple pleasure in history or for more serious study, this exciting book gives many answers to why the world is the way it is today and what lessons can be learned from the past for the new millennium.

1950

1951

THE 20TH CENTURY YEAR BY YEAR relives the events of the last 100 years with stunning contemporary photographs and newspaper-style stories. In these fact-packed pages, you can rediscover the people, events, and ideas that have shaped our lives.

The year-by-year approach makes the information easy to find for all the family. Each year has a double-page spread, an example of which is shown below. It is annotated to explain the features that make this chronicle of this century unique and informative.

◀ *Color bar at top of the page signposts the year.*

▶ *Each decade has a different colored bar running down the right hand page for easy access.*

1956

▲ *A different colored panel shows each new decade.*

1956

▲ *Icon for the year featured is enlarged for quick reference.*

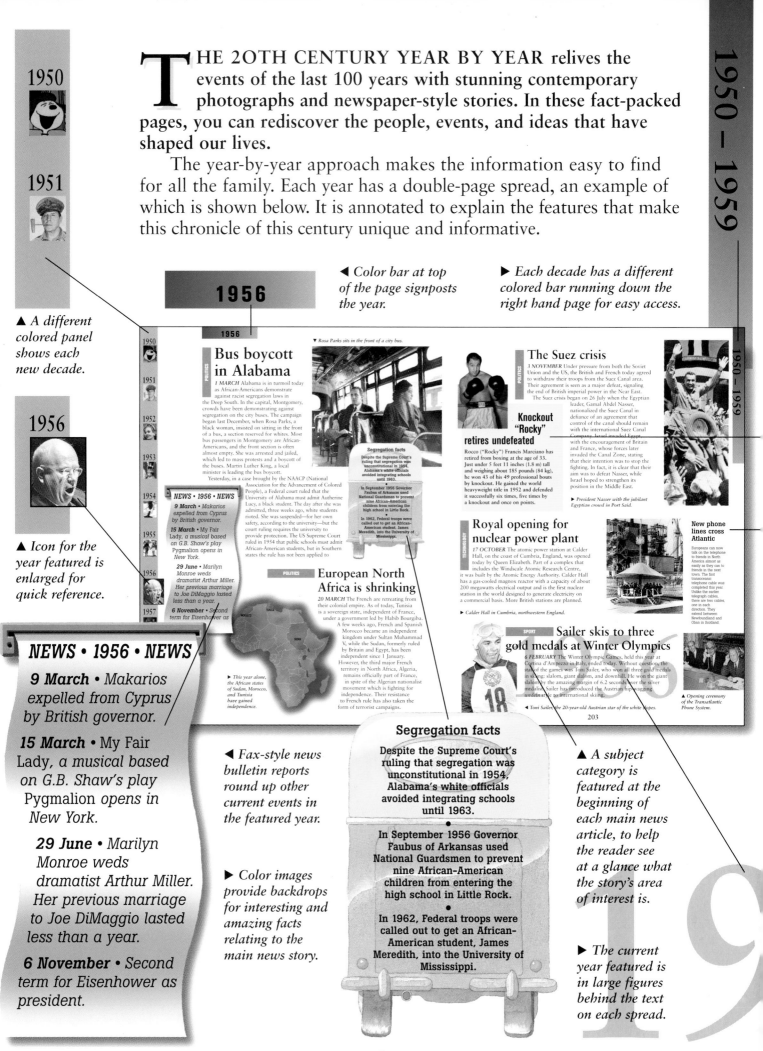

Bus boycott in Alabama

POLITICS

1 MARCH Alabama is in turmoil today as African-Americans demonstrate against racist segregation laws in the Deep South. In the capital, Montgomery, crowds have been demonstrating against segregation on the city buses. The campaign began last December, when Rosa Parks, a black woman, insisted on sitting in the front of a bus, a section reserved for whites. Most bus passengers in Montgomery are African-Americans, and the front section is often almost empty. She was arrested and jailed, which led to mass protests and a boycott of the buses. Martin Luther King, a local minister is leading the bus boycott.

Yesterday, in a case brought by the NAACP (National Association for the Advancement of Colored People), a Federal court ruled that the University of Alabama must admit Autherine Lucy. The day after she was admitted, three weeks ago, white students rioted. She was suspended—for her own safety, according to the university—but the court ruling requires the university to provide protection. The US Supreme Court ruled in 1954 that public schools must admit African-American students, but in Southern states the rule has not been applied to

▼ *Rosa Parks sits in the front of a city bus.*

Segregation facts

Despite the Supreme Court's ruling that segregation was unconstitutional in 1954, Alabama's white officials avoided integrating schools until 1963.

In September 1956 Governor Faubus of Arkansas used National Guardsmen to prevent nine African-American children from entering the high school in Little Rock.

In 1962, Federal troops were called out to get an African-American student, James Meredith, into the University of Mississippi.

POLITICS

European North Africa is shrinking

20 MARCH The French are retreating from their colonial empire. As of today, Tunisia is a sovereign state, independent of France, under a government led by Habib Bourguiba. A few weeks ago, French and Spanish Morocco became an independent kingdom under Sultan Muhammad V, while the Sudan, formerly ruled by Britain and Egypt, has been independent since 1 January. However, the third major French territory in North Africa, Algeria, remains officially part of France, in spite of the Algerian nationalist movement which is fighting for independence. Their resistance to French rule has also taken the form of terrorist campaigns.

▶ *This year alone, the African states of Sudan, Morocco, and Tunisia have gained independence.*

The Suez crisis

POLITICS

3 NOVEMBER Under pressure from both the Soviet Union and the US, the British and French today agreed to withdraw their troops from the Suez Canal area. Their agreement is seen as a major defeat, signaling the end of British imperial power in the Near East.

The Suez crisis began on 26 July when the Egyptian leader, Gamal Abdel Nasser, nationalized the Suez Canal in defiance of an agreement that control of the canal should remain with the international Suez Canal Company. Israel invaded Egypt, with the encouragement of Britain and France, whose forces later invaded the Canal Zone, stating that their intention was to stop the fighting. In fact, it is clear that their aim was to defeat Nasser, while Israel hoped to strengthen its position in the Middle East.

▶ *President Nasser with the jubilant Egyptian crowd in Port Said.*

Knockout "Rocky" retires undefeated

Rocco ("Rocky") Francis Marciano has retired from boxing at the age of 33. Just under 5 feet 11 inches (1.8 m) tall and weighing about 185 pounds (84 kg), he won 43 of his 49 professional bouts by knockout. He gained the world heavyweight title in 1952 and defended it successfully six times, five times by a knockout and once on points.

Royal opening for nuclear power plant

TECHNOLOGY

17 OCTOBER The atomic power station at Calder Hall, on the coast of Cumbria, England, was opened today by Queen Elizabeth. Part of a complex that includes the Windscale Atomic Research Centre, it was built by the Atomic Energy Authority. Calder Hall has a gas-cooled magnox reactor with a capacity of about 200 megawatts electrical output and is the first nuclear station in the world designed to generate electricity on a commercial basis. More British stations are planned.

▶ *Calder Hall in Cumbria, northwestern England.*

New phone lines cross Atlantic

Europeans can now talk on the telephone to friends in North America almost as easily as they can to friends in the next town. The first transoceanic telephone cable was completed this year. Unlike the earlier telegraph cables, there are two cables, one in each direction. They extend between Newfoundland and Oban in Scotland.

SPORT

Sailer skis to three gold medals at Winter Olympics

6 FEBRUARY The Winter Olympic Games, held this year at Cortina d'Ampezzo in Italy, ended today. Without question, the star of the games was Toni Sailer, who won all three gold medals in skiing: slalom, giant slalom, and downhill. He won the giant slalom by the amazing margin of 6.2 seconds over the silver medalist. Sailer has introduced the Austrian hip-wagging *wedeln* style to international skiing.

▶ *Toni Sailer, the 20-year-old Austrian star of the white slopes.*

▲ *Opening ceremony of the Transatlantic Phone System.*

203

NEWS • 1956 • NEWS

9 March • Makarios expelled from Cyprus by British governor.

15 March • My Fair Lady, a musical based on G.B. Shaw's play Pygmalion opens in New York.

29 June • Marilyn Monroe weds dramatist Arthur Miller. Her previous marriage to Joe DiMaggio lasted less than a year.

6 November • Second term for Eisenhower as

NEWS • 1956 • NEWS

9 March • Makarios expelled from Cyprus by British governor.

15 March • My Fair Lady, *a musical based on G.B. Shaw's play* Pygmalion *opens in New York.*

29 June • Marilyn Monroe weds dramatist Arthur Miller. Her previous marriage to Joe DiMaggio lasted less than a year.

6 November • Second term for Eisenhower as president.

◀ *Fax-style news bulletin reports round up other current events in the featured year.*

▶ *Color images provide backdrops for interesting and amazing facts relating to the main news story.*

Segregation facts

Despite the Supreme Court's ruling that segregation was unconstitutional in 1954, Alabama's white officials avoided integrating schools until 1963.

In September 1956 Governor Faubus of Arkansas used National Guardsmen to prevent nine African-American children from entering the high school in Little Rock.

In 1962, Federal troops were called out to get an African-American student, James Meredith, into the University of Mississippi.

▲ *A subject category is featured at the beginning of each main news article, to help the reader see at a glance what the story's area of interest is.*

▶ *The current year featured is in large figures behind the text on each spread.*

▼ *Yellow boxes are used to feature the more lighthearted popular and cultural news stories.*

Knockout "Rocky" retires undefeated

Rocco ("Rocky") Francis Marciano has retired from boxing at the age of 33. Just under 5 feet 11 inches (1.8 meters) tall and about 185 pounds (84 kg), he won 43 of his 49 professional bouts by knockout. He gained the world heavyweight title in 1952 and defended it successfully six times, five times by a knockout, and once on points.

About the special spreads

This chronicle of 20th-century events also features 30 special spreads, each focusing on a particular theme or idea which had a major impact on the history and development of this century. The subjects examined in this way highlight a range of cultural, scientific, technological, and historic milestones or episodes which left, or will leave, their mark on humankind's progression in the world.

The twentieth century has witnessed an incredible leap forward in the advancement of knowledge. At the start of the century we were just getting to grips with the incredible feat of flying, and now as the century draws to an end we are pushing farther and farther out into space—with all the amazing discoveries that this brings. Cultural beliefs and ideologies have shaped the way people think and behave—the features on terrorism, counterculture, communism, youth culture, Nazism, and Fascism explore the way in which these "movements" have shaped the course of our history. The special spreads give us an invaluable understanding of some of the major elements that have made the twentieth century what it is.

New phone lines cross Atlantic

We can now talk on the telephone to friends in North America almost as easily as we can to friends in the next town. The first transoceanic telephone cable was completed this year. Unlike the earlier telegraph cables, there are two cables, one in each direction. They extend between Newfoundland and Oban in Scotland.

▶ *The special spreads feature additional interesting facts and information.*

◀ *Stories in the side columns feature innovations or new inventions and scientific break-throughs and current popular trends.*

1900
1901
1902
1903
1904
1905
1906
1907
1908
1909

1900

As the new century dawned, many people in the US and Europe looked forward to the continuing success of their economies and cultures, which dominated the world.

In the first decade of the 20th century, when electricity, telephones, and automobiles became part of daily life, it seemed that technological progress was limitless. Although Britain's empire continued to span the globe, the US was emerging as a superpower.

▲ *One of the entrances to Paris' brand-new Métro system.*

Cakewalk craze!

The cakewalk is the latest dance to hit fashionable ballrooms. Couples form a square with the men on the inside and strut around the square. They are eliminated one by one by judges, who consider the elegance of the men, the grace of the women, and the inventiveness of the dancers. The remaining pair win a decorated cake.

Exhibition facts

The construction site extended over 547 acres (221 hectares).

•

The 350-foot (106-meter) Great Wheel had 80 cars, each holding 20 people.

•

There were 76,000 exhibitors: 36,000 from France and 40,000 from overseas.

•

The exhibition made a profit of five million francs.

•

A whole gallery of the Palais de l'Industrie was devoted to the car, which was barely five years old.

CULTURE

World exhibition opens with style

14 APRIL The International Exhibition opened in Paris today. The exhibition, held to celebrate the new century, is the biggest ever seen in Europe. It was officially opened by the president of France, Emile Loubet, who, in his address, called for world peace. The exhibition is viewed by the world as a sign that France is determined to assert its imperial power.

The exhibition features "palaces" and outstanding attractions from every major nation. This is the third international exhibition to be held in Paris: the first was in 1878 and the second in 1889, when the Eiffel Tower was built. Later this year, in July, Paris is also due to host the Olympic Games.

▼*Paris, with the exhibition buildings in the foreground.*

Métro arrives!

TRANSPORT

19 JULY The Paris Métro (underground railroad) opened today, almost 40 years after the world's first system in London. Many of the stations are decorated in the popular Art Nouveau style. Some of the trains that will run on the Métro's 119 miles (192 km) of track have rubber tires, giving Parisian commuters an exceptionally smooth ride.

▲ *British troops face Boer forces on the outskirts of Mafeking.*

Turning point in Boer War

WAR

30 SEPTEMBER British commander-in-chief Lord Roberts assured London today that the year-old Second Boer War will soon be over. The Boers, who are descendants of Dutch settlers in South Africa, have proved skillful fighters. In the "Black Week" of December 1899, the British forces suffered three serious defeats. Britain sent reinforcements and achieved an historic victory at Mafeking in May, driving the Boers from their positions. But the Boer forces have only been scattered, not captured, so the war may drag on.

New camera in US

The Eastman Kodak Company today introduced a new camera. The Kodak "Brownie" costs just one dollar and is the first camera to have a removable film container. This means that the film can be unloaded and sent back to the factory for processing. Previously, the entire camera had to be returned.

The Kodak Camera

"You press the button, we do the rest."

OR YOU CAN DO IT YOURSELF.

The only camera that anybody can use without instructions. As convenient to carry as an ordinary field glass. World-wide success.

The Kodak is for sale by all Photo stock dealers. Send for the Primer, free.

The Eastman Dry Plate & Film Co.   ROCHESTER, N. Y.

Price, $25.00 – Loaded for 100 Pictures.
Re-loading, $2.00.

Minoan finds

ARCHEOLOGY

19 MARCH The British archeologist Sir Arthur Evans today announced the discovery on the island of Crete of a great palace where ancient kings must have lived. The palace of Knossos dates from about 3000 B.C. Crete was home to the advanced Minoan civilization. The palace walls are decorated with pictures, many of which show double-headed axes and minotaurlike bulls.

▼ *Wall paintings in the ancient palace of Knossos.*

Siege of Peking lifted

WAR

14 AUGUST Western forces today raised the 56-day-long siege of Peking, and defeated the so-called Boxer Rebellion of patriotic Chinese against foreign exploitation of China. Members of the secret Boxer organization were prominent in the recent events, in which European missionaries and Christian Chinese were killed and Peking's foreign embassies were besieged. The Western allied force of 10,000 British, French, American, and German troops met fierce resistance from the rebels before entering the city.

◄ *One of the Chinese rebels who attacked "foreign devils" in China.*

Zeppelin flight

TRANSPORT

2 JULY The German Count Ferdinand von Zeppelin piloted his LZ-1 airship on its maiden voyage today. The craft was launched from a floating hangar near Friedrichshafen. Unlike a balloon, the LZ-1 is a rigid airship. It has an aluminum frame formed from 16 hoops, connected and stiffened by wire stays. The outer skin is made of cotton fabric, and the 16 gas bags inside are lined with goldbeater's skin, a thin membrane taken from the intestines of cattle. The bags are filled with hydrogen gas, which is lighter than air and gives the craft its lift. Two 16-hp engines give the airship a potential top speed of 14 miles per hour (23 km per hour), and it is steered by means of large rudders mounted at the rear.

Meccano invented

TECHNOLOGY

30 NOVEMBER A revolutionary new mechanical building system for children was patented today by Briton Frank Hornby. He had been in the habit of making metal accessories for his sons' railroad set, but was dissatisfied with their lack of interchangeable parts. So he came up with the idea of using perforated copper plates, joined together by miniature nuts and bolts. His first construction set will allow you to build a crane with realistically moving parts.

▲ *Freud (front left) with his colleagues.*

Freud's book of dreams

SCIENCE

14 OCTOBER The publication today of *The Interpretation of Dreams* by the Austrian doctor Sigmund Freud lays the basis of the new science known as psychoanalysis. Freud claims that people with certain nervous disorders may be cured by talking about their dreams. Dreams, Freud maintains, contain symbols that can reveal much about a person's suppressed memories and desires. He believes that all dreams are the fulfillment of a person's wishes. His ideas have attracted a great deal of interest, although not everybody agrees with him.

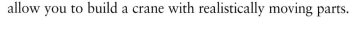

◄ *Freud's patients lie on this couch during sessions.*

US wins first Davis Cup

The US men's tennis team have today won the very first Davis Cup competition, beating the British pair of A.W. Gore and Roper Barrat. Unable to master their American opponents at the Longwood Cricket Club in Boston, the British team suffered a decisive defeat by three matches to love. The cup was given by the US player Dwight F. Davis as the prize in a team competition between the US and Great Britain.

Russians occupy Manchuria

POLITICS

◄ *Until the invention of the rigid LZ–1 airships, flight was only possible in balloons like this early powered one.*

3 SEPTEMBER Russia today has formally put areas of Manchuria in northeastern China under its military rule. On 13 August Russian Cossacks clashed with Chinese troops and put them to flight. Since then several towns along the Amur River have been occupied and Chinese residents banished. The Russian governor of the huge Amur district, General Gribsky, explained that the Russian action was a warning to Manchurians to respect Russian power.

▲ *A battery of Russian soldiers overlooking the Liao Plain, which is on the Manchurian front in northeastern China.*

First hamburger

The hamburger is the latest food fad to hit the US. Made of a ground-beef patty seasoned with chopped onions, the hamburger is eaten like a sandwich. The New Haven restaurant that offers the new dish is believed to have been inspired by the cuisine of German immigrants.

NEWS • 1900 • NEWS

2 January • First electric bus runs in New York.

4 April • Prince of Wales survives an assassination attempt in Brussels.

22 May • Minimum age of miners in Britain raised from 12 to 13.

16 August • World's first book of stamps issued in US.

31 August • Coca-Cola drink goes on sale in Britain.

Planck's quantum theory

SCIENCE

14 DECEMBER German physicist Professor Max Planck has revealed his new theory about the nature of energy, and it has turned conventional physics on its head. According to Planck's quantum theory, energy, like matter, is made up of particles. He calls each energy particle a quantum. According to his theory, energy radiates (flows out) in small packets of quanta instead of continuously, as previously thought.

Planck arrived at his theory after observing the way in which heat is radiated. The theory allows scientists to calculate a precise measure of units of energy, such as heat, light, and radio waves.

► *Max Planck.*

▼ *The luxury transatlantic liner Deutschland.*

Deutschland gets Blue Riband

TRANSPORT

13 AUGUST Just a day after the transatlantic speed record between the US and Europe was set by the *Kaiser Wilhelm der Grosse* of the North German Lloyd Line, the Hamburg America liner *Deutschland* has captured the coveted blue riband. The blue riband, or blue ribbon, is awarded to the passenger liner making the fastest transatlantic crossing. The *Deutschland's* speedy passage knocked eight hours off the *Kaiser Wilhelm's* record crossing of five days, nineteen and three-quarter hours.

1900
1901
1902
1903
1904
1905
1906
1907
1908
1909

ROYALTY

Queen Victoria is dead

22 JANUARY Queen Victoria died today at Osborne, her seaside home on the Isle of Wight. The Queen was 81 and had reigned for 63 years, the longest reign of any British monarch. Crowned in 1838 at the age of 18, she was thought frivolous at first because of her fondness for gaiety and dancing. The people began to warm to her after she met and fell in love with her cousin Prince Albert. They married in 1840 and had nine children, several of whom have married into other European royal families. The current German Kaiser is her grandson, and the Russian Tzarina is her granddaughter.

On Prince Albert's death in 1861, the grief-stricken Victoria largely withdrew from public life, and for 40 years she wore the black clothes of mourning. Toward the end of her reign Victoria emerged from seclusion and regained her interest in current events until the latter part of 1900, when her health began to fail and she retired to Osborne.

Close shave in US

It was announced today in the US that next year is to see the introduction of a new type of razor. The gadget is the idea of King Camp Gillette, an inventor and businessman. Although the idea was actually patented in 1895, it has taken several years to perfect the manufacture of a suitable blade. The hoe-shaped, double-edged blade is designed to be used until blunt, then thrown away and replaced with a new one.

▶ *Gillette's razor comes in a stylish new box, too.*

◀ *Queen Victoria's funeral cortège (procession) passes through the grounds of Windsor Castle.*

First Mercedes

TRANSPORT

31 MARCH The Daimler motor company has today unveiled a revolutionary automobile. It was made for Emile Jellinek, the Consul-General of the Austro-Hungarian Empire in Nice, who has named it Mercedes for his daughter. The car is an improved version of the model made by Daimler for the Consul-General in 1899. It boasts a four-cylinder, 5.9-liter, water-cooled internal combustion engine. It does not look like a horse-drawn carriage and can reach a speed of 53 miles per hour (85 kilometers per hour).

New disks

The first gramophone disks have gone on sale. The one-sided disk, issued by His Master's Voice record company, features the voice of Enrico Caruso, the great Italian tenor, singing an aria from Leoncavallo's opera *I Pagliacci (The Clowns).*

First Nobels

CULTURE

10 DECEMBER The first Nobel awards were made today. Funded by a legacy from the Swedish chemist Alfred Nobel, the awards will be made annually to individuals who make outstanding contributions in the fields of literature, chemistry, physics, peace, and medicine. Among the recipients this year was the German physicist Wilhelm Roentgen for his discovery of X-rays.

▼ *Nobel made his fortune from explosives.*

NEWS • 1901 • NEWS

26 February • *Boxer Rebellion leaders beheaded in Peking (Beijing).*

18 May • *Total eclipse of the sun photographed in Mauritius.*

24 June • *Paris critics acclaim first Picasso show.*

2 July • *Nearly 400 die in New York heatwave.*

9 September • *Artist Henri Toulouse-Lautrec dies, aged 36, in France.*

▼ *Jewish settlers in Palestine live in tent cities until houses are built.*

Jews flee to Palestine

POLITICS

1901 Russian Jews are flooding into Palestine to settle in agricultural colonies financed by Baron Rothschild. They are fleeing the continued violence against them in Russia, where mobs are robbing and attacking Jewish communities. The authorities turn a blind eye to these crimes because anti-Semitism is official government policy. Tzar Nicholas II is unsympathetic because he believes that Jewish people are responsible for many strikes in Russia and the organization of revolutionary terrorism.

Beans hit Britain

FOOD

1901 Baked beans in tomato sauce have just been introduced to Britain. This tasty new food is produced by the American firm, H.J. Heinz of Pittsburgh. The beans are on sale at Fortnum and Mason, the London department store. A single can is expensive, costing £1.50, but each one is guaranteed to contain a piece of pork!

POLITICS

President McKinley assassinated

14 SEPTEMBER President William McKinley died early today from the gunshot wound he suffered eight days ago at the hands of a Polish anarchist, Leon Czolgosz. He is the third American president to be murdered. It was hoped that the president would recover from his ordeal, but he suddenly took a turn for the worse. Vice President Theodore Roosevelt was summoned to McKinley's bedside in Buffalo, New York, traveling as swiftly as possible by horse-drawn carriage and a special train. Unfortunately, Roosevelt was too late to see the president, and he took the oath of office late today, 12 hours after McKinley had died.

◄ *An artist's impression of the moment Czolgosz shot McKinley at a fair in Buffalo.*

"Nickelodeons" popular

Audiences in the US are flocking to the first "nickelodeons." These storefront establishments charge eager customers a nickel to see about an hour's worth of moving pictures, hence the name. Enthusiastic they may be, but the pioneer moviegoers need to have patience, since the programs are frequently interrupted by technical problems, such as a projector breakdown or some other machinery malfunction.

▲ *The Australian flag.*

POLITICS

Birth of Australian Commonwealth

1 JANUARY Some 50,000 people have flocked to Melbourne to celebrate the birth of the Commonwealth of Australia in which the separate Australian colonies have become one nation. The prime minister, Mr. Edmund Barton, has already announced the formation of the first Federal Cabinet, in which he also holds the post of foreign minister. The occasion is greatly heightened by the good news of the strong Australian economy. Better defense has certainly been one motivation for this change; another has been the wish for more effective Asian immigration control; and the third has been the desire for free trade between the Australian colonies.

White House's Black guest

POLITICS

16 OCTOBER American President Theodore Roosevelt angered opponents of racial equality when he invited Booker T. Washington, the noted reformer and teacher, to dine at the White House. Born a slave, Washington became a believer in education rather than political agitation as a means of uniting Blacks and Whites. When a college to train Black teachers was opened in 1881, Washington became its first principal. He has since become the recognized leader of Black Americans.

▶ *Washington and Roosevelt dine together.*

Wuppertal monorail

TRANSPORT

1 MARCH Today saw the opening in Germany of the world's first suspended monorail (above). Conceived by German engineer Eugen Langen, the monorail consists of a single elevated track beneath which the railroad cars run. The entire system covers the 8 miles (13 km) from Vohwinkel to Barmen, much of it above the Wupper River.

Booth cleans up

English civil engineer Hubert Cecil Booth has patented an electric vacuum cleaning system. Using a powerful electric pump, Booth's system sucks air along a hose and through a cloth filter. He was inspired by an American railroad-car cleaner that blew dust into a container. Booth tried the reverse process, testing his theory by sucking through his handkerchief laid over the arm of a chair.

Fingerprint first

Police in London are now using fingerprinting to prevent fraud in prisons. This system, which records the unique patterns on a person's fingertips (which can be seen on the bottle below), thereby identifying them, was first used in the Indian Civil Service to prevent people from claiming pensions fraudulently.

Art Nouveau style

ART

1901 The Art Nouveau ("new art") movement is becoming increasingly popular. This ornamental style, characterized by long wavy lines and flowing plant forms, was encouraged by Louis C. Tiffany's lampshades and the recent Paris exhibition. First appearing around 1890, Art Nouveau is an attempt to create a new language of decoration. The term itself was coined by a gallery in Paris that exhibited much of this work.

◀ *Art Nouveau has influenced many forms of decoration, including posters.*

1901

1902

1903

1904

1905

1906

1907

1908

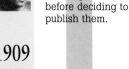

1909

▼ *A locomotive traveling on the Trans-Siberian Railroad.*

TRANSPORT

Moscow to Vladivostok

1902 The Trans-Siberian Railroad, the longest railroad line in the world, has opened for traffic. It stretches 5,777 miles (9,297 km) from Moscow to Vladivostok, on Russia's Pacific coast, and is due to be fully completed by 1904. Construction began in 1891, and there have been great difficulties to overcome. Long bridges had to be built to cross the wide Siberian rivers; deep marshes had to be filled in; and workers had to cope with extremes of temperature during construction. In addition, the steep land around Lake Baikal means that it has not been possible to continue the track around it. Ferry steamers will carry trains across the lake and the rest of the journey will be through Manchuria on the Chinese Eastern Railroad. The entire trip will take more than 10 days, and there are more than 1,000 stations along the route.

ARCHITECTURE

Flatiron Building completed

1902 The completion of the distinctive Flatiron Building in New York marks the beginning of a new age in building in the city. Its architect, Daniel H. Burnham, pioneered the use of the steel skeleton frame or cage construction that changed the skyline of Chicago during the 1880s. Conventional brick and masonry buildings cannot be built any higher than 16 stories, but with cheap steel construction and the availability today of efficient passenger elevators, the sky is truly the limit. The first of these very tall buildings, or skyscrapers, was the Home Insurance Building in Chicago, built by William Le Baron Jenney in 1884. The demand for office space in modern cities means that the skylines of these cities is likely to change dramatically in the next few years.

▶ *The building is named Flatiron because of its shape.*

Peter Rabbit delights

In bookstores now is *The Tale of Peter Rabbit*, by English author Beatrix Potter, featuring Peter Rabbit and other animal friends. Miss Potter has decorated her simple text with her own watercolor illustrations. Potter wrote the stories for the sick child of a former governess before deciding to publish them.

DISASTERS

Kembla disaster

31 JULY An explosion at the Mount Kembla colliery in New South Wales, Australia, today killed more than 90 men— the worst mining disaster in Australian history. The Mount Kembla mine was thought to be particularly safe—so safe, in fact, that miners wore lamps with naked flames. These were believed to be the reason for the explosion, causing the gas, known as firedamp, to ignite. The explosion led to a landslide that covered the main shaft and trapped 250 miners underground. Of these, 96 were killed.

Aswan dam finished

10 DECEMBER The massive Nile dam at Aswan, 590 miles (950 km) south of Cairo, was declared complete today. The construction has taken four years and required a workforce of 11,000. The dam is just over 1¼ miles (2 km) long. It has been built to contain the annual floodwaters of the Nile and to release them gradually throughout the dry season. A 199-mile (320-km) long lake is already building up behind the dam.

▲ *The dam is 132 feet (40 meters) high.*

NEWS • 1902 • NEWS

9 February • Barnum and Bailey Circus Siamese twins separated in Paris.

28 May • Thomas Edison invents the battery.

31 May • Boers surrender to the British in South Africa.

9 August • King Edward VII crowned in Westminster Abbey.

29 September • French writer Emile Zola dies after gas fumes leak into his bedroom in Paris.

Pele erupts

8 MAY Some 30,000 people were reported killed by poisonous volcanic fumes when Mount Pele, the largest mountain on the island of Martinique, in the French West Indies, erupted today. According to reports, every building in the capital city of St. Pierre was destroyed. St. Pierre is the largest town in the French West Indies and a major commercial center.

▼ *This map shows the route of the submarine cable.*

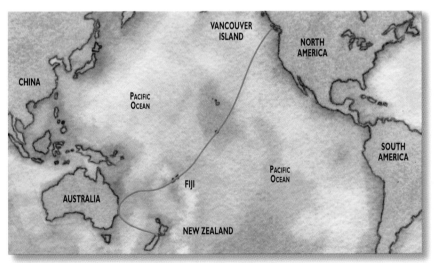

New cable spans Pacific

31 OCTOBER The world has become a little bit smaller with the laying of the undersea telegraph cable from Vancouver Island on the west coast of Canada across the Pacific Ocean, via Fiji, to Australia and New Zealand. The cable has a single conductor wire insulated with gutta percha, a natural resin, and protected by galvanized iron armor wires.

As with the earlier transatlantic cables, the new cable is suitable for telegraph communication alone; it can transmit only one signal at a time. The increasing number of telephone users will have to wait before they too can speak to someone on the other side of the world.

Méliès the moon man

Georges Méliès, the French filmmaker, unveiled his latest work today. *A Trip to the Moon* shows a voyage into space by rocket, as well as fantastic forms of life on other planets. This latest example of Méliès' "special effects" has attracted large crowds. Méliès has made over 100 short films at his Paris studios and has aroused great interest in the new medium by creating special tricks and effects not possible in any other media.

1900
1901
1902
1903
1904
1905
1906
1907
1908
1909

1903

◄ *The Wright brothers fly into history in Kitty Hawk. The first flight attained a height of only 9 feet (3 meters).*

Wright brothers' first flight

TRANSPORT

17 DECEMBER Just after 10:30 am, in Kitty Hawk, North Carolina, a powered airplane made the first controlled and sustained flight ever. Designed by brothers Orville and Wilbur Wright, biplane *Flyer 1* achieved an initial flight of some 118 feet (36 meters). The flight lasted just 12 seconds, but history has been made. The Wright brothers, who own a bicycle shop in Dayton, Ohio, have been experimenting with flight since 1896. By 1900 they had gained sufficient confidence to build their first biplane glider, which they tested in Kitty Hawk. The craft eventually carried a passenger, and in 1901 they flew a larger glider for 387 feet (118 meters). The Wrights then set out to make a powered flight by building a four-cylinder, lightweight gasoline engine. Fitted to the glider, this drives two propellers through a system of chains and gears. *Flyer 1* has no wheels, but is launched from a trolley rolling along a greased track. Today's flight is the result of testing by the brothers in a wind tunnel they have built near their home.

Around the world in six hours

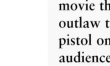

On 11 July the French magazine *Temps* carried out an amazing experiment, sending a telegram right around the world. The telegram was sent at 11:55 am and arrived back at 5:55 pm. Never before has a single message been sent so far. The success of the experiment proves the value of modern communications.

Great Train Robbery in US

A new movie has taken American audiences by storm. *The Great Train Robbery* is a novel eight-minute movie made by Edwin Porter featuring nonstop action sequences with no caption boards. The result is a thrilling story about a gang of outlaws who hold up a train. The robbers are then chased by the sheriff's posse and eventually caught. At the end of the movie the chief outlaw turns his pistol on the audience and fires at them! This dramatic ending makes the movie very popular.

Aspirin goes on sale in Germany

SCIENCE

10 OCTOBER The Bayer Company of Germany has today offered a drug called aspirin for sale. Used as a general pain reliever, it is an effective remedy for headaches due to anxiety or overwork.

The new drug was developed by a Bayer chemist, Felix Hoffman, to relieve his father's rheumatism. Aspirin was at first derived from salicylic acid, an extract of willow bark, but in 1899 Bayer developed a way of making it synthetically.

◄ *Outlaws get up to mischief in a scene from* The Great Train Robbery.

Teddy bears (and Teddy Roosevelt)

A company has been formed in the US to make fur-covered toy bears. Inspired by President Roosevelt's refusal to shoot a baby grizzly bear on a hunting trip in 1902, company owner Morris Michton asked his wife to make a small stuffed toy bear. He put the bear in the front window of his store, and it sold within five minutes. The bears proved so popular that by the end of the day he had orders for a dozen more.

SPORT

Red Sox win first World Series

13 OCTOBER The American League Boston Red Sox today beat the astounded National League Pittsburgh Pirates by five games to three in the first World Series ever. This competition sets the National League winners against the breakaway American League winners in a five-out-of-nine-game tournament. Formed in 1876, the National League strongly resisted any attempts to form a rival league. It lost the battle in 1901 when the Western League was expanded to form the American League.

SPORT

Garin's Tour de France

19 JULY The first Tour de France was won today by French cyclist Maurice Garin. The Tour is a 19-day road race across France, devised by the journalist and

promoter Henri Desgrange. Stretching more than 1,864 miles (3,000 km) through France, the grueling course starts in Paris and passes through Lyons, Marseilles, Toulouse, and Bordeaux before finishing in Paris. The race is divided into six stages, each of which varies in length and severity. Only 20 of the original entrants finished the race. Garin reached the finishing line more than two hours ahead of his nearest rival, the unknown cyclist Pothier, "the butcher of Sens."

▲ *Despite early objections, the National League allowed the Series to take place.*

◄ *Maurice Garin (left), rode to victory in the first Tour de France.*

SCIENCE

Prize for Marie and Pierre Curie

10 DECEMBER Marie Curie (far right), the French scientist, today became the first woman to win a Nobel prize. She shares the award with her husband, Pierre (right), and Henri Becquerel for the work they have done to explore the mystery of radioactivity. Marie Curie has discovered that many elements are radioactive, including thorium, polonium, and radium.

NEWS • 1903 • NEWS

26 February • Inventor of rapid-fire gun, Richard Gatling, dies.

3 March • British explorers set new Antarctic record by reaching the farthest point south.

11 June • Serbian king shot dead by rebels.

16 June • Henry Ford forms automobile company in Detroit.

10 October • Emmeline Pankhurst forms group to fight for the right to vote for British women.

QUEST FOR FLIGHT

▼ *After the success of* Flyer, *the Wright brothers built many new planes. This one is in England in 1910.*

Human beings have always wanted to fly and have been trying to design flying machines for centuries. Even the great 16th century artist Leonardo da Vinci made studies of aerodynamics and flying apparatus.

The first airplane that flew successfully by its own power was made by the American brothers Orville and Wilbur Wright. It eventually made flights up to 853 feet (260 meters) long over a beach in North Carolina in 1903. The Voisin brothers in France were making airplanes commercially the very next year. However, it was the need for military aircraft in World War I that prompted rapid advances in aviation technology.

First aviators

The Wright brothers' flight on 17 December 1903 lasted for less than a minute but was a triumph. Their airplane, called *Flyer*, weighed 605 pounds (275 kilograms) and had a tiny engine with a propeller. Movable wing tips enabled the direction of the plane to be controlled. The Wright brothers' achievement made them famous and they went on to develop many more planes.

◀ *Frenchman Louis Blériot in his Type XI airplane was the first person to fly across the English Channel (1909).*

Charles Lindbergh

Only 23 years after the Wright brothers took to the air, a young American pilot became the first person to fly solo non-stop across the Atlantic. His name was Charles Lindbergh and his journey from New York to Paris took 33½ hours. The 3,600-mile (5,800-km) flight in his plane, *Spirit of St. Louis*, ended on 21 May 1927 in Paris. Lindbergh was greeted by huge cheering crowds and became an instant international hero.

Modern airplanes emerge

In the 1920s and 1930s, airplanes provided a new form of transportation. Regular commercial flights between London and Paris began in 1919, transatlantic flights in 1939. Flying boats (aircraft that can land on water) were often used at first because they did not need airports, but the Douglas DC-3 "Dakota" was the biggest success.

Airplanes grew safer, larger and faster, especially after World War II, during which new types of aircraft, such as helicopters, were developed. By the 1950s, jet-powered airplanes began to replace ships for long-distance travel.

▲ *Concorde was the first supersonic (faster than the speed of sound) passenger airliner. It went into service in 1976.*

Flight facts

France: The first people to fly ascended in the Montgolfier brothers' balloon in 1783.

•

Brazil: Alberto Santos-Dumont built the first microlight aircraft in 1907.

•

Germany: The first jet aircraft to fly was a Heinkel He 178 in 1939.

•

US: More than 300,000 warplanes were built from 1941 to 1945.

▶ *Workers build a Concorde. The plane was developed by British and French firms.*

▼ *In less than 100 years, the airplane has developed from a fragile kitelike contraption into a highly sophisticated people mover—or a formidable weapon.*

▲ *LVG CV1, 1917*

▲ *De Havilland Comet, 1949*

▲ *Panavia Tornado GR1A, 1986*

▶ *DC-3 "Dakota," 1934*

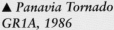

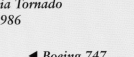

◀ *Boeing 747 Jumbo Jet, 1969*

1900	
1901	
1902	
1903	
1904	
1905	
1906	
1907	
1908	
1909	

1904

Nobel prize for Pavlov

SCIENCE

10 DECEMBER Ivan Pavlov (near left) was today awarded a Nobel prize for his work on the digestive system. The Russian scientist has discovered that nerve messages from the brain play a vital role in digestion. He cut a dog's food pipe and found that even when the food the dog chewed did not enter the stomach, the stomach still produced digestive juices. By contrast, when key nerves were cut, no juices were produced, even when the food reached the dog's stomach. Pavlov also discovered that if a bell rang every time a dog was fed, the animal eventually salivated (produced saliva in the mouth) at the sound of the bell alone. Pavlov calls this a conditioned reflex as opposed to inborn, or inherited, reflexes.

Russia goes to war after Japanese raid

WAR

10 FEBRUARY The Russian fleet stationed at Port Arthur, in northern China, came under attack last night from Japanese torpedo boats. In addition, yesterday 8,000 Japanese troops landed in Korea to begin a march on Seoul, the capital. In Tokyo the Japanese emperor officially declared war, blaming Russian ambitions in Korea and Manchuria for the conflict. The first news of the attack was rushed to the tzar, attending an opera performance in St. Petersburg. Officials waited until the end before informing him, so as not to spoil his evening.

▲ *A Japanese gun crew in action.*

Caruso the star!

Enrico Caruso, the great Italian tenor, has the world at his feet. He is currently appearing at New York's Metropolitan Opera in Donizetti's *L'Elisir d'Amore*. The 30-year-old star is paid nearly $1,000 for each performance and has just made his first US recording, a 10-inch disk of the aria "La Donna è Mobile" from Verdi's *Rigoletto*. Caruso will thus be the first singer to be heard by future generations.

Peter Pan flies in London

ENTERTAINMENT

28 DECEMBER The new play by Scottish writer James Barrie, *Peter Pan—or the Boy Who Wouldn't Grow Up*, which opened last night at the Duke of York's Theatre, is certain to be the hit of the season. It stars Nina Boucicault as Peter and Gerald Du Maurier as Captain Hook and proves unquestionably that today's audiences definitely believe in fairies. Although he has no children of his own, Barrie became guardian to the five sons of his close friend Sylvia Llewellyn Davies. *Peter Pan*, it is reported, first appeared in the stories that Barrie created for these boys.

New York subway opens

TRANSPORT

27 OCTOBER The New York City subway system began operating today. The Broadway and Fourth Avenue Line has been put into service after four years' work. Engineers who designed the subway took advantage of experience gained from New York's earlier "elevated" railroad and from studies of the London Underground. One of the major features of the new system is multiple tracks, which make it possible to run express services that bypass some stations.

◀ *The new underground subway will run in addition to the elevated railroad.*

Hopes for Entente Cordiale

TREATIES

8 APRIL This morning Great Britain and France signed a historic agreement, which aims to resolve all outstanding differences between them. A compromise has been reached over territorial and fishing rights around the world. Visits between the French president and the British king last year paved the way for the entente.

Degree for Helen Keller

PEOPLE

1 SEPTEMBER Helen Adams Keller, a 24-year-old deaf and blind woman, graduated today from Radcliffe College in Cambridge, Massachusetts. At the age of 19 months, Keller was struck by a serious illness that left her blind, deaf, and unable to talk. In 1887 the young Keller began to be schooled by a partially sighted teacher called Anne Sullivan, who taught her to read and write in braille. Accompanied by Miss Sullivan, Keller attended the Horace Mann School for the Deaf in Boston. From there she went on to college, still with Miss Sullivan, who would "spell" the lectures into Keller's hand.

◀ *Helen Keller is pictured in cap and gown at her graduation.*

NEWS • 1904 • NEWS

8 January • Pope Pius X forbids wearing of low-cut evening gowns.

22 March • A US newspaper carries first color photographs.

1 April • Henry Royce's engineering firm produces its first car.

6 May • British forces fight with Tibetans.

9 May • British explorer Sir Henry Morton Stanley dies at 63.

28 September • Woman arrested for smoking in New York.

Ice-cream cone debut!

Ladies at the World's Fair in St. Louis were today seen enjoying one of the latest new foods, the ice-cream cone. Invented by Italian immigrant Italo Marcioni, the cone is made from flour, milk, and sugar and means that ice cream can be enjoyed while walking around, without the need for a bowl, plate, or spoon.

POLITICS

A Bloody Sunday in St. Petersburg kills 500

22 JANUARY Thousands of strikers and their families, marching through St. Petersburg to petition Tzar Nicholas II for better working conditions, were fired on today by Russian troops. Many were killed and many more were wounded. This tragedy, on what is already being called "Bloody Sunday," was the result of a march led by a priest, Father George Gapon. The demonstration began at noon and was headed by the priest, carrying a cross, while strikers and their families carried icons, banners, and the tzar's portrait. Arriving at the Winter Palace, the marchers were met by lines of infantry. The troops, it was reported, had been given firm orders to disperse any crowds, and without warning they opened fire on men, women, and children, staining the snow with blood. Father Gapon managed to escape, but other strike leaders were seized. The massacre has destroyed popular trust in the tzar as a fatherly protector of the poor. Tzar Nicholas was away for the weekend at his country palace.

▼ *Russian troops disperse the strikers outside the Winter Palace in St. Petersburg.*

▲ *This scene from the Russian film* Battleship Potemkin *shows the mutinous crew assembled on the warship's deck.*

Potemkin's mutiny

POLITICS

27 JUNE Sailors aboard Russia's most powerful warship, the *Potemkin*, have mutinied, throwing their officers into the sea. The trouble started when a sailor complained about poor food. When he was shot by the first lieutenant, the crew became inflamed and, joined by eight officers, they threw the commander and several other officers overboard. The crews of two torpedo boats also joined in. The port of Odessa, where the ship is anchored, has been in a state of anarchy, with strikes, shootings, and explosions commonplace.

Brighter bulbs arrive

The latest light bulbs are brighter and last longer thanks to the use of a new material for the filament of the bulbs. Until now, filaments were made from vegetable fiber, which has a short life. The new type of filament is made from carbonized cellulose, giving more light and a significantly improved life span.

INCANDESCENT LAMPS.

Crazy for postcards!

Postcard fever, already rife in Europe, has truly caught on in Britain. According to a report by the British Postmaster-General, postcards are increasing in popularity. Over 700 million postcards were delivered in the year ending 31 March 1904. But some people never received theirs. Over 300,000 packets were mailed with an incorrect address on them! Many included money, and one package contained jewelry worth more than £2,000.

▶ *A sepia postcard sent by President Roosevelt to his mother.*

◀ *King Haakon VII of Norway poses with Queen Maude and Prince Olaf.*

Norway is independent

POLITICS

7 JUNE The Storting, the parliament of Norway, today declared the union with Sweden to be dissolved. In 1814, Norway had entered into a union with Sweden under which the Swedish monarch ruled both countries. Norway, however, spent the rest of the 19th century struggling to assert its independence and attempting to preserve its own culture. Norwegians have now voted to reestablish their own monarchy by electing Prince Charles of Denmark to be King Haakon VII of Norway.

Fauves in Paris

ART

1 OCTOBER A group of artists exhibiting in the new *Salon d'Automne* has been dubbed "Les Fauves"—the wild beasts, by a critic. Painting pictures with primary colors straight from the tube, these artists maintain that color itself is a vital means of expression. The leader of the group, Henri Matisse, has painted a portrait of his wife that has scandalized onlookers. What has been described as "violence on the walls" has provoked strong reactions from some members of the public.

▶ *Still Life by Matisse.*

▲ *The brilliant young scientist, Albert Einstein.*

Einstein and his new theory of relativity

SCIENCE

1 JULY The publication of a novel scientific theory, called *Special Relativity*, by Albert Einstein, a German-born physicist, has turned the scientific ideas of Isaac Newton upside down. According to Einstein, there is no such thing as absolute time or motion. Everything depends on the observer. Suppose a rocket passes by the planet Earth. From the Earth the rocket seems to shrink, and time on the rocket seems to be running slow. For the rocket pilot, however, time seems to be running normally on board, but seems to be running slow on Earth. The most striking implication of the theory is that mass is a form of energy, and that a small amount of mass would be equivalent to a huge amount of energy. Einstein derived the equation $E=mc^2$, where E is energy, m is mass, and c is the speed of light. The only absolute, he maintains, is the speed of light.

Pizzas get hot in New York

FOOD

1905 The famous Italian pizza—a Neapolitan invention—has made its debut in New York City. A flat disk of dough topped with olive oil, tomatoes, and mozzarella cheese, the pizza is baked quickly and served while it is still hot. It has been brought to New York by the growing Italian community and is certain to become a popular treat.

"Little Nemo in Slumberland" appears

A brand-new comic strip has been launched in the *New York Herald* to popular acclaim. "Little Nemo in Slumberland" is the creation of cartoonist Winsor McCay. Little Nemo visits Slumberland each night where he meets unusual characters who act as his guides. The dream world depicted in the strip is gentle, exciting, and humorous, and the cartoon is bound to be a hit.

▲ *A few frames from the* Little Nemo *comic strip.*

Von Suttner wins Nobel prize

PEOPLE

10 DECEMBER Bertha von Suttner, the Austrian novelist and noted pacifist, won the Nobel Peace Prize today. The daughter of an impoverished Austrian field marshal, in 1876 she became Alfred Nobel's secretary-housekeeper at his Paris residence. After only a week, however, she returned to Vienna and secretly married Baron Arthur von Suttner. Though she saw Nobel only twice after 1876, she corresponded with him until his death in 1896. Their last meeting in August 1892 followed a peace congress in Bern. It is believed that her increasing identification with peace movements and her letters on the subject to Nobel caused him to institute a peace prize. Her novel, *Die Waffen nieder!* (*Lay Down Your Arms!*), has been influential.

26

NEWS • 1905 • NEWS

2 January • Russian garrison at Port Arthur surrenders to Japanese

24 March • Jules Verne, French author, dies.

4 April • Over 10,000 die in earthquake in Lahore, India.

25 August • Eight crew of the Potemkin sentenced to death.

5 October • Wright brothers fly for 38 minutes.

30 December • Tzar's troops crush workers' revolt, killing 10,000.

Anna Pavlova in *Swan Lake*

1905 The young Russian ballerina Anna Pavlova (right) has danced a wonderful new ballet solo entitled "The Dying Swan," written specially for her. Pavlova is just 23 but joined the Imperial Ballet six years ago and is well on her way to becoming a prima ballerina. The piece has been created by the eminent choreographer Michel Fokine. Pavlova's performance displays grace, poetry, and magic.

ENTERTAINMENT

"Die Brücke" group set up

ART

7 JUNE A group of four Expressionist artists in Germany have come together today to form "Die Brücke," or The Bridge. Its founders, Karl Schmidt-Rottluff, who gave the group its name, Fritz Bleyl, Erich Heckel, and Ernst Ludwig Kirchner are students at the Dresden Technical School. The group aims to be a focus for revolutionary elements. The paintings and prints by Die Brücke artists are executed in a style that stresses bold outlines and strong colors.

"Blues" thrives in US

The "Blues," folk music of rural African Americans, is thriving in towns and cities, particularly on Beale Street, in Memphis, Tennessee. The music is accessible to untrained singers and musicians, but W.C. Handy, an enterprising songwriter and bandleader from Alabama, is keen to set up the first Blues publishing company.

Stieglitz opens gallery

ART

NOVEMBER Photographer Alfred Stieglitz has opened a gallery in New York City to exhibit the work of his radical group, the "Photo-Secession." The group is dedicated to the recognition of photography as a creative art equal to that of painting, a cause for which Stieglitz has long fought. Stieglitz is known for his critically acclaimed pictures in rain, snow, and at night.

▶ *The cornet is W.C. Handy's favorite instrument. He has worked as a minstrel show bandleader.*

1900
1901
1902
1903
1904
1905
1906
1907
1908
1909

TECHNOLOGY

New era on the high seas for Britain

10 FEBRUARY Britain's sea power took a giant technological leap forward today when King Edward VII launched the Royal Navy's latest battleship. HMS *Dreadnought* is the fastest, largest warship on the high seas. It boasts 10 giant 12-inch guns, making her able to fire on enemy ships while staying out of the range of torpedoes.

First Lord of the Admiralty, Sir John Fisher, ordered work to begin on the revolutionary battleship after a report suggested Britain's safety depended on radical improvements in the quality of its fleet. Experts suggest the ship will be capable of taking on the enemy even if it is outnumbered 10 to 4, but some fear the launch of the new ship will only speed up the arms race between Britain and Germany.

▲ *Britain's fleet rules the waves.*

Automatic Entertainer a hit in Chicago

Here's something new to get the dancers on the dance floor. The John Gabel Company has produced the latest in entertainment with an ingenious device called The Automatic Entertainer. Just punch in your selection and the machine will play your choice from a store of recorded disks held inside.

DISASTERS

San Francisco rocked by gigantic earthquake

19 APRIL At 5:13 am the California city of San Francisco was shaken to its foundations by what will surely prove to be the most disastrous earthquake ever to hit this beautiful coastline. Huge and devastating fires caused by broken gas mains are now raging out of control all over the city. At least 1,000 people are already feared dead, and the city's inhabitants are fleeing for their lives. Martial law has been declared, and this afternoon four looters were shot.

▼ *A scene in downtown San Francisco after the earthquake.*

NEWS • 1906 • NEWS

7 February • *Liberal Party win British election.*

23 May • *Norwegian playwright Henrik Ibsen dies, aged 78.*

27 June • *Hungarian Ferenc Szisz wins first Grand Prix motor race, at Le Mans, France.*

24 August • *Kidney transplants performed on dogs in Toronto.*

22 October • *French artist Paul Cézanne dies, aged 67.*

Vesuvius erupts

DISASTERS

7 APRIL A terrifying flow of lava is spreading unstoppably across the Italian countryside, following the eruption of Mount Vesuvius near Naples. The army is bringing in emergency food supplies, but many communities remain cut off and the roads are jammed with people trying to escape the rain of soot and ash from the sky. Casualties are difficult to estimate at the moment, but the town of Ottaiano has been obliterated, and 100 people in Naples were killed when roofs collapsed under the weight of ash.

▲ *A huge ash cloud rises above Vesuvius.*

▲ *Celebrations marked the opening of the Simplon Tunnel.*

Simplon Tunnel opens

TRANSPORT

1 JUNE The Simplon Railroad Tunnel has opened between Switzerland and Italy after eight years of construction. At 12½ miles (20 km) long, the tunnel is the world's longest. Workers have had to endure difficult conditions, including temperatures of 120°F (49°C) and massive underground floods. The structure is the brainchild of German engineer Alfred Brandt, who devised a new type of hydraulic rock drill and radical new tunneling methods to allow construction to proceed. Exhausted by overwork, Brandt died in 1899 and so did not see the tunnel completed.

Algeciras talks on Morocco crisis end

POLITICS

31 MARCH Talks aimed at settling the Moroccan question—in which Germany disputes France's claim to a special role in the country—ended with a compromise being reached in Algeciras today. Negotiators from the rival countries expressed satisfaction with the outcome. This recognizes France's special position, while accepting Germany's demand that all countries should have equal access to commercial opportunities.

TRANSPORT # Silver Ghost appears

15 MARCH A new luxury motor car has made its debut. Rolls-Royce's Silver Ghost (left) has earned its name because it has a near-silent six-cylinder engine.

Kellogg's breakfast cereal company

William Kellogg has founded the Battle Creek Toasted Corn Flake Company to market a new kind of crunchy cereal invented by accident. Apparently the hot corn cereal got left too long in the pan one day in the kitchen at his brother John Kellogg's Battle Creek Sanitarium, producing crisp flakes—something new for everyone's breakfast table all around the world.

Balloon racers in the news

It has been a big year for hot-air balloon enthusiasts. In July, seven balloons took part in Britain's first race sponsored by the *Daily Mail* newspaper. Now US Army Lieutenant Frank Lahm has flown all the way from Paris to Whitby in Yorkshire, in northern England, to win the first international race.

1900
1901
1902
1903
1904
1905
1906
1907
1908
1909

1907

PEOPLE

Record immigration into the US

20 FEBRUARY Following anxieties about the record number of people entering the US, Congress has passed an Immigration Act saying that new arrivals can be barred from the country if it is thought likely their entry could damage US labor conditions. The Act also allows for the exclusion of some people of oriental origin. The move comes after violent agitation in California against Japanese workers last year.

Of the current US population, 14 percent were born in another country, but immigrants may actually make up as much as half of the workforce. The latest wave of new arrivals has come not from Britain, Ireland, and Germany, countries from which many earlier immigrants hailed, but mainly from southern and eastern Europe. Every year since the 1880s, at least 50,000 Russian Jews have been seeking new lives, free of persecution, in the US, but the most recent spate of anti-Semitic attacks in tzarist Russia has triggered a massive increase in the exodus from there. This year has seen record numbers of immigrants passing through New York's Ellis Island, the entry point for immigrants since 1892. In a single day 11,747 passed through, and before the year is out one million will have arrived.

▼ *New arrivals view the New York skyline.*

▲ *A US residence certificate.*

Boy scouts formed

LEISURE

29 JULY Robert Baden-Powell, famous for his heroic exploits during the Boer War, has formed an organization for boys inspired by army scouts. His aim is to make good citizens for tomorrow by encouraging discipline, unselfishness, and a sense of duty.

Earlier this month 20 boys, some from private schools such as Eton and Harrow and others from the East End of London, took part in an experimental camp on Brownsea Island, on England's south coast. They learned outdoor skills as well as first aid and lifesaving. Baden-Powell hopes to make the Scouts into an international movement for boys.

▼ *Baden-Powell (left) with his wife (center).*

▲ *A scene in a Montessori kindergarten.*

Maria Montessori sets up kindergartens in Italy

PEOPLE

1907 Dr. Maria Montessori has set up her first school, or children's house, in a slum district of Rome. The 37-year-old doctor, the first woman in Italy ever to be awarded a medical degree, has had remarkable success teaching mentally handicapped children. She now hopes to achieve equally dramatic results applying her revolutionary methods to nonhandicapped children from deprived backgrounds.

Dr. Montessori's method involves directing a child's spontaneous energies of mind and body rather than subjecting them to conventional teaching. In this way she expects to teach children under five to read and write, and to turn out children who love work and discipline and can concentrate for long periods without strain.

Kipling wins Nobel prize

LITERATURE

10 DECEMBER Rudyard Kipling has become the first English author to receive the prestigious Nobel Prize for Literature. Born in India in 1865, Kipling is acknowledged as the foremost poet and storyteller of the British Empire.

After schooling in England, Kipling became a globetrotting journalist, picking up the exotic backgrounds which give his writings such vivid life. By the time he returned to London in 1889 he was already well known, but

his *Barrack Room Ballads* (1892), which introduced the public to such characters as Danny Deever and Gunga Din, made him a popular favorite. He is perhaps best known now for his children's stories, especially his two *Jungle Books* of 1894 and 1895 and the *Just So* stories which he published four years ago.

◀ *Rikki-Tikki-Tavi the mongoose from one of Kipling's* Jungle Books.

Florence Nightingale receives OM

PEOPLE

29 NOVEMBER The Lady of the Lamp, Florence Nightingale, aged 87, today became the first woman ever to receive the Order of Merit. During the Crimean War, 50 years ago, Miss Nightingale organized the reform of the British Army's facilities for the sick and wounded. She cleaned up the hospital at Scutari and, by insisting on strict hygiene and offering good food, she improved the lives of British soldiers. Miss Nightingale trained in a European nursing school and after the war she set up the first modern school of nursing in Britain.

The Ziegfeld Follies

Audiences at theaters on New York's Broadway are thrilling to a new kind of musical revue. Inspired by Paris' famous *Folies Bergère*, producer Florenz Ziegfeld has mounted a lavish entertainment called *The Follies of 1907*, starring his wife, French-born beauty Anna Held. Mr. Ziegfeld hopes to make his *Follies* a yearly event.

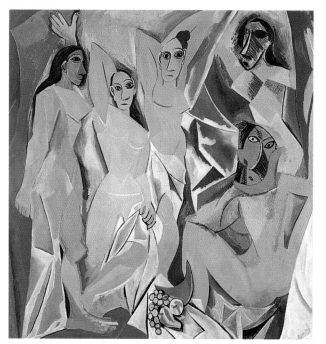

▲ *In* Les Demoiselles d'Avignon, *by Pablo Picasso, each figure is made up of various shapes, which show different views of the subject at the same time.*

Pablo Picasso in Parisian art shock

ART

MARCH The Paris art world is used to surprises but the latest painting on show from Spanish-born Pablo Picasso, 26, has shocked everyone. *Les Demoiselles d'Avignon* shows five female figures in various stages of undress. But their bodies and the drapes have been distorted into strange, geometrical shapes that break all the rules of the conventional art world, such as composition and perspective.

Picasso is a young artist used to reinventing himself in new styles. For years he painted only in blue. Then he switched to a predominantly rose-colored palette. But this canvas is a radical step even for him. Some see the influence of Paul Cézanne in this extraordinary new painting, others point to the similarities between the masklike faces of the two right-hand "demoiselles" and African masks exhibited in Paris earlier this year. With this painting Picasso marks the beginning of a new way of viewing visual reality in art. He paints objects as he thinks of them and there is often more than one view point.

Hagenbeck Zoo mimics nature

ENVIRONMENT

7 MAY The world-renowned animal dealer and trainer Carl Hagenbeck has transformed the way captive animals are shown to the public at his new zoological gardens at Stellingen near Hamburg. Gone are the small, restrictive cages of the ordinary zoo, in which pathetic, unhappy creatures pace miserably. Herr Hagenbeck has gone to great lengths to try to imitate the natural habitats of his animals, which are kept in large, uncovered pits with no bars. This arrangement should be a model for all zoos in the future.

▲ *Feeding time for the walruses and penguins at the Hagenbeck Zoological Gardens.*

Bakelite debut

Belgian-born chemist Leo Baekeland has named an amazing new material after himself. Bakelite (a hard, chemically resistant plastic that does not soften when heated and does not conduct electricity) is a phenolformaldehyde resin which begins as a liquid and can be molded into any shape. This synthetic resin is thought to be the material of tomorrow.

Finnish women finish first in elections

POLITICS

15 MARCH Last year, after a total reform of its parliamentary system, Finland became the third country in the world after New Zealand and Australia to give women the vote. Today, Finnish women are the first in the world to win seats in a national parliament. The bulk of the deputies-elect come from the Social Democratic Party—which holds the majority of seats—and includes women from different social backgrounds. "Votes for Women" campaigners around the world are now waiting to see which country will be next. As their campaign gathers momentum, suffragettes in Britain and the US are determined their turn will come soon.

▲ *Miina Sillanpää, first female deputy-elect.*

MUTT AND JEFF—Eight Dollars Is Some Money

Augustus Mutt appears in the papers

The name of Mr. Augustus Mutt, who is always looking for his big break, may soon be familiar to people all over the US. The San Francisco *Chronicle* is the first newspaper in the world to run a comic strip adventure every day of the week, including Saturdays. The creator of the strip is Bud Fisher, a sports columnist from Chicago who has moved to California. The daily comic is seen as an attempt to boost circulation in the cutthroat world of newspapers. Mutt's popularity will be assured next March when he is set to meet his future sidekick, Jeff, in the unusual setting of an insane asylum.

▲ *Mutt and Jeff pursue their hilarious antics frame by frame in the full-color comic strip.*

DISASTERS

India struck by killer bubonic plague

1907 Scientists working for the Second Indian Plague Commission say they are now satisfied beyond doubt that bubonic plague is carried by rat fleas. The Commission's conclusion is that the only way to halt the spread of the plague, which has claimed an estimated six million victims in India in the last 10 years, is to introduce strict quarantine rules for shipping and to set up rat extermination programs worldwide.

The deadly disease killed a quarter of the population of Europe in the Middle Ages but had almost disappeared by the end of the last century. Symptoms include the characteristic buboes, or black swellings in sufferers' armpits and groin that give the disease its name, as well as headaches, a fever, and vomiting. Eventually victims lose consciousness and die.

The current outbreak is thought to have started in China some 50 years ago. In 1894 it reached the busy port of Hong Kong, from where it was spread via the rats on board ships to places as far apart as California, South Africa, and Argentina. India, however, remains the worst affected country.

▲ *An exhibit in Bombay demonstrates the dangers of rats and fleas to locals.*

SPORT

Italian aristocrat wins world's longest auto race

10 AUGUST Prince Borghese of Italy has beaten five other competitors to win the world's longest automobile race ever. The drivers set off from Peking (Beijing) in China two months ago to cover 8,000 miles (12,874 km) of rough roads on their way to the finishing line in Paris. The race nearly didn't start at all after problems obtaining documents of safe passage in China. Apparently the Chinese suspected a plot to find a way to invade their country. In Mongolia, by contrast, the inhabitants were said to be thrilled by the speed of the horseless carriages. Borghese nearly fell at the last hurdle when a Belgian policeman stopped the Italian aristocrat for speeding.

▼ *During the rally one of the competitors got stuck in the rail tracks.*

NEWS • 1907 • NEWS

25 April • A bill proposing building a channel tunnel between France and England withdrawn in British parliament.

10 June • Lumière brothers announce a new color photography process.

13 September • Lusitania completes record Atlantic crossing.

13 November • French inventor Paul Cornu makes first vertical takeoff flight in prototype helicopter.

Sidebar timeline (left margin):

1900
1901
1902
1903
1904
1905
1906
1907
1908
1909

Ford's Model T finally in the USA

1 OCTOBER The "motor car for the multitudes," promised by American car manufacturer Henry Ford, is finally on sale. At a price of just $850, the Model T Ford brings driving within the reach of the ordinary man and woman. The car is being built on a production line, a new system of manufacturing invented by Mr. Ford, which helps to keep down costs.

The car is not a beauty and has already been nicknamed the "Tin Lizzy," but it has a three-point suspension and is made of a tough, light steel alloy, guaranteed to smooth out the bumps on rough country roads. Powered by a four-cylinder, 20-horsepower engine and specifically designed for ease of maintenance, the Tin Lizzy cruises comfortably at a speed of 25 miles per hour (40 km per hour).

Henry Ford himself took the very first Model T for a spin around Detroit in the summer and pronounced himself "tickled to death" with it. He then put the car through its paces when he went on a grueling hunting trip in the mountains.

Some of Ford's backers are said to be unhappy at the manufacturer's determination to switch all production to his low-cost cars, but Ford is convinced that this is the way to go into the future. Next year he hopes to build as many as 25,000 Model Ts.

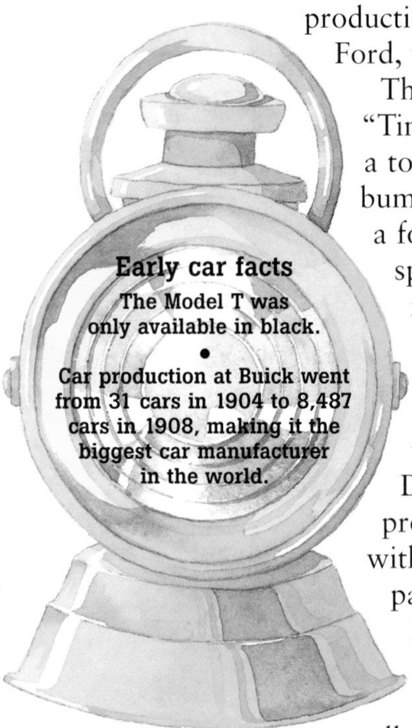

Early car facts
The Model T was only available in black.
•
Car production at Buick went from 31 cars in 1904 to 8,487 cars in 1908, making it the biggest car manufacturer in the world.

▲ *The Model T was the first car with left-hand drive.*

Ottoman Empire seethes with unrest

24 JULY Sultan Abdul Hamid II of Turkey, the ruler who calls himself "the Shadow of God," has been forced to order all districts of the Ottoman Empire to hold elections for parliament after widespread unrest. The Young Turk revolutionary movement, which has its own name for the Sultan—"the old spider"—is demanding freedom of religion, education, and the press, and a return to the constitution of 1876 which was set aside by the Sultan after just one year.

An uprising began earlier this month throughout the Turkish army in Macedonia. The Young Turks, currently in exile in Paris, immediately aligned themselves with Major Ahmed Niyazi, leader of the rebel faction, and the revolt spread rapidly. The Ottoman Empire is likely to be weakened, and European states may take the chance to try to grab parts of its territory.

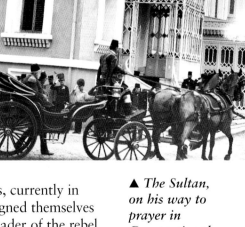

▲ *The Sultan, on his way to prayer in Constantinople, rides in an open carriage.*

Johnson: new boxing champion

On 26 December, a big, raw-boned 6-foot (1.8 meter) tall Texan named Jack Johnson became the first black heavyweight boxing champion of the world. Police had to step in to halt the bruising encounter in Sydney, Australia, in the 14th round after defending champion Tommy Burns, who won his world heavyweight title two years ago, had been knocked unconscious for several seconds.

◀ *Jack Johnson in fighting form.*

NEWS • 1908 • NEWS

1 February • *King Carlos and Crown Prince Luiz of Portugal assassinated.*

7 March • *Germany launches the Nassau, its version of HMS Dreadnought.*

14 May • *Franco-British Exhibition opens in London at White City.*

14 September • *General Motors formed in Detroit, Michigan.*

5 October • *Austria annexes Bosnia-Herzegovina.*

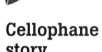

Cellophane story

A new transparent material made from cellulose has been produced by Dr. Jacques Brandenberger, a Swiss chemist. Dr. Brandenberger hopes to get backing from the Comptoir de Textiles Artificiels, a giant rayon producer, to manufacture the product, which he calls cellophane, as a wrapping material for food.

Royal row in Congo

19 AUGUST One of the great scandals of colonial Africa may be coming to an end. The Belgian parliament has finally voted to annex the Congo from its own king. It will pay Leopold II the equivalent of approximately $7.5 million in return for his giving up control of the colony, an enormous tract of land in central Africa, some 80 times the size of Belgium. King Leopold has ruled there as absolute monarch for the last 22 years. The government in Brussels was finally forced to act after international attention was focused on the cruelties perpetrated by their ruler on the unfortunate inhabitants of the region.

▼ *Belgian settlers bring industrial machinery to the Congo.*

Anne to steal hearts

1908 Lucy Maud Montgomery has published her first novel, *Anne of Green Gables*. It is a delightful tale about a spirited, unconventional orphan girl who finds home and happiness in a small town in Canada with an elderly brother and sister. Miss Montgomery, who has worked as a journalist and schoolteacher, is said to have drawn on her own childhood experiences on Prince Edward Island in creating the rural community of Avonlea where her heroine, Anne, lives. The book's charm seems certain to earn it a place in the hearts of readers the world over.

▲ *Pu Yi (right) with his father and brother.*

Pu Yi: China's boy emperor

POLITICS

2 DECEMBER The new Emperor of China is a boy not yet three years of age. Pu Yi ascends the throne following the mysterious deaths in November of both the previous emperor and the Dowager Empress Tzu Hsi. The 73-year-old empress, who was ruling as regent, began her political career as a stunningly beautiful concubine. Her power was particularly resented by Europeans because she supported the anti-Western Boxer rebels of 1900.

Pu Yi will live in the Imperial Palace in the Forbidden City, a large area of the capital protected by a high wall which extends for 2½ miles (4 km). His father will act as regent until he comes of age.

New lines for old curves

The political freedom being sought by militant suffragettes is echoed in the latest ladies' fashions. Dresses now favor a slim, straight figure, rather than the S-bend Venus de Milo curves of the "Gibson Girl."
To emphasize the longer look, the new corsets hardly go in at the waist.

▶ *The exaggerated curves of the Gibson Girl are on the way out.*

▲ *Queen Alexandra presents prizes to winners at the White City Stadium.*

London Olympics held at White City

SPORT

30 JULY Controversy over the result of the marathon was settled today at the Olympics when Queen Alexandra presented a special gold cup to Dorando Pietri. Pietri crossed the line first in the marathon, but was disqualified after the exhausted runner received medical attention and assistance from stewards during his final lap of the magnificent new White City Stadium. The stadium also hosted the swimming events—in a specially constructed temporary pool.

With over 2,000 participants and 21 different sports, the London Olympics have been hailed as a tremendous success. This follows games in Paris and St. Louis which failed to live up to the hopes of the founder of the modern Olympic movement, Baron de Coubertin. However, disputes between the athletics associations of Britain and the US, centered around the fact that all the judges were British, have marred the games.

Nellie scoops beauty contest

An 18-year-old British girl named Nellie Jarman has won the first international beauty contest, staged at the Pier Hippodrome in Folkestone, England. She beat off challengers from England, France, Ireland, and Austria.

"W.G." retires from cricket

SPORT

31 AUGUST Summer will never be the same again. W.G. Grace, that grand old man of cricket whose ample frame and bushy beard have come to symbolize the summer game for thousands of enthusiasts, has retired. Now nearly 60, Grace has been playing since 1865. He scored 54,211 runs and took 2,808 wickets in first-class matches.

Wright air crash fatality

TRANSPORT

17 SEPTEMBER Flying has claimed its first victim. Lieutenant Thomas E. Selfridge was killed today in a crash at Fort Myer, Virginia. Selfridge was accompanying pioneer aviator Orville Wright on a demonstration flight for the US Army.

A large crowd of spectators, from both the army and the press, watched in horror as a blade on the left propeller of Mr. Wright's biplane broke off and the aircraft's rudder system was torn to shreds. The plane plummeted from a height of some 75 feet (23 meters), badly injuring Mr. Wright. In spite of efforts to save his life, Lieutenant Selfridge suffered a fractured skull and died.

▲ *Lt. Selfridge lies dead at the crash site.*

British women call for the vote

POLITICS

21 JUNE A huge crowd of 200,000 people gathered today in London's Hyde Park to call for British women to be given the vote. Christabel Pankhurst, cofounder with her mother Emmeline of the Women's Social and Political Union, a body dedicated to winning suffrage for women, was the leading speaker. Miss Annie Kenney, who with Christabel took part in the organization's first public demonstration in Manchester three years ago, also addressed the meeting. Miss Kenney noted the number of men in the crowd who had come to voice their support for "the cause."

The W.S.P.U. has been involved in a number of controversial incidents since it moved its campaign to London two years ago. Earlier this year 50-year-old Emmeline Pankhurst was sentenced to six weeks in Holloway prison for obstructing the police within the area of Parliament. Mrs. Pankhurst wrote vividly of the unpleasant conditions she experienced in Holloway. About the same time, police arrested 50 suffragettes who attempted to smuggle themselves into Parliament inside a large furniture van.

▲ *A suffragette addresses a rally.*

Sicilian town ripped apart by earthquake

DISASTERS

28 DECEMBER The Sicilian town of Messina, the second-largest on the island, is a heap of rubble today following the most violent earthquake recorded in European history. Rescuers are searching desperately for survivors trapped beneath fallen buildings, while aftershocks continue to shake the region. The quake has caused a massive sea wave, or *tsunami*, which has carried death and destruction across the straits of Messina to Calabria, the southernmost part of mainland Italy, where the town of Reggio has also been devastated.

The death toll in Messina is hard to estimate, but some believe up to half of its 150,000 inhabitants may have lost their lives. A huge international response has been promised. British ships based in Malta will probably help in the rescue and evacuation of victims.

▶ *The scene of destruction in Messina after the record-breaking quake.*

1900
1901
1902
1903
1904
1905
1906
1907
1908
1909

General Electric toaster

Here's something new to add to the list of recent gadgets designed to make life easier for the modern housewife. The General Electric Company has invented an electric toaster, designed to make a perfect slice of toasted bread. Electric coils inside the machine heat up and turn the bread a golden brown. Delicious!

1909

▲ *Blériot's monoplane outside its hangar, and Blériot himself in flying gear (inset).*

TRANSPORT

Blériot first to fly the Channel

25 JULY Frenchman Louis Blériot, 36, made history today when his monoplane landed at Dover Castle after a 36-minute flight across the English Channel from France to England. The intrepid flyer had to wait five days for the right weather conditions for his 25-mile (40-km) flight, and even then he got lost in the clouds and only found his landing area with the help of a journalist waving the French tricolor flag. He made his historic flight without the use of a compass, navigating by following ships traveling to Dover. As the first man to fly the Channel, Blériot beats two of Europe's other top aviators, Hubert Latham and Count de Lambert, and wins the prize of £1,000 offered by the *Daily Mail* newspaper. Although the French government supplied a rescue ship, it was thankfully not needed.

Blériot's magnificent achievement is even making governments take notice since his flight has proved that planes are capable of crossing previously impassable geographical boundaries.

POLITICS

Prince Ito slain

26 OCTOBER Prince Ito Hirobumi, who was Japan's first prime minister, has been assassinated while visiting Manchuria. The assassin has been identified as a Korean patriot, which suggests that Prince Ito's recent role in crushing the Korean national struggle cost him his life. Twenty-five years ago, the 68-year-old statesman played a major role in the modernization of Japan. In spite of his title, he was of fairly humble origin. His father was a farmer who did well enough to buy into the nobility.

NEWS • 1909 • NEWS

1 January • Old Age Pension first introduced in Britain.

17 February • Royal Commission proposes no more children to be kept in workhouses.

27 April • Sultan of Turkey deposed.

3 May • Reporters use wireless for first time.

16 July • 12-year-old boy becomes Shah of Persia.

10 September • Freud and Jung begin first US tour.

Mary takes the biscuit

Dewy-eyed sweet 16-year-old Mary Pickford is the star of the new movie *Her First Biscuits*. "You're too fat and too little," was movieman D.W. Griffith's comment when she first presented herself for a movie career, but Miss Pickford is a tough cookie who never takes no for an answer. Born plain Gladys Mary Smith in Toronto, Canada, she has been charming theater audiences since she was just five years old.

▲ *A new star, Mary Pickford.*

Peary reaches North Pole

QUESTS

21 DECEMBER Eight months after US explorer Robert E. Peary announced he had become the first man to reach the North Pole his claim has been officially accepted. Peary reached the top of the world at the sixth attempt, but Frederick Cook, who has accompanied Peary on earlier expeditions, then said he had reached the pole nearly a year earlier. Cook was exposed as a fraud by Inuit (Eskimos) who reported him turning back some 20 miles (32 km) short.

◀ *Peary and his party raise the Stars and Stripes at the North Pole.*

New speed record set at Brooklands

TRANSPORT

1909 The brand-new course at Brooklands, England, saw a world speed record for automobiles when top French driver Victor Hémery, at the wheel of the "Lightning Benz," clocked an amazing 127 miles per hour (205 km per hour). The "Lightning Benz" was specially built at the Benz factory in Mannheim, Germany. The new record proves that, although steam-powered cars can achieve high speeds, gasoline-driven cars have a decided edge over steam when it comes to breaking records.

▲ *The new "Lightning Benz."*

First youth hostel opens in Germany

LEISURE

1909 Schoolteacher Richard Schirrmann is opening a dormitory in his school for the use of young travelers during their vacation. In August the schoolteacher got caught in a thunderstorm with his hiking party in Westphalia. With nowhere else to stay, the group ended up sleeping in the village school. Schirrmann is now promoting the idea of a national network of such inexpensive accommodation across Germany.

▶ *Burg Altena in Germany: the first youth hostel.*

Johannsen names the "gene"

Danish botanist Wilhelm Johannsen is creating a new science. His latest publication argues that there is a basic unit of heredity, which he calls a gene, hidden in the cells of every biological system, from the princess beans, which he studies, right up to man. Johannsen maintains that genes are responsible for an individual's inherited traits.

Death of Geronimo

PEOPLE

17 FEBRUARY The Chief of the Chiricahua Apache tribe, Geronimo, has died at Fort Sill, Oklahoma, at the age of 80. From 1860 to 1875 Geronimo was a name that struck fear into the heart of Mexicans and Americans alike, as Geronimo and his braves raided along the border. When the Chiricahua were moved to a new reservation in Arizona, Geronimo fled to the Sierra Madre Mountains until his capture in 1886. Eventually, he became a rancher and rode in President Roosevelt's inaugural parade three years ago. Geronimo's Apache name was Goyathlay, which means "the one who yawns."

Timeline

1910

1911

1912

1913

1914
1915

1916
1917

1918

1919

1910

The decade that would bring the bloodiest war ever fought in Europe and revolution in Russia began with most people quite unaware of the dangers which lay ahead. The British Empire was still intact. The Royal Navy still ruled the waves. In the US the economy was growing fast and no one had much time to spare for the intricacies of European politics.

But times were changing. Women were agitating more and more strongly to be allowed to participate in the democratic process, and the growing pace of scientific advance was beginning to affect the lives of ordinary people.

Sickle cell anemia

James Herrick, Professor of Medicine at Rush Medical College, has published a fascinating paper, describing what appears to be a new kind of anemia. Herrick has observed strange, crescent-shaped (or sickle-shaped) red cells in the blood of an African-American patient suffering from anemia (below). He believes the cells are associated with the disease.

Comet facts
- Comets are actually "dirty snowballs" made of ice and dust.
- Halley's Comet is visible from the Earth every 76 years.
- Halley's Comet features in the Bayeux Tapestry, created in 1066.

Comet flashes by Earth

SCIENCE

20 MAY The great, fiery ball of Halley's Comet with its spectacular tail streaming out across the heavens is just 13 million miles (21 million km) from the Earth today. Weather conditions permitting, it should be quite a sight in the evening skies for the next few days. Scientists say this is the closest the comet will come to our planet, but some are not convinced. The US particularly seems to be gripped by Comet Fever with predictions that the world is about to come to an end in a terrible collision. In Chicago pills are on sale to the gullible, supposed to act as an antidote to poison gases in the tail of the comet. In New York it was reported that passengers leaped from a moving trolley shouting, "Comet!" after a brick landed on the roof. The comet is named after Sir Edmond Halley (1656–1742), the British astronomer who first correctly predicted when it would appear. The comet will next be seen in 1986.

▶ *A fanciful view from the US of Halley's comet.*

Japan to take Korea

POLITICS

24 AUGUST Japan announced today that it intends to formally annexe Korea, the so-called Hermit Kingdom, this week so that it becomes a Japanese territory. Korea was a disputed area throughout the 1800s. Since the treaty of 1905, which ended the war between Japan and Russia, Japan has been in complete control of Korea. Nevertheless, this week's move is likely to spark trouble on the streets of the Korean capital, Seoul.

Portugal becomes a republic

POLITICS

4 OCTOBER King Manuel of Portugal is tonight a fugitive from his own country in the British colony of Gibraltar, following an armed uprising in Lisbon. This morning dissident elements in the Portuguese Navy shelled the capital, while the sound of artillery and rifle fire filled the streets. Forces loyal to the king seem to have been rapidly overcome, and the rebels marched through the city chanting "Long live the republic!"

The last 10 years have seen the assassination of King Manuel's father and brother, and today's developments have not come as a complete surprise. The provisional government in Lisbon is thought likely to abolish the monarchy altogether.

▼ *Wassily Kandinsky.*

▶ *Artillery in action in Portugal.*

Father's Day in US

CULTURE

19 JUNE Today in the town of Spokane, Washington, Mrs. John B. Dodd led citizens in celebrating for the first time what she is calling "Father's Day." Mrs. Dodd hopes to set aside the third Sunday in June each year as a special day for fathers, but whether the idea will spread beyond the confines of Spokane remains to be seen. There is already a movement in Pennsylvania for the setting up of a day to honor mothers.

The birth of jazz

An exciting new music called jazz is emerging from the city of New Orleans. It has its origins in the African-American community. Played on a small group of instruments, jazz combines strong rhythms with improvisation, especially by the trumpet player. It remains to be seen if this new music will catch on.

▶ *Jazz musicians in New Orleans.*

Kandinsky and the birth of abstraction in painting

ART

1910 Wassily Kandinsky, a 44-year-old Russian painter, now the leader of a group of avant-garde artists in Munich, has written a treatise calling for a new kind of art which he calls "abstract." Kandinsky no longer attempts to represent the world around him: his canvases are made up of apparently random colors, lines, and shapes with which he hopes to "make close contact with the human soul." His aim is to make painting more like music, which is able to express general ideas and deep emotions without the "distraction" of trying to represent nature.

Revolution in Mexico

20 NOVEMBER Today is the day for the people of Mexico to rise up and throw off the dictatorship of President Porfirio Diaz, according to opposition leader Francisco Madero. President Diaz has ruled Mexico with an iron fist for more than 30 years, refusing to tolerate any opposition. As a result, Mexico's wealthy families have grown richer, but the peasants have largely been ignored, and their plight has become more desperate.

Last year Diaz himself sparked excitement when he told American reporter James Creelman he thought his country was now ready for democracy. The 79-year-old dictator also seemed to indicate he would not be a candidate for election in the forthcoming presidential election of 1910. However, he later announced he was running for election after all, and Francisco Madero, who is a son of one of Mexico's richest families, decided to lead the campaign against him.

In June of this year Madero was arrested. In September the Chamber of Deputies declared that Diaz had been reelected. The following month Madero escaped from prison and fled across the border to San Antonio in Texas from where he plans to finance the revolution in his country.

▲ *Pancho Villa, leader of the Mexican Revolution, rallies the rebels.*

Movie audiences crow over newsreels

Charles Pathé is to take his successful newsreels to the US for the first time. Pathé Brothers was one of the first movie companies to film actual events. First shown in England more than 10 years ago, the company's latest series, *Pathé-Journal*, appeared in France in 1908. Newsreels cover important subjects such as coronations, state funerals, and sports events. They are usually shown before or in between main features.

▲ *Louis Botha, first Union president.*

South Africa establishes Union

21 MAY South Africa becomes a union today when the South Africa Act, promised by Britain after the Second Boer War, comes into effect. The Cape Colony, the Transvaal, the Orange River Colony, and Natal have united to make up the new Union of South Africa. Negotiations over the constitution have been long and hard. The Boers have won a concession by which the electoral system in the British-dominated Cape—which allowed some black and mixed-race people to vote—will not apply in Union-wide elections.

Clean-living girls Guide the world

LEISURE

31 MAY Three years after the formation of the Boy Scouts, Sir Robert Baden-Powell and his sister Agnes have founded the Girl Guides. The aim is to teach girls the virtues of obedience, clean living, and resourcefulness.

The scouting movement is spreading throughout the world. This year the Boy Scouts of America was formed by William Boyce. The US also has its own version of the Girl Guides, called the Camp Fire Girls, started by Dr. and Mrs. Luther Gulick, with the three watchwords of work, health, and love.

▲ *Girl Guide troop lines up for inspection.*

▲ *DuBois gained a Ph.D. from Harvard University.*

NAACP founded: reform is on its way

POLITICS

1 MAY Black American radicals and white reformers have joined to create the National Association for the Advancement of Colored People (NAACP). A key figure in the new movement is 48-year-old W.E.B. DuBois, who has devoted his life to the fight for equality for the black people of the US. DuBois is the leader of the group called the Niagara Movement, which has joined with concerned white Americans to form the new organization, based in New York.

Professor DuBois has spent the last 13 years at Atlanta University studying the conditions under which African-Americans live in the southern states. He will now be working fulltime for the NAACP at its headquarters.

Fun on wheels

The craze of roller skating which is sweeping the US and western Europe has achieved a new respectability. Figure dancing on four-wheeled skates is now a recognized sport, and a system of judging has been developed based on that used in ice-skating.

The world loses Mark Twain

LITERATURE

21 APRIL One of the world's best-loved authors, Mark Twain, has died. He was the creator of the popular American fictional heroes Tom Sawyer and Huckleberry Finn.

Born Samuel Langhorne Clemens, Twain grew up near the Mississippi River, which became the background for his greatest stories. He became a riverboat pilot later in life, and he took his *nom de plume* from the pilot's cry "mark twain," meaning two fathoms, a depth only just safe for navigation by shallow-draft Mississippi steamers.

Twain's greatest success as an author came in the 1870s and 1880s. Despite this, he went bankrupt in the 1890s and had to tour the world giving humorous lectures to pay his debts. Twain, who also had a dark side to his humor, once called humans "evolution's failure," because they had the only evil hearts in the entire creation.

◀ *Huckleberry Finn became a classic American character.*

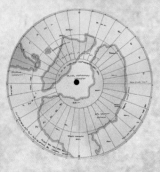

▲ *An old map (as drawn by early explorers) of the South Pole (black dot). It appears as if the pole is in the sea, but in fact this area is buried under ice all year round.*

RACE TO THE POLES

In the late 19th and early 20th centuries there was a sudden burst of polar exploration. Expeditions from several countries set off to the fog and ice of the Arctic Ocean or the glaciers and icebergs of Antarctica.

One purpose of these expeditions was scientific research, but there were other motives. Sometimes national rivalry played a part; sometimes the desire to be famous. It became a race to the poles. The explorer Robert Peary intended to be the first man to reach the North Pole, while Roald Amundsen was determined to be first at the South Pole.

The South Pole

The race to the South Pole was between the British expedition led by Captain Robert Falcon Scott and the Norwegian explorer Roald Amundsen. Scott and his team of 11 men set out with motorized sleds, ponies, and dogs from Cape Evans on 24 October 1911. The sleds soon failed and the horses had to be shot when it became too cold. Amundsen's base camp was 60 miles (96 km) closer to the South Pole than Scott's. An experienced Arctic explorer, he used Inuit (Eskimo) methods of travel. He reached the pole first, on 14 December 1911, five weeks before the exhausted and depleted British team.

Scott's last journey

Only five of Scott's original team reached the South Pole. Scott and two others lived to attempt the return journey but died in a blizzard about 11 miles (18 km) from safety. They never saw their ship *Terra Nova* (below) again.

▲ *Roald Amundsen was on his way to the Arctic when he heard of Peary's success, so he went south instead.*

◀ *The Norwegian flag flies at the South Pole. The Norwegians used dogs to pull sleds and for meat. Scott's men ended up pulling their own sleds, loaded with rocks for scientific study back home.*

▲ *An old map showing the North Pole, located in the permanently frozen sea.*

◀ *Peary took lessons from the Inuit on how to manage a dog team.*

The North Pole

The first attempt to reach the North Pole was made by a British naval officer, Edward Parry, in 1827. Among later expeditions, the best was led by the Norwegian Fridtjof Nansen in 1893–96 in a specially designed ship, the *Fram* (it later carried Amundsen to the Antarctic). Although the ship became frozen in the ice, the current carried it toward the pole as Nansen predicted. He then tried to reach the pole with skis and canoes. His attempt failed, but broke the "farthest-north" record by 162 miles (260 km).

The American Robert Peary made his first Arctic expedition in 1891. He led six expeditions altogether, the last in 1909. He laid down supplies in advance on the route he would take, leaving a final dash to the pole of 155 miles (250 km). With a companion, Matt Henson, and four Inuit, he reached it on 6 April 1909. Not everyone believed Peary's account, and another American, Frederick Cook, claimed to have reached the pole a year earlier. But even fewer believed Cook.

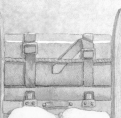

North Pole
1909 Peary triumphs as Cook's claim is proved to be false.

South Pole
1911 Roald Amundsen is the first man to reach the South Pole.

1912 Robert Falcon Scott reaches the Pole—five weeks after Amundsen.

Hood and mittens

Pemmican

◀ *Polar explorers carried special equipment and food, such as fur-lined clothing and canned dried meat, called pemmican.*

1910
1911
1912
1913
1914
1915
1916
1917
1918
1919

▲ *The long pigtail symbolized the old ways of the Manchu Dynasty. Here one boy cuts another's hair.*

POLITICS

China becomes a republic

29 DECEMBER Dr. Sun Yat-sen, a leading advocate of reform in China for 30 years, has been named provisional President of the Chinese Republic. Sun Yat-sen, who is a Christian, trained as a doctor in Hong Kong under Dr. James Cantile, a noted specialist from London. Five years ago Cantile intervened to prevent his ex-pupil being taken back to almost certain death in China by agents at the Chinese legation in London.

From modest beginnings as leader of a secret society operating in Tokyo, Japan, Sun has managed to strengthen his position as leader of the Revolutionary Alliance and mobilize strong support for a constitution. The main supporters of the constitutional movement are young intellectuals, as well as gentry and wealthy merchants who resent the commercial privileges that have been granted to foreigners since the middle of the 19th century. Sun arrived in Shanghai on Christmas Day, having sailed from France.

The declaration of a republic comes after two months of violent civil war, following an uprising in central China. The rebellion was led by units of New Army troops, encouraged by revolutionary groups not affiliated with Sun Yat-sen. In an attempt to stem the tide of rebellion, the emperor, Pu Yi, who is only five years old, took the advice of the prince regent, Prince Chun, and granted a constitution at the end of last month. The move came too late. Two weeks ago Prince Chun was forced to resign. Reports indicate that he has been taken from the Forbidden City under armed guard.

A national convention is to be called to devise a new constitution for China, but it is almost certain that the monarchy will be abolished, bringing to an end the Manchu Dynasty, which has ruled China for 300 years. Many people feel that weak rulers have been responsible for the problems that China has been experiencing.

Massive hit for Irving Berlin

"Alexander's Ragtime Band" is the most popular hit of the year. Written by Russian-born songwriter Irving Berlin—who started out as a singing waiter in New York's Bowery—the catchy tune is not actually ragtime at all. That hasn't stopped the newspapers from crowning Berlin the King of Ragtime.

Nijinsky stars at the Ballets Russes

The Ballets Russes (Russian Ballet), founded in 1909 by impresario Sergei Diaghilev, has a huge hit on its hands in Paris following the opening night of its new ballet *Petrushka*. It stars 21-year-old Vaslav Nijinsky, who has astounded the ballet world in the last few years with his gravity-defying leaps.

Everything, including the sets, dancing, and music adds up to a fantastic new art.

▶ *A portrait of one of the stars of the Ballets Russes.*

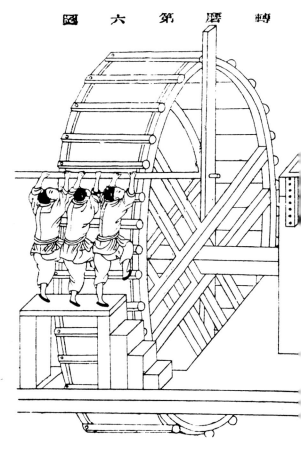

▲ *The old ways—a treadmill in ancient China.*

NEWS • 1911 • NEWS

3 January • Shoot-out between police and anarchists in London, England.

5 May • Mexican revolutionaries oust dictator, President Diaz.

22 June • Coronation of King George V.

5 November • Calbraith Rogers makes first coast-to-coast flight in US.

31 December • Marie Curie wins her second Nobel prize.

ART

Mona Lisa stolen from the Louvre

22 AUGUST There are red faces at the Louvre Museum in Paris today after it was discovered that the most famous painting in the world, Leonardo da Vinci's masterpiece the *Mona Lisa*, was stolen during the night. No one knows how the museum's extensive security system was breached. The *Mona Lisa* was painted in about 1504, when Da Vinci was 52 years of age and living in Florence, Italy, having returned there from Mantua and Venice. The masterpiece, with its subtle smile, is so well known that art experts believe it will be impossible for the thief to sell the painting anywhere in the world.

▲ *Leonardo da Vinci's* Mona Lisa.

ENTERTAINMENT

Film studio first in Hollywood

OCTOBER The Nestor Film Company has opened the first movie studio in the small California community of Hollywood, Los Angeles. Situated on the intersection of Sunset and Gower, the building had been a tavern until it was shut down by antialcohol activists. With its year-round sunshine providing good light for filming, California is fast becoming a favorite location for moviemakers. Whether more will choose to base themselves in Hollywood, only time will tell.

▲ *A film set at Nestor's new studio.*

Explorer finds lost city

US explorer Hiram Bingham reports one of the greatest archeological discoveries of all time. Exploring some 2,000 feet (610 meters) up in the Andes Mountains in Peru, Bingham has found the lost Inca city of Machu Picchu. Unvisited for centuries and never discovered by the Spanish conquistadors, the beautifully constructed stone buildings are overgrown, but survive almost intact.

▼ *Hiram Bingham in front of his tent.*

SPORT

Salchow is world champion again

3 FEBRUARY Swedish-born master of the ice-rink Ulrich Salchow has become world figure-skating champion for a record 10th time. Three years ago he won the first Olympic gold medal awarded for the sport. Salchow has given his name to a tricky and spectacular maneuver involving a jump and a full turn in the air.

Jigsaw puzzle craze

Jigsaw puzzles are all the rage on both sides of the Atlantic. The puzzles were first made in the 18th century when dissected maps were used as a way of teaching geography.

Timeline
1910

1911

1912

1913

1914

1915

1916

1917

1918

1919

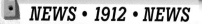

17 January • Robert Scott reaches the South Pole.

14 February • Arizona becomes the 48th state.

28 February • First parachute jump.

1 March • Suffragettes smash store windows in London.

30 July • Yoshihito becomes Emperor of Japan.

23 September • Mack Sennett releases first Keystone Cops movie.

▲ *The drama of the sinking ship is captured in this painting.*

DISASTERS

Titanic tragedy

15 APRIL Just before midnight, the SS *Titanic* rammed an iceberg and shattered the hull on the front starboard (right) side. At 2 o'clock this morning, it slid to the bottom of the Atlantic Ocean, taking with it 1,513 passengers and crew. The maiden voyage of this glittering liner, pride of the White Star Line, has ended in tragedy off Newfoundland.

The *Titanic* has been the most talked about ship in recent years. Reporters invited on board described it as a floating palace complete with an elegant ballroom, magnificent staterooms, indoor gardens, and even a swimming pool. At 892 feet (272 meters) long, it was not only the world's largest ship, but also the most technically advanced. The double-bottomed hull was divided into 16 watertight compartments that were supposed to make the *Titanic* unsinkable.

Investigators will be asking tough questions. Why was the ship steaming through an icefield at a speed of 23 knots? Why was the rogue iceberg not spotted earlier? And why did the *Titanic*, which was capable of holding about 3,500 people, only have lifeboats for 1,178?

SOS signal adopted

Ships in trouble have been using the signal SOS for four years now, but this year the US adopted it as the official distress signal, making the use of SOS universal. Ships communicate with each other using Morse code. The wireless operator taps out letters as combinations of short tones (dots) and long ones (dashes). In Morse, SOS is instantly recognizable as a cry for help and will save many lives.

WAR

Balkan victory

4 DECEMBER Today, just over two months after Bulgaria and Serbia launched an attack on the neighboring Ottoman Empire, Turkish troops have surrendered. Turkish rule in the Balkans, the mountainous countries in southeastern Europe, has been destroyed.

The turning point came at the bloody battle of Lule Burgas last month, at which the Bulgarian army triumphed.

Today's news is the final nail in the coffin of the once glorious Ottoman Empire, founded by the Turks in about 1300 and known since the 1850s as "the sick man of Europe."

▼ *Ottoman Empire recruits line up in Constantinople.*

SPORT

Triumph for Jim Thorpe

22 JULY A Sauk from Prague, Oklahoma, is the sensation of this year's Olympic Games in Stockholm. Jim Thorpe (left), whose tribal name is Wa-Tho-Huck (Bright Path), won a gold medal in the pentathlon and set a world decathlon record of 8,412.96 points. Sweden's King Gustav V congratulated Jim, saying "Sir, you are the greatest athlete in the world." Unsure how to address royalty, he replied: "Thanks, king."

SCIENCE

"Continents have drifted," says Wegener

JANUARY The German scientist Alfred Wegener noticed that the shapes of South America and Africa would fit neatly together if placed side by side. After comparing rocks and fossils from South Africa and Brazil, he has come up with a fascinating new theory that millions of years ago the seven continents we know today were all once part of a single landmass, which he calls Pangaea. Since then the continents have drifted apart, but as yet nobody understands why.

250 million years ago.

135 million years ago.

65 million years ago.

Today's continents.

Painters find a use for scraps

Over the last two years, two young artists from the Parisian group known as the Cubists have been developing an exciting new way of painting. Pablo Picasso and Georges Braque paint objects as if they were being seen from many angles at once, so that the viewer's idea of the object is challenged. Favorite images include newspapers and the human figure. They have also begun to experiment with collages, sticking scraps of various materials onto canvas.

▲ *A still life painting by Georges Braque.*

ARCHEOLOGY

Sculpture stuns the world

7 DECEMBER A 3,000-year-old sculpture has been found in almost perfect condition by German archaeologists in Egypt. The highly painted limestone bust is of Queen Nefertiti, wife of the ancient Egyptian pharaoh Akhenaton IV, who lived around 1360 B.C.

Most ancient Egyptian sculptures are painted according to a set of strict rules that make everyone look the same. This beautiful sculpture, however, allows Queen Nefertiti's regal character to come through. The bust may well be the first true portrait of a person.

SPORT

Annual boat race comes to soggy end

28 MARCH The annual Oxford versus Cambridge University boat race on the Thames River in London ended with both crews soaked to the skin. Battling against strong winds and creating large amounts of spray, the Cambridge boat rapidly sank, while Oxford struggled to the end with their feet in swirling water. The umpire has ordered a rematch in two days time.

1910

1911

1912

1913

1914

1915

1916

1917

1918

1919

1913

Albert Schweitzer's hospital in Lambaréné

16 APRIL A new hospital has opened at Lambaréné, by the Ogooué River in French Equatorial Africa (now Gabon). It will treat the thousands of people in the area suffering from malaria, leprosy, and other tropical diseases. The man who has funded the hospital, and helped to build it with his own hands, is none other than Albert Schweitzer, the world-famous writer and concert organist.

Schweitzer grew up in Germany and studied hard to become a musician, a pastor, and an academic. At the age of 30, he kept an old promise to devote his life to helping other people. He gave up his teaching career to study medicine, and started to raise money by giving organ recitals. He sailed to Africa this year with his wife, Helen, who trained as a nurse in order to help him. The hospital is a converted chicken shed. Local people have already started to come for treatment, but they prefer to sleep outside the clinic and to bring their own goats and chickens for food.

Cartier chip claim

A French chef named Cartier claims to have perfected a new way to cook potatoes. He slices them very thinly before deep-frying them in oil. This claim would surprise George Crum, who first served a similar dish in 1853 at the Moon Lake Lodge in Saratoga Springs, New York. Crum invented the potato chip in a fit of temper after being asked to slice his French fries ever thinner. Now they are catching on worldwide.

▲ *Workers add bodies to Model T Fords.*

93 minutes to assemble a Ford

7 OCTOBER Henry Ford, whose Model T is the world's favorite automobile, today pushed the button of his latest invention: the moving assembly line. Until today, the car chassis has stopped at each point of the assembly line; now, it just keeps moving.

The time needed to make a car has dropped from 12½ hours to 93 minutes, the price has dropped from $850 in 1908 to just $440 today. Assembly workers complain that the work is boring, but they like the wages, which have gone up from $2 to $5 a day.

Domestic fridge in Chicago and Germany

How to keep food fresh in the summer months has always been a problem, particularly in hot countries. Well-off households have used ice-chests—cabinets kept cool by a block or blocks of ice—for decades, but in the last few years machines that make their own ice have become available in Europe. These "refrigerators" are very expensive, but cooks in the grand households that can afford them say that they are an enormous asset in the kitchen.

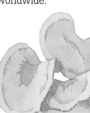

TRANSPORT

World's largest railroad station opens in NYC

2 FEBRUARY New Yorkers have another reason to be proud of their city today with the opening of Grand Central Station, the world's largest. Set in the heart of Manhattan, the station covers an area of 47 acres (19.2 hectares) and has 48 tracks.

The highlight of the station is its superb main concourse. Lit by high windows, it has a sweeping staircase and a vaulted ceiling with gold stars shining out of a deep blue background. There is also a big clock, under which passengers will be able to meet.

PEOPLE

Suffragette martyr dies

8 JUNE The fight for women to have the right to vote (women's suffrage) in Britain gained its first martyr today when 38-year-old Emily Davison died. Four days ago she was seriously injured when she tried to seize the reigns of the king's horse while it was racing in the Derby at Epsom, Surrey.

NEWS • 1913 • NEWS

18 March • King George of Greece assassinated.

3 April • Suffragette Emmeline Pankhurst jailed for three years.

29 June • Women in Norway win the vote.

23 September • Roland Garros becomes the first to fly the Mediterranean.

17 November • German Kaiser bans soldiers from dancing the tango.

12 December • Stolen Mona Lisa is recovered.

ARCHITECTURE

Manhattan skyline reaches new heights

24 APRIL The Manhattan skyline has just become even higher. At 792 feet (241 meters), the Woolworth Building, which was opened today by President Wilson, is the tallest building in the world. It took an army of workmen four years to complete the 55-story building, at a cost of $13.5 million. The Woolworth Building is made of strong concrete on a steel frame, but is covered in molded terracotta, which gives it a delicate appearance similar to a Gothic cathedral.

▶ *The Woolworth Building was designed by Cass Gilbert.*

◀ *Young composer Igor Stravinsky.*

MUSIC

Audience boos new music

29 MAY The audience at a theater in Paris did not enjoy tonight's ballet, the first performance of a piece called *The Rite of Spring.* They shouted, booed, whistled, and walked out, drowning out the music and forcing the composer, Igor Stravinsky, to hide backstage. The music, unlike anything ever heard before, is discordant, strongly rhythmical, and at times very loud.

1910

1911

1912

1913

1914

1915

1916

1917

1918

1919

Zip up and relax

Mary Phelps Jacob, a wealthy American woman, is tired of being laced tightly into whalebone corsets. Instead, she has gathered two handkerchiefs into a cup shape, sewn them together and tied them around the back with pink tapes creating a soft, comfortable but supportive garment. As Miss Jacobs is a fashion leader it is likely this new "brassiere" will catch on. Meanwhile, Gideon Sundback, a Swedish engineer based in Hoboken, New Jersey, has perfected a machine to make slide fasteners. These new fasteners hold clothes together by using a slide to lock or unlock metal teeth on either side of the opening. They could put buttons out of business.

WAR

European war with one shot

4 AUGUST Early this morning, Germany invaded Belgium. At 11 o'clock, Great Britain declared war on Germany. These events were sparked off by the assassination on 28 June of the heir to the Austrian throne, Franz Ferdinand, in Sarajevo—the main city of Bosnia.

As a result, Austria, which has controlled Bosnia for six years, attacked Serbia, accusing it of helping the Bosnian-Serb assassin; Russia, Serbia's ally, prepared to defend Serbia; and Germany, honoring historic ties with Austria, declared war on Russia. This morning's attack on Belgium is really a prelude to an invasion of Russia's faithful ally France, but also draws Britain—long pledged to help defend Belgium in case of invasion—into the conflict.

The underlying causes of this war have been festering for years. Germany has wanted to win more colonies around the world. Britain has wanted to protect its empire. Russia has long been nervous of its German neighbor. All sides believe the war will be over by Christmas.

▲ *Both Ferdinand and his wife were murdered.*

WAR

Europe's troops are ready for battle

12 AUGUST After 10 days of feverish activity, the French, German, and British armies are now ready to fight. It is the fastest mass mobilization of troops in history, mainly thanks to the skilled use of railroads. The French authorities, for example, have used 4,064 trains to move troops eastward to the front. The British Expeditionary Force, which will join France in the defense of Belgium, has assembled at ports, ready to sail.

All the major nations on Europe's mainland have huge armies of conscripts—healthy young men who have to do two or three years' military service by law. Russia called up over a million troops last month, and Germany has at least 1.5 million men in the field already. Britain, however, has a much smaller volunteer army and will need to take measures to encourage more young men to sign up.

▲ *German troops in Brussels, capital city of Belgium.*

WAR

Hindenburg triumphs

31 AUGUST The German General von Hindenburg has scored the first real triumph of the war. With 160,000 men he has routed a Russian force of 210,000 at Tannenberg (near the Polish border), expelling them from their main stronghold in East Prussia.

Four days ago Hindenburg drew up his forces to face the invading Russians. He captured the road and the railroad, cutting off lines of supply, and surrounded them. Yesterday the Russians started to retreat, but were trapped by heavy German bombardment.

Short-cut canal opens early

TRANSPORT

15 AUGUST The SS *Ancon* today made the 40-mile (64-km) journey along the Panama Canal, marking the opening—six months ahead of schedule—of a short cut that will change the face of the Earth. The canal, which opens a sea passage through the narrow strip of land joining North and South America, will cut journeys from the Caribbean to the Pacific by up to 7,000 miles (11,300 km)—a boon to shipping.

▲ SS Ancon, *the first ship to pass through the canal.*

▼ *The German chief of staff, von Schlieffen.*

From English lord to jungle king: Rice Burroughs' Tarzan

He was born the son of a British nobleman, but was abandoned as an orphan child in the African jungle. Raised by a tribe of apes, he can swing from tree to tree and communicate with other animals. He is Lord Greystoke, better known as Tarzan.

This amazing character was created this year by the American novelist Edgar Rice Burroughs in a book called *Tarzan of the Apes*. An exciting new adventure story, Burroughs' book should soon turn out to be a bestseller.

A chief's war plan

WAR

30 SEPTEMBER The German attack on France has been conducted according to a plan finalized in 1905 by the German chief of staff, Alfred von Schlieffen. The idea was to crush the French army quickly and capture Paris while the Russian enemy is still mobilizing on the eastern front, and then swing east to attack Russia.

German troops entered France through Belgium, but were stopped by a strong counterattack at the Marne. Alfred von Schlieffen's plan for winning the war quickly is in shreds.

Victory at the Marne

WAR

10 SEPTEMBER In a major victory for the Allies, General Joseph Joffre's men have driven the German army back from the Marne River and saved Paris from invasion. Joffre secretly collected troops in Paris as the German army tried to encircle the city. Some French troops were rushed to the battlefront in a fleet of taxis and succeeded in mounting a surprise attack on the Germans.

The German commander, Helmuth von Moltke, has ordered a retreat to the Aisne River. His men are digging themselves into trenches. The Allies are also digging in, just a few hundred yards away.

NEWS • 1914 • NEWS

17 March • Winston Churchill urges Britain to build more warships.

13 April • Opening night of Pygmalion, by George Bernard Shaw.

31 July • World stock exchanges close for duration of war.

27 September • Russia invades Hungary.

1 October • Turkey closes Dardanelles Strait.

14 November • Ottoman sultan declares jihad (holy war) on Allies.

◄ *French troops advancing at the Battle of the Marne.*

53

1910
1911
1912
1913
1914
1915
1916
1917
1918
1919

1915

All ships are targets of U-boats

WAR

7 MAY Twenty minutes after being struck by two torpedoes this afternoon, the Cunard liner *Lusitania* sank below the waters of the Atlantic off the coast of Ireland. It was on a return journey from New York to Liverpool with over 1,900 passengers and crew on board, when a U-boat (a German submarine) surfaced nearby and fired its deadly weapons. Some 1,200 people, including 124 Americans, are now believed to have died.

Today's attack is a violent response to the Allied blockade of German ports, which is stopping supplies from reaching that country. Germany now considers every ship in the waters around Britain to be a fair target for attack, and the *Lusitania* was carrying a large cargo of war supplies, including millions of rifle bullets.

▼ *A U-boat, having just torpedoed a merchant ship, stops to pick up survivors.*

Americans will be outraged by the news. The use of submarines to attack shipping is against international law, and President Wilson, who is said to have had several friends on board the ship, is expected to make a strong protest. Last week the German authorities warned US citizens not to travel on the *Lusitania*, which suggests that this attack had long been planned.

Because they are invisible until they reach the surface, U-boats are powerful weapons of surprise.

▼ *U-boats are armed with deadly torpedoes as well as a deck gun.*

Italy joins Allies

WAR

23 MAY The Allies gained a new partner today when Italy declared war on its old ally, Austria. Until now, Italy has kept out of the war, but when Austria refused to hand over territories in the Balkans claimed by Italy, demands for war grew. Last month the Italian prime minister, Antonio Salandra, approved the signing of a secret treaty with France, Russia, and Britain. They have promised to help Italy win its territorial claims in exchange for Italian support. It should be remembered, however, that Italy is short of both money and arms.

POUR LA FRANCE
VERSEZ VOTRE OR

L'Or Combat Pour La Victoire

STÜTZT UNSRE
FELDGRAUEN
KRIEGSANLEIHE
ZERREISST
ENGLANDS
MACHT
ZEICHNET

The propaganda war

WAR

1915 Since war broke out, the word "propaganda" has been given a new meaning. From a Latin word meaning "to spread," applied to religious beliefs, it now refers to the influencing of public opinion in general. Germany used it first, in posters and newspaper reports designed to boost morale. They even marked the sinking of the *Lusitania* with a souvenir medal.

Britain joined in with the *Report on Alleged German Outrages in Belgium*. The 300 pages are full of unconfirmed eyewitness reports, designed to make readers angry.

◄ *French (far left) and German (left) propaganda posters.*

Camera is the star in Griffith's latest movie

The latest movie by director D.W. Griffith (below) opened tonight. *The Birth of a Nation*, which tells the story of the formation of the Ku Klux Klan just after the Civil War, opens a new chapter in the history of cinema. Griffith has made the camera perform: scenes fade in and out, close-ups reveal the emotions of the actors and actresses, and scenes are interwoven to show that they are happening at the same time.

▲ *Allied soldiers blinded by gas.*

WAR

Ypres gas attack

22 APRIL This evening, near the town of Ypres, on the Western Front, German troops unleashed their latest weapon, poisonous chlorine gas, on the Allies. Choking, blinded, and frightened, soldiers in the front line fled. It was left to brave Canadian troops, fighting to their last man, to halt the attack of the advancing German army.

Poet's death is tragic loss

The death today of Rupert Brooke, one of the most promising young poets of his generation, will sadden many. Brooke will long be remembered for his writing, which paints an idealized image of war and nobility in death. His vision, however, is increasingly at odds with the reality being experienced by the soldiers fighting in the trenches.

POLITICS

Ku Klux Klan lives again

4 DECEMBER Inspired by D.W. Griffith's movie masterpiece *The Birth of a Nation*, Colonel William Simmons has relaunched the Ku Klux Klan in Atlanta, Georgia. The Klan is a secret society, born in the 1860s just after the Civil War but banned since 1872. Members wear sinister hooded costumes, and their aim is to maintain white control in America—mainly by keeping the black population in fear and poverty.

NEWS • 1915 • NEWS

13 January • 29,000 die in Italian earthquake.

6 June • German U-boats ordered not to sink passenger liners.

5 September • Tzar takes command of Russian army.

12 October • Germans execute English nurse Edith Cavell for helping Allied prisoners to escape.

10 December • Ford Motor Company produces millionth car.

▼ *Allied troops fighting at Gallipoli.*

WAR

Gallipoli dead

20 DECEMBER Tonight, the Allies finally abandoned their main positions on the Gallipoli peninsula. Troops, mainly from Australia and New Zealand, landed here in April, in response to a request from the Russians for Allied help in their campaign against Turkey. The Turkish army has mounted an iron defense of the peninsula, which guards the Dardanelles Strait at the entrance to the Sea of Marmara. The Allies have fought a disastrous, disorganized campaign, suffering huge casualties but achieving nothing.

◄ *Ku Klux Klan members burn a wooden cross.*

CIVILIANS IN WAR

▼ *A charity in Berlin feeds children whose fathers are away fighting.*

World War I, or the Great War, was a devastating experience for everyone involved. This was a war fought by ordinary people as well as by professional soldiers. The people who stayed at home were also part of the war machine: most civilian factories began making vitally important guns and military goods.

A whole generation of men left home and went to their deaths in the trenches. This meant that many women never married, and some spent the rest of their lives in mourning. A lot of soldiers who survived returned with physical injuries or "shell shock," a state of mental collapse caused by constant bombardment.

Children's life at home

Countless children went hungry because the British navy blockaded German ports and German U-boats targeted ships coming to Britain. Feeding the troops took priority, and soon mothers spent large parts of each day lining up for food. In 1915, Germany started issuing "bread tickets," which limited the amount each household could buy. In Britain, children were upset when the government rationed sugar in 1917; butter, margarine, jam, and meat followed.

Games imitated the real world, and children played at being air aces, wounded heroes, and brave nurses. New boardgames gave them the chance to catch Kaiser Bill or mount a sea battle. Children also played more practical roles. Girls helped their mothers to knit sweaters for the soldiers, and British Boy Scouts helped the coastguard watch the shores.

▼ *Aiding the war effort—children in New York help to grow their own food in plots near their homes.*

"Goodbye, Daddy!"

A scene repeated at railroad stations and ports across the world was that of children kissing their soldier fathers goodbye, never knowing when they would see them again. Millions of children were too young to know what was happening and did not recognize their fathers when they came back from the front.

▶ *A US private on his way to Europe says goodbye to his family.*

Women take over "men's" work

In order for men to go to war, they had to be released from work. For the first time, women took jobs that had always been thought too hard or too responsible for them. They seized the opportunity to learn new skills, earn their own wages, and contribute to the war effort. Women porters, guards, and inspectors on the railroads; women bus and van drivers; female coal porters (using special, smaller sacks), and mailwomen were all new sights. "Land girls" stepped in to do the work of young farmers. Women also worked in munitions factories, performing heavy industrial work such as making shells, guns, and explosives. When the men returned, they expected to get their old jobs back, and at the end of the war many women returned to household work—but their prospects had changed forever.

▲ *London policewomen warn people of Zeppelins.*

▶ *A woman welds metal parts together in a factory—traditionally a man's job.*

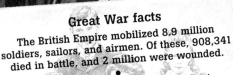

Great War facts

The British Empire mobilized 8.9 million soldiers, sailors, and airmen. Of these, 908,341 died in battle, and 2 million were wounded.

•

30,633 civilians were killed in U-boat attacks and air raids.

•

In total, more that 8 million people were killed, and about 20 million others were wounded.

•

The British war effort cost about £8 billion.

◄ *Captain T. E. Lawrence.*

1910

1911

1912

1913

1914

1915

1916

1917

1918

1919

▲ *The harsh Arabian desert is difficult fighting terrain.*

Curvy bottle for Coca-Cola

A very unusual bottle appeared in the stores, bars, and diners of the US this summer, when the Coca-Cola Company started to sell its fizzy drink in a curvy bottle designed by the Root Glass Company of Terre Haute, Indiana. The bottle is based on the shape of the cola nut, one of the drink's "secret" ingredients. The owners hope that the distinctive shape will help them sell more.

► *The muddy trenches of Verdun, where soldiers are fighting the bloodiest battle on the Western Front.*

POLITICS

Arabs bid for independence

31 OCTOBER In June, the tribes of Arabia and Jordan, long ruled by the Turks, made their bid for independence. Hussein ibn Ali, the emir (ruler) of Mecca, proclaimed an Arab revolt against the Ottoman Empire and forced the Turkish garrison in Mecca to surrender. He then swiftly sent his sons Faisal, Abdullah, and Zeid to take control of key cities such as Taif, Jeddah, and Medina.

Although the Arabs have had major successes fighting in their traditional way, it is now clear that they really need a modern style of army. This month, to help him make reforms, Hussein has welcomed a group of British officers to Jeddah. They include a 28-year-old intelligence officer, Captain Thomas Edward (T.E.) Lawrence, who speaks Arabic and is familiar with the area and its customs. Lawrence has been appointed liaison officer between the British Army and Prince Faisal. It is his aim to ensure that the Arab tribes, who have so far fought separately, now fight together.

WAR

Agony at Verdun

25 JUNE Whatever the outcome of the Great War, the French people will remember 1916 as the "year of Verdun." It is four months since Germany launched a massive attack on the historic fortress of Verdun on the Meuse River in northeastern France. In strict military terms Verdun is not a vital position for the French or the Germans, but it has huge symbolic significance for France, and the Germans have calculated that the French will do anything to defend their fortress. So far, over 600,000 men have died in the Battle of Verdun, and still the French soldiers, led by General Pétain, are holding out against the vicious assault by the Germans that aims to destroy their morale.

British fleet limps back from Jutland

WAR

1 JUNE The German and British fleets are making their way home from the North Sea this morning after the first great naval clash of the war. Yesterday morning, Admiral Scheer led the German High Seas Fleet out of their harbors in an attempt to break the Allied blockade of the German coast. The British Grand Fleet, under Admiral Sir John Jellicoe, sailed to meet it.

Both commanders were unaware that they were about to meet an entire fleet. Neither was prepared for the scale of the battle and the heavy losses. Both sides claim victory; but the British confidently predict that the German fleet will not dare to leave port again.

Mystic monk murdered

PEOPLE

30 DECEMBER Grigori Rasputin, a disheveled monk believed by the tzar and his family to have mystical healing powers, has long been the most hated man in Russia. His interference in politics infuriated a group of patriots led by Prince Felix Yusupov.

Last night Yusupov tried to kill Rasputin with chocolate cakes laced with cyanide. When this failed he tried other methods, finally succeeding in drowning the monk in a river.

NEWS • 1916 • NEWS

27 January • Conscription introduced in Britain.

21 February • Germany attacks Allies at Verdun.

29 April • British troops surrender to Turks at Kut el-Amara.

1 July • Allies launch offensive on River Somme, France.

7 November • Jeannette Rankin becomes first US Congresswoman.

7 December • David Lloyd George becomes British Prime Minister.

Brave Earl Kitchener dies

PEOPLE

5 JUNE Tonight Earl Kitchener of Khartoum, the British War Secretary, went down with the cruiser HMS *Hampshire* after it hit a mine near the Orkney Islands. Kitchener was last seen standing calmly on deck as the badly holed cruiser started to sink. Britain has lost a great, if much criticized, hero. It is Kitchener's finger that points from the army recruitment posters.

Defiant art at the Cabaret Voltaire

Visitors to Zurich should head for the Cabaret Voltaire, a "literary nightclub." The artists and writers who meet there are inventing a new style of art that has no rules. If an object is chosen by an artist, or shown in a gallery, then it is art. The movement's name is Dada (French for "rocking horse"). The name was chosen at random from a dictionary by members of the group.

▶ *Man Ray, a Dadaist.*

◀ *Irish freedom fighters.*

Irish Easter rising is over

POLITICS

29 APRIL Today the Irish rebellion is over and Irish independence from Britain is a distant dream once again.

The rebellion began on Easter Monday, when rebels set fire to the courthouse in Dublin and shot at sentries guarding the castle. The rebel leader, poet Padraic Pearse, bravely declared Irish independence from the steps of the captured post office. The rebellion was quashed by the British in a violent counterattack with troops and a gunboat.

Timeline:
1910
1911
1912
1913
1914
1915
1916
1917
1918
1919

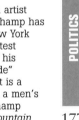

POLITICS

Russian Revolution promises "Peace, land, bread"

7 NOVEMBER Today Russia experienced its second revolution in a year when the Bolsheviks seized power in the capital, Petrograd (St. Petersburg). There has been virtually no bloodshed. The first revolution occurred in March and forced the tzar, Nicholas II, to abdicate after his troops refused to fire on rioting crowds protesting against food shortages. A provisional government was formed, promising reforms that would make Russia into a democracy.

The new government was welcomed by nearly all classes, but no one could agree about what kind of state should replace the tzardom. The confusion and turmoil gave the Bolsheviks their chance to seize power.

The Bolsheviks are an extreme revolutionary group led by Vladimir Lenin and Leon Trotsky. They are followers of the German philosopher Karl Marx and believe in a state in which all private property is abolished. A small party, the Bolsheviks have gained influence in the cities through the control of workers' councils, called soviets. Their promise of "Peace, land, bread" has a strong appeal for the people.

▼ *Bolshevik artillery prepare to fight in the streets of Moscow during the second 1917 Revolution.*

▶ *Bolshevik soldiers guard the door to Lenin's room.*

Is this art?

The French artist Marcel Duchamp has startled New York with the latest example of his "ready-made" sculpture. It is a urinal from a men's toilet. Duchamp names it *Fountain* and has signed it R. Mutt 1917. He bought it from a plumbers' merchant. Duchamp was one of the founders of Dada, the movement that attacks the whole idea of art, and of common sense.

POLITICS

Uncle Sam needs you

6 APRIL The President of the United States, Woodrow Wilson, today signed a declaration of war against Germany. He told Congress: "The world must be made safe for democracy." The US now joins Britain and France in the world war.

Since independence in 1776, the US has always avoided becoming involved in the quarrels of Europe—the policy known as isolationism.

Until today, President Wilson has remained neutral, attempting to start peace talks between the warring powers. But attacks by German submarines on ships in the Atlantic and the discovery early this year of a secret German plan to persuade Mexico to declare war on the US have provoked a dramatic reversal of policy.

I WANT YOU FOR U.S. ARMY
NEAREST RECRUITING STATION

NEWS • 1917 • NEWS

31 March • Recordings by the Original Dixieland Band introduce a wider audience to jazz music.

17 September • Germans defeat Russians and capture Riga (Latvia).

15 October • Supposed German spy Mata Hari executed in France.

2 November • British Balfour Declaration supports the creation of a national home for Jews in Palestine.

◀ *US government poster depicting Uncle Sam, the symbol of the US, encouraging men to join the army.*

▲ *Gotha GV bomber.*

"Buffalo Bill" Cody dies

William F. Cody, the Wild West star, died at the age of 70 on 10 January. He had once been a professional hunter and earned his nickname of "Buffalo Bill" supplying buffalo meat to gangs building the transcontinental railroad in the US. Later, he became an actor in touring companies, and in 1883 organized his first Wild West show, with mock stage-coach hold-ups and "Indian fights." His shows were very popular in the US and Europe and helped to form the image of what life was like in the "Wild West."

TECHNOLOGY

Fast attack from new German bomber

13 JUNE A sinister new development in warfare took place today when German aircraft bombed east London. Over 100 people, including children, are said to have been killed in the raid. The attack took place in broad daylight, and although the bombers met antiaircraft fire, none was hit. London has been attacked before, by the large, slow airships called Zeppelins, which were easier to shoot down than fast-flying planes.

The planes in today's raid were Gotha GVs, biplanes with twin Mercedes engines. They can fly at nearly 100 miles per hour (160 km per hour) for more than 500 miles (800 km) and carry six 110-pound (50-kg) bombs.

WAR

Costly battle in Flanders mud

6 NOVEMBER Allied troops have finally captured the ridge at Passchendaele, northeast of Ypres in Flanders. Field Marshal Sir Douglas Haig's aim of dislodging the Germans from this stretch of high ground has been achieved, but a battle that should have lasted two days has taken three terrible months.

This is the third battle to be fought in the area around Ypres, and troops have been trying to advance across thick mud, pockmarked with deep, water-filled shell craters. Torrential rain has added to their difficulties. Losses on both sides are thought to be shockingly high. Many of the men lost their lives by drowning in the mud.

▼ *Wet weather and heavy shellfire have turned Flanders into a mudbath.*

Vision at Fatima

A strange story is starting to emerge from the Portuguese village of Fatima, north of Lisbon. Two young girls and a small boy claim to have seen visions of the Virgin Mary, mother of Jesus. Although the oldest of the girls is only 10, people are taking the children seriously. From the descriptions of the visions and the sophisticated words that they use, it is hard to believe that the children have made up the entire story.

WAR

No more retreat for Italians

12 NOVEMBER The Italians have managed to hold their front in the northeast of Italy, despite a disastrous setback in the previous two weeks. On 24 October Austrian and German troops launched a fearsome attack on weak Italian defenses in Caporetto. The Italian commander General Cadorna was forced to retreat. Thousands of men were killed, about 275,000 were taken prisoner, and nearly as many deserted. However, with the aid of British and French reinforcements, the Italians are now standing firm again.

1910
1911
1912
1913
1914
1915
1916
1917
1918
1919

1918

End of Romanov dynasty

▼ *Tzar, Nicholas II, the Tzarina Alexandra, and their children, photographed before the Revolution.*

17 JULY The Russian tzar, Nicholas II, his wife, and their children have been brutally murdered in cold blood. The massacre took place last night in the cellar of the house where they were held under guard by the Bolshevik (Soviet) authorities. There appear to be no survivors in spite of rumors that the princess Anastasia escaped.

After a republic was declared in Russia during the March Revolution last year, the royal family were guarded by the provisional government. At first, they stayed in some comfort in Tobolsk, but in April 1918 they were moved to Ekaterinburg, a grim town in central Russia. With civil war raging, Ekaterinburg was in danger of being overrun by Czech forces fighting with the White (anti-Bolshevik) Russians. To prevent the royal family becoming the pawns of the White Russians, the local commissar had them murdered, with Bolshevik government permission. The family doctor and servants were also killed. This grim massacre ends the dynasty of the Romanovs, who have ruled Russia since 1613.

Russia is out of the war

3 MARCH Russia has pulled out of the war. Today, representatives of the new Bolshevik (Soviet) government agreed a peace treaty with the Germans and Austrians at the city of Brest-Litovsk in Belarus.

Russian casualties in the war have been higher than those of any other country, and the Bolsheviks have been eager to end the war since they came to power. Although expected, the treaty is unwelcome for Britain and France as it removes a major part of the alliance.

▼ *Russians and Germans agree the treaty at Brest-Litovsk.*

Big Bertha: giant "secret" weapon

24 JUNE A colossal German gun today shelled Paris from a distance of over 75 miles (120 km). Total casualties since it began firing in March are about 1,000, and French morale has suffered a heavy blow.

This monster has a barrel 110 feet (33.5 meters) long and weighs 200 tons. It fires its shells 12 miles (18 km) high, where there is little drag from the atmosphere. At such great range, it is highly inaccurate, but Paris is too big a target to miss. Big Bertha is thought to be a giant howitzer. Similar guns were used in Belgium at the beginning of the war.

▶ *Big Bertha, the German's monster gun.*

Women get the vote

28 DECEMBER Results of the British general election were declared today—the first in which women have been allowed to vote.

The long campaign for women's suffrage (the right to vote) was led by a group of women who were nicknamed the suffragettes. As a result of the part played by women in the war effort, opposition has finally faded, and the act giving women the vote was passed with little resistance in June. However, only women over 30 may vote, while men may vote at 21.

Work for the girls

1918 The war has changed the position of women in society, probably forever. Thousands of women in all the warring countries are now doing work in industry that was previously done only by men. But women's work is not confined to peaceful industries. They are also to be found in branches of the armed forces.

Auxiliary women's services have existed before, mainly for nurses, but this is the first time that women have been granted full military rank and status. They are not being trained to fight but, by taking over some of the administrative and other jobs in the army, servicewomen are freeing more men for a fighting role.

◀ British female soldiers on motorbike patrol.

▲ *British and German aircraft in a "dogfight."*

Red Baron loses final "dogfight"

21 APRIL The Red Baron (above right) will fly no more. This once-feared great German fighter ace was shot down and killed today in a dogfight above the war-torn area of the Somme.

Baron Manfred von Richthofen gained his nickname from one of his aircraft, a red Fokker Dr. 1 triplane. He had been a fighter pilot for two years and is said to have been responsible for the destruction of up to 80 Allied aircraft.

A gentleman, who once treated a captured British pilot to an excellent dinner, the Baron was a cool and ferocious opponent in the air.

Allies to "bag" the enemy

18 JULY Three days after the Germans renewed their offensive on the Marne sector of the front in northern France, the Allies have launched a counterattack, under the command of the French general, Pétain.

The attack is being aimed against the west flank of the "bulge" in the lines, made when the Germans advanced earlier in the year. The Germans extended their front still farther three days ago, when some divisions succeeded in crossing the Marne River. Pétain's aim is to turn the "bulge" into a "bag," capturing the German troops inside it. His forces include 500 tanks.

▶ *Allied forces go into action at the Second Battle of the Marne.*

The war is over—peace at last

11 NOVEMBER Today, the lamps in Europe can be relit. The war—the cruelest and costliest war in European history—is over. An armistice has been agreed, and at 11 o'clock this morning the guns that have thundered over the Western Front for four long years at last fell silent. Instead, church bells are triumphantly ringing in peace.

A month ago, the Allies were planning their next campaign. But the string of Allied successes since August has finally cracked the resolve of the German government and the military high command. It was the supreme commanders, Hindenburg and Ludendorff, the most successful generals in the whole war, who insisted on an armistice.

Germany had not yet been invaded, and military experts say that it could have continued the war, but there is no doubt that the country is exhausted. The German people have had enough. They have agreed to evacuate French territory including Alsace-Lorraine, former French provinces held by Germany since 1871. All major weapons, including ships, are to be surrendered, and Allied troops will be stationed in Germany as far east as the Rhine River.

▲ *Woman wearing a flu mask.*

Flu epidemic rages on

The worldwide epidemic of Spanish flu continues. The total deaths so far are estimated at more than 20 million, in the worst outbreak ever.

In spite of its name, there is no evidence that this flu began in Spain. Instead, it seems to have started in the Middle East. This pandemic disease is the worst since the bubonic plague, or Black Death, killed one third of the population of Europe in the 1300s.

▶ *In the US, flags come out to celebrate the Armistice.*

▼ *Thousands lie buried in European cemeteries.*

Armistice facts

In the US, the press mistakenly reported the Armistice four days too early. Americans have celebrated twice.

•

In London, celebrating crowds hijack buses and total strangers embrace.

•

Lieutenant Ernst Jünger, a German officer, is in a hospital recovering from the latest of the 14 wounds he has suffered since 1914.

War claims a generation

1918 The Great War has been the costliest in European history. It is thought that there are around 8.5 million dead, with many more seriously wounded.

The casualties are mainly young men, creating a shortage of leaders for the next generation. Many children will grow up without ever knowing their fathers. For the men who have survived, returning to normal life could be extremely difficult.

Much of northern France and southern Belgium is in ruins. The cathedral of Reims, where medieval French kings were crowned, is a shell. The financial costs are huge. One estimate puts them at nearly $100 billion. The European nations are heavily in debt: the Allied powers owe the US over $7 billion. Only the US has escaped without damage to its infrastructure. There are no real victors.

Habsburg empire collapses

POLITICS

16 NOVEMBER Republics have been proclaimed in Austria and Hungary, marking the collapse of the Austro-Hungarian empire. The Poles, Czechs, and Slovaks, who were also part of the empire, gained independence last month.

The emperor Karl has left the imperial capital of Vienna and gone into exile. He is the last of the Habsburg dynasty, rulers of the empire and a major power since the Middle Ages.

Boundaries for the new republics, including those of a much-reduced Austria, will be determined at a later date.

◀ *Crowds in front of the Reichstag, Berlin.*

NEWS • 1918 • NEWS

14 January • French statesman Joseph Caillaux, who opposes the war, arrested for treason.

5 March • Moscow replaces Petrograd (St. Petersburg) as Russian capital.

23 April • Irish general strike against British proposal to introduce conscription.

29 May • Czech forces in Russia join "White" Russians in the civil war against the "Red" Bolshevik government.

Germany becomes a republic

POLITICS

9 NOVEMBER Today Philip Scheidemann, a member of the Social Democrat Party, announced that Germany is now a republic. He was speaking from the Reichstag in Berlin.

Germany is in the grip of a revolution, and Scheidemann had been racing to make the announcement ahead of the left-wing faction of the Social Democrats and other extremist groups. He has succeeded in seizing power for the more liberal elements of his party.

The kaiser, Wilhelm II, has abdicated and fled to Holland. His chancelor, Prince Max of Baden, has ceded power to the Social Democrat leader, Friedrich Ebert. A new constitution will now have to be decided.

Points for peace

TREATIES

8 JANUARY President Wilson (left) today published his statement of war aims in the form of 14 points. They are intended to be the basis for peace negotiations at the end of the war.

The points include free and open negotiations between nations; free trade and freedom of the seas; reduction of weapons of war; and restoration of lands occupied by Germany, including the French provinces of Alsace-Lorraine held by Germany since 1871. The last of the 14 points calls for a league of nations, which would guarantee the independence of nations threatened by powerful neighbors.

Ape boy hits big time

Tarzan of the Apes, which opened in New York on 27 January, is already a big success. The film, based on the book by Edgar Rice Burroughs, is the story of a British aristocrat's son (played by Elmo Lincoln) who is abandoned in the jungle as a baby and brought up by apes. Although the scenery looks more like a stage set in California than a tropical forest in Africa, no one is complaining. We will no doubt be seeing a lot more of Tarzan in the future.

1910

1911

1912

1913

1914

1915

1916

1917

1918

1919

1919

ENTERTAINMENT

Stars form new film company

17 APRIL Four of the biggest stars in Hollywood are forming a new, independent film company, called United Artists. The stars plan to distribute their own movies and build a production studio. An independent movie studio will be a challenge to the big Hollywood companies that have monopolized the distribution of movies until now. Hollywood companies have also been in the habit of holding their stars under contract at a fixed salary, depriving them of a share of the large profits their movies are earning.

The stars who are taking this daring step are Mary Pickford, "America's sweetheart," who is said to have signed a studio contract worth over $1 million dollars; her husband, Douglas Fairbanks, famous for his athletic performances in adventure films; D.W. Griffith, the outstanding director who made the first Hollywood epic, the three-hour-long *The Birth of a Nation*; and Charlie Chaplin, the British-born comic genius celebrated for his character of the "little fellow" underdog who somehow comes out on top. Chaplin is probably the most famous of the four.

Lest we forget

11 November is the first anniversary of the Armistice. For two minutes at 11 o'clock, silence reigned throughout the countries of the British Empire and its Allies in the war. People stopped in the streets, workers put down their tools, children were held quietly by their mothers as all remembered those who lost their lives in the Great War. Armistice Day has been declared an annual day of mourning.

▲ *Mary Pickford signs for United Artists, watched by Fairbanks (left), Chaplin (center), Griffith (second from right), and lawyers.*

NEWS • 1919 • NEWS

10 March • Emergency food supplies shipped to Germany to aid the starving.

23 March • Mussolini founds the Italian Fascist Party.

10 April • Emiliano Zapata, Mexican peasants' leader, betrayed and shot during Mexican Revolution.

13 April • British troops fire on unarmed crowd in Amritsar, India, killing 400.

TREATIES

Treaty is too severe

21 JUNE The official end of the war came today when a peace settlement was reached at Versailles, near Paris. Representatives of nations involved in the Great War signed the treaty. It is 200 pages long and has taken five months to finalize. Many minor affairs still remain to be settled.

The treaty is highly controversial. Some experts say that the penalties imposed on Germany by the treaty are too severe. It demands an initial payment of 20 billion gold marks and 27,150 square miles (70,312 square km) of land to be surrendered to neighboring states. The Germans, who disclaim responsibility for the war, have been forced to sign. Many feel that German resentment could lead to another war.

◄ *Allied leaders at Versailles.*

Daring Italian poet seizes city of Fiume

Gabriele D'Annunzio, an Italian poet, war hero, playwright, and adventurer has seized the city of Fiume, on the Adriatic Sea in Dalmatia. Fiume was being held by the Allies until its status could be decided. D'Annunzio declares that the city belongs to Italy and, supported by 300 volunteers, has thrown out representatives of Allied governments and set himself up as dictator, or sole ruler. The Italian government officially condemns his bold action, but the Italian people are delighted. D'Annunzio, like his fellow countryman Mussolini, believes in government by a single strong leader.

◀ The poet D'Annunzio and supporters.

WAR

German navy scuttles High Seas Fleet

21 JUNE The German High Seas Fleet is at the bottom of the sea. At noon, on an agreed signal, the crews opened the stopcocks and sent the ships plunging to the seabed.

When the fleet surrendered at the end of the war, about 70 ships were interned at the naval base of Scapa Flow, off the Orkney Islands. They were not handed over to British command, but were carefully observed from a distance. Now, only a few ships are still afloat.

The German admiral said that he was obeying an order given at the start of the war—no German ship should be surrendered.

▲ A German warship sinks to its watery grave in Scapa Flow.

POLITICS

Lady Astor takes her seat

1 DECEMBER American Lady Nancy Astor took her seat in the British Parliament today, breaking a centuries-old tradition—she is the first female member to sit in the House of Commons. Her husband held the same seat until he moved to the House of Lords on becoming the second Lord Astor. Lady Astor's wit will be a welcome addition.

SCIENCE

Scientists "split" the atom

1 JUNE The brilliant New Zealand-born scientist Ernest Rutherford, of Manchester University, England, has succeeded in "splitting" the atom.

Traditionally, scientists believed that the atom was nature's smallest building block and could not be divided into smaller particles. The discovery that hydrogen atoms contain a positive nucleus and negative electrons undermined this belief. In a sensational new experiment, Rutherford has split a nitrogen atom into atoms of oxygen and hydrogen by bombarding it with subatomic alpha particles.

▲ Ernest Rutherford.

TRANSPORT

Sandwiches sustain transatlantic pilots

14 JUNE Aviation history was made today when a Vickers Vimy aircraft crash-landed at Clifden in the west of Ireland. She had flown nonstop from St. John's, Newfoundland, taking 16 hours and 12 minutes. The pilot was Captain John Alcock, a well-known British air ace in the recent war, and his navigator was Lieutenant Arthur W. Brown. They flew through fog and sleet, sustained by sandwiches.

An American, Lieutenant Albert C. Read, flew across the Atlantic last month, but had to stop in the Azores to refuel.

▼ Alcock (center, with a model of his aircraft) and Brown (right) on a British ship after their flight.

1920

New clashed with the old in the 1920s. An explosion in new fashions and entertainments thrilled many, but some were too poor to take part and turned back to traditional ways.

In Europe and North America, people flocked to the new cinemas and dance halls. Jazz music and dances such as the Charleston were popular. Women demanded greater equality with men. The US authorities tried to ban alcohol, and in the south the racist Ku Klux Klan was revived. Businesses boomed in the US, but the end of the decade saw the onset of economic gloom.

1920
1921
1922
1923
1924
1925
1926
1927
1928
1929

▲ *The new hairdryer is sure to be a big hit.*

Handheld hairdryer on sale

It is now easier than ever to try the latest hairstyles at home. Here comes a secret weapon for home grooming—the new handheld hairdryer. The adventurous also have the chance to try the permanent wave, or perm— a revolutionary way of curling straight hair. You can now change the color of your hair, too, with the new synthetic hair dyes.

▼ *Gangsters have a violent reputation, as this movie scene shows.*

LAW

Alcohol goes down the drain

16 JANUARY It's goodbye to saloon bars. The US Constitution's 18th Amendment, which bans making, transporting, or selling alcohol, took effect at 12:01 o'clock today. Americans wanting to raise a glass to toast in the new decade must fill it with nothing stronger than water.

It is a day of triumph for religious groups who have fought a long campaign for the banning of alcohol. Many states have already passed prohibition laws— Maine did so in 1851, and 26 states have followed its lead since 1917.

Some fear that people will go "underground" to secret drinking dens. In cities such as Chicago, it is rumored that the gangsters who run the prostitution business are already organizing an illegal operation making and selling alcoholic drinks, which would turn in huge profits. Jim Colosimo, Johnny Torrio, and Al "Scarface" Capone are known to be operating there already.

If the gangsters make a fortune out of illegal alcohol, it will only increase the threat that they pose to law-abiding Americans. When big profits are at stake, the gangsters will be desperate to come out on top in power struggles with rival gangs, unleashing a spiral of violence in American cities.

Prohibition facts
In 1929 in New York City, there were an estimated 100,000 illegal drinking dens. • Official figures show that 1,000 people had been killed or poisoned by impure alcohol by 1929.

▲ *US government officials empty barrels of beer.*

SPORT

Black Sox play dirty

28 SEPTEMBER Eight of baseball's top stars were suspended today after being accused of deliberately losing last year's World Series against the Cincinatti Reds. The players from the Chicago White Sox are believed to have been bought off by a New York syndicate, and three of the players have already confessed. Many gamblers have made a fortune out of the result. Nicknamed the "Black Sox," the eight players face a lifetime ban from baseball.

Nations meet for peace

TREATIES

11 FEBRUARY The first council meeting of the League of Nations took place in London today. The international organization has been set up to settle arguments between countries and keep peace. Statesmen from Britain, France, Japan, Italy, Belgium, Spain, Brazil, and Greece made up the council, but there was no delegate from the US.

The US voted against joining the League because it does not want to become involved in other countries' disputes.

The League was established under the Versailles Treaty last year. Critics say that without the US, the League will not be strong enough to keep international peace. Many countries still disagree over the boundaries imposed on them under the treaty.

▲ *League of Nations council members held an informal meeting in Geneva earlier this year.*

Famine looms as chaos reigns

DISASTERS

MARCH A civil war has broken out in the former Russian Empire between the Bolshevik government and its enemies. The war is wreaking havoc on the Russian economy, especially agriculture. Both sides have begun to seize grain from the peasants at bayonet-point. In response, the peasants have stopped sowing for next year. If the situation continues, there will be a famine once current food stocks are used up, putting millions of lives at risk.

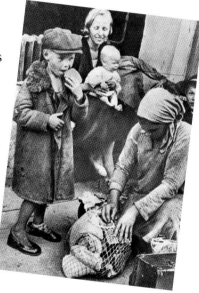

US election on the air

TECHNOLOGY

2 NOVEMBER The results of today's presidential election have been announced to the US in the nation's first radio broadcast. Frank Conrad and Donald Little were the broadcasters for KDKA, a radio station based in Pittsburgh, Pennsylvania.

Although fewer than 1,000 radio sets received the broadcast, interest in the radio is growing and radio set sales are expected to rise.

Today's results mark the start of weekly broadcasts by KDKA. For the record, Warren Harding won the race for the White House.

▲ *The site of the first KDKA broadcast.*

Top baseball star now playing for big bucks

Big money spoke loudly today when the New York Yankees signed the Boston Red Sox's 26-year-old star Babe Ruth for a record £78,000. Babe, whose real name is George Herman Ruth, helped the Red Sox win the World Series, baseball's top trophy in 1915, 1916, and 1918.

▶ *Babe Ruth hit a record 29 home runs for the Red Sox last season.*

Psychiatric help with ink blots

SCIENCE

1920 Swiss psychiatrist Hermann Rorschach has been showing his patients pictures of ink blots. The patients are encouraged to talk about whatever comes into their head when they see the blots and to talk about anything else they associate with that word or image—a process known as free association.

Rorschach then compares the responses made by his patients to the ink blots. He says this gives him an insight into different mental disorders.

▲ *Treaty negotiators hope that dividing Europe up into smaller countries will reduce the chance of war.*

1920

Europe gets facelift from new treaties

TREATIES

4 JUNE The map of Europe has been redrawn as a result of treaty negotiations following the Great War of 1914–18. Today Hungary signed the Treaty of Trianon with the Allies, losing Slovakia to Czechoslovakia, Transylvania to Romania.

Last year, Austria lost most of its half of the old Austro-Hungarian empire when it was redistributed under the Treaty of Saint-Germain. This created the two new countries of Czechoslovakia and the Kingdom of Serbs, Croats, and Slovenes.

Bulgaria lost some of its land to Greece and the Kingdom of Serbs, Croats, and Slovenes under the Treaty of Neuilly last year. The treaty also makes Poland an independent country once more. Before the war, some of it was part of the Russian empire.

The negotiators hope that the chance of war will be reduced by larger national groups having their own land. However, tensions still exist between some of the groups within countries.

R.U.R. coins the term "robot"

R.U.R., (*Rossum's Universal Robots*), the new play by Czech writer Karel Capek, tells the story of factory robots who rise up against their inventors and conquer the world. In his play, Capek invents the word "robot," taken from the Czech word "robota," which means forced labor.

▲ *The last sultan, Mohammed VI, parades the streets.*

End of great Ottoman Empire

TREATIES

10 AUGUST The great Ottoman Empire died today when Turkey signed the Treaty of Sèvres, losing four-fifths of its empire. Turkey's neighbor Greece has gained a lot of the land, including the islands in the Aegean Sea, the area of Thrace (on the Turkish-Greek border), and the port of Smyrna.

At its peak in the 1500s, the Ottoman Empire ruled large areas of southeastern Europe, northern Africa, and the Middle East. Some Turks, led by Kemal Atatürk, are now vowing never to give up land where Turks outnumber other peoples.

Elegant new detective graces literary scene

Hercule Poirot, a retired Belgian policeman with a carefully groomed moustache and an egg-shaped head, is the hero of *The Mysterious Affair at Styles*, written by British writer Agatha Christie. In her novel, Poirot helps his friend Captain Arthur Hastings find the murderers of Emily Inglethorp.

Mrs. Christie is well equipped to write murder mysteries. During the war in 1914–18 she mixed drugs in a hospital dispensary— so she knows a lot about medicines and poisons. *Styles* is published in the US this year, and will be available in England next year.

◄ *Mystery writer Agatha Christie.*

Puzzling new German movie draws crowds

ENTERTAINMENT

27 FEBRUARY The Cabinet of Dr. Caligari opened today in Berlin. Directed by Robert Wiene, the movie looks nothing like the real world. Houses lean at crazy angles and furniture is pulled out of shape.

The movie is based on the style of Expressionism. This is a movement in painting and writing that highlights the artist's vision and emotions rather than showing the real world in solid dimensions. The movie's designers have distorted things in the movie to emphasize terror and also to indicate the hero's unbalanced mind.

In the film, Dr. Caligari puts Cesare, a sleepwalker, on show at fairgrounds, but at night Cesare murders Dr. Caligari's enemies. *The Cabinet of Dr. Caligari* has a sinister twist in the tale—it later becomes clear the story is being told by a madman in an asylum.

▲ *Joselito was a brave and fearless bullfighter.*

Great matador Joselito dies tragic death in bullfight

Followers of the Spanish sport of bullfighting are in mourning. Joselito, born Juan Gomez in 1895 and hailed by some as the greatest matador of them all, has died in a bullfight. With his friend and rival Juan Belmonte, Joselito brought a daring new skill to the arena. No matador before had let the bull come so close. In bullfights the matadors must face the bull in the arena and kill it—or be killed or injured.

▶ The Cabinet of Dr. Caligari *has been described as a "madman's fantasy."*

NEWS • 1920 • NEWS

16 May • Frenchwoman Joan of Arc (1412–31) is declared a saint by Pope Benedict XV.

24 May • The Olympic Games open in Antwerp, Belgium.

5 September • Hollywood star Fatty Arbuckle is charged with the murder of actress Virginia Rappe.

7 September • Margaret Gorman wins the first "Miss America" beauty contest.

▲ *Suffragettes celebrate voting victory.*

US women celebrate the vote

POLITICS

26 AUGUST Suffragettes—campaigners for women's right to vote in elections—are rejoicing tonight. US Secretary of State Bainbridge Colby today signed papers approving the US Constitution's 19th Amendment, which gives adult women the right to vote.

American women have been calling for the vote for more than 70 years. Elizabeth Stanton, a leading antislavery campaigner, first demanded it at a women's rights convention in 1848. Today's leaders Alice Paul and Carrie Chapman will remember the women who were not here to savor the hour of triumph.

1920

1921

1922

1923

1924

1925

1926

1927

1928

1929

ENTERTAINMENT

Chaplin's latest movie *The Kid* is big hit

▼ *Charlie Chaplin with Jackie Coogan in* The Kid.

6 JANUARY An accident-prone tramp has won a special place in moviegoers' hearts. *The Kid*, the latest film from British actor-director Charlie Chaplin, once again stars "Charlie," the little man with bowler hat, cane, and baggy pants.

The film is being advertised as "a picture with a smile—perhaps a tear," and there is no doubt that it touches viewers' feelings. In a memorable scene, Charlie the tramp falls asleep and dreams of heaven. All the characters, including the policemen who have been pestering him, are transformed into angels.

Charlie is an innocent in a world full of danger. His trusting nature always seems to lead him into trouble. Of his costume Charlie explains, "I wanted to create a satire on man—the cane for his dignity, the mustache for his vanity, the boots for the cares that weigh him down."

Chaplin was born in London in 1889. He later toured the US in a vaudeville show and was signed by Hollywood producer Mack Sennett. In 1913 Chaplin made his debut in *Making a Living*, directed by Sennett.

The Kid is Chaplin's first feature-length film. With a budget of over £310,000, it is one of the most expensive movies ever made.

New chic perfume

French clothes designer Gabrielle "Coco" Chanel has launched her latest success, the perfume Chanel No 5, named after her lucky number. She has also been changing the look of women's fashion. Coco is now setting women free from tight-fitting corsets, with shorter skirts and low-heeled shoes. She started designing women's clothes in Paris after the 1914–18 war.

LAW

Outrage at verdict for Sacco and Vanzetti

14 JULY The verdict reached by a jury in Dedham, Massachusetts, has caused a political storm across the US tonight. Italian-born Nicola Sacco and Bartolomeo Vanzetti have been found guilty of murdering a factory paymaster and guard last year and stealing their wages, but none of the evidence has been linked to them.

▼ *Supporters believe the pair have been set up.*

Some people claim that the pair are being punished for their political beliefs—they are known anarchists. Sacco and Vanzetti could receive the death penalty when they are sentenced.

TREATIES

New Irish free state established

6 DECEMBER A treaty signed in London today has created the Irish Free State. It is a British dominion of 26 Irish counties. Six counties in Ulster, Northern Ireland, will remain part of the United Kingdom. The treaty ends a two-year conflict between the British authorities and the Irish Republican Army (IRA). But those who have campaigned for a united country, such as the Sinn Fein members pictured below, are bitterly disappointed—Irish Free State parliament members are now required to take an oath of allegiance to the British monarch.

◄ *Eamon de Valera.*

▶ *Michael Collins and Arthur Griffith.*

World Games for women only

The Women's World Games were held recently in Monte Carlo in protest over the fact that women are not allowed to compete in track and field events at the Olympic Games. Women were not allowed near the Olympic Games when they were held in ancient Greece. According to some reports they were put to death if they were caught watching the men perform. Baron Pierre de Coubertin, president of today's International Olympic Committee, is determined that women should not take part in the track and field events. Women have competed in the games since 1900, but only in the tennis and swimming events.

▲ The start of the 50-meter race at the Women's World Games, won by Miss Lines from England.

Winning skyscraper

German architect Ludwig Mies van der Rohe has designed a tall office building that looks like a wall of glass. Van der Rohe, 35, entered a competition in 1919 to design a skyscraper alongside the Friedrichstrasse railroad station, in Berlin. His plans call for it to be made entirely of steel and glass and to feature jagged edges. He believes that using man-made materials is appropriate for the modern age.

▲ A girl from Inner Mongolia wearing the customary headdress.

POLITICS

Mongolian independence

10 JULY Outer Mongolia is now independent from China, but the reins of power are held by the Soviet Red Army. The Soviets came to the aid of Mongolians when the Russian White Army, which was defeated by the Communists in the Russian civil war of 1918–20, invaded the Mongolian capital, Urga, and killed many Mongolians. Inner Mongolia, however, remains a part of China.

NEWS • 1921 • NEWS

25 January • The first women to serve on a divorce court jury are sworn in, in London.

23 April • American sprinter Charles Paddock sets new 100-meter record of 10.4 seconds.

11 May • Germany agrees to pay war costs of nearly $10 billion in reparation over 42 years.

10 December • Albert Einstein wins the Nobel Prize for Physics.

▲ The design for the Glass Skyscraper.

SCIENCE

One step closer with diabetes breakthrough

27 JULY Frederick Banting and Charles Best, who lead a group at the University of Toronto, Canada, have given hope to people suffering from diabetes.

Most people with diabetes are unable to produce insulin, a substance that controls the amount of sugar in their blood. If the level of sugar rises too high or falls too low, it can be dangerous. The disease can lead to numbness and sometimes blindness.

Banting and Best have succeeded in extracting insulin from dogs. In their experiments, this insulin cured diabetes in other dogs. This result has given scientists hope that insulin can be used to treat diabetes in humans.

▲ C. H. Best.

▼ F. G. Banting.

LAW

Sweden abolishes capital punishment

8 MAY Both houses of the Swedish Riksdag, or parliament, voted to abolish the death penalty in Sweden today. It has not been used in Sweden for 11 years.

Capital punishment provokes heated political debate worldwide. Its supporters believe that the threat of death stops people from committing crimes. Its opponents argue that no one has the right to order a person's death.

The death penalty has already been abolished in Portugal (1867), the Netherlands (1870), and Norway (1905). It is still in use in Britain for murder, treason, piracy, and some forms of arson. In the US, six states currently do not use the death penalty—Michigan, Wisconsin, Maine, Minnesota, South Dakota, and Kansas.

1920
1921
1922
1923
1924
1925
1926
1927
1928
1929

1922

Discovery of Egyptian king's tomb

30 NOVEMBER Two British archeologists have discovered a breathtaking collection of 3,000-year-old burial treasure. On 26 November, Howard Carter and Lord Carnarvon opened the tomb of Tutankhamen, pharaoh of Egypt, who died in 1323 B.C.

The tomb lies in the Valley of the Kings, near Luxor in central Egypt, and consists of several rooms. In the burial chamber, Tutankhamen's body lies preserved as a "mummy" by a special technique the ancient Egyptians used for preserving the bodies of the dead.

Tutankhamen's mummy is encased in three coffins. Covering the mummy's head is a solid gold mask. It shows Tutankhamen as Osiris, the ancient Egyptian god of the underworld. Several pieces of jewelry are inside the coffin and bound into the mummy's wrappings.

In the tomb's other rooms are weapons, clothes, drinking vessels, furniture, statues—even a chariot. One cup, made of alabaster, shows the young pharaoh as a white lotus flower. Its inscription expresses the hope that Tutankhamen will spend "many millions of years sitting with his face to the cool breeze, his eyes beholding happiness."

Tutankhamen died aged 18. He was the son-in-law of Pharaoh Akhenaton, who oversaw changes in religious custom to the worship of one god only. Tutankhamen restored religion to the old way of worshiping many deities, but he achieved little else. His name is not well known to historians, but this find will change that.

▲ *Tutankhamen's mummy lies in an inner coffin made of solid gold. The outer coffins are made of wood.*

Tutankhamen's tomb unleashes curse

NOVEMBER Rumor has it that Howard Carter and Lord Carnarvon invoked an ancient curse when they disturbed the tomb of Tutankhamen. Egypt is a land of fantastic legends, and many people believe that the archeologists have broken a powerful curse that forbids the disturbance of the kingdom of the dead. Old inscriptions threaten disaster to "the living who come to violate the tombs."

Howard Carter and Lord Carnarvon have been searching for Tutankhamen's tomb for 10 years and were just about to give up. Now that they have made their exciting discovery, they plan to excavate the tomb with great care.

Ancient Egypt facts
The embalming of mummies began in Egypt in 2500 B.C.

• A group of funeral urns, called canopic jars, were used to contain the vital organs of a body before it was embalmed.

• The mummies of pharaohs were buried in boats because the Egyptians believed this would help them travel to the next world.

▶ *Howard Carter supervises his finds.*

74

New vampire villain thrills movie crowds

Movie audiences have been bitten by a new bug—the horror movie. *Nosferatu*, directed by the German F. W. Murnau, tells the terrible tale of a vampire, a living corpse that feeds on human blood. The movie's heroine, Mina, sacrifices herself to the vampire because she knows this will destroy the monster.

Murnau's is the first movie version of the 1897 novel *Dracula* by Irishman Bram Stoker. Other moviemakers are sure to take note.

◄ *Nosferatu, played by Max Schreck, must keep away from daylight to avoid going up in smoke.*

▲ *Ontario Hydro uses water to generate electricity.*

World's largest hydro-electric station opens near Niagara Falls

1922 The Queenston-Chippawa station opened this year on the Niagara River in Ontario, Canada. It is now the world's largest hydroelectric station.

Hydroelectric power stations generate electricity from the energy of falling water. The Niagara area boasts one of the most obvious places to generate hydroelectric power—the thundering waterfall of Niagara Falls is about 197 feet (60 meters) high.

Entrepreneurs have been experimenting with generating power here since 1881. The first hydroelectric power generated on the US side was in Buffalo, New York State, before 1900. A second station was built on the Canadian side of the Falls, and it sent its first power to the nearby city of Toronto in November 1906.

▲ *French delegates sign the Washington treaty.*

Navies cut down to size

6 FEBRUARY The naval arms race that has been going on since the end of the 1914–18 war has been put on hold. Delegates from the US, Britain, Japan, France, and Italy today signed a treaty in Washington guaranteeing that their countries will build no new battleships or cruisers for 10 years.

The treaty also agrees to limit the total number of warships each country will have. Some existing ships will have to be scrapped. The US, for example, will be getting rid of 25 ships.

Treaty with a secret arms clause

16 APRIL Soviet Russia and Germany have agreed to establish trading and diplomatic links. Officials signed the Treaty of Rapallo while attending a conference in Genoa, Italy. Other European powers were also negotiating with the Soviets to establish trade, and they are concerned at this new alliance. It is reported that the treaty has a secret clause which allows Germany to build weapons and carry out military research on Russian territory, and Germany will help build up the Soviet arms industry.

▲ *Ministers in Italy.*

New trends for male students

Students at Oxford University, England, have started a new trend: flapping trousers with an extremely generous cut. Known as Oxford bags, the slacks were given the seal of approval when the Prince of Wales wore the new style. Bright ties, suede shoes, and caps or soft hats are also popular with men.

▲ *The new style Oxford bags.*

BBC Radio founded

The BBC (British Broadcasting Company) made its first regular news broadcast on 15 November. Founded on 18 October, the BBC is owned by radio manufacturers keen to promote the wonders of their machines. The BBC is offering a mixture of news, discussion, and music and has appointed John Reith as general manager.

SCIENCE

Nobel for atomic discovery

10 DECEMBER Danish scientist Niels Bohr has been awarded the Nobel Prize for Physics for his breakthrough in the understanding of the atom.

An atom was thought to be the smallest particle of a substance, and it was believed that atoms could not be broken down into anything smaller. Bohr built on the ideas of New Zealand-born physicist Ernest Rutherford, who claimed that each atom had a central nucleus and electrons that orbited it, like the planets orbiting the Sun in the solar system. Bohr says that electrons can leap from one orbit to another, giving off energy only when they jump between orbits.

Bohr developed his theory in 1913, but scientists today, including Albert Einstein, are gripped by it. The theory explains accurately the way in which atoms give off energy.

▼ *Niels Bohr has helped scientists to understand the atom.*

NEWS • 1922 • NEWS

18 March • Indian nationalist Mahatma Gandhi is jailed for six years for civil disobedience.

7 April • Two airliners in first midair collision near Paris; seven die.

12 April • Hollywood star Roscoe "Fatty" Arbuckle is acquitted of the murder of actress Virginia Rappe.

12 May • A 20-ton meteor hits Blackstone, Virginia, making a crater 500 square feet (46 square meters).

New "flapper girl" takes US by storm

She drinks and smokes, wears lipstick, and swears in public. She wears shapeless dresses that hide her curves, but she is happy to let the young men see her ankles and lower legs. She has her hair cut short in a "bob," but then she hides it beneath a cloche hat. A new type of woman has hit the streets of American cities. The magazine *Vanity Fair* has found a name for her—the "flapper."

The women who went to work during the Great War and who won the vote in 1920 are not going to go back to the old ideals of womanhood. They have proved that they are equal to men. They are happy to say what they think—and even to admit that they enjoy sex. The older generation cannot understand it.

◀ *The new flappers have bewildered the older generation.*

Mussolini goes to Rome

30 OCTOBER An army of 24,000 black-shirted fascists marched into Rome from Naples two days ago in a naked bid for power—and were welcomed by enthusiastic crowds. Tonight the fascist leader Benito Mussolini is prime minister of Italy. He paraded three times on the balcony of the royal palace with King Victor Emanuel while the crowd roared its approval.

The success of the fascists' bold move forced Victor Emanuel to summon Mussolini to Rome. The king was afraid that if he stood up to the fascists it might provoke civil war and he could lose his throne.

Mussolini founded the *Fasci di Combattimento* in March 1919 to combat socialism. The party won the financial backing of many Italian businessmen who were nervous at the spread of strikes. Last year Mussolini declared himself *Il Duce*, or leader, of the fascists. He and his followers are now riding a wave of popular support.

▲ *Mussolini inspects his fascist troops.*

Death of last castrato marks end of an era

21 APRIL Alessandro Moreschi, the last known castrato, has died today aged 63. Castrati were male singers who were castrated before puberty to prevent their voices from growing deeper.

The practice began in Italy in the mid-1500s. Boys were castrated between 6 and 8 years of age. They sung in the finest church choirs, such as the Sistine choir, which sings for the pope in the famous Sistine Chapel in the Vatican. The first castrati entered the Sistine choir in about 1565. Castrati also took the leading roles in operas, including Caesar, in *Julius Caesar* by George Frederick Handel, and Orfeo, in *Orfeo ed Euridice* by Christophe Willibald Gluck.

Moreschi was born at Montecompatri, near Rome, in 1858. From 1883 to 1913 he was a member of the Sistine choir. In 1902–3 Moreschi made some recordings, which show off the clear tone and vocal power of the castrato voice.

▲ *Alessandro Moreschi, the last castrato.*

New poem echoes feelings of despair in modern world

OCTOBER T.S. Eliot's latest poem, *The Waste Land*, breaks new ground in poetry. Eliot, an American poet living in London, published the long and unsettling poem in the first issue of his new literary magazine, *The Criterion*.

The Waste Land seems to express people's feelings of despair and pointlessness since the 1914–18 war. Its disjointed style contains fragments of other languages, everyday speech, references to myths and religions, and echoes of other books. It appears to conclude that the modern world is old and tired and that no hope exists.

The poem's new departure from style resembles that of *Ulysses*, an astonishing novel published this year in Paris by Irishman James Joyce. It uses the myth of Homer's Greek hero Ulysses, or Odysseus, to describe the events of one day in 1904, in Dublin, Ireland.

Weissmuller breaks 60-second barrier

Johnny Weissmuller has become the first man to swim 100 meters in less than one minute. The 18-year-old swam the distance in 58.6 seconds, knocking 1.8 seconds off the existing record. Weissmuller is originally from Romania but came to the US with his family in 1908 and settled in Chicago.

▶ *Johnny Weissmuller broke four world records recently.*

RADIO POWER

Radio began as the "wireless telegraphy" invented in the late 1890s by Italian-born Guglielmo Marconi. In 1899 the *New York Herald* sponsored him to broadcast news of the America's Cup yacht race by following its progress from a ship.

Over the next 20 years, inventions such as the radio valve, the vacuum tube, and the regenerative circuit took wireless telegraphy into millions of homes. The new medium had a huge impact on everyday life. Until television came along, radio was the most important source of information.

▼ *Orson Welles directed* War of the Worlds. *The play went out on the Columbia Broadcasting System (CBS).*

▲ *When* War of the Worlds *was broadcast, many Americans prepared to attack the invaders, and roads clogged as families fled from the "advancing" Martians.*

Radio play causes panic

On 31 October (Hallowe'en) 1938, *War of the Worlds*, a highly realistic play about a Martian invasion of New Jersey, was broadcast. All over the US, listeners responded to the play as if it were a live news report, resulting in chaos as people fled from the advancing aliens. The play's impact showed how seriously people took what they heard on the radio.

Radio facts

Radio waves were discovered by German physicist Heinrich Hertz in 1888.

At least 120 million people regularly listen to the BBC's World Service, making it the world's largest radio audience.

The number of sunspots on the Sun affects the distance radio waves travel around the Earth at any given moment.

Radio at war

"Nation Shall Speak Peace unto Nation" read a plaque at the BBC's London headquarters, which opened in 1932, but with the outbreak of World War II, radio became a key weapon in the propaganda offensive. The BBC began its wartime overseas broadcasts by repeating the opening notes of Beethoven's Fifth Symphony, which are the same as the Morse code for the letter V (for victory), and people living in occupied Europe risked their lives to tune in to information that provided hope and support to resistance movements.

Although the Nazis were masters of the art of propaganda, their wartime broadcasts were ineffective. The renegade Englishman William Joyce, who made programs aimed at English-speaking listeners, was mocked for his upper-class "Lord Haw Haw" accent. Meanwhile, "Tokyo Rose" made programs that aimed to demoralize American soldiers in the Pacific. Like Lord Haw Haw, she was unintentionally entertaining.

▶ *"Lord Haw Haw" (above left); Charles de Gaulle (above), whose broadcasts from exile in London kept alight the "flame" of the French Resistance; "Tokyo Rose" (right).*

Selling it on the air

Radio advertising was controversial at first, but by the late 1920s it was the way most American radio stations made money, as businesses competed to sponsor the most popular programs. When leading lady Marion Davies gave a talk called "How I Make Up for the Movies" for the Mineralava beauty product company, the offer of autographed photographs was taken up by hundreds of listeners.

Politicians were quick to exploit radio's potential for direct access to people. Hitler liked to bypass political opponents by presenting key policies in his radio speeches to the German people.

▶*For New Yorkers, the "Radio Queen" was regarded as a style goddess.*

Timeline

1920

1921

1922

1923

1924

1925

1926

1927

1928

1929

Republic born out of Ottoman Empire

29 OCTOBER Today Mustafa Kemal proclaimed Turkey a republic and himself its first president.

Mustafa Kemal, the leader of the Turkish nationalists, led the army that drove out the Greeks last year from the port of Smyrna. After Turkey's defeat in the Great War and the loss of the non-Turkish territories in the Ottoman Empire, Mustafa Kemal was determined to keep all of Asia Minor within the borders of a modern Turkish state. At the peace conference in Lausanne last year, he succeeded in getting other European countries to agree to Turkey's new borders.

However, thousands of Greek-speaking Orthodox Christian refugees have been left living in squalid emergency camps as a result of the recent upheavals. Greece has already taken over a million refugees. The new Turkey also worries the Kurdish people, who regard part of it as their national homeland.

Ottoman Empire facts

As part of his policy of persuading his people to use Western-style last names, in 1934, Mustafa Kemal adopted the last name Atatürk, which means "Father of the Turks."

•

Atatürk banned the wearing of traditional fezzes, like this one.

◀ *Mustafa Kemal, the founder of the republic of Turkey, is pictured with his wife.*

Instant chocolate success

A new chocolate bar has gone on sale in the US. The "chocolate malted milk in a candy bar" is called the Milky Way, and it has been an instant success. Three years of research went into developing the chocolate bar, which has resulted in the employment of a fulltime sales staff.

Marathon dancing craze hits US

Lured by the promise of huge cash prizes, men and women are flocking to competition halls hoping to out-dance everyone else. But what sounds like an easy way of earning money often turns into a nightmare—competitors, cheered on or taunted by spectators and stewards, often dance until they drop!

▼ *Dancers in Washington after 40 hours.*

Salt tax leaves bitter taste

FOOD

24 MARCH The Indian Council of State is bringing back the unpopular tax on salt to balance the budget. This tax will affect everyone, irrespective of caste, creed, or region because salt is essential for preserving and preparing food. Indian politician Mr. Sastri protests that the Council members, many of whom are British, do not appreciate the realities of Indian life or the effect this new tax will have on households that are already struggling.

NEWS • 1923 • NEWS

16 February • American blues singer Bessie Smith records "Down-hearted Blues."

5 March • Montana and Nevada introduce the first US pensions of $25 a month.

4 April • Earl of Carnarvon, supposedly under the "curse of Tutankhamen," dies after an insect bite.

12 August • Italian Enrico Tirboschi swims the English Channel in a record 16 hours 33 minutes.

▼ *Lenglen says her tennis style is inspired by Russian ballet.*

Fifth Wimbledon for Lenglen

SPORT

6 JULY Suzanne Lenglen, the 24-year-old French tennis ace, has won the Ladies' Singles at Wimbledon, again. Miss Lenglen, who won her first champion's title in France when she was 15 years old, first amazed Wimbledon in 1919 and has dominated the women's game ever since.

With her short dress and practical headband, not to mention her powerful overhand serve and forehand drive, Miss Lenglen is a thrilling player to see in action. Quite a change from the demure days of summer 1884, when Miss Maud Watson won Wimbledon's first ladies' tournament. Wimbledon began in 1877, when all of the competitors were men.

New store to sell cheaper goods

The first "supermarket," a general store selling many different kinds of goods, has opened in San Francisco. The goods are sold more cheaply than in specialized stores because the goods are bought in bulk. This may signal the beginning of the end of the butcher, the baker, and the fishmonger.

▲ *Shoppers can help themselves.*

Millions made homeless as earthquake destroys Japan

DISASTERS

16 SEPTEMBER The most catastrophic earthquake in recorded history has devastated Tokyo, the largest city in Japan, and Yokohama, its most important seaport. As many as 300,000 people have perished—and this figure looks set to rise—and at least 2 million people have lost their homes.

The massive quake, caused by a sudden movement along a fault or crack in the Earth's surface, happened without any warning. Those buildings which did not immediately collapse were soon engulfed by fires started by smashed gas pipes and burst oil tanks.

More than a million survivors have fled the ruined, smoking city for the surrounding countryside, but even here they are not safe. The Fukoro, Chiyo, and Takimi rivers have already burst their banks, causing severe flooding and more homelessness. Typhoons are expected, and the refugees living in crowded, unhygienic camps are at risk from infectious diseases such as dysentery and cholera.

As they wait in line for emergency riceball rations, many of the survivors are still too shocked to believe what has happened. It will be months, maybe years, before Japan's capital begins to recover.

◄ *Tokyo's citizens help to clear up after the devastating earthquake.*

ECONOMICS

Hyperinflation hits Germany hard

22 JUNE As life savings and fixed pensions become worthless, and storekeepers give up in despair, many of Germany's hapless citizens are turning to barter. A housewife will exchange homemade sausages for a new pair of shoes, and a doctor will treat the children of the mechanic who fixes his car. For now, people are coping as best they can with hyperinflation, but there's no sign of any let-up on the war reparations front.

The economic crisis has been caused by the occupation of the Ruhr by French and Belgian troops after Germany's failure to meet reparation payments. But most Germans feel that Germany is being asked to pay too much too soon for a war which was not all its fault. Britain and the US are willing to reduce the reparations, but France and Belgium, which were occupied by German forces during the war, want complete "satisfaction." The result is economic chaos and depression in Germany's towns and cities.

▶ *Money fit only for burning is the grim reality facing most Germans.*

POLITICS

Soviet succession looms as Lenin suffers stroke

9 MARCH Vladimir Ilyich Lenin, the founder and leader of the Soviet Union, has suffered another stroke. Despite being bedridden from previous attacks, the 53-year-old communist leader has continued to rule with the aid of a team. But after this latest stroke, which has left him paralyzed and subject to fits of unconsciousness, it is unlikely he will continue to rule from his bed.

Lenin is a trained lawyer but made plans that fueled the communist revolution. As a leader he is admired for his personal integrity. In his absence, Grigori Zinoviev, Leon Kamenev, and Joseph Stalin are in control, although Leon Trotsky is thought to be Lenin's favorite as the country's next leader.

◀ *A healthier Lenin addresses the crowds.*

Moving pictures are a family affair for Warner Brothers

Brothers Harry, Albert, Jack (pictured below), and Sam Warner have moved from the business of showing pictures in cinemas to the business of making them in studios. Warner Brothers want to make entertaining, not necessarily expensive, movies that connect with the lives of 20th-century people: "I'd rather take a 50-mile hike than crawl through a book," says Jack Warner.

Criminal activity to be monitored worldwide

LAW

23 SEPTEMBER Police from 20 countries have gathered in Vienna to launch the International Criminal Police Organization. "Interpol," the new organization's telegraph address, is beginning to stick as its everyday name, and it aims to meet every year in a different capital city to share information on criminal activity and new criminal identification technologies. As air travel becomes more common, this kind of liaison will be extremely important, but Interpol will steer clear of crimes with a racial, religious, or political aspect.

▲ *Interpol will share data to combat crime.*

Time magazine launched

The first issue of an American weekly magazine, *Time*, is making news in its own right. The brainchild of Henry Luce, a Presbyterian missionary's son, and his Yale classmate, Briton Hadden, *Time* already has 12,000 subscribers, but it's sure to attract many more. Its publishers aim to inform readers of the latest international events and trends in politics, arts, sports, and fashion.

▲ *Time magazine's emphasis is on personalities combined with a lively mix of pictures and news stories.*

Trouble brews at beer-hall putsch

POLITICS

9 NOVEMBER Members of the National Socialist German Workers' Party, known as the Nazis, have attempted to take control of the government of Bavaria, a state in southern Germany. The Nazi's leader, Austrian-born Adolf Hitler, started the political uprising yesterday in Munich's biggest beer hall, a regular venue for political meetings, just minutes before the dictatorial state commissioner of Bavaria was due to present a lecture about political dictatorship. Hitler stormed in and declared that if he had political power, he would tear up the Versailles Treaty, which he thinks is unfair and calls the "Diktat." Most Germans blame the Treaty for most of the country's problems.

During the Great War, Hitler himself only rose to the rank of corporal, but his partner in this uprising is General Erich von Ludendorff, the aristocratic hero of Germany's wartime victories. Ludendorff organized a march through the city in an attempt to win the support of the army, but the marchers met police resistance.

The Bavarian government quickly defeated the putsch. Ludendorff is under house arrest, and it seems Hitler will be imprisoned. But the Nazis have a lot of popular sympathy, and their distinctive swastika flags can be seen all over Munich.

▲ *Hitler's attempt to seize power draws the crowds.*

Death of exotic stage star mourned by many

ENTERTAINMENT

26 MARCH The first, some say the greatest, international star of the stage, Sarah Bernhardt (left), has died at her home in Paris. In keeping with her mysterious image, Miss Bernhardt herself never revealed her age, but it is known that she was 78 years old. Her love affair with the theater began when her mother took her to a play, hoping to discourage her from becoming a nun. The treatment worked, and Bernhardt was 16 when she made her stage debut at the *Comédie Française* in 1862.

1920

1921

1922

1923

1924

1925

1926

1927

1928

1929

Olympics in snow and ice

The first festival of winter sports has ended at Chamonix in the French Alps. Competitors from 18 countries took part in the events. The medal winners were mostly from Scandinavian countries, where perfect skiing and skating conditions occur naturally.

Paavo Nurmi wins five Olympic golds

SPORT

30 JULY The undisputed star of the 1924 Olympic Games just held in Paris is the phenomenal Flying Fin, Paavo Nurmi. In spite of the stifling heat, Nurmi won five gold medals. In the space of two hours, he won the 1,500-meter and 5,000-meter runs, in both of which he also set new Olympic records. Another notable medal winner was Scottish sprinter Eric Liddell. His strict religious beliefs meant he had to miss his best event, the 100-meter race, because the heats were happening on a Sunday. He switched to the 400 meters and still came in first.

It is almost 30 years since the first modern Olympic Games took place in Athens in 1896. Frenchman Baron Pierre de Coubertin had the idea of reviving the games that the ancient Greeks held every four years between 776 B.C. and A.D. 395, and he still heads the international committee that organizes the modern Olympic Games. Although he himself is not an athlete, he is dedicated to the highest ideals of sportsmanship. These ideals mean that Olympic competitors have to be amateurs—they cannot make money out of sports.

Baron Coubertin introduced the spectacular torch ceremony and had the idea of including a marathon event, which was not part of the ancient Olympics. Another big difference is clothes. Ancient athletes competed naked, but Baron Coubertin drew the line at reviving nudity!

Olympic facts

The Olympic emblem of five interlaced circles represents the five continents.

•

Ancient Greeks measured time in "Olympiads" or four-year intervals.

•

Women did not compete in the ancient Olympic Games; instead they had their own games in honor of the goddess Hera.

▲ *Finnish runner Paavo Nurmi broke two Olympic records in under two hours.*

NEWS • 1924 • NEWS

28 September • *Gandhi refuses to break his fast as an appeal for peace between Muslims and Hindus.*

17 October • *It is announced that climbers Andrew Irvine and George Mallory have died climbing Mount Everest.*

4 November • *Texas elects first woman governor, "Ma" Miriam Ferguson.*

2 December • *Charlie Chaplin marries 16-year-old Lita Grey.*

"Sick" murderers say killing was an experiment

LAW

31 MAY Nineteen-year-old "rich kids" Richard Loeb and Nathan Leopold have confessed to the murder of 14-year-old Bobby Franks. Both boys come from millionaire families and had no need of the $2,000 ransom that they demanded from the victim's parents.

They say they kidnapped and killed Bobby Franks to see how he reacted to his ordeal and to test their wits against police detectives with "inferior minds." Defense will argue "not guilty," claiming that the boys' ability to judge right from wrong has been distorted by their unusually privileged backgrounds.

▲ *Gershwin's music matches the vitality of city life.*

MUSIC

Rhapsody in Blue thrills audience

12 FEBRUARY The audience in New York's Aeolian Hall last night enjoyed the first performance of an unusual piece, *Rhapsody in Blue*, by dynamic young jazz pianist and composer, George Gershwin. He describes his latest work as "an experiment in modern music," and if its success so far is anything to go by, it is already a classic work.

POLITICS

New kingdom is born

20 OCTOBER Two kingdoms have become one under the rule of Ibn Saud, the emir of Nejd. Occupying most of the Arabian peninsula, Nejd in the interior and Hejaz by the Red Sea coast, the new realm of Ibn Saud will be called Saudi Arabia. The joint capitals are Riyadh and Mecca. As the birthplace of the prophet Mohammed, Mecca is Islam's holiest city, and all Muslims try to visit it at least once. Ibn Saud has pledged to protect all persons, property, and holy places.

POLITICS

Lenin's last wish is denied after his death

28 JANUARY Thousands of mourners are still flocking to Moscow to pay their respects to Vladimir Ilyich Lenin who died last week. In spite of his request for a simple burial, the government has just announced that Lenin's body will be enbalmed and put on permanent view in a mausoleum in Red Square.

Lenin's pallbearers were all prominent Bolsheviks: Kalinin, Bukharin, Tomsky, Kamenev, Molotov, and Stalin, but Trotsky wasn't present. Some say Stalin gave Trotsky the wrong date.

ART

New Surrealist manifesto inspired by psychoanalysis

1924 The fiery young French poet André Breton has published the Surrealist manifesto, which defines the movement as "pure psychic automatism." He believes that art should not be limited by unimaginative rules or fixed ideas. Instead, Surrealist artists, such as Pablo Picasso and Joan Miró, go with the flow of their dreams and fantasies. They are inspired by the psychoanalytical movement and by "primitive" peoples. Breton's outrageous ideas have struck a chord among rising young painters, filmmakers, poets, and photographers.

▶ **Dutch interior** *by Surrealist Joan Miró.*

▲ *The* New Orleans *on its record-breaking trip.*

First round-the-world flight takes 175 days

US Army pilots John Harding and Erick Nelson have just landed in Seattle, Washington, after a record flight of 27,000 miles (43,500 km). They were the pilots of the *New Orleans*, which is the first plane to circumvent the globe. It was one of four that attempted the journey, but only two succeeded (the other was the *Chicago*).

1920

1921

1922

1923

1924

1925

1926

1927

1928

1929

Monkey business trial ends in guilty verdict

SCIENCE

21 JULY Biology teacher John Thomas Scopes has been fined $100 for teaching Darwin's theory of evolution to schoolchildren in Tennessee. A new state law outlaws the teaching of ideas that contradict Old Testament stories about how the world was made. Fundamentalist American Protestants are using this law to fight what they believe to be the immoral theory that human beings are related to apes.

Mr. Scopes was prosecuted by former presidential candidate William Jennings Bryan, who argued that the Bible's version of creation is exactly how things happened. But after being questioned by Scopes' defense lawyer, Clarence Darrow, Bryan had to agree that the creation process may have lasted longer than seven days.

Darwin, who was educated as a Protestant clergyman, delayed the publication of his theory for 20 years because he was afraid of its effect on Christian belief. Although his theory of evolution is backed up by fossil evidence, the Tennessee judge ruled against hearing any scientific evidence.

▲ *Darwin's theory of evolution claims that human beings are related to apes, an idea some people consider immoral.*

▶ *Scopes' lawyer Clarence Darrow with prosecutor William Jennings Bryan (right).*

Death of China's revolutionary leader

PEOPLE

12 MARCH Sun Yat-sen, the venerable leader of China's democratic revolution, has died of cancer in Peking. He led the campaign against the last Manchu emperor in 1911 and founded the Kuomintang, the Chinese nationalist party. Sun Yat-sen died without fulfilling his dream of a united, democratic China, but his followers are determined to achieve it.

General Chiang Kai-shek, Sun's brother-in-law, is to be Sun's successor. A military rather than a political leader, Chiang Kai-shek has recently returned from Moscow, where he studied the techniques of the Red Army. Since 1923 the Kuomintang army, now 40,000 strong, has received substantial advice and aid from Soviet Russia.

◀ *Sun Yat-sen was known as the Father of the Republic.*

86

▲ *Bauhaus philosophy is about simple, functional beauty.*

ARCHITECTURE

Bauhaus school to move to Dessau

MARCH The famous Bauhaus school of architecture and design is to move from Weimar to Dessau in Germany because the city's new nationalist government has withdrawn financial support. The nationalists think the Bauhaus movement is "too cosmopolitan," and the public resent their taxes going toward the school.

The Bauhaus movement was founded in 1919 by the architect Walter Gropius. The aim of the school was to train craftsmen, painters, and sculptors to work on projects in which all their skills would be combined. The Bauhaus team includes people such as painters Wassily Kandinsky and Paul Klee, architect and designer Marcel Breuer, and architect Ludwig Mies van der Rohe.

▼ The Street *by New Realist artist George Grosz.*

LITERATURE

Hitler publishes autobiography

18 JULY Adolf Hitler has published his political ideas in *Mein Kampf* (*My Struggle*). He worked on it when he was imprisoned for his role in the Munich putsch in 1923.

In his book, Hitler reveals that he never finished school because his mother couldn't afford to let him stay there after his father died. One of his teachers, however, says his failure was due to personality, not poverty.

Hitler also analyzes the effectiveness of propaganda techniques and talks of his resolve to establish *lebensraum* (living space) for the Aryan race.

Revolution horror brought to life in Eisenstein film

Soviet director Sergei Eisenstein's latest movie is *The Battleship Potemkin*, the story of the famous 1905 warship. The main set was the sister ship of the real *Potemkin*, and the cast included sailors of the Soviet Black Sea Fleet and ordinary people from Odessa. The movie features a grim massacre scene filmed on the Odessa Steps.

Keep racking your brains

Chicago's health authority has announced that crosswords are a good form of mental exercise. This contradicts British Optical Association's president W. R. Baker's claim two months ago that the popular newspaper word puzzles are a cause of eye strain and headaches.

ART

New exhibition shocks public

14 JUNE Germany's *Neue Sachlichkeit*, or New Realist, artists have just opened their latest show in Mannheim. Unlike the Expressionists, the New Realists are not interested in exotic or primitive subjects. Instead they depict the reality of life in the modern urban and industrial age. Politicians, prostitutes, pimps, and tramps all have a place in the highly detailed paintings of such New Realists as Otto Dix and Georg Grosz. As long as chaos and corruption are the reality in Germany, they say that genuine art-lovers should not expect to see pretty pictures of flowers.

◀ *Otto Dix is a major exponent of Germany's New Realism.*

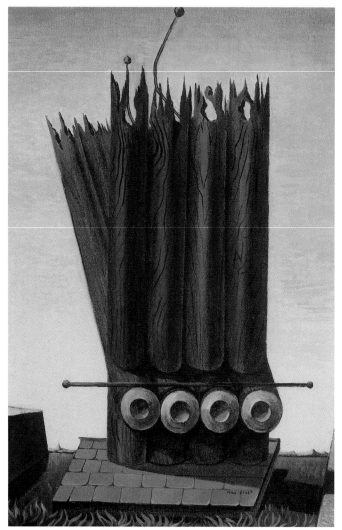

▲ The Forest, *a Surrealist painting by the German Dadaist artist Max Ernst.*

First exhibition by Surrealist artists inspired by dreams

ART

14 NOVEMBER An unusual art show has opened at the Galerie Pierre in Paris. Hans Arp, Giorgio de Chirico, Paul Klee, Max Ernst, Joan Miró, André Masson, Pablo Picasso, and Man Ray are among the Surrealist artists whose work is exhibited.

Although this is their first group show, the Surrealists do not regard themselves as members of a formal organization, or a particular "school" of painting. The only rule of Surrealism is that there are no rules. True Surrealists trust in the creative power of the imagination and the unconscious. The Italian artist Giorgio de Chirico doesn't belong to the Paris-based group, but the dreamlike scenes that he painted before and during World War I are admired by Surrealists, so works by him are in the Galerie Pierre show on that basis.

As well as dreams and fantasies, the Surrealists' art responds to unusual raw materials. Max Ernst uses burlap sacks, leaves, thread, and wood for a technique called frottage, by which an image is first suggested by a natural shape or texture. For his "automatic" images, André Masson sometimes uses sand, and he often paints directly from the tube.

The leading spokesman for the Surrealist movement is poet André Breton. The Café Cyrano, near Breton's home, is one of the group's regular meeting places, where they get together to discuss their art and new ideas. Marcel Duchamp, another great figure of French avant-garde art, is not represented at this show—he is currently devoting his time to chess.

NEWS • 1925 • NEWS

26 February • Reports suggest that the Leaning Tower of Pisa will eventually collapse.

17 March • A tornado hits Illinois, Indiana, and Missouri, killing 900 people and injuring 3,000.

2 May • A US Navy seaplane sets a new record by remaining in the air for 28½ hours.

12 December • The first "motel" is opened in San Luis Obispo, California.

Witty writer honored with Nobel prize

LITERATURE

10 DECEMBER George Bernard Shaw, the celebrated Irish dramatist, has been awarded the Nobel Prize for Literature. Now 69 years old, Mr. Shaw was in his forties, with a string of unpublished— some say unpublishable—novels to his credit, when he switched to writing the plays that have brought him such acclaim.

His latest play, *St. Joan*, has been such a critical and commercial success in Britain, Ireland, the US, and on the Continent that he is now a wealthy man. In fact, he is so well off that he has declined the £7,000 cash prize.

Shaw is a man of many causes, including socialism, vegetarianism, and feminism, but he pursues them all with such wit and charm that he manages to persuade more people than he offends. Facets of his own personality are revealed in the character of the phonetics expert, Henry Higgins, in *Pygmalion*, which is one of his most popular plays.

Sensational new dancer excites audiences in Paris

27 OCTOBER The toast of the French capital is Miss Josephine Baker, the star of the American dance troupe "La Revue Nègre." Her flimsy costumes, made of fruit and feathers, leave little to the imagination. The French writer Colette says that she has the grace of a panther—a compliment reflected by the American dancer's habit of taking her pet leopard for walks on the Champs Elysées.

Born 19 years ago in Missouri, Miss Baker joined a traveling theater company when she was only 13. She is now thinking about making Paris her home.

▲ *Miss Baker wearing one of her thrilling costumes.*

New snappy camera

The amateur action photographer's dream camera is here. The new Leica is lightweight and inconspicuous, and it can take 36 negatives on a single loading of 35-mm film. Already dubbed the "candid camera," the versatile Leica is the invention of amateur photographer Oskar Barnack, who works as a microscope specialist at the famous E. Leitz optical works in Wetzlar, Germany.

Europe's hopes for peace

1 DECEMBER The governments of seven European nations—Belgium, Britain, Czechoslovakia, France, Germany, Italy, and Poland—have confirmed the international borders that were drawn up after the Great War. They met in Locarno, in the neutral country of Switzerland. Of particular importance is a new understanding between Germany and France—Germany's foreign minister, Gustav Stresemann, says that this is Europe's best hope for permanent peace. Instead of continuing to occupy the Rhineland region for 15 years, the Allies have agreed to withdraw. After Locarno, another world war is less likely.

◄ *The German delegation at the Locarno conference.*

Straight-faced Keaton goes west in latest film

In the star comedian's new film, *Go West*, a soft-hearted "tenderfoot" makes friends with a cow and ends up taking her everywhere. This crazy story gives Buster Keaton plenty of opportunities for gags and stunts, but no matter how funny he is, he never loses his trademark solemn face, which has earned him the nickname "Great Stone Face." Hilarious Keaton joined the family vaudeville act when he was 4, and went into motion pictures when he was 19, about 10 years ago.

Road safety measures to curb traffic chaos

29 SEPTEMBER Britain's Ministry of Transport has decided that the number of cars on modern roads calls for new safety measures. To start with, indelible white lines will be painted on main roads to separate streams of traffic and to highlight dangers. In London, colored traffic lights will require drivers to stop and wait their turn.

Other countries, such as the US, are taking similar action. With the increasing availability of inexpensive cars, rules of the road are becoming a matter of life and death—25,000 Americans have been killed in car accidents in just one year.

1920

1921

1922

1923

1924

1925

1926

1927

1928

1929

Winnie-the-Pooh set to capture hearts

LITERATURE

14 OCTOBER Alan Alexander Milne has produced another delightful children's book. The character of the title, Winnie-the-Pooh, is a teddy bear of "little brain" who belongs to a six-year-old boy named Christopher Robin. They live in Hundred Acre Wood with several other memorable characters: a morose donkey called Eeyore, a cheerful Piglet, a boisterous Tigger, a pedantic Owl, and a kangaroo mother (Kanga) and baby (Roo).

The adventures of these animal characters were inspired by the toys and games of A. A. Milne's own young son, a real-life Christopher Robin, and the book's distinctive illustrations (pictured below) are by E. H. Shepard. Given the success of Mr. Milne's book of verse, *When We Were Very Young*, which has been reprinted 13 times since it was first published two years ago, his latest book is sure to be a winner with young and old readers alike.

▲ *A. A. Milne, author of the Winnie-the-Pooh stories.*

▲ *The inspiration for* Winnie-the-Pooh, *A. A. Milne's son Christopher Robin hugs his mother.*

▲ *Christopher Robin meeting with the Hundred Acre Wood gang outside the tree trunk house.*

▲ *Pooh Bear stands on a chair to reach his honey jar.*

New epic film hailed as masterpiece

Ramon Novarro, the young star with the romantic Latin looks, stars in the latest film version of the best-selling novel *Ben-Hur*. It tells the story of a rebellious Jewish nobleman who survives life as a Roman slave and gladiator to encounter Jesus and is reunited with his true love and his family. The sea battle and chariot race scenes are as spectacular as they are realistic, and the *New York Times* has hailed the movie as a "masterpiece of study and patience, a panorama filled with artistry."

▶ Ben-Hur *is set in ancient Rome.*

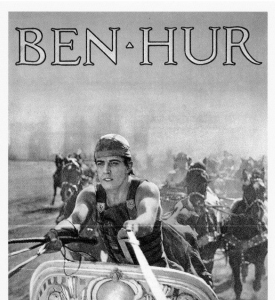

BEN·HUR

▲ *The new British Commonwealth of nations is shown in pink on the map above. It includes Canada, Australia, Newfoundland, New Zealand, and South Africa.*

GB to head new Commonwealth

POLITICS

20 NOVEMBER The former colonies of the British Empire—Canada, Australia, Newfoundland, South Africa, and New Zealand—are to become dominions within a "Commonwealth" of nations. It was agreed at a meeting in London that Britain, the "mother country," is now in partnership with the dominions. The king's title is to be "George V, by the Grace of God, of Great Britain, Ireland, and the British Dominions beyond the Seas, King, Defender of the Faith, Emperor of India." The Irish Free State has been included in the alliance but does not have to accept royal sovereignty.

Muscle man brings hope for "weeds"

Body-builder Charles Atlas has opened a gym where ordinary New Yorkers can do his exercise regime and acquire an impressive physique like his own. Atlas, who was born Angelo Siciliano, takes his name from the giant of Greek mythology who supported the weight of the heavens upon his shoulders.

▲ *Charles Atlas shows off his strength.*

Discovery of ancient worlds

ARCHEOLOGY

18 FEBRUARY Five Maya cities have been discovered in the Yucatán peninsula in Mexico. Much of ancient American civilization remains a mystery, but it is thought that these stone complexes date back to around A.D. 300. Their inhabitants may have been the priestly astronomers who devised the sacred Maya calendars and organized important religious festivals.

Like the Egyptians, their script was hieroglyphic, but scholars are still puzzling over the meaning of Maya symbols. Some answers may yet be uncovered in the dense forests of Mexico.

▲ *This detail is taken from a Maya pot.*

◀ *Emperor Hirohito.*

Death of Gaudí

ARCHITECTURE

10 JUNE The great Catalan architect, Antonio Gaudí, has died in Santa Cruz Hospital, three days after being knocked down by a trolley-bus in his beloved Barcelona.

The 74-year-old had been working on a spectacular church dedicated to the Holy Family, the Templo Expiatorio de la Sagrada Familia. He began work on it in 1882, but did not expect the building to be completed in his own lifetime.

In his work, Gaudí tried to fuse nature with geometry so that the buildings seemed to have grown rather than been built.

▶ *Gaudí's Sagrada Familia church.*

Hirohito becomes emperor of Japan

POLITICS

25 DECEMBER As of today, Crown Prince Hirohito is the emperor of Japan, though his subjects, who regard him as a god, never refer to him by that name. To them, he's Tenno or Tenno Heika, meaning Son of Heaven. Unlike any of his imperial ancestors, the 25-year-old emperor has visited Europe, and is also a dedicated marine biologist. He is the 124th direct descendent of the first Japanese emperor, Jimmu.

SPORT

Gertrude Ederle is first woman to swim Channel

6 AUGUST A 19-year-old New Yorker, Gertrude Ederle, is the first woman to swim from France to England, and she's swum the Channel in the record time of 14 hours and 31 minutes. This is more than two hours faster than the time of the previous record-holder, the Italian swimmer Enrico Tiraboschi, who lives in Argentina.

Two years ago Miss Ederle won a bronze medal in the 400-meters freestyle at the Paris Olympics, but the solo English Channel event presented her with a more daunting challenge. She crossed from Cap Gris Nez on the French coast and reached the Kent coast after withstanding severe cold, strong tides and currents, and an unfriendly wind.

◀ *Cross-Channel swimmers Gertrude Ederle (right) and Lilian Cannon pose with their trainer.*

▲ *Unrest rocks the streets of Warsaw during coup.*

Fritz Lang's vision of the future

The new Expressionist German movie *Metropolis* imagines life in the year 2000—and it is not a cheerful scenario. Armies of antlike workers swarm through the factories of a vast underground city. They are kept in their place by a saintly girl called Maria, but disaster strikes when she is replaced by an evil robot, also called Maria, the invention of a crazy scientist. Nothing like *Metropolis* has been seen before. Its director, Austrian-born Fritz Lang, was training as an architect when he became a movie director. This interest is apparent in the spectacular sets of his imaginary metropolis.

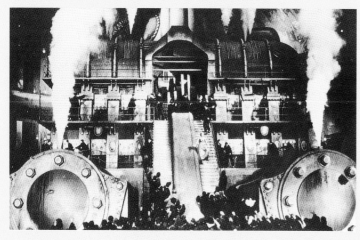

POLITICS

Pilsudski seizes power in Poland

13 JUNE After a successful coup d'etat in Poland, Pilsudski is a dictator in all but name. He has been made commander of the army by the president and by the cabinet, and he cannot be overruled by them or by acts of parliament.

Pilsudski tried to retire from political life three years ago, but it seems as if he changed his mind to support the overthrow of Poland's chaotic parliamentary government. A true patriot, he has been imprisoned twice by Poland's former Russian rulers. But Pilsudski is a military man rather than a politician, and it remains to be seen how he will treat Polish democrats who are opposed to his dictatorial new role.

◀ *Symbols of the Muslim (far left) and Hindu communities.*

QUESTS
Byrd says he flew over North Pole

13 MAY Last week, US Navy aviators Floyd Bennett and Richard Byrd claim they flew their Fokker trimotor plane to the North Pole from Spitzbergen in Norway and back in 15½ hours. The aptly named Byrd, who flew to Greenland last year, is now planning an Antarctic flight. Meanwhile in Nome, Alaska, an international team of pioneer aviators has just landed safely, having flown over the North Pole in an airship.

▲ *Richard Byrd.*

RELIGION
Hindu's and Muslim's clash

24 APRIL Calcutta is once again the scene of violent fighting between the Muslim and Hindu communities. The death toll is not yet known because bodies are still being collected.

The current troubles began some weeks ago, after outraged Muslims responded to rumors of a Hindu atrocity by arming themselves and taking to the streets. Now rival gangs are on the rampage, and it is not safe for a Hindu to be among Muslims, or a Muslim to be among Hindus.

ENTERTAINMENT
Houdini's last magic

31 OCTOBER Harry Houdini, the agile magician who could free himself from chains, straitjackets, and handcuffs, has died. He had boasted to a class in Montreal that his stomach muscles could withstand powerful punches. One of the students then hit him twice above the abdomen. On his return to the US, surgeons removed his appendix but peritonitis had set in. He was born in Hungary as Erich Weiss, but it is as Harry Houdini, the master escapologist, that he'll be remembered.

▲ *Harry Houdini in chains.*

POLITICS
General strike in Great Britain

8 MAY "Not a penny off the pay, not a minute on the day!" That is the slogan of Britain's miners. It has been a week since their dispute with mine owners became a "general strike" involving thousands of workers. To feed London's millions, a central milk and food depot has opened in Hyde Park, while volunteers and soldiers are helping to keep essential services running. So far there has been no serious violence, but feelings are running high.

NEWS • 1926 • NEWS

1 January • *Americans own 61 percent of the world's telephones, Europe 27 percent.*

12 January • *The Pasteur Institute in Paris announces the discovery of an anti-tetanus serum.*

21 April • *Princess Elizabeth, first baby of Britain's Duke and Duchess of York, is born.*

23 August • *Film idol Rudolph Valentino dies of a ruptured appendix at the age of 31.*

Dancer stretches out in new studio

Just three years after arriving in New York, 31-year-old Martha Graham is opening a dance studio on Fifth Avenue. She wants to work closely with accompanist and composer Louis Horst, who publishes the influential journal *Dance Observer*. Miss Graham is respected as a dramatic and powerful dancer, but is also a choreographer. Purity of line and freedom from ornamentation characterize her style.

ROARING TWENTIES

After World War I the US economy boomed, giving this period the name "roaring twenties." The high-living atmosphere was partly due to the Prohibition law passed in 1920, which forced people into the fashionable speakeasies (drinking clubs) in search of illegal alcohol.

Radios, record players, and Hollywood movies popularized American music, dances, and fashions in Europe. But the decade that began with a roar ended with a crash. After the panic selling of shares on the US stock exchange, share prices slumped, banks collapsed, and businesses went bust. Unemployment doubled worldwide in a year. The Depression had begun.

Saxophone

Cotton Club and jazz music

In New Orleans at the turn of the century, European and African traditions fused in the music of the time, giving jazz its characteristic "ragtime" (ragged time) sound. In 1917, when the US Navy closed its New Orleans base, many pioneering jazz musicians moved to other American cities such as St. Louis and Chicago, taking their distinctive sound with them.

In New York that same year, the Original Dixieland Jass Band from New Orleans made the first jazz recording. Most people first heard jazz on the radio, but an important venue for the popular new music was the Cotton Club in Harlem, New York. It opened in 1922 and its manager, Owney Madden, was rumored to be a leading figure in New York's Prohibition underworld.

The Cotton Club could seat 700 people and was decorated in a "primitive" style, which may have inspired Duke Ellington to develop his influential "jungle sound"; his orchestra was one of its regular performers. Other influential Cotton Club artistes were Ed "Snakehips" Tucker, Evelyn Welch, Bill Robinson, orchestras led by Cab Calloway, Andrew Preer, and Louis Armstrong, and singers such as Lena Horne and Ivie Anderson. In 1936 the Cotton Club moved to Broadway and 48th Street, and jazz was established as a musical category of its own.

◀ *Louis Armstrong, the jazz virtuoso, was born in New Orleans. Nicknamed "Satchmo," he first learned to play the trumpet in reform school.*

▶ *The Cotton Club hired many famous African-American entertainers and staff, but it did not generally admit black people as customers.*

Twenties' fashion

The clothes of the 1920s reflected the optimism of young people, who were keen to make up for the time lost to World War I.

Fashionable young women, known as flappers because they were frivolous or because of the Charleston's arm movements, scorned the stiff corsets, voluminous petticoats, and cumbersome skirts of their grandmothers. Their dresses were low-waisted and their hems were high, and they wore makeup and costume jewelery.

Stylish accessories

When she was a Red Cross worker during the war, Gabrielle "Coco" Chanel decided to modernize women's impractical clothes. She began by adjusting men's jackets to fit women, and after the war she set up her own fashion house in Paris. By 1924 her easy-to-wear short skirts and collarless jackets designed for slim, active women were all the rage.

The 1920s brought a new informality and a new classlessness for men. They no longer had to be gentlemen of leisure to wear a certain kind of hat or a suit. An Oxford University student fashion for wide-legged slacks, known as "Oxford bags," became popular in the US.

The Charleston

The frenetic, extravagant spirit of the roaring twenties was epitomized by the Charleston. Named after the South Carolina town where it began, it spread all over the US and had caught on in European capitals by 1925. It was especially popular with flappers, whose Charleston outfits included swinging beads and fringes. Film star Joan Crawford was a famous flapper.

▶ *The energetic Charleston involved bending the knees and kicking out the legs.*

Roaring 20s facts

The first "talk" of the first "talkie" film was "You ain't heard nothing yet!" said by Al Jolson in *The Jazz Singer*, 1927.

•

By 1927, as a result of Prohibition, there were 30,000 speakeasies in New York City.

•

The sale of 16 million shares resulted in the Wall Street Crash on 29 October, 1929.

▲ *The cloche hat was fashionable in the 1920s. Pulled down over the ears, it was highly practical for "motoring."*

▶ *Movies helped to popularize fashions. This outfit was influenced by* The Sheik *(1921), starring Rudolph Valentino.*

1920

1921

1922

1923

1924

1925

1926

1927

1928

1929

▲ *Lindbergh standing in front of his airplane,* the Spirit of St. Louis.

▲ *Charles Lindbergh in his leather flying hat and goggles.*

Flying ace conquers Atlantic

TRANSPORT

21 MAY At 10:22 pm this evening US pilot Charles Lindbergh landed his single-engined monoplane, *Spirit of St. Louis*, at Le Bourget airfield in Paris, France, having flown from New York. A huge crowd gathered to welcome him after his record-breaking 33½-hour solo flight across the Atlantic. He had no navigational instruments except a compass, could not use charts in the cramped cockpit, and was unable to see straight ahead because extra fuel tanks blocked his forward view. The *Spirit of St. Louis* is a modified version of a civil aircraft. Its fuselage is constructed from steel tubing and the wings are of wood, both covered in fabric. Captain Lindbergh, son of a wealthy Congressman, taught himself to fly after buying his own aircraft. He joined the US Army Flying Corps, and later flew for the airmail service. He has survived several forced landings and once had to bail out when he got lost in fog and ran out of fuel. He now wins a $25,000 prize as the first man to fly the Atlantic alone.

Ten-year-old virtuoso is a star

In Paris on 6 February, the musical world was astounded by a brilliant performance of Lalo's *Symphonie Espagnole*—a very difficult piece for violin. It was played faultlessly by a boy called Yehudi Menuhin, who is just 10 years old. The son of Russian-Jewish parents, Yehudi was born in New York. He gave his first public performance at the age of seven, so he is already a veteran of the concert hall. This is likely to be the start of a successful career.

Chinese Nationalists take Shanghai

POLITICS

21 MARCH Chinese Nationalist troops today marched into Shanghai. This great international city, which has many foreign residents and businesses, was taken with little resistance.

The forces of the northern warlords, who still control the government in Peking, melted away as the Nationalists, led by Chiang Kai-shek, marched in. The international area, which was guarded by European troops, was not invaded.

The alliance between the Chinese Communist Party and Chiang's Nationalists is likely to become very strained under the pressure of recent events as both battle for control of the country.

12 February • Portuguese dictator António Carmona defeats popular uprising against his rule.

29 March • Henry Segrave breaks Malcolm Campbell's land speed record at 200 miles per hour (323 km per hour).

29 June • First total eclipse of the sun visible in Britain for 200 years.

14 September • Dancer Isadora Duncan killed when her scarf catches in car wheel.

▲ *The Weissenhof Estate provides a beautiful and practical living environment.*

ARCHITECTURE
New estate heralds change in standards

23 JULY A remarkable new housing area was opened to the public today at Weissenhof, on the outskirts of Stuttgart in Germany. It consists of 60 units of housing.

The group behind this development is the Werkbund, a group of artists, architects, and industrialists who promote modern design. The structure is intended to match perfectly the needs of modern living, while being very cheap to build because of the use of prefabricated parts. Residents will enjoy excellent living standards.

"Talkie" is a big hit

Hollywood history was made when *The Jazz Singer,* starring Al Jolson (third from left), opened on 6 October. Until now the only sound in movies has been music recorded on disks, but the new Vitaphone disks used in this movie include speech. The sound is recorded while the movie is being shot. Many actors will need voice training to do this.

POLITICS
Trotsky expelled from Party

15 NOVEMBER Leon Trotsky, who was Lenin's right-hand man during the Bolshevik (Communist) Revolution in Russia in 1917, has been expelled from the Communist Party of the Soviet Union and dismissed from his official posts.

Since Lenin's death in 1924, Joseph Stalin has been emerging as the new leader of the Soviet Union. Many members of the party have criticized the policies of the central government, but Stalin has been quick to quell opposition. Besides Trotsky, several other leading opponents have been expelled.

Some say Stalin is trying to secure unity in the party, while others say that his motive is simply to increase his own power.

◄ *While in exile, Trotsky goes fishing.*

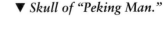

Road signs made standard

Driving in the US will soon become easier as a result of the introduction of the same type of road signs across the country. At present, road signs vary from state to state. A board of experts set up by the federal government has recommended a system of road markings and signs for standard use.

ARCHEOLOGY
Ancient skull found in Peking

▼ *Skull of "Peking Man."*

1927 An ancestor of modern humans has been found in a cave near Peking. He was identified as a new species from a single fossil tooth by Davidson Black, a Canadian professor teaching in China. Discovery of more remains will no doubt confirm Dr. Black's judgment. "Peking Man," or *Sinanthropus pekinensis,* lived about 350,000 years ago.

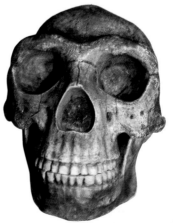

1920	
1921	
1922	
1923	
1924	
1925	
1926	
1927	
1928	
1929	

1928

SCIENCE

Miracle mold discovered: could save millions of lives

30 SEPTEMBER Doctors are excited by a recent discovery made by Alexander Fleming, a Scottish scientist working at Queen Mary's Hospital, London. It seems that a certain mold, similar to that which grows on stale food, may be able to cure dangerous infections. The mold is called *Penicillium notatum*, and the miracle substance it produces has been named penicillin.

Professor Fleming, who is known for his work on typhoid vaccines, found the mold growing on a plate containing bacteria which had stood for several days on his lab bench. The bacteria were a variety of *Staphylococcus*, which are responsible for many infections in humans, including abscesses and pneumonia. He noticed that around the patches of mold the bacteria had completely disappeared. It seems that a chemical in the mold kills the bacteria.

So far, it looks as though the chemical is harmless to humans, and it may kill other harmful bacteria besides *Staphylococcus*. The next step is to extract the penicillin and begin tests to see how effective it is.

▶ *The pencillin mold growing in Fleming's petri dish.*

▼ *The Harlem Globetrotters make the game of basketball fun.*

Harlem Globe-trotters trot the globe

The amazing Harlem Globetrotters have been delighting audiences far from home this year. Formed in Chicago in 1926, they are a team of professional basketball players. They started off touring small American towns, traveling in a beat-up car. Now they are going abroad. They play the game as an entertainment, and crowds gasp at their technical skills and laugh at their clowning, sometimes with trick basketballs.

▲ *Fleming at work in his laboratory.*

Penicillin facts

The discovery was an accident.

•

Fleming found that penicillin still worked when diluted 800 times.

•

Penicillin is unique because it does not harm human cells.

ECONOMICS

New pact means world peace

27 AUGUST Another step was taken toward world peace today when the Kellogg-Briand pact was signed in Paris. Fifteen of the world's most powerful nations agreed not to go to war except to defend themselves. The pact is named after the the French foreign minister, Aristide Briand, who first proposed such an agreement between France and the US, and the US secretary of state, Frank B. Kellogg.

▼ *Delegates sign the Kellogg-Briand pact.*

TECHNOLOGY

Doctors take to the skies

15 MAY An Australian doctor now visits his patients by airplane. The new service has been set up by John Flynn, a Presbyterian minister, to cover the huge, thinly settled area of central Australia. Patients can contact the flying doctor at Cloncurry, Queensland, by radio.

▲ *A patient breathes with the aid of an iron lung.*

Five-Year Plan for a modern USSR

1 OCTOBER As part of the intense effort to turn the Soviet Union into a modern industrial state, Stalin's first Five-Year Plan goes into effect today. It sets targets for every industry in the country, and there are hopes that it can be completed ahead of time.

A similar "revolution" is taking place in the countryside, where the peasants are finding that their smallholdings are to be transformed into collective farms, to be worked under state control.

Medics hope metal marvel will save lives

12 OCTOBER An "iron lung," or "tank respirator," was first used today to help a young patient in Boston Children's Hospital in Massachusetts. The metal marvel is a machine that helps patients to breathe when their own lungs do not work.

The device was invented by Philip Drinker at Harvard University, near Boston. It looks like a large metal tank with a hatch at one end. The patient is placed inside the tank and the hatch is closed. Only the patient's head sticks out, and a rubber ring fits tightly around the neck to ensure that the tank is airtight. When the pressure inside the tank is lowered, the patient's chest expands and air is drawn into the lungs. When the pressure is raised again, the air in the lungs is expelled. By alternately lowering and raising the pressure, a patient can be "ventilated," or made to breathe, for a long time.

The young patient in Boston was suffering from poliomyelitis (polio). An infectious disease, polio is caused by a virus. It is more common in the US than other countries, and is especially dangerous to children. The disease causes paralysis, usually of the arms and legs, but in severe cases the respiratory system is paralyzed so the victim cannot breathe. More iron lungs are being built, and doctors hope they will save the lives of many more polio victims.

NEWS • 1928 • NEWS

13 March • Hundreds die as dam bursts near Los Angeles, California.

8 June • Chiang Kai-shek's Nationalist forces capture Peking.

20 June • Roald Amundsen, Norwegian polar explorer, killed on Arctic rescue flight.

30 July • US inventor George Eastman demonstrates moving pictures in color.

1 November • German airship Graf Zeppelin completes return flight to US.

Sharp Schick's close shave

Men who cut themselves shaving, even with a safety razor, are hopeful that the new electric shavers are the answer, since earlier models did not work. Joseph Schick's invention is better. A thin metal screen passes over the face. Hairs stick through the holes and are cut off by a blade moving rapidly back and forth. These new razors will probably be very popular with women as well.

▶ *Producers of the new electric razors claim it gives a close shave.*

◀ *Huge dams provide power for Soviet industry.*

Talking mouse is major attraction

19 SEPTEMBER The long lines for the children's matinee at the Colony Theater in New York City will be longer this month. The star attraction is *Steamboat Willie*, a short cartoon made by Walt Disney. The film does for cartoons what *The Jazz Singer* did for other motion pictures last year. It is the first cartoon to have a soundtrack and is designed to show off the latest advances in film technology, with the cargo of a riverboat, complete with animals, turning into an orchestra.

The star of the movie is a mouse called Mickey. He was invented last year by Walt Disney's old friend and partner, Ub Iwerks, and was first called Mortimer Mouse. He was renamed Mickey and has appeared in two short silent movies: *Plane Crazy* and *Gallopin' Gaucho*. Walt Disney himself does Mickey's squeaky voice. More Mickey Mouse shorts, including some in color, are being planned at the Disney studio in Hollywood, so we can expect those matinee lines to get longer.

▲ *Mickey Mouse and his girlfriend Minnie Mouse.*

"Duke" plays the Cotton Club

1928 The liveliest place to be in New York at the moment is the Cotton Club in the district of Harlem. Jazz is popular everywhere now, but the Cotton Club is the place to hear the latest "big band" jazz. Duke Ellington, composer, piano player, and bandleader, has been the star since last year. He is a national celebrity, thanks to radio broadcasts, and is planning foreign tours.

Ellington's jazz style is totally unique and has already started to influence other musicians and composers.

◀ *Edward Kennedy "Duke" Ellington leads his band from the piano.*

Woman claims to be Russian princess

6 FEBRUARY A mysterious immigrant arrived in New York today. Her name is Mrs. Chaikovsky, and she claims to be the Princess Anastasia, one of the daughters of the last tzar of Russia. The whole Russian royal family was murdered in 1918, but there have been rumors that some members of the family may have escaped. The son of the tzar's doctor, who was also murdered, says Mrs. Chaikovsky is definitely Anastasia, but other people are doubtful.

▲ *Anastasia— dead or alive?*

◄ *Engineers prepare the first rocket car for a test run.*

German rocket car shoots ahead

TRANSPORT

23 MAY The engineer and industrialist Fritz von Opel drove his amazing rocket-powered car during a successful test today. The first rocket car made its debut on 15 March this year, but this is an improved version, called the *Opel-Rak 2*. It achieved a speed of more than 143 miles per hour (230 km per hour) at the Avus racecourse near Berlin.

The speedy car was built by Opel and the engineer Max Valier. Opel is the grandson of Adam Opel, whose family firm began making cars in 1898. In spite of Opel's success, nobody is suggesting that the family car of the future will be rocket-powered. Rockets are more likely to be used in different ways—in the US, Robert Goddard hopes that they can be used to explore space, and experiments with rocket-powered flight are also being conducted by the Soviets.

Suffrage for women in the United Kingdom

POLITICS

7 MAY The British House of Commons today passed the Equal Franchise Bill. It gives all women over 21 the right to vote. There was no opposition. British women first gained the right to vote in a parliamentary election in 1918, but only if they were over 30. Now, all adult citizens, male and female, have equal rights—at least on election day.

◄ *At the Olympics, women had previously only competed in events such as swimming.*

Emil saves the day

This year's surprise bestseller in Germany is *Emil und die Detektive* (*Emil and the Detectives*), by Erich Kästner. The star of the book is 10-year-old Emil Tischbein, the son of a poor widow, who goes to Berlin to stay with his grandparents. On the train he is robbed and sets out after the suspected thief. When he reaches Berlin, he is helped by local schoolchildren. They eventually catch the thief, who turns out to be a dangerous bank robber. Emil gets the reward and becomes famous.

▶ *One of the illustrations from the book.*

Women athletes in Olympics

SPORT

12 AUGUST The ninth Olympic Games since the modern games began in 1896 ended in Amsterdam, Netherlands, today. About 3,000 competitors took part. They came from 46 countries, compared with only 13 countries in the 1896 games. There were also more medal-winners from countries outside Europe and North America, such as Argentina and Japan. For the first time women, who in previous Olympics were limited to sports such as swimming, competed in athletics. The gold medal in the women's 100 meters was won by Elisabeth Robinson of the US.

101

1920

1921

1922

1923

1924

1925

1926

1927

1928

1929

▼ *Best Actor Emil Jannings with his award.*

First Academy Awards

Hollywood honored its finest on 16 May when the Academy of Motion Picture Arts and Sciences announced its first awards. All the winners received a 13-inch (33-cm) gold-plated figure of a man standing on a reel of film. The awards ceremony is to be held annually.

SCIENCE

Evidence of Big Bang explodes universe myths

1929 American astronomer Edwin Hubble has produced the first evidence to back up the Big Bang theory. This is the idea that the universe was once concentrated in a single point that exploded with a huge force (big bang) and has been rushing apart with the momentum of this event ever since.

Scientists already know that the Earth revolves around the Sun and that the Sun is one of many stars in a vast system called the Milky Way galaxy. Hubble demonstrated five years ago that the Milky Way is not the only galaxy—there are others far out in space. Now he has shown that these galaxies are moving away from us, which proves that the universe is expanding. He has also discovered that the farther away the galaxies are, the faster they are moving. Hubble uses the powerful telescope at the Mount Wilson Observatory in the US to roam the galaxies.

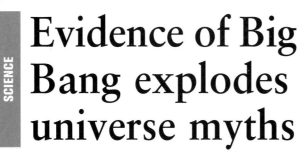

▲ *Edwin Hubble, who proved other galaxies exist outside of ours.*

Universe facts
Hubble worked out that the universe is 2 billion years old—but scientists now think it may be 7 times older than that.

• There are about 100 billion stars in our galaxy.

▲ *An unsuccessful investor tries to sell his car for $100.*

ECONOMICS

Wall Street crash brings despair to investors

24 OCTOBER Panic swept the New York stock exchange on Wall Street today as the bottom fell out of the market in stocks and shares. Investors ordered their brokers to sell at any price and during the day 12,894,650 shares were sold. The US has been booming, with many shares bought on credit, but now the bubble has burst. Some have seen vast fortunes wiped out, but many smaller investors also face ruin. At least 11 people have committed suicide. The effect is sure to be felt worldwide.

Intrepid Tintin appears

Tintin, a teenage news reporter with a taste for adventure, made his debut today in the Belgian newspaper *Le Vingtième Siècle* (*The Twentieth Century*). He is the hero of a comic strip drawn by Hergé, the pen name of Belgian author and artist Georges Rémi. Tintin has distinctive red hair and is followed everywhere he goes by his white dog Snowy. The young hero needs all his wits to survive.

▼ *Tintin with faithful Snowy.*

Peasants hit by hardship in USSR

ECONOMICS

27 DECEMBER Peasants in the Soviet Union are being forced to give up their land and join large collective farms, which are intended to provide workers with food. This is part of the Five-Year Plan launched by the Soviet leadership last year to propel the Soviet Union into the forefront of European nations. Many peasants oppose the program, known as collectivization, and have killed and eaten their cattle rather than handing them over. Resisters risk being sent to camps in Siberia.

▲ *Russian peasants are opposed to joining the collective farms.*

Death of a legend

PEOPLE

13 JANUARY Wyatt Earp, the famous gambler and frontier lawman of the West, died today in Los Angeles.

During the 1870s Earp worked for the US marshal in Dodge City, Kansas. In Tombstone, Arizona, on 26 October 1881, Wyatt, two of his brothers, and friends Doc Holliday and Bat Masterson clashed with the Clanton family in the infamous gunfight at the O.K. Corral.

Wyatt portrayed himself as an honest man to writer Stuart Lake. He in fact made money from gambling and prostitution.

▲ *Wyatt Earp (sitting, center) and friends.*

Novel hits hard

LITERATURE

DECEMBER A hard-hitting novel about the horror of trench fighting in the Great War was a bestseller in Germany this year. *All Quiet on the Western Front*, written by war veteran Erich Maria Remarque, tells the story of German schoolboys who enlist to fight for their country but then have to cope with dirt, disease, and death in the trenches. Work will soon begin on a Hollywood movie of the book.

The St.Valentine's Day massacre

LAW

14 FEBRUARY Police are convinced that gangster Al Capone ordered the shooting of seven members of a rival gang led by "Bugsy" Moran in a beerhouse raid today. Since his friend Johnny Torrio retired in 1925, Capone has had total control over Chicago's illegal business in prostitution, gambling, and liquor, and does not want to share the profits with any rival.

Some of the gangsters involved in the killings posed as police officers wearing police uniforms, which has outraged Police Commissioner William Russell. He says he has "never known a challenge like this."

▲ *Al Capone.*

NEWS • 1929 • NEWS

11 February • Vatican City is created in Rome.

4 April • Pioneer German car designer Carl Benz dies, aged 84.

1 July • Popeye the Sailor Man makes his comic strip debut in the US.

29 August • German airship Graf Zeppelin lands in New Jersey, after flying around the world.

29 November • US Navy Commander and explorer Richard Byrd flies over South Pole.

SOCCER & BASEBALL

Two sports rule the world. Soccer, also called "association football" or just "football" in Britain, is the most popular sport in large parts of the globe. Every four years the top soccer-playing countries compete in the World Cup Finals, and fans take great pride in the performance of their national team. Most countries also have soccer leagues, in which town or city clubs compete.

In the US baseball is so popular it is known as the national pastime. The highlight of the baseball season is when the winners of the top professional leagues—the American League and the National League—play each other in the World Series. Soccer and baseball are not only big businesses; thousands of people enjoy playing them.

Tools of the trade

In baseball, the batter wears a protective helmet and uses a rounded bat 42 inches (106 cm) long. The pitcher hurls a leather-covered ball at the batter. The catcher squats behind the batter, wearing a heavy catcher's glove as well as a padded chest cover, helmet, and wire mask for protection.

Helmet

Ball

Bat

Fielder's glove

◀ *Babe Ruth began as an all-rounder—he could pitch and field as well as bat—but his fame rests on his batting for the Yankees. In his career he hit 714 home runs. Ruth died in 1948, aged 52.*

Stadium stars

Between them, Babe Ruth and Joe DiMaggio produced 34 years of baseball heroics for the New York Yankees. Ruth signed for the Yankees from the Boston Red Sox in 1920. In his first season he scored a record 54 home runs, which means that when batting he hit the ball either off the field or so far that he was able to run around all four bases before the fielders threw the ball back. In 1927 he hit 60 home runs—and his record stood until 1961. Babe retired in 1935.

The following year DiMaggio joined the Yankees from the San Francisco Seals—and hit 29 home runs in his first season. The Yankees then won the World Series four years in a row from 1936 to 1939. DiMaggio, who retired in 1951, had one other claim to fame—he married the actress Marilyn Monroe.

▶ *It is very difficult for a batter to hit the ball to safety every time he bats, but DiMaggio did that a record 56 games in a row in 1941.*

▶ The team from Uruguay won the Olympic soccer competitions in 1924 and 1928, and were favorites to win the World Cup.

Uruguay wins the first World Cup

A national holiday was declared in Uruguay after they beat Argentina 4–2 in the first soccer World Cup on 30 July 1930. Members of soccer's international governing body FIFA agreed in 1928 to hold a World Cup competition, to take place every four years beginning in 1930. Only four European teams—Romania, France, Belgium, and Yugoslavia—took part.

▶ Since 1974 the trophy has been called The FIFA World Cup.

Pelé—one of the greatest soccer players

The Brazilian striker Pelé scored 1,090 goals in 1,114 games for his Brazilian club Santos. He first made his debut in a good Brazilian team at the age of 16 in 1957. The following year he scored two goals in the World Cup final when Brazil beat Sweden. For the last two years of his career he played for the New York Cosmos in the US. He retired on 1 October, 1977, after an exhibition match between Santos and the Cosmos in Giants Stadium, New York.

World Cup winners

1930	Uruguay	(beat Argentina 4–2)
1934	Italy	(beat Czechoslovakia 2–1)
1938	Italy	(beat Hungary 4–2)
1950	Uruguay	(beat Brazil 2–1)
1954	West Germany	(beat Hungary 3–2)
1958	Brazil	(beat Sweden 5–2)
1962	Brazil	(beat Czechoslovakia 3–1)
1966	England	(beat West Germany 4–2)
1970	Brazil	(beat Italy 4–1)
1974	West Germany	(beat Holland 2–1)
1978	Argentina	(beat Holland 3–1)
1982	Italy	(beat West Germany 3–1)
1986	Argentina	(beat West Germany 3–2)
1990	West Germany	(beat Argentina 1–0)
1994	Brazil	(beat Italy 3–2)
1998	France	(beat Brazil 3–0)

1930

1931

1932

1933

1934

1935

1936

1937

1938

1939

1930

Unemployment and poverty dominated the lives of many people in Europe and the US at the beginning of the 1930s. Franklin Roosevelt was elected president in 1932, offering a "new deal" for Americans through a wide-ranging recovery program. Dust storms in midwestern states starting in 1933 forced many farmers to abandon their land and move on. In Europe, political turmoil caused bloodshed. The bitter Spanish Civil War lasted from 1936 to 1939. The extreme nationalist and racist Nazi Party came to power in Germany, imprisoning and killing thousands of Jews while many others were forced to flee. The end of the decade saw the onset of the second "world war" within 25 years.

▼ *Fish, fruit, and vegetables can be kept fresh by freezing.*

▼ *"Mahatma" means "great soul." Gandhi's march helped focus anti-British feeling in India.*

PEOPLE Gandhi defies law in salt march

6 APRIL Indian nationalist campaigner Mahatma Gandhi and his followers arrived on the Indian coast yesterday after a protest march of about 300 miles (500 km). Gandhi organized the march as a challenge to the British government's law banning Indians from making their own salt. Today, on a beach facing the Gulf of Cambay in northwestern India, he picked up a piece of natural sea salt in order to show his defiance of the law.

Gandhi has been a leading campaigner against British rule in India for over 10 years. He wants his supporters to refuse to cooperate with the authorities until Britain allows India to govern itself. He insists that all protests should be peaceful, although Gandhi has told his supporters to be ready for "the worst, even death, for defiance of the salt tax." He seems prepared to go to jail over the issue.

Birdseye spots gap in market

New York businessman Clarence Birdseye has perfected a method of fast-freezing food to preserve it. His products are the first frozen foods to taste almost as good as fresh. Birdseye was inspired by trips to Labrador in eastern Canada, where locals freeze food in winter.

SCIENCE New neighbor for planet Earth

13 MARCH The Lowell Observatory in Flagstaff, Arizona, announced today that astronomer Clyde Tombaugh has discovered a new planet. It is likely that this new planet will be called Pluto. Tombaugh found the planet while searching photographs of the night sky taken in late January. At its farthest from the Sun, Pluto is 4.6 billion miles (7.4 billion km) from the Earth.

▲ *An artist's impression of Pluto (left).*

Art Deco skyscraper opens for business

ARCHITECTURE

DECEMBER The ultramodern Chrysler building has opened in New York. Designed by William Van Alen, it has a striking steel spire and a sleek streamlined form. Characteristic of the Art Deco style, which originated in Europe in the 1920s, streamlining is inspired by the designs of ships and locomotives.

Selassie crowned

POLITICS

2 NOVEMBER Prince Ras Tafari was today crowned Emperor Haile Selassie of Abyssinia (Ethiopia) in northeastern Africa. He wore a magnificent velvet robe of crimson trimmed with gold for his coronation. Representatives of foreign governments and spearbearing tribesmen watched as the prince, regent of the country since the revolution in 1916, paraded through the streets.

▶ *Haile Selassie.*

▲ *The new Chrysler building is 1,046 feet (319 meters) high— the world's tallest building to date.*

Fortresses to protect France

WAR

DECEMBER French workers have begun building a line of concrete forts (below) along France's border with Germany. It is the idea of French war minister André Maginot, who argues that the forts will protect France forever against German invasion. The plan is to build with the thickest concrete and install heavy guns.

NEWS • 1930 • NEWS

24 April • British aviator Amy Johnson lands in Australia after completing the first solo flight from Britain by a woman.

1 July • The Greyhound Company opens a bus service covering the US.

7 July • British writer Arthur Conan Doyle, creator of Sherlock Holmes, dies aged 71.

5 October • British R101 airship crashes on its first flight, killing 44 people in France.

Nazis in open racist displays

POLITICS

13 OCTOBER In parliament today, Nazis clashed with Communists. Nazi supporters ran riot outside, howling "Down with the Jews!" and even attacking some Jewish-owned shops.

The new German parliament began sitting today following last month's election in which the National Socialist German Worker's Party, led by Adolf Hitler, took a big step closer to power. The National Socialists—or Nazis—are now the second largest party after the Socialists. Critics thought that the Nazis' extreme policies—especially their open racism against Jewish people—would not be popular with enough people for them to win votes, but they have been proved wrong.

Bombshell Dietrich— an overnight star

The movie *The Blue Angel*, released today, looks set to make an overnight star of the actress Marlene Dietrich. She plays a dancehall singer, Lola Lola, who marries but then abandons a German professor played by Emil Jannings. Director Josef von Sternberg saw Dietrich in a revue and insisted on casting her despite studio objections.

▲ *Marlene Dietrich in the role of Lola Lola.*

Timeline

1930

1931

1932

1933

1934

1935

1936

1937

1938

1939

ARCHITECTURE

Empire State scrapes New York skyline

1 MAY A shining beacon of hope in the middle of the Great Depression, New York's Empire State Building was formally opened today. At 1,250 feet (381 meters), the 102-story office block at the corner of 34th Street and Fifth Avenue is the tallest building in the world. The time it took to build is another record—an army of laborers took 6 months to complete a task that the architects thought would take 18 months.

Former New York Governor Alfred Smith cut the tape and President Hoover pushed a button that lit up the building, before everyone tucked into a giant cake shaped like the building.

The Empire State Building, with its strong vertical lines and square appearance, is a spectacular addition to the city's skyline and has a mooring mast for airships at the top. Its owners hope that it will become the New York terminal for air travelers from around the globe. But meanwhile, they are struggling to rent the building. New Yorkers are already calling it the "Empty State" building.

▲ *Empire State Building.*

New game is a bit of a scrabble

Alfred Butts, an unemployed architect, has dreamed up a new game. You have to make up words using randomly chosen letters, and each letter is worth a different number of points. Butts does not know what to call the game—perhaps the "scrabble" for high-scoring letters will suggest a name.

TREATIES

Japanese occupy Manchuria

28 OCTOBER Today the US Secretary of State has negotiated a truce in the three-week-old Manchurian War, in which Japan has claimed Manchuria, a vast area of land in northeastern China. The League of Nations is using this time to study the situation. The trouble started on 18 September, when Japan alleged that China had sabotaged the Japanese-owned South Manchurian Railroad. But in fact Japan has long wanted to capture the rich natural resources of the area and was just waiting for an excuse to invade. Japan now has its sights set on the port of Shanghai.

▶ *Chinese prisoners in Manchuria.*

POLITICS

Spain becomes a republic

14 APRIL King Alfonso XIII and the Spanish royal family are on their way to Paris tonight—Spain has become a republic. The king realized his time was up when Spaniards voted overwhelmingly for the Republicans in the municipal elections.

Since 1923, the King has ruled as a dictator, with the help of General Miguel Primo de Rivera. But Rivera died last year, leaving the King exposed to attack after eight years of grinding poverty and bad government. Both Alfonso and Spain's new leaders hope that today's events will prevent Spain from collapsing into civil war.

▲ *Republicans celebrate in Spain.*

CULTURE

United States gets national anthem

3 MARCH Ever since the War of Independence, Americans have been singing "The Star-Spangled Banner" at patriotic occasions. But only today has it become the official national anthem. The noble tune is based on an old English drinking song; the stirring words were written in 1814 by Francis Scott Key.

POLITICS

Coalition takes over as Labour falls in Britain

24 AUGUST The worldwide depression today destroyed Britain's Labour government. With international banks refusing to accept British currency, Prime Minister Ramsay MacDonald has formed an all-party "National Government" as an emergency measure during the crisis.

MacDonald's new cabinet contains Liberals and Conservatives—including Stanley Baldwin, the Conservative leader.

Win money and lose a spouse in Nevada

Nevada is renowned for being a sparsely populated desert state, but a new law passed this year by state legislators in Carson City looks set to change all that.

By legalizing gambling and relaxing laws on divorce, the state of Nevada hopes to boost its revenue. People are already flooding into the town of Las Vegas to play the tables.

▲ *Gambling—Nevada's the winner!*

TECHNOLOGY

World loses one of its greatest inventors

18 OCTOBER With the death of Thomas Alva Edison this morning, the world has lost one of the greatest inventors in history. Edison was always fascinated by science and chemistry, but his schoolteacher said he was "addled."

His first invention was the "ticker tape" machine to print stock exchange results. He went on to create, or improve, the telephone, the gramophone, the electric light, the battery, and motion pictures.

▶ *Thomas Edison with a motion picture projector. He has been granted patents for more than 1,000 inventions.*

1930

1931

1932

1933

1934

1935

1936

1937

1938

1939

▲ *Bread lines are common in the US.*

Sydney bridge

Sydney Harbour Bridge has opened, linking the center of the city with the suburbs to the north. It took nine years to build the 1,650-foot (503-meter) long structure. It is the largest single-span bridge in the world. Sydneysiders are mockingly, but fondly, calling it "The Coathanger."

Depression facts

Between 1929 and 1932:

14 million Americans (1 in 4) out of work.

●

2.25 million Britons out of work.

●

Farm prices halved.

●

44 percent of US banks failed.

ECONOMICS

Depression hits Western world hard

DECEMBER As the year draws to a close, a poignant song sums up the economic depression that has swept the world. "Brother, can you spare a dime?" by Jay Gorney and Yip Harburg puts into music the question on millions of unemployed workers' lips. The grinding slump triggered by the 1929 Wall Street Crash is now in its fourth year.

One in five of the world's labor force is out of work; factories are dark, machines idle, and docks silent. Because workers have no money, sales of goods are down, so more factories close and unemployment goes on rising. People are eating at soup kitchens, repairing holes in shoes with cardboard, and patching up the rips in their clothes. Different countries seek different solutions. In Britain, 3,000 hunger marchers presented the government with a petition. Americans see Franklin Delano Roosevelt, their new president-elect, as a savior. Germans, meanwhile, are gravitating toward Adolf Hitler's National Socialist (Nazi) Party.

POLITICS

F. D. Roosevelt is elected president

8 NOVEMBER Americans today threw out President Herbert Hoover, blaming him for the continuing deep economic depression. They have placed their trust in the Democrat candidate, Franklin Delano Roosevelt (F.D.R. for short).

Although he is unable to walk because his legs are paralyzed by polio, Roosevelt undertook an energetic campaign, traveling the length and breadth of the country by train.

He promised Americans a "New Deal" to end poverty, including new laws on wages and prices, and government spending on roads and public buildings.

▶ *Roosevelt (right) traveled over 12,427 miles (20,000 km) during his campaign.*

110

Dribble wizard goes professional

SPORT

MARCH Soccer star Stanley Matthews has made his debut for Stoke City soccer club in Great Britain. The 17-year-old Matthews was signed up by Stoke City in February this year, as a right winger. Born and educated in Staffordshire, England, Stanley is a player with immense talent, and his ball control skills are earning him the nickname "the wizard of the dribble." Stoke City club has agreed to pay this talented young man a wage, so he is now a "professional" player.

▲ *Stanley Matthews.*

▲ *Antonio Salazar.*

From professor to dictator

POLITICS

5 JULY Portugal has followed Italy's lead and turned fascist. Today Antonio Salazar, a former professor of economics, became Portugal's premier, with total power to run the country as dictator.

Four years ago he became finance minister, and made great economic improvements. He is planning to set up the Estado Novo (new state)—a reborn Portugal with a new constitution.

Earhart flies into history

TRANSPORT

21 MAY Amelia Earhart, America's intrepid woman aviator, nicknamed "Lady Lindy," made history today when she landed her Lockheed Vega at Culmore, Northern Ireland, just under 16 hours after leaving Newfoundland. She is the first woman to fly solo nonstop across the Atlantic Ocean.

Amelia Earhart already holds the altitude record of 19,000 feet (5,800 meters) for flying in an autogyro—an aircraft with a thin, rotating wing — which she set last year.

▼ *Amelia Earhart and her Lockheed Vega airplane.*

Alexander Calder invents mobile new art form

Philadelphia-born sculptor Alexander Calder trained as a mechanical engineer. This helped him to create a new art form this year.

Calder has wired together pieces of steel, brass, and painted aluminum to make perfectly-balanced constructions called mobiles. When the mobiles are suspended in the air, the slightest breeze makes them move.

◀ *Calder and one of his mobiles.*

NEWS • 1932 • NEWS

4 January • Indian Congress Party made illegal; Gandhi arrested.

2 March • Aviator Charles Lindbergh's baby son is kidnapped.

10 April • Paul von Hindenburg reelected as President of Germany.

6 May • Russian maniac assassinates French President.

12 May • Lindbergh baby found dead.

6 November • Nazi Party loses 34 seats in German election.

France wins sixth Davis cup

SPORT

31 JULY The "Four Musketeers" have done it for the sixth year in a row. In the final of the Davis Cup tennis competition, held in Paris, the four-member French team have defeated the US by three matches to two. They hope next year to equal the American feat of seven straight wins between 1920 and 1926.

BUILDING OF THE CITIES

The growth of cities has dominated the 20th century. People migrate from the country to the city because of better job prospects. In some parts of Europe and North America, this migration was in full swing in the 1800s, and it has spread in the last 100 years. Almost half of the world's population will live in cities by the year 2000. More than three-quarters of people already live in cities in Australia, North America, and parts of Europe.

Cities are always changing. Rundown areas are rebuilt and old buildings are destroyed. New ones take their place. Many cities, like Tokyo and Hamburg, needed major rebuilding after being devastated by bombs during World War II.

▲ A view of the New York skyline with Brooklyn Bridge in the foreground.

◄ A construction worker rests during the building of the Empire State Building. The Chrysler Building stands in the background.

City transportation

City dwellers once had to walk to work. But more cars, trains, and buses allowed people to live farther away from the city. At the end of the 20th century, city transportation faces a crisis. Public systems are struggling to cope with the numbers that use them. The subway is so crowded in Tokyo that staff have to push commuters into full trains.

◄ Rush hour on a Tokyo tube.

Population increases cause cities to expand

Industrial cities in Europe and North America, such as London and New York, expanded vastly in the 1800s, and have continued to grow in the 1900s. São Paulo in Brazil and Mexico City in Mexico now more than match them, having exploded in size after 1950. Mexico City had 5 million people in 1960 and 17 million in 1985. Thirty-one million people are predicted to be living there by the year 2000.

Booming populations force cities to expand. Where space is severely limited, room is found for housing and offices by putting up taller and taller buildings. The best-known example is Manhattan in New York City, home to some of the tallest buildings in the world—the Empire State Building, built in just six months in 1931, has 102 storys and is 1,250 feet (381 meters) tall. Other cities, for example, Los Angeles or London, tend to sprawl outward, eating up the surrounding countryside.

▲ *This picture, taken in 1962, shows Chinese refugees living in floating boat slums in Aberdeen, Hong Kong Island.*

▼ *A homeless woman begs on the street in Buenos Aires, Argentina.*

Poverty and the homeless

Life is harsh for the poorer inhabitants of cities. Because cities are crowded, there is a shortage of houses and apartments—people with little money end up homeless or are forced to live in a dirty, overcrowded place. Most cities have rundown areas where nobody wants to live and where crime and violence are common. Those who suffer most are often the people who come to cities looking for work. In the 1990s it was common to see homeless people sleeping on the streets in cities such as New York or London. Beggars plead with tourists and workers for money. In some parts of the world, the homeless build their own makeshift housing out of tires or scraps of metal, creating "shanty towns," usually on the city outskirts. Experts say that in Latin America as many as 5 million families live in shanty towns.

City facts

On a clear day you can see 50 miles (80 km) from the top of the 1,250-foot (381-meter) of New York's Empire State Building.

•

The 60-story Woolworth building, which opened in 1913 in New York, had room for 14,000 workers.

•

The number of cities with more than one million inhabitants in the world had risen from 16 in 1900 to 67 in 1950 and 250 in 1985.

•

Figures compiled in the 1980s showed that there were more telephones in the city of Tokyo than in the whole of Africa.

Worldwide centers of financial control

City-based banks and financial trading houses control the world economy. Financial decisions taken on stock exchanges in Tokyo, New York, and London can determine whether businesses thousands of miles away succeed or fail. In most cities this economic power is concentrated in one area—the financial district, where the main banks and traders have their offices. In New York it is on Wall Street in Lower Manhattan. But the flow of money throughout cities is what keeps them alive. The very wealthy often live in cities or are drawn there to spend their money.

▶ *Traders at the London International Financial Futures and Options Exchange have an effect on economies worldwide.*

1930
1931
1932
1933
1934
1935
1936
1937
1938
1939

▶ *Swastika and eagle, the Nazi insignia.*

▼ *Nazis salute their leader.*

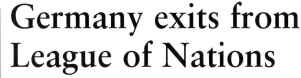

POLITICS

Adolf Hitler is the new Chancellor

30 JANUARY Torchlight parades in towns and cities across Germany tonight mark the appointment of Adolf Hitler as chancellor (prime minister). President von Hindenburg sent for Hitler, the 43-year-old leader of the National Socialist German Workers' (Nazi party for short) Party, after the other parties failed to agree to form a government.

The Nazis are the largest party in the Reichstag (parliament), with 196 seats. Hitler, a fiery public speaker, blames trade unions, Communists, and above all the Jews for Germany's humiliating defeat in the Great War. He believes that Germans are a "master race" whose destiny is to rule Europe, cleansing it of Jews and enslaving "inferior races" such as the Russians.

In recent years Hitler's promise of work for everybody has attracted millions of Germans. There is huge discontent among these people because of the high amount of unemployment since the end of the war. Hitler intends to get the job done by ruling as a dictator.

Reichstag goes up in smoke

POLITICS

27 FEBRUARY Tonight firemen are desperately struggling to extinguish the blazing Reichstag, Germany's parliament building in Berlin. The historic building looks doomed as flames shatter the glass-domed ceiling and gut the interior.

Police have detained a young Dutchman, Marinus van der Lubbe, on suspicion of arson. Adolf Hitler and the president of the Reichstag, Hermann Goering, blame the fire on communists. They intend to assume emergency powers to wipe out any opposition.

Germany exits from League of Nations

NATIONS

14 OCTOBER In a surprise move, Germany has withdrawn from the League of Nations, the organization set up to keep peace after the 1914–18 war. It is the latest in a series of radical moves. The Nazi regime has banned political opponents, burned "subversive" books, boycotted Jewish businesses, and hounded Jews and communists from public office. A new prison camp at Dachau houses political opponents. Even Germany's Boy Scout movement has been replaced by a new association—the Hitler Youth.

▲ *Fire rages uncontrolled in the historic Reichstag.*

◀ *Top left: Kurt Weill (on the right).*
Top right: Thomas Mann.

▲ *Bottom left: Bertolt Brecht.*
Bottom right: Arnold Schoenberg.

Artists flee Germany

ART

15 OCTOBER Adolf Hitler today laid the foundation stone for the House of German Art in Berlin. Yet creative people (many of whom are Jews and left-wingers) are leaving Germany, driven out by an official policy that demands that they glorify Nazism. Condemned as "degenerate," Expressionists, Surrealists, and avant-garde composers can no longer practice their art in Germany.

"Bodyline" controversy

SPORT

19 JANUARY English cricketers have won the third Test at Adelaide, but their "bodyline" tactics have sparked off a bitter wrangle. Australia's batsmen were bowled a barrage of fast bouncers on the leg side, and could only defend themselves by sending the ball into the hands of strategically arranged fielders. The Australians say it just isn't cricket.

NEWS • 1933 • NEWS

28 March • Germans ordered to boycott Jewish businesses.

3 April • British biplanes fly over Mount Everest.

23 June • Hitler dissolves all opposition political parties.

12 August • Winston Churchill warns that Germany is rearming.

23 August • Mahatma Gandhi released from Poona jail.

5 December • Prohibition ends in US; alcohol is legalized.

▲ *"Bodyline" cricketers Voce, Larwood, and Mitchell (left to right).*

Big ape beats box office

Amazing special effects have made *King Kong* the smash movie hit of the year. King Kong is an escaped giant gorilla who rampages across New York.

Audiences are being thrilled by this exciting movie, which ends with Kong on top of the Empire State building, holding a screaming woman, Fay Wray, in one hand as he swats away fighter planes.

▲ *Scary posters sell Kong to the public.*

Roosevelt to aid Dust Bowl areas

ECONOMICS

12 MAY President Roosevelt's "New Deal" to get the American economy out of depression took a step forward today with the passing of the Agricultural Adjustment Act, which sets out a national farming policy. The act aims to help America's impoverished farmers including those in the Dust Bowl areas.

▼ *Dust storms traveling at 90 miles per hour (145 km per hr) threaten farms in the "panhandle" area.*

1930
1931
1932
1933
1934
1935
1936
1937
1938
1939

1934

POLITICS

Mao's march for freedom

▼ *Mao was one of the founding members of the Chinese Communist Party in 1921.*

21 OCTOBER Around 100,000 Chinese Communists have fled from their stronghold in Kiangsi in southeastern China, where they have been besieged by their Nationalist enemies. The Communists are marching northwest, commanded by Chu Teh Mao Tse-tung, who lost the leadership of the Kiangsi Communists earlier this year. The marchers are heading for the Communist-controlled area near Tsuni, a few hundred miles away. If they decide to go farther, the prospects are tough. Aside from Kiangsi, the other main area of China controlled by the Communists lies around Yan'an, 6,000 miles (10,000 km) away. For months the Communists have been pinned into the area around Kiangsi by the powerful Nationalist Army led by Chiang Kai-shek. The Communists and Nationalists are former allies—they fought together against Chinese warlords in the mid-1920s. But in 1927 Chiang Kai-shek turned against them, and the Communists began building up support in the countryside.

Long March facts

The Communists reached Yan'an after marching for 368 days. They crossed 24 rivers and 18 mountain ranges.

•

One-third of the 100,000 Communist marchers were killed in the first three months of the "Long March."

POLITICS

Austrian Chancellor murdered by Nazis

25 JULY A band of Austrian Nazis have brutally killed Austrian Chancellor Englebert Dollfuss. They stormed into Dollfuss' office and shot him in the throat and left him to die. The Nazis took other ministers hostage and demanded to be allowed to go to Germany. A deal was agreed, then cancelled when it was found that Dollfuss was dead. More than 150 Nazis are in custody in Vienna.

German Nazi leader Adolf Hitler says he has disowned the Austrian party, but Italian dictator Benito Mussolini has put troops on standby, nervous that the Germans might invade Austria.

▶ *A poster depicting the murder of Dollfuss by Austrian Nazis.*

New Disney bird on cartoon-movie scene

A bad-tempered bird has joined the colorful line-up of animal characters assembled by American cartoonist Walt Disney. Donald Duck made his debut th year in *Wise Little Hen*. The first Disne character, Mickey Mouse, was introduc in 1928 and last year appeared in the fi Technicolor cartoon, *Flowers and Trees*

▼ *Donald Duck (below right) joins Mickey Mouse and Pluto the dog as Disney favorites*

Germany: Night of the Long Knives

POLITICS

30 JUNE Early this morning leading Nazi Ernst Roehm was hauled from his bed at a hotel near Munich and shot. Roehm was leader of the Nazi Party's *Sturmabteilung* (SA)—the "storm division" of street fighters. He is one of many top SA figures to have died in a purge launched last night by party leader Adolf Hitler.

It is said that the SA leaders were hatching a plot to replace Hitler, but rumors suggest that Hitler made a calculated political decision to get rid of the SA himself. As the Nazi Party rose from obscurity, the SA stormtroopers in their uniform of brown shirts became a widely feared sight, and they used street violence to frighten opponents. Now that Hitler is chancellor he feels that the Brown Shirts could ruin the Nazi's relationship with the German Army.

▶ *Captain Roehm, right, with Lieutenant Brueckner.*

▲ *Mao Tse-tung is a leading figure among the marchers.*

▲ *A Sioux, from one of the Native American tribes.*

Italy wins second World Cup

SPORT

10 JUNE Italy's World Cup performance today in Rome was a great propaganda victory for fascist dictator Benito Mussolini. The team gave the straight-armed fascist salute before beating Czechoslovakia 2–1. Argentinian players descended from Italians—Guaita, Monti, and Orsi—were key players for Italy.

It is the second time the World Cup has been held, and Italy is the first European country to win the trophy. The first cup was won by Uruguay in Montevideo in 1930.

Reorganization Act for Native Americans

POLITICS

JUNE A new US Government act has given Native Americans the right to own their reservation lands as tribes once again. Almost 50 years ago, the Dawes Act of 1887 split the reservations up into small units of up to 160 acres (65 hectares) each. Congress wanted the Native Americans to farm these plots, but much of the land was sold to white Americans. The new Indian Reorganization Act also allows the tribes to govern themselves, and the government's Bureau of Indian Affairs is offering to help Native Americans develop the reservation lands.

▲ *Soccer's World Cup trophy.*

Don't forget to "Pass Go"

Millions of Americans now have the chance to play the ruthless tycoon with the new boardgame, Monopoly. Squares on the board represent property, and the aim is to buy the most valuable squares and charge other players high rent. The winner makes a fortune, but the losers slide into bankruptcy.

▼ *The new boardgame appeals to people of all ages.*

▲ *Bonnie clowns about with her partner Clyde.*

LAW

Luck finally runs out for Bonnie and Clyde

23 MAY After defying the law for almost two years, the infamous duo Bonnie and Clyde drove into a police ambush in Louisiana. They were shot dead by police officers armed with submachine guns. More than 50 bullets were found in their bodies.

In a 21-month spree Bonnie Parker and Clyde Barrow, both in their mid-20s, robbed banks, gas stations, and restaurants across the Southwest. Time and again they escaped the police—once after 200 lawmen had blockaded a picnic site in Iowa. In April 1933 they had to drive through a garage door to make their getaway. Their adventures made a good story for the newspapers, which cast a glow of romance around the young couple. But notorious bankrobber John Dillinger dismissed Bonnie and Clyde as "punks" and said that they were "giving bankrobbing a bad name."

Bonnie worked as a waitress in Dallas, Texas, before teaming up with Clyde when he was released from prison in 1932. They killed at least 12 people, including 6 policemen, during their two-year crime spree. Police caught up with them today after reportedly being tipped off by one of Clyde's friends.

Wimbledon ladies play in shorts

Female players were allowed to wear shorts instead of skirts at Wimbledon this year for the first time. This must have brought the British players luck—Fred Perry won the men's singles (the first British win since 1901), and Dorothy Round won the ladies' singles, as well as the mixed doubles with Ryuki Miki from Japan.

POLITICS

New Mexican president brings hope to country

2 JULY Lázaro Cárdenas, once a soldier in the Mexican Revolution, is the new president of Mexico. He represents Mexico's first national revolutionary party, the Partido Nacional Revolucionario (PNR), and says that he will carry through the PNR's plans for social change, which include giving farmland to peasants.

The Mexican Revolution began in 1910 after a landowner, Francisco Madero, stood up to General Porfiro Diaz, who had ruled as a dictator for 34 years. Madero became President in 1911, but was overthrown in 1913, and civil war followed.

The revolution was won in 1917 by the army. A new constitution declared that the church and government should be separate; natural resources such as oil should be owned by Mexico and not foreign businessmen; and land should be given to native Mexican tribes. These principles are slowly being put into practice, but Cárdenas is under pressure to move more quickly.

NEWS • 1934 • NEWS

17 January • A prospector in South Africa finds a 726-carat diamond, the third largest in the world.

24 February • England's great composer Sir Edward Elgar dies, aged 76.

7 April • Two seaside towns crash into the sea after cliff crumbles in Norway; 57 die.

1 August • Blues singer "Leadbelly" is freed from jail after writing a song begging for a pardon in Louisiana.

◀ *Lázaro Cárdenas during his election campaign, when he toured the country.*

New state-of-the-art pool for London Zoo penguins

LEISURE

JUNE The recently opened penguin pool at London Zoo is already a favorite with visitors. Built entirely of reinforced concrete, the sunken pool is oval in shape. Two spiral ramps, on which the penguins clamber and waddle, rise out of it, and visitors can watch from the ground level.

The architectural group Tecton, formed two years ago by Russian architect Berthold Lubetkin with recent London graduates, designed the pool. It has delighted Peter Chalmers-Mitchell, the zoo's director, who asked the architects to create the pool. Tecton has also designed a gorilla house for the zoo.

▲ *Penguins entertain visitors in their new pool at London Zoo in Regent's Park.*

Pedestrian safety is main concern in traffic trial

TRANSPORT

12 JUNE Sixty pedestrian crossings have been put in use today in central London to protect British pedestrians. Figures show that 22 people are killed in road accidents every day in Britain.

The crossings are part of an official trial and have been created in places where traffic lights or policemen control the flow of traffic. Cars turning right or left must yield to pedestrians on the crossings, but pedestrians must keep out of the way of cars driving straight ahead. If the trial is successful, the crossings will be introduced nationwide.

Censure to make artists follow Stalinist line

ART

1934 Soviet leader Joseph Stalin is stamping his authority on the USSR by killing or imprisoning political opponents and by imposing strict standards on artists and writers. The new style, known as Socialist Realism, advocates that socialist society should be portrayed in art; artists must produce paintings or books that appeal to working people and have an optimistic, uplifting spirit. Soviet officials condemn modern artists such as Pablo Picasso or Georges Braque because they think they are too concerned with artistic form.

СОМОЛ-УДАРНАЯ БРИГАДА ПЯТИЛЕТКИ

◀ *A poster portraying workers.*

Dancing duo Fred and Ginger have plenty of style and class

Hollywood's latest double act is as irresistible as the comic partnership of Laurel and Hardy. But newcomers Fred Astaire and Ginger Rogers, stars of this year's hit musical film *The Gay Divorcee*, are dancers, and they seem perfectly matched.

In the 1920s, Fred was a great star of theatrical musicals in New York where he performed with his sister Adele. When she retired in 1932, he came to Hollywood. Ginger's first success was winning a dance contest when she was a teenager, and she went on to star in vaudeville shows and in New York. She made her Hollywood debut three years ago.

Astaire and Rogers performed together for the first time only last year, in a segment of the musical film *Flying Down to Rio*. *The Gay Divorcee*, directed by Mark Sandrich, is their first full-length film together. Astaire starred in the show on Broadway and was a natural choice for the film.

▲ *The Gay Divorcee is based on Cole Porter's musical.*

NAZIS AND FASCISTS

The years between the end of World War I in 1918 and the beginning of World War II in 1939 saw the introduction and the rise of right-wing dictatorships in several European countries.

After the chaos and insecurity of the Depression years, many people longed for the stability promised by dictatorial leaders, even if it gave the leaders total authority. Individual citizens had few rights and many duties in states such as Nazi Germany and Fascist Italy.

▲ *The fascist symbol is an ax made from rods.*

▼ *Hitler and Mussolini in Berlin at the 1936 Rome-Berlin Axis meeting.*

Dictators and their lust for power

Adolf Hitler was inspired by the success of Benito Mussolini in Italy. Soon after he became prime minister in 1922, Mussolini changed the election rules so that he controlled parliament. Likewise, when Adolf Hitler became Germany's chancellor in 1933, he lost no time in passing the Enabling Law which gave him absolute power.

Mussolini and Hitler had similar aims—they wanted the central government to control the economy. Hitler wanted to expand Germany into central and eastern Europe, and Mussolini wanted Mediterranean and African colonies for Italy. In 1936, Fascist Italy and Nazi Germany formed an alliance, the Rome-Berlin Axis, but they were not equal partners—Nazi Germany was more powerful and extreme. One sign of Hitler's domination was that Mussolini started to persecute Italian Jews.

▼ *Mussolini addresses the crowds in Treviso, Italy.*

▼ *Hitler's power was asserted by carefully organized displays of mass support.*

▲ *Many women fought in the civil war.*

▲ *General Franco, the Spanish dictator.*

Spanish uprising

General Franco led the Nationalists to victory against the left-wing government in the Spanish Civil War from 1936 to 1939. Nazi Germany and Fascist Italy supported Franco's rebels, while Soviet Russia backed the Republican government.

▼ The Nazi Party's rally in Nuremberg in September 1935.

Youth movements

No one could escape the influence of Mussolini's fascist ideology in Italy. Boys had to join a junior army corps called the *Balilla*, in which they were drilled for their future role as fascist soldiers. Girls were encouraged to think of themselves as future wives and mothers because the Italian Empire would require millions of colonists as well as soldiers.

An important part of fascist policy was the Battle for Births. Mothers of more than six children were awarded medals, soldiers were ordered to salute pregnant women, and men had to pay special taxes if they did not get married.

The Nazis were equally concerned with the loyalty of Germany's youth. When Hitler told German parents, "Your child belongs to us already," he meant that the Nazi state was exclusively responsible for educating children "physically, intellectually, and morally in the spirit of National Socialism."

Schoolchildren and students in Germany were encouraged to join Nazi youth organizations, one being the Nazi boy scout movement called Hitler Youth. Through sports, parades, and patriotic songs, Hitler Youths were trained as potential soldiers and workers for the Third Reich's war machine.

Nazi and Fascist facts

Mussolini was expelled from school for stabbing another boy.

•

The lights of Mussolini's office were kept on at night to keep up his superhuman image.

•

Hitler wore glasses, but his speeches were typed in specially enlarged letters so he did not have to wear them in public.

◄ Fascist policy included preparing children for their part in the future Italian Empire.

1930

1931

1932

1933

1934

1935

1936

1937

1938

1939

▲ *Shirley Temple, in a scene from one of her early movies, has a life insurance policy with Lloyd's.*

ENTERTAINMENT

Shirley Temple becomes youngest Oscar winner ever

27 FEBRUARY Seven-year-old Hollywood star Shirley Temple can do no wrong. She is the proud holder of a Special Academy Award for "her outstanding contribution to screen entertainment during the year 1934." This year she was the top box-office attraction in the US.

Miss Temple—the hot property of Twentieth Century Fox studios—receives 15,000 fan letters a week. Her admirers can buy Shirley Temple nursery equipment, dolls, and coloring books.

The young star started her career at the age of three in *Baby Burlesks*, mimicking adult actresses such as Marlene Dietrich. Her first feature-film part came at the age of 4, in 1932. But Miss Temple's breakthrough was in 1934, when she had a string of hits including *Bright Eyes*—in which she sang the fans' favorite "On the Good Ship Lollipop"— *Little Miss Marker, Now and Forever,* and *Stand Up and Cheer.*

▲ *Shirley Temple with* Bright Eyes *costars.*

▼ *A Jewish family is jeered at in the street.*

ECONOMICS

Stakhanovite award introduced in USSR

8 SEPTEMBER Workers in the Soviet Union have been given a new incentive to increase production. Today Alexis Stakhanov, a coal miner from Donetsk in the Ukraine, won a special award for digging 175 tons of coal. The new "Stakhanovite movement" has been introduced by Joseph Stalin, under whom the Soviet authorities are imposing central control and order in all aspects of people's lives. Workers are told they must learn to be punctual and disciplined and to work hard in the service of the state.

Electric guitar goes into production

The Michigan–based guitarmaker, Gibson, has launched its first electric model, the ES150. Lloyd Loar, a worker at Gibson, tried out electrical amplification for the guitar back in 1924. The ES150 launch follows the success of electric Hawaiian guitars developed by Adolph Rickenbacker and George Beauchamp.

Campbell sets land speed record

Today British driver Malcolm Campbell became the first man to break the 300-mile-per-hour barrier. He averaged 301.337 miles per hour (484.955 km per hour) over Bonneville Flats, Utah, in his specially designed car, *Bluebird*. Campbell first set the land speed record in 1924. Today he also broke his own previous record of 276.8 miles per hour (445.5 km per hour) set last March at Daytona Beach, Florida.

◄ *Malcolm Campbell.*

Mussolini leads troops in Abyssinia invasion

WAR

2 OCTOBER Italian troops invaded Abyssinia in Africa today. Bombing aircraft led the onslaught, hitting the border settlement of Adowa. Abyssinian Emperor Haile Selassie called on his people to defend their country.

The war has blown up after clashes last November on the border between Abyssinia and Italian Somaliland, and Abyssinia asked the League of Nations for help. Italy's Fascist leader Benito Mussolini appeared to be willing to negotiate at first, but it seems he decided to go to war. Troops have been building up in Italy's African colonies—Italian Somaliland and Eritrea—since February. Mussolini wants to create an empire like that of ancient Rome.

▲ *Abyssinians salute a poster of Mussolini in this Italian propaganda photo.*

Germany begins conscription

WAR

16 MARCH Nazi leaders today declared that they are reintroducing conscription, five days after announcing the creation of a new German air force, the Luftwaffe. The moves amount to a public rejection of the Versailles Treaty, which ended the 1914–18 war and strictly limited German military strength. German leader Adolf Hitler wants an army of 500,000—five times larger than that allowed by the Versailles Treaty.

The Nazis say that their conscription is in response to Britain's recent announcement of rearmament. Insiders say that Germany has been secretly rearming for two years.

◄ *A member of Hitler's military signals to round up the men.*

Public to voice their opinions

A former teacher of journalism from Iowa has been blazing a trail at one of New York's top advertising agencies. In 1932 the Young and Rubicam agency hired George Gallup, pictured below, to investigate public opinion for its clients. "Opinion polls" have yet to catch the public imagination, but Gallup is sure that he can prove their worth during the next presidential election. This year he founded the American Institute of Public Opinion.

New Nazi laws remove Jewish rights

POLITICS

15 SEPTEMBER Nazi leader Adolf Hitler today announced new laws that exclude Jews from German life. In a speech at the Nazi Party's Nuremberg Rally he decreed that Jews are no longer German citizens—they are "subjects of the state." He also said that it was illegal for Jews to marry German citizens or to have sexual relations with them.

Hitler and the Nazis claim that human races are not equal—they say that the Aryan race, which includes the Germans, is the highest while the Jewish one is the lowest. Jews, they assert, are *untermenschen* (less than human) and weaken Aryan Germans if they mix with them. As a result, German Aryans are refusing to do business with Jewish people. Jewish workers have been banned from working in public services and have had their pensions and the right to vote taken away. Many Jews have already left Germany and many more are sure to follow.

COMIC CRAZY!

Popeye, Tintin, Wonder Woman, Superman, Spider Man, and the Incredible Hulk—comic strips have given us some of the best-loved heroes and heroines of the 20th century. Almost all the comic-strip greats made the leap from newspapers or books to radio shows, television cartoons, and movies. Comics are not just for children—American soldiers read about Captain America and Superman right through World War II.

Craze for comics

Space hero Buck Rogers became famous in the newspaper strip launched by Dick Calkins in 1929. Tough detective Dick Tracy first hit the streets in a newspaper cartoon in 1931. Comic strips already had a place in newspapers, but the comic book did not become popular in the US until later in the 1930s. Many great comic heroes and heroines first appeared in the 1930s and '40s: Batman, Captain Marvel, Wonder Woman, and, of course, Superman, who made his debut in 1938.

In Britain, comics had been around for a long time. But about the time that Superman took his first bow, the well-known comics *Dandy* and *The Beano* appeared, featuring characters such as Dennis the Menace.

During World War II, some comic books became more violent. Parents and teachers claimed comics were corrupting young people. This whipped up a scare and even led to investigations in Congress. But the comics were as popular as ever.

◀ *Boys read 3-D comics with special glasses at a boys' club in New York.*

Superheroes to the rescue

In the 1960s Marvel Comics unleashed a new breed of superhero. They included the Amazing Spider Man, the Incredible Hulk, Iron Man, and a muscular Scandinavian warrior named the Mighty Thor. Four young heroes—Marvel Girl, the Angel, the Iceman, and the Beast—made up the X-men. Captain America also made a comeback.

The superheroes took on the forces of evil—a terrifying collection of opponents. Once Iron Man had to deal with the Mysterious Melter, and Spider Man confronted Kraven the Hunter. Fluid, forceful drawing and zany dialogue made the books popular. Storylines were usually bizarre—the treatment was never too serious. Marvel Comics proved a great hit with college students as well as younger people.

◄ *Created by René Goscinny and Albert Uderzo, Asterix the Gaul appeared in 1959.*

◄ *Marvel's superhero Spider Man swings through the air and climbs walls like a spider.*

Intrepid Tintin

Belgian artist Georges Rémi (seated), with the pen name Hergé, launched the detective-reporter Tintin in a newspaper strip in 1929. Hergé and his team created fresh, unusual stories, which were translated into English. Tintin's dog Milou became Snowy and detectives Dupont and Dupond became Thomson and Thompson.

1930

1931

1932

1933

1934

1935

1936

1937

1938

1939

▶ *The International Brigade (fighting for the Spanish Republic) holding Franco's forces at Madrid.*

Facts about the Spanish Civil War

During the siege of Madrid, food supplies were limited to 2 ounces (57 g) per person per day.

•

About 100,000 people were murdered in cold blood or killed in mass executions.

•

Volunteers from all over the world fought for both sides.

Fashion for earlobes

The trend for pierced ears is reported to be growing fast in the world of fashion, especially among younger women. Clip-on earrings are easily lost, and women who want to wear valuable pearls or diamonds in their ears do not want to run that risk. Ear piercing is nothing new. It was done in ancient times, on men as well as women.

Franco's rebels spark Civil War

WAR

▲ *Spanish people flee their villages as fighting spreads, seeking refuge from Franco's troops.*

19 JULY A military revolt that broke out in Spanish Morocco two days ago now presents a major threat to the Republican government of Spain. The rebels were led by General Franco, who today arrived in Cadiz to direct the rebellion on the Spanish mainland. Franco has the support of nationalists and other right-wing political groups, as well as aid from Fascist Italy and Nazi Germany; the Republicans have support from the Socialists, communists, and the Soviet Union.

In 1931, soon after the dictator General Primo de Rivera and King Alfonso XIII fled into exile, the Republic came into existence. Because of new governmental reforms, divisions remained in Spain. On the right were the church, the army, and landowners; on the left, the workers, peasants, and most people from the Basque country and Catalonia. In 1933 a nationalist (center-right) government took over, cancelled all the new reforms, and crushed protests. But in February this year a coalition of Leftist parties gained power, threatening revolutionary changes. Amid growing violence, army officers and other conservatives planned the rebellion. Franco is expected to win because he has the army on his side, but the Republic is organizing resistance.

▼ *The Jarrow Crusaders march toward London.*

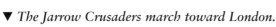

Jarrow Crusaders protest

ECONOMICS

5 OCTOBER Crowds of sympathizers in Jarrow, on Tyneside, northern England, watched as 200 unemployed men began a protest march in London today. They are led by the local member of parliament, Ellen Wilkinson, and carry a petition signed by 12,000 people, demanding help from the government. Although the worst of the Great Depression is over, unemployment is still very high in Durham, South Wales, Clydeside, and Lancashire. In Jarrow, the town's main employer went out of business in 1933. Two-thirds of working men are unemployed, with no prospect of jobs unless new industry is attracted to Tyneside.

◀ *Edward VIII's official documented declaration of his abdication in favor of his brother.*

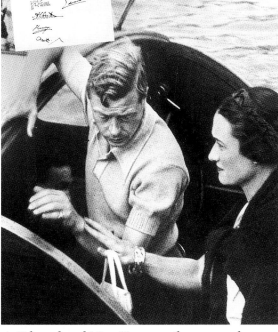

▲ *Edward and Mrs. Simpson, the woman he wants to marry, on vacation after his abdication.*

Popular Front fuels social reforms in France

3 JUNE The elections in France have been won by the Popular Front, led by Léon Blum. The Front is a coalition of socialists and other leftist parties, including communists.

The main concern of the new government is social reform. Blum is expected to introduce a shorter working week and paid vacations, and to reduce the power of bankers and industrialists. Strikes by workers in factories are forcing employers to recognize the strength of working-class feelings, and most people agree that reforms are overdue. But they are likely to cause other problems, such as the weakening of the French franc and inflation. These economic problems may destroy the Popular Front's unity.

▲ *Children march in a Communist pro-Popular Front demonstration in Paris.*

Abdication of love

11 DECEMBER In a radio broadcast today, Edward VIII, king of England since 20 January, abdicated from the throne. He explained that he felt unable to carry out his duties as king "without...the support of the woman I love." He meant Mrs. Wallis Simpson, a fashionable, middle-aged, American woman who has divorced one husband and is married to her second. This royal love affair has been kept secret in Britain, although widely reported in foreign newspapers. The King's moving speech, written for him by Winston Churchill, brought tears to many eyes.

Henie wins third Olympic gold

28 FEBRUARY At this year's winter Olympic Games, Sonja Henie of Norway has won her third Olympic gold medal for figure-skating, equaling the record set by Gillis Grafström of Sweden in 1928. Miss Henie won her first gold medal in 1927 at the age of 14. Since then she has won 10 successive world titles. This will be her last Olympic title; she is planning to go professional.

▲ *Sonja Henie on her way to her third successive Olympic figure-skating victory.*

Porsche's people's car

The German chancellor, Adolf Hitler, opened a new car factory on 26 February that will make a car called the Volkswagen, meaning "people's car." A small, four-seater family car, it should be cheap to run and reliable. The brainchild of well-known car designer Ferdinand Porsche, it this is the German equivalent of the Model T Ford that turned ordinary Americans into motorists. Its air-cooled engine is at the rear, and the luggage space is under the hood. The Volkswagen looks very much like a large beetle, and many motoring experts doubt that it will ever be successful.

▶ *German chancellor Adolf Hitler gives his blessing to the new "people's car."*

Diego Rivera, the Mexican muralist

8 DECEMBER The extraordinary Mexican painter Diego Rivera today celebrates his 50th birthday.

His murals, huge frescoes mostly done on the walls of public buildings, are generally inspired by socialist ideals and have brought about a revival of fresco painting in the US and Latin America. Some of Rivera's finest works depict Mexican history and society.

Last year Diego Rivera completed his series of paintings for the grand staircase of the presidential palace in Mexico City, an enormous work. As a young man he spent 13 years in Europe and was influenced by the old Renaissance masters, who also specialized in wallpaintings. He experimented with the revolutionary movements in European art, such as Cubism, but when he returned to Mexico in 1921, he devoted himself to the new, popular-art movement, with large murals picturing Mexican life. His paintings are bold, dramatic, and easy to understand.

Vitamin pills on the market for first time

1936 It is now possible to obtain vitamins in pill form. Vitamins are organic substances that are needed for a healthy diet, though only in tiny amounts. The name "vitamin" was invented in 1912, but the existence of such substances was known earlier. More vitamins undoubtedly remain to be discovered.

▲ *An extract from Rivera's mural about Mexico's struggle for independence.*

◄ *Diego Rivera and his wife, Frieda Kahlo.*

A Night at the Opera with the marvelous Marx brothers

The latest movie of those hilarious clowns, the Marx Brothers opened in New York on 22 May. In *A Night at the Opera* Groucho (below right), Chico, and Harpo wreak havoc in the pompous world of opera. It is full of sidesplitting set pieces, ending with the boys reducing a performance of *Il Trovatore* to a complete shambles. Before making the movie, they tried out the main scenes on the stage, touring several cities with their writers in the audience. This is their best movie since *Duck Soup*.

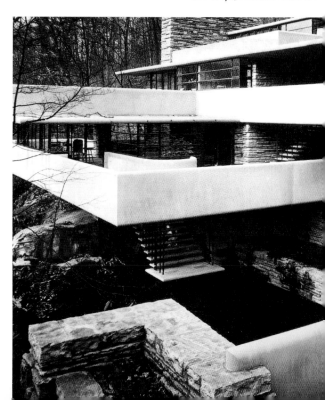

128

Jesse Owens, star of Berlin "Propaganda" Olympics

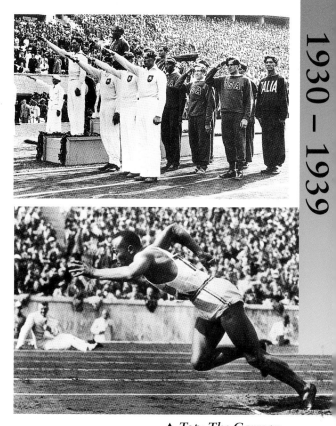

16 AUGUST The Olympic Games in Berlin, capital of Germany, ended today. As far as the athletic events themselves are concerned, the games were a big success, with about 5,000 athletes from 53 countries taking part. Many records were broken, including in the 1,500 meters, in which New Zealander Jack Lovelock (first) and Glenn Cunningham of the US (second) both beat Cunningham's old world record. However, Adolf Hitler's government turned the games into a political event. Hitler intended them to be a showcase for his Nazi regime.

The star of the games was the US sprinter Jesse Owens, who broke five world records in one day last year in the US. He won four Olympic gold medals (100 meters, 200 meters, long jump, and 4 x 100-meter relay). That was bad news for Hitler, because, apart from being a non-German, Owens is black. The Nazis believe that the so-called Aryan race is superior and that blacks, like Jews, belong to a lesser breed. As the crowd cheered Owens, who won worldwide admiration for his sportsmanship and good humor as well as his fabulous running, Hitler hurriedly left the stadium.

▲ *Top: The German 400-meters relay team (front), at the medal ceremony. Above: Jesse Owens, star of the games.*

Germany defies the Treaty of Versailles

▲ *German troops march in to Cologne, in the Rhineland.*

7 MARCH German troops today marched into the Rhineland, the region in Germany close to the borders of France and the Low Countries. After the Great War, the Treaty of Versailles laid down that the Rhineland should remain a demilitarized zone. Hitler is proposing a new agreement to ensure peace in Europe, and the French and British will probably take no action against Germany.

Frank Lloyd Wright's Falling Water

8 JUNE A fascinating house, Falling Water, designed by the American architect Frank Lloyd Wright, is being built in Bear Run, Pennsylvania. The career of Wright, who is 67 today, seemed to be over, but he has surprised everyone by designing two revolutionary new buildings (the other is an office building in Racine, Wisconsin).

Wright believes that buildings should be part of the landscape. Falling Water is a luxurious weekend house for Edgar Kaufmann, owner of a department store in Pittsburgh. It makes daring use of reinforced concrete: part of the house is cantilevered (attached at one end only) out over a waterfall, and stonework connects the concrete with the natural rock.

◀ *Falling Water springs from the natural rock of Pennsylvania.*

NEWS • 1936 • NEWS

5 May • Italian forces capture Addis Ababa, capital of Abyssinia.

19 May • German train sets speed record of just under 124 miles per hour (200 km per hour).

6 September • Beryl Markham becomes first woman pilot to fly the Atlantic solo.

1 October • The BBC begins TV transmissions with sound.

23 October • Hitler sends German bombers to aid Franco.

1930

1931

1932

1933

1934

1935

1936

1937

1938

1939

1937

▶ *The exploding Hindenburg collides with the mooring mast as it crashes.*

NEWS • 1937 • NEWS

30 May • Twelve workers shot dead by police and security guards in American steel strike.

2 July • American pilot Amelia Earhart disappears during round-the-world flight.

8 July • Peel Report recommends partition of Palestine into Arab and Jewish areas.

29 November • Emergency telephone number 999 introduced in Britain.

DISASTERS

Hindenburg explodes in a ball of fire

6 MAY The greatest disaster in air travel occurred today when the German airship *Hindenburg* crashed in Lakehurst, New Jersey. The airship, built by the German firm of Zeppelin, was the world's first transatlantic airliner. Measuring 804 feet (245 meters) in length and kept in the air by 7,062,895 cubic feet (200,000 cubic meters) of hydrogen, it could travel at speeds of 82 miles per hour (132 km per hour) and was equipped with a library, lounge, and cocktail bar. It began regular flights 12 months ago, taking 60 hours to fly from Frankfurt to Lakehurst.

The accident occurred while the airship was preparing to land during a thunderstorm. As it approached the mooring mast during a lull in the storm, the hydrogen caught fire and the airship exploded in flames. Thirty-four passengers and crew and a member of the ground staff were killed in the explosion, probably caused by static electricity igniting the hydrogen gas. The disaster is bound to destroy people's confidence in airship travel, and flights across the Atlantic are unlikely to restart.

WAR

Threat of major war as Japan invades China

13 AUGUST The Japanese today bombed Shanghai in an horrific attack which killed thousands of Chinese citizens. Pictures of the devastation of this Chinese port have shocked the world. Since July of this year the Japanese have been attacking Chinese cities and ports—Shanghai is the latest victim in a list of atrocities.

Japan has held Manchuria since 1931 and was known to have further designs on Chinese territory, but the motive for trying to start a major war is unclear.

▲ *A child in the bombed ruins of Shanghai.*

Golden Gate Bridge opens with a bang

27 MAY The longest suspension bridge in the world, which took over four years to build and cost $35 million, was opened today. It spans the entrance to San Francisco Bay and is 4,199 feet (1,280 meters) long. About 200,000 people crossed it on the first day, and as darkness fell, the bridge was the setting for a spectacular fireworks display.

▶ *Construction workers make final adjustments.*

Spain: bombing of ancient Guernica

▼ *Only soldiers walk the ruined streets of Guernica now.*

26 APRIL The German Condor Legion today launched a devastating air raid on Guernica, the ancient capital of the Basques. They destroyed the town with bombs, then machine-gunned the streets, killing or wounding about one-third of the total population. By order of Hitler, the Legion is in Spain to help Franco in the Spanish Civil War. It appears that the attack on a target of no military importance was intended to inspire terror.

George VI crowned

12 MAY Cheering crowds lined the route to Westminster Abbey today as Prince Albert, Duke of York, younger son of the late King George V, was crowned king of England. His wife, the former Lady Elizabeth Bowes-Lyon, was crowned queen. The couple, who have two young daughters, succeeded to the throne unexpectedly when Edward VIII abdicated six months ago. The king has taken the name George in honor of his father. He is a shy man with a stammer, but he is likely to be a more reliable monarch than his elder brother.

Stalin's rule of terror

12 JUNE There are reports from Moscow of new developments in Stalin's brutal attempts to destroy all opponents of his rule. Following the purges of political figures and intellectuals, especially those linked with Trotsky (Stalin's rival who is in exile), Stalin has turned against the army. Marshal Tukhachevsky, a great Russian war hero and chief of the general staff, and several other generals were shot after a secret "trial."

In January, 17 prominent men were sentenced to death. Most confessed to charges of treason, perhaps to save their families from persecution. The sentences were not appealed and executions followed quickly.

▶ *Karl Radek, the leading political writer in the Soviet Union, was sentenced to 10 years in prison in the January trial.*

Fonteyn's performance is a triumph

A brilliant young dancer, Margot Fonteyn, stunned the audience at London's Sadler's Wells ballet this January with her performance in *Giselle*. Though only 18, her exquisite style and sympathy for the music mark her as a fitting successor to Alicia Markova, who retired in 1935. She was picked to succeed Markova as prima ballerina by Ninette de Valois, who runs the Sadler's Wells ballet school, where Fonteyn studied.

◀ *Fonteyn with Robert Helpmann, who partnered her as the Prince in* Giselle.

1938

1930

1931

1932

1933

1934

1935

1936

1937

1938

1939

Persecution of Jews gets worse

POLITICS

10 NOVEMBER The pavements of Berlin and other German cities are still strewn with broken glass after the night of terror they're calling *Kristallnacht* (crystal night). Last night more than 7,000 Jewish shops were wrecked and looted by uniformed Nazi thugs, and if their owners dared to protest they were beaten up in full view of jeering Nazi supporters. Hundreds of synagogues were also burned down.

Although it is clear that the attack was highly organized, Josef Goebbels, in charge of Public Enlightenment and Propaganda, is claiming that the pogrom was done by anti-Semitic Germans acting on their own initiative. When Adolf Hitler came to power in 1933, about 600,000 Jews were living in Germany. Since then about half of them have left because of the increasing persecutions. After *Kristallnacht*, no one can be optimistic about the future of Germany's Jewish communities.

▲ *Before last night's attack, some Jewish people had already been forced out of business.*

▲ *Neville Chamberlain waves the new agreement triumphantly in London.*

Munich peace agreement

TREATIES

30 SEPTEMBER Visibly relieved, British Prime Minister Neville Chamberlain returned from the four-power conference in Munich today and told the news reporters at Heston Airport that the Czechoslovakian crisis is over. According to the agreement reached in Munich, which has been signed by Britain, France, Germany, and Italy, Adolf Hitler will be allowed to take over the German-speaking Sudeten district of northwestern Czechoslovakia, on condition he leaves the rest of Czechoslovakia alone. "I believe it is peace in our time," Chamberlain says, but Czechoslovakia's leaders are not convinced. They say it is peace at the expense of their country.

NEWS • 1938 • NEWS

26 January • Australia celebrates 150th anniversary of European settlement.

30 June • The first Superman *comic strip* appears.

29 July • The Dane Jenny Kammersgaad is the first person to swim the 37-mile (60-km) Baltic in 40 hours 9 minutes.

31 October • "War of the Worlds" radio play sparks off widespread panic about Martians invading the US.

Germans occupy Czech Sudeten region

WAR

5 OCTOBER After marching across the border at the head of his invading army, Adolf Hitler has been treated to a hero's reception in Eger, the principal town of the Sudeten region of Czechoslovakia. The Fuhrer told the cheering crowds "I am able to greet you for the first time as my people, and I bear you the greetings of the whole German nation... This greeting is at the same time a vow. Never again shall this land be torn from the Reich."

The occupation of Sudetenland is a direct result of the agreement made in Munich last month by Britain, France, Germany, and Italy, in which the Czech government had no say. The mood in Prague is grim, and Czechoslovakian President Benes has resigned.

▲ *German troops are warmly welcomed in Linz, Austria.*

Benny Goodman plays at the Carnegie Hall

After his performance at New York's Carnegie Hall, Benny Goodman, the undisputed master of "swing," is also the darling of serious concert audiences. He formed his band four years ago and soon attracted a wide audience for his style of jazz music. Fans caused so much chaos when Goodman played at the Paramount Theater last year that the event became known as the Paramount Riot. Goodman has also worked with Gershwin and Béla Bartók.

WAR

Germany extends borders with Austria annexation

13 MARCH Austria is now part of Hitler's Germany, proclaimed today by the Anschluss (meaning union) in the Austrian city of Linz. To judge by the number of swastikas decorating the streets, the Anschluss is popular with locals, but in these parts the Nazi Fuhrer is a local boy made good. Thousands of terrified Jewish families, however, are planning to leave because of the Nazis' anti-Semitic beliefs.

Although Britain and France are expected to make some protest, Hitler is confident that he will experience no serious international opposition to his latest acquisition.

SCIENCE

Extinct "living fossil" catch excites scientists

22 DECEMBER Scientists are still trying to make sense of the living coelacanth, *Latimera chalumnae*, which has just been trawled up from the ocean depths near East London in South Africa. The bizarre fish has been called a "living fossil" because it is exactly like members of the ancient suborder Coelacanthini, fossil remains of which have been found all over the Earth, leading to the assumption that it became extinct 70 million years ago.

The living coelacanth is longer and heavier than its fossil ancestors, which were closely related to some of the first animals to walk on land 350 million years ago.

▼ *People in Eger, Sudetenland, greet the German troops as they claim the country as their own.*

▼ *Nestlé hopes that the new instant coffee will convert tea addicts.*

FOOD

Nestlé produces instant result with new coffee

1 APRIL Forget about grinders and percolators—for a cup of coffee, all you need is a spoonful of Nescafé and hot water. The convenient new instant coffee is the result of years of research by scientists at the Nestlé company's Swiss laboratory.

Nestlé hopes to be producing the instant coffee powder for the European market next year. The pick-me-up beverage is sure to convert millions of tea addicts into coffee lovers. That is also the hope of Brazil's hard-pressed coffee growers. For the past few years they have been accumulating such huge coffee surpluses that they have had to destroy some of the harvest in order to prevent the already low coffee prices from sinking even further.

HIS FIRST FULL LENGTH FEATURE PRODUCTION! Walt DISNEY'S **Snow White** in the Marvelous MULTIPLANE TECHNICOLOR and the Seven Dwarfs

"Grumpy, let me see YOUR hands!"

▲ *Walt Disney's stunning new movie is an international hit.*

ENTERTAINMENT

Disney's first feature-length cartoon film

7 FEBRUARY British film censors have just given Walt Disney's *Snow White and the Seven Dwarfs* an "A" certificate, which means that British movie fans of all ages will soon be acquainted with Happy, Sleepy, Bashful, Sneezy, Grumpy, Dopey, and Doc: the seven dwarfs of Disney's stunning new movie. Their memorable songs—"Whistle While You Work," "Hi-Ho, Hi-Ho, It's Off to Work We Go"—have already caught on all over the world, and they are rivaling Mickey Mouse in the cartoon character popularity stakes.

As the first feature-length cartoon movie, *Snow White and the Seven Dwarfs* was something of a gamble for Walt Disney, but three years of hard work and two million drawings have paid off in more ways than one. In addition to its commercial success, *Snow White and the Seven Dwarfs* is enjoying critical acclaim as a work of art. Fantasy based on authentic reality is Disney's winning principle. Images and experiences of real castles and real forests inspired the vivid landscapes and architecture of *Snow White*. The Gothic style of Swedish-born artist Gustaf Tenggren, for example, lends great power to the scene in which the princess is lost in the forest. The cartoon Snow White princess is as wide-eyed, innocent, and girlish as her illustrated storybook predecessor, and Disney intends to carry on working in a traditional style to make a whole series of classic cartoon fairytales.

First tennis player to win Grand Slam

SPORT

2 JULY The brilliant young American player Donald Budge has set a new sports record after defeating "Bunny" Austin in the men's singles final at Wimbledon. Budge has won all four of the world's major tennis tournaments—the Australian, British, French, and US championships—in the same year to become the world's first "Grand Slammer." This must rank as a lifetime achievement for any sportsman, but some Budge-watchers have not yet recovered from his amazing victory over the German champion, Baron Gottfried von Cramm, in the Davis Cup final in Wimbledon last year. Veteran British champion William Tilden said that had been one of the finest games of tennis he had ever seen. Tennis fans expect to see many more US players—they have won all five titles at this year's Wimbledon tournament.

▶ *Grand Slammer Donald Budge.*

WAR

Spitfire brought into service by RAF

15 JULY One thousand people responded in a single day when the Royal Air Force launched a recruitment campaign last month. Now Britain's air force is to be supplied with 1,000 more Spitfire fighter planes. The scale of this order shows how seriously the British government is taking the threat of another war, in which national air defenses will be crucial. The Spitfire (above) is said to be a superb machine for intercepting enemy aircraft, a match for the best German fighter plane, the Messerschmitt 109. Besides boosting Spitfire production, Britain's Air-raid Precautions (ARP) include issuing everybody with a personal gas mask. Air-raid shelters will be provided, but children living in places most at risk from air attacks will be evacuated to safer areas.

Largest transatlantic passenger ship launch

TRANSPORT

27 SEPTEMBER The world's biggest ocean liner, the *Queen Elizabeth*, was launched from John Brown's shipyard on Scotland's Clyde River today. The latest ship of the Cunard White Star Line, which has been built for the transatlantic passage, weighs 80,000 tons.

The queen of England was about to start the christening ceremony when the massive ship's restraining beams broke and it started to roll forward. In the nick of time, the Queen pushed the champagne bottle forward so that it crashed against her namesake's bow just before it slipped into the water.

▲ *The* Queen Elizabeth*: Cunard's Superliner and the world's largest liner.*

◀ *The plant's compressor weighs 8,000 tons.*

Cooling system gets rid of hot air

TECHNOLOGY

26 JULY Legislators are enjoying a new air conditioning plant which has been designed to cool the Capitol and Senate house office buildings in Washington.

The system works like a fridge. The chemical Freon is used to refrigerate 12,240,000 gallons (46,330,000 liters) of water daily, and this chilled water is sent over a single pipeline circuit to the various buildings, where it cools the air blown through local conditioning systems. Similar systems have been in use in textile factories, where a controlled atmosphere is crucial for the quality of cotton yarn, and it will not be long before air conditioning is available for offices and homes.

Britain sets new world steam-engine record

The British steam engine *Mallard* made history today when it set a new record of 125 miles per hour (202 km per hour) on the London to Newcastle line. The speed was kept up for more than 5 miles (8 km), and the engine's designer, Nigel Gresley, was on board to record it.

Journalist patents novel new pen

Hungarian journalist Lazlo Biró has patented a new invention, the ballpoint pen. It can write 200,000 words without blotting, smudging, or needing to be refilled. A tiny tube within the pen carries ink to the attached "ballpoint" nib. This new invention has mass-market potential.

"Queen Helen" wins eighth Wimbledon

SPORT

2 JULY Helen Wills Moody has won the ladies' singles title at Wimbledon for a record eighth time. Once again she defeated her rival, fellow-American Helen Jacobs, whom she faced before in the finals of 1929, 1932, and 1935. Both players attended the University of California and learned the game at the Berkeley Tennis Club, where they were coached by the legendary Pop Fuller. Now 32, Miss Moody won her first Wimbledon ladies' singles title 11 years ago, and earned the nickname "Queen Helen" of the tennis court because of her icy self-confidence.

▲ *German soldiers fly the SS flag in Danzig.*

WAR

World War II fears as Germany invades Poland

1 SEPTEMBER The first blitzkrieg (lightning war) started yesterday evening when men dressed in Polish army uniforms appeared to attack a German radio station and German customs station near Germany's eastern border. But these "Polish" soldiers were in fact German prisoners, and their actions were planned by Heinrich Himmler's *Schutzstaffel* (SS) to justify a full-scale invasion of Poland.

It was dawn when the *Wehrmacht* force of 1.25 million men, including six armored divisions and eight motorized divisions with armored units, began to stream over Germany's border with Poland. The Luftwaffe is now raining bombs on the Polish railroad system. Adolf Hitler has made no secret of his determination to "reclaim" areas of Poland, especially the Danzig corridor, which Germany lost after World War I. At the same time, Soviet Russia has designs on Poland's eastern frontier, which is one reason why Joseph Stalin and Adolf Hitler agreed their Non-Aggression Pact one month ago.

Hitler's foreign minister, Joachim von Ribbentrop, persuaded him that Britain and France, who had already committed to defending Poland against German aggression, would not do much more than protest about the blitzkreig. It seems Ribbentrop guessed wrongly, because Britain and France are now asking Germany to withdraw from Poland within two days or face them as Poland's military allies. If Hitler does not respond to this ultimatum, Europe's latest crisis could escalate into another world war.

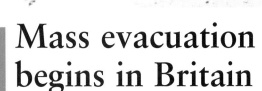

◀ *German troops dismantle border barriers in Poland.*

▼ *Young evacuees wait for the trains which will take them to safety.*

PEOPLE

Mass evacuation begins in Britain

2 SEPTEMBER Although Britain is not yet officially at war—Germany has until 11 o'clock tomorrow to withdraw from Poland—the Air-raid Precautions (ARP) have been put into effect.

In the last few days there has been an exodus of children from the major cities and towns. Equipped with their personal gas masks, a small bag, and enough food for a day, the young evacuees gather at their schools. From there they are transported to major railroad stations, where special trains are taking them to safer homes in the countryside. Parents do not know where their children will end up, or how long they will be separated from them. There seems, however, to be a calm and orderly atmosphere.

Sikorsky builds first practical helicopter

TRANSPORT

14 SEPTEMBER Russian-born aviationist Igor Sikorsky has invented another helicopter, and this one actually works! Sikorsky designed and built the first helicopter in 1909, but it did not work so he turned his genius to fixed-wing airplanes. After studying the work of Blériot and Zeppelin in France and Germany, Sikorsky immigrated to the US. Now he has his own aircraft business on Long Island and it is expected that his new direct-lift flying machine will benefit US marine and naval forces.

▲ *Sikorsky flys his VS-300, one of the first effective helicopters, above the Vought-Sikorsky field in Bridgeport, Connecticut.*

▲ *Hitler and Mussolini at a meeting last year.*

Long-awaited Hollywood premiere

Gone With the Wind can now be seen. It has been famous ever since producer David O. Selznick started searching for the actress to play Scarlett O'Hara, the heroine of the popular novel on which the movie is based. Many people were surprised when he cast an English actress as the capricious Southern belle, but no one who has seen the catlike Miss Vivien Leigh's performance can question that choice. The movie is 3 hours and 45 minutes long, but the cast and the subtle use of Technicolor mean that the Civil War epic is certain to be a major success at the box office.

Nazi and Fascist steel alliance

TREATIES

22 MAY The foreign ministers of Nazi Germany and Fascist Italy have signed the "Pact of Steel" to become a fully fledged military alliance. In the event of Italy or Germany becoming involved in a war with each other's country, they are pledged to come to each other's aid "with all their military forces." Mussolini, who fancies himself as an orator, first thought of calling the new arrangement the "Pact of Blood." Despite the warlike words, observers believe Italy is not prepared for a major war.

Nonaggression for Hitler and Stalin

TREATIES

23 AUGUST Hitler and Stalin (center) are to be partners in "nonaggression." Today, their foreign ministers, Joachim von Ribbentrop (left) and Vyacheslav Molotov (right), signed the agreement between Nazi Germany and Soviet Russia not to attack one another. This alliance has surprised Western powers, who now think that a European war is inevitable.

▼ *After his DDT "bath," Chang, an elephant at the Central Park Zoo in New York, is free from winged pests.*

DDT is answer to every farmer's prayers

SCIENCE

1939 Dichlorodiphenyltrichloroethane is not a name that trips lightly off the tongue, but when it is available as DDT farmers, cattle ranchers, housewives, and doctors will be singing its praises. For thousands of years livestock and crops—and human beings—have been at the mercy of pests such as fleas, mites, ticks, locusts, and caterpillars. The new synthetic insecticide is so toxic to these destructive, irritating creatures that once they have absorbed it they cannot pester anyone or anything that grows.

Some people are saying, however, that DDT is too good to be true. A dose of it might preserve a cabbage from caterpillars without killing off a worm, but what happens to the robin that eats a hundred of those contaminated worms? And what happens to the fox that eats that robin? But right now, scientists are more interested in the benefits of DDT. Besides promising a future of healthy bumper crops, the wonder chemical may help to win the battle against malaria. No one can complain about that.

◄ *The amazing new insecticide, DDT.*

ICI begins polythene production

Imperial Chemical Industries has produced the world's first "plastic," called "polythene." The light, transparent material was first discovered by Reginald Gibson and Eric Fawcett after a laboratory accident six years ago, but full-scale polythene production started this year. Polythene is sure to change our lives in many ways, but for now it is an ideal material for insulating underwater cables.

Graf Spee scuttled by crew

WAR

18 DECEMBER The *Graf Spee*, the pride of the German Navy, was sunk last night by her own crew. For weeks now, the battleship has been menacing ships in the South Atlantic and the Indian Ocean. Three British Royal Navy cruisers, the *Exeter*, the *Ajax*, and the *Achilles*, converged for the day-long Battle of the Plate River, which sent a badly battered *Graf Spee* into Montevideo harbor. When the Uruguayan government threatened to seize the ship, Hitler himself authorized the *Graf Spee's* destruction. Such an end was considered more glorious than further defeat by the Royal Navy. As the *Graf Spee* began to explode, her distraught captain, Hans Lansdorf, shot himself in the head.

▼ *The latest fashion aid.*

▼ *The* Graf Spee *sinks after being blown up in Montevideo harbor.*

Pan Am go transatlantic

TRANSPORT

3 MARCH In Washington today the First Lady, Mrs. Franklin D. Roosevelt, named Pan American Airways' pioneering flying boat the *Yankee Clipper*. Also known as a Boeing 314, *Yankee Clipper* made history just over a week ago when she landed safely in Baltimore, having carried passengers across the Atlantic at a cruising speed of 145 miles per hour (230 km per hour). Inside, the *Yankee* is more like a luxury liner than the ocean-racing clippers of old. Besides her palatial flight deck, she contains a private honeymoon suite and a 14-seat dining room.

▲ *Passengers board a Pan Am flight.*

NEWS • 1939 • NEWS

17 January • *Nazis ban Jews from driving, going to concerts, movies, and theaters, and from working as dentists, vets, and pharmacists.*

24 January • *An earthquake in Chile kills 30,000 people.*

1 April • *The Spanish Civil War officially ends.*

26 June • *France ends public executions.*

20 July • *A five-year-old boy is chosen to be Tibet's new Dalai Lama.*

Winter War along Mannerheim line

WAR

30 NOVEMBER The Finns claim to have pushed the Russians back over their border, along a 150-mile (240-km) front. Soviet Russia is eager to gain control of the main military approaches to Leningrad, which includes the Finnish part of the Karelian isthmus.

Stalin ordered the Soviet invasion when the Finns refused to surrender Karelia, and no one imagined that Finland would be capable of offering any resistance. But to Russia's embarrassment, the small Finnish army has put up a brilliant defense along the Mannerheim line so far.

▲ *A Finnish family flees the fighting.*

Nylon stockings to fashion ladies' legs

Nylon stockings are now on sale at $1.15 a pair. That's not cheap but stockings made of artificial silk are longer- and harder-wearing than stockings made of natural silk, and just as sheer, so they're highly popular. People have admired the silkworm's ability to produce fibers for centuries, and with the miracle of Nylon that ability has been successfully imitated. Nylon was discovered back in 1937 by chemist Wallace Carothers of the du Pont company. It can also be used to make parachutes.

Hitler escapes bombing

WAR

8 NOVEMBER A huge bomb wrecked a Munich beer cellar tonight, moments after Adolf Hitler had left the building. 0He had been making his traditional speech on the anniversary of the Munich putsch, which began in the cellar in 1923. People are assuming that the bomb was meant to kill Hitler. Suspects include two British Secret Service

▲ *Munich beer hall lies in ruins.*

agents and the communist carpenter who has been arrested at the Swiss border with a photograph of the beer-hall interior in his possession. But the "assassination attempt" might also be a propaganda stunt designed to encourage sympathy for Hitler, who will attend the funeral of the blast's seven victims.

THE MOVIES

At the beginning of the 20th century, motion pictures began as a new kind of popular entertainment. By the 1920s the first theaters were giving way to luxurious picture palaces. Hollywood conquered the world with the first "talkies" in the late 1920s. The 1930s saw the golden age of Tinseltown, with giant movie studios, lavish musicals, and glamorous stars. Television threatened to replace the movies in the 1950s, but the video revolution of the late 1970s helped to revive the cinema-premiered feature film.

Movie stars of the silver screen

Silent movie stars, such as Theda Bara, Mary Pickford, Gloria Swanson, Douglas Fairbanks, and Rudolph Valentino, became famous for playing the same type of character over and over again in their films. With the coming of sound in 1929–31, stars had to have voices and accents to match their screen personalities and actions. The first spoken endearments of 1920s heartthrob John Gilbert disappointed his fans, but when Greta Garbo made her talkie debut as a streetwise prostitute—"Gimme a viskey with ginger ale on the side and don't be stingy, baby"—her Swedish accent only added to her mystique. Charlie Chaplin, who made his first appearance as the little tramp in 1914, was so popular in that role that he waited until 1940 before playing his first speaking part as Adenoid Hynkel in *The Great Dictator*. Buster Keaton and Harold Lloyd were Chaplin's main rivals, but their heyday was the silent era. By contrast, Oliver Hardy and Stan Laurel only became stars after 1927, when they could be heard as well as seen by audiences. Together they appeared in more than 200 movies, including 27 feature films.

▲ Greta Garbo, the "Swedish Sphinx," epitomized Hollywood glamour.

▶ Laurel and Hardy were film's most successful comedy act.

Leading young ladies of the world of Hollywood movies

Shirley Temple (1928–), who sang, danced, and acted her way through a string of hit musicals between 1934 and 1940, was the most popular child star ever. Her stage career began when, at the age of three, she mimicked Marlene Dietrich and other leading ladies of the day. She won an Academy Award for her first film, *Bright Eyes*, in 1934. In her film roles, she helped eccentric adults out of difficult situations by being charmingly direct and honest. A whole industry—Shirley Temple dolls, coloring books, and dresses—developed around her curly-haired image, and she was genuinely talented and worked very hard.

Judy Garland (1922–69), who was born Frances Gumm, was only three when she joined her sisters on stage. She later changed her name and was pushed into a solo career by her mother, whom she described as "the real-life Wicked Witch of the West." Judy Garland was 17 years old when she starred as Dorothy in *The Wizard of Oz*. In the movie she sang "Over the Rainbow," which was to become her theme tune. Unlike Shirley Temple, Judy Garland's career lasted beyond her teens, but while she was coping with the pressures of juvenile stardom, she became addicted to sleeping pills and dieting drugs.

▲ *Judy Garland won an Oscar for her role as Dorothy in* The Wizard of Oz.

Movie facts

According to one story, the Oscar award got its name from movie star Bette Davis, who thought the statue resembled her Uncle Oscar.

• Movie stars can start fashion crazes— Greta Garbo did for berets what Marlene Dietrich did for slacks.

• The real name of famous screen cowboy John Wayne was Marion Morrison.

◄ *In* Safety Last *(1923), Harold Lloyd climbs up a skyscraper for the love of his girl.*

▲ *Perky, golden-haired Shirley Temple, seen above as Heidi, touched the hearts of millions of moviegoers.*

The magic and wonder of Walt Disney

Walt Disney's animated films involved millions of drawings and years of work, but the results appealed to everyone. Disney (right) pioneered the feature-length cartoon with *Snow White and the Seven Dwarfs* (1938), which was followed by *Pinocchio* (1940), *Fantasia* (1940), *The Reluctant Dragon* (1941), and *Dumbo* (1941). Then, in 1942, *Bambi*, the story of a forest deer (left), was released. Unlike previous Disney cartoons, there were no human characters, but the animals, notably the comic rabbit called Thumper, had convincing personalities. The cartoon movie, a Disney favorite, was based on a novel by Austrian writer Felix Salten.

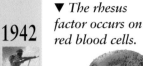

1940
1941
1942
1943
1944
1945
1946
1947
1948
1949

1940

The first half of the decade was dominated by a global war in which some 55 million people were killed, more of them civilians than military people.

After the war, shattered nations slowly pieced themselves together again. But after the horrors of Auschwitz and Dresden, and after Hiroshima, the world would never be the same. By the end of the decade, confrontation—a stand-off between the capitalist West and the communist East—was back. This was the start of the "Cold War."

◀ *Charlie Chaplin as dictator "Hynkel," dancing with the globe.*

▼ *The rhesus factor occurs on red blood cells.*

Rhesus blood factor is discovered

Austrian-born immunologist Karl Landsteiner, who won a 1930 Nobel prize for pioneering work on blood groups, has now discovered the rhesus factor. Named for the monkey species in which it was discovered, the Rh factor is a reaction that can occur in the blood of a mother and fetus, causing abortion or dangerous illness in the newborn.

ENTERTAINMENT

Chaplin as "The Great Dictator"

15 OCTOBER Charlie Chaplin, the world's most famous clown, has released a new movie. *The Great Dictator* is the first movie in which he speaks, and it has some superb comic moments. But above all it mocks Adolf Hitler, parodied by Chaplin as Adenoid Hynkel—complete with uniform, silly salutes, and temper tantrums.

Hynkel's nonsensical harangues attract hordes of admiring followers. When he meets fat Italian dictator Benzino Napoloni, played by Jack Oakie, the stage is set for high jinks. The movie closes with a warning from Hynkel: people should learn to love, not hate, each other. As members of the audience pick their way home through the blackout, hearing the hum of aircraft above, perhaps even caught in an air raid, they know exactly what he means.

Charlie Chaplin facts

Charlie Chaplin's movie career started in 1914 and ended in 1967. In that time he made 89 films, 35 them in 1914.

•

He was nominated for seven Oscars and won one (*Limelight* 1952).

•

Chaplin was an actor, director, writer, photographer, choreographer, and composer.

WAR

Nazi blitzkrieg stuns Europe

28 MAY Belgium today surrendered to Germany, who less than three weeks ago launched a devastating attack on the Low Countries. The "phony war" in Europe, a lull in war campaigns from September 1939, when Germany invaded Poland, to April 1940, when they invaded Denmark and Norway, ended on 10 May, when 200,000 German troops pushed toward the North Sea.

No one was prepared for the German blitzkrieg (lightning war) tactics—the swift tanks and armored vehicles, backed by Ju87 Stuka divebombers.

▲ *A German tank among the rubble of a Belgian town.*

▲ *A painting by Charles Cundell depicting the withdrawal from Dunkirk.*

Operation Dynamo

WAR

4 JUNE A flotilla of ships has whisked 338,226 Allied troops (mainly British) across the English Channel from Dunkirk. German tank forces had advanced with such speed in May that British, French, and some Belgian soldiers were encircled and trapped around the port of Dunkirk. The men saved represent a victory snatched from the jaws of defeat.

Operation Dynamo, as the evacuation is called, started on 27 May. Under heavy air and land attack, the Allies battled to hold onto Dunkirk while the evacuation took place. Fog over the Channel allowed ships to make their crossing undetected.

Jeeps jump into US

This fall the US military took delivery of a prototype new car: the Willys General Purpose Vehicle. The GPV—or "jeep" for short—is a tough, open-sided automobile designed to help battlefield reconnaissance. Its four-cylinder engine gives it a top speed of about 65 miles per hour (105 km per hour), and its high ground clearance and four-wheel drive mean that the jeep can handle almost any terrain, no matter how rough. If it goes into mass production, this go-anywhere car will be a great asset to an army.

Hitler triumphant in France's defeat

WAR

23 JUNE Yesterday the French surrendered to Germany. General Wilhelm Keitel watched them sign their surrender in a train carriage in the forest of Compiègne. The irony of the meeting place was not lost: in this same carriage 22 years ago, the Allies accepted Germany's armistice at the end of the Great War.

The blitzkrieg tactics that conquered the Low Countries were even more effective in France. Around 1.5 million French troops were taken prisoner as the German panzer divisions swept to the Atlantic coast. Today Hitler triumphantly toured Paris, which fell nine days ago. Britain is next on his list.

▶ *Hitler in front of the Eiffel Tower touring Paris after its fall.*

Trotsky assassinated

ASSASSINATIONS

21 AUGUST Leon Trotsky (left) Lenin's trusted helper during the Russian Revolution and the creator of the Red Army, has been assassinated by an agent of Joseph Stalin. Trotsky and Stalin were sworn enemies, and since 1929 Trotsky has been in exile in Mexico. His assassin, a Spaniard calling himself Frank Jackson, smashed his skull with an ice pick.

Royal Navy scuttle French

WAR

3 JULY Determined to prevent France's warships from falling into German hands, the Royal Navy today launched a lightning strike on the French fleet. In five minutes of ear-splitting bombardment, a squadron of British ships sank three battleships berthed at Oran, Algeria. Over 1,200 French sailors are feared dead; six ships, including the *Strasbourg*, got away.

Vice-Admiral Sir James Somerville, leading the operation from HMS *Hood*, took the grim decision to scuttle the ships after the French commander refused to join the British or to disarm his ships or scuttle them himself.

The young Dalai Lama, dressed in peasant clothes, at Kumbum Monastery.

RELIGION

Child Dalai Lama enthroned in Tibet

22 FEBRUARY Tibet has a new ruler: a five-year-old boy from a small settlement in the northeast of this remote country. Today he was enthroned as the 14th Dalai Lama, making him the spiritual and political leader of the country.

The people of Tibet, the world's highest country, are fervent Buddhists and believe that we each have an immortal soul which simply moves to another body when we die. When the 13th Dalai Lama died in 1933, his spirit transferred itself to a newborn baby. Senior Tibetan monks, or lamas, began the search immediately—and were helped by magical omens. Rainbows beckoned them to travel northeast of Lhasa, the capital; the head of the 13th Dalai Lama, whose body awaited burial, also slowly turned to the northeast. These portents, combined with visions, inspired a group of lamas to disguise themselves as traders and go to the village of Takster. They were welcomed into a farmhouse, where two-year-old Lhamo Thondup grabbed a set of beads which had belonged to the 13th Dalai Lama. "You are a lama from Sera," he told the astonished lama of Sera. Later, shown a selection of objects, the boy picked out those which had belonged to the last Dalai Lama, saying: "They are mine." Today the boy was renamed Tenzing Gyatso and begins a harsh apprenticeship into the mysteries of Tibetan religion.

◀ Potala, the winter palace of the Dalai Lamas, in Lhasa, built in the 17th century.

NEWS • 1940 • NEWS

8 January • Butter, sugar, and bacon are rationed in Britain.

15 February • Hitler orders U–boat commanders to attack all ships heading for Britain.

12 March • End of war between Russia and Finland.

10 June • Italy declares war on the Allies.

27 September • Japan signs Tripartite Pact, aligning itself with Italy and Germany.

POLITICS

Churchill becomes prime minister

▼ Winston Churchill, the new prime minister of Great Britain.

13 MAY Winston Churchill today addressed the House of Commons for the first time as Britain's prime minister. Three days ago, Neville Chamberlain's government collapsed in the face of furious criticism from all sides. The king summoned Churchill, a veteran politician, to form a coalition government that would unite all the parties.

Churchill has always spoken out against Hitler and against Chamberlain's policy of giving in to his demands. His speech today was characteristically determined: "I have nothing to offer but blood, toil, tears, and sweat," he said, pledging to "wage war against a monstrous tyranny, never surpassed in the dark, lamentable catalogue of human crime."

Battle of Britain

17 SEPTEMBER Hitler has called off Operation Sealion, the planned invasion of Britain. It is a triumph for the brave young pilots of the Royal Air Force, who have fought off attacks from Herman Goering's numerically superior Luftwaffe.

The battle started just over two months ago, when Hitler demanded that Goering win control of the skies over Britain. The British have the advantage of superb Spitfire and Hurricane fighter planes, sophisticated communications and radar systems, and a top-secret facility at Bletchley Park, which has cracked the Luftwaffe's Enigma code. Goering made a strategic error on 7 September, when he switched tactics to bomb Britain's cities instead of its airfields.

▶ *Boys look at the ruins of their bombed school.*

▲ *A German air gunner in a Dornier DO-17.*

Life in the Warsaw ghetto

19 NOVEMBER A Pole was executed today for throwing bread into the Warsaw ghetto—the area where all the city's Jews must live. On 16 October Hans Frank, Poland's German governor, ordered all Poles to leave the area and moved in Jews from the rest of Warsaw. Four days ago, on 15 November, he imprisoned the ghetto's 400,000 residents, setting up armed guards at its entrances and exits.

Nearly a third of Warsaw's population is now crammed into 2.5 percent of the city's area. Jews cannot leave to go to work and depend on German food rations set at 300 calories per person per day—Germans are allocated 2,300. Hans Frank wants to starve the Jews to death.

▲ *Streets have been walled up to imprison the residents of the ghetto.*

Haw Haw has the last laugh

FEBRUARY Millions of Britons are tuning their radios to "Lord Haw Haw" the drawling propagandist who broadcasts from Hamburg every evening. But far from sapping British morale, his sneering tirades—delivered in a peculiar aristocratic accent and always beginning "Jairmany calling!"—are unintentionally very funny. People listen and laugh.

▲ *Charles de Gaulle, exiled but still fighting.*

Cave art found at Lascaux

A group of teenagers today discovered an incredible prehistoric art gallery in a cavern at Lascaux, in southern France. Marcel Ravidat and friends are the first for 14,000 years to see pictures of wild animals painted by ancient people. In one scene, a man seems to be falling after being butted by a speared bison.

De Gaulle rallies the French

18 JUNE France may have fallen to the Germans, but the French are undefeated according to General de Gaulle. Two days ago, he escaped to England. With the support of the British government he will lead the "Free French." In a radio broadcast he declared: "Whatever happens, the flame of the French resistance must not go out and it will not go out."

1940

THE HOMEFRONT

In 1938, Nazi Germany took control of Austria and parts of Czechoslovakia. When the Nazis invaded Poland in September 1939, Britain and France declared war. By June 1940 most of western Europe was under Nazi control. Germany invaded Russia in 1941, breaking the nonaggression pact they both had made in 1939. The US entered the war as an Ally in 1941 after Japan attacked Pearl Harbor in Hawaii.

Germany surrendered in May 1945; Japan in August after US forces dropped the first atomic bombs on Hiroshima and Nagasaki. Although much of the fighting had taken place in Europe, there were few parts of the world where the six-year-long conflict had no impact.

Cities suffer widespread destruction from air raids in World War II

The bombing of the defenseless Basque town of Guernica by the German air force during the Spanish Civil War showed how vulnerable cities and civilians were to a new kind of offensive. From the beginning, World War II was waged from the sky. Radar helped to intercept bombers so that they could be shot down before they had hit their targets. Hitler's Luftwaffe aimed to destroy British war industries and undermine the spirit of resistance, and the British RAF and the US Air Force tried to do the same to Germany's morale and key industries.

During the first phase of the bombing of Britain, known as the Blitz (7 September to 2 November, 1940), London was bombed intensively every night. For the next phase other important cities were also bombed—Coventry most catastrophically—and, finally, Britain's western ports. May 1941 saw the last heavy German air raid, on Birmingham. About 30,000 people died in the Blitz, over half of them in London, and thousands lost their homes.

Toward the end of the war, the Allies bombed the historic German city of Dresden. This raid, in which 130,000 people died, was criticized because the city was crammed with refugees fleeing from the Eastern front. It was carried out to demonstrate how well the Allies were collaborating to bring about Germany's defeat.

▲ *A young survivor sits among the devastation after the Luftwaffe's 1939 attack on Warsaw. The Polish capital was bombed to destroy Polish resistance.*

▼ *In February 1945, Dresden was reduced to a smoking ruin by RAF and US Air Force bombers.*

▲ *Parts of Tokyo lie in ruins after a US air strike in 1945.*

Children suffer separation from their families

Before war broke out, the British government had made plans to evacuate the children living in London and other cities considered to be most at risk from air raids. The first evacuation began on 1 September, 1939, two days before the actual declaration of war, and involved nearly 1.5 million children.

There were two more major evacuations, when the Blitz began and during the 1944 wave of "doodlebug" rocket attacks.

But the discomforts and upsets of homesick British child evacuees were nothing to the fate of Jewish children in Europe. Over six million Jews, including children, were murdered by the Nazis during World War II. Just before the war, 10,000 Jewish children from Nazi-ruled parts of Europe were allowed to take refuge in Britain. Most of them never saw their parents again.

▲ *As the Nazis advanced across Europe, refugees fled with only their most basic possessions.*

▲ *Young British evacuees were taken by train to safer areas.*

◀ *Gas masks were issued to schoolchildren.*

▶ *Young evacuees were each given an identification label.*

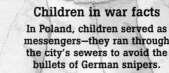

Children in war facts

In Poland, children served as messengers—they ran through the city's sewers to avoid the bullets of German snipers.

•

Tens of thousands of German children died in firestorms caused by air raids; in Japan thousands of children were killed by atomic bombs in Hiroshima and Nagasaki.

▲ *Underground subway stations served as air-raid shelters in London.*

Food rationing for everyone

▲ *Children gathered blackberries in England as part of their contribution to the war effort.*

All luxuries and many necessities were hard to obtain during World War II. Basic foods—meat, butter, fats, bacon, cheese, milk, eggs—were rationed in Britain and Germany, but bread and potatoes, which were plentiful in Britain, were also rationed in Germany. The US rationed some canned goods, sugar, and coffee, but not as much as Europe. Rationing was not as unpopular as some people had feared because it was regarded as fair.

▼ *You could not buy anything without your ration book.*

1940

1941

1942

1943

1944

1945

1946

1947

1948

1949

Konrad Zuse's Z3 computer

German aeronautical engineers have started to use an extraordinary electronic machine to calculate the behavior of prototype airframes in flight. The machine, called the Z3 by its creator, Konrad Zuse, is the world's first electronic computer. It takes three seconds to perform a calculation using the binary system. Because of the war, Zuse's work is secret, but he is far ahead of other scientists in developing a form of artificial intelligence, based on "Plankalkül," a special type of computer language.

◄ *Konrad Zuse and his computer.*

WAR

Japanese attack Pearl Harbor— US enters war

8 DECEMBER At 5:10 pm today, President Roosevelt declared war on Japan. He wore a black armband in memory of the 2,403 people killed in yesterday's surprise attack on the US Pacific Fleet berthed at Pearl Harbor, Hawaii.

The Japanese attack was part of a brilliant strategy to seize control of the entire Pacific. As Admiral Chuichi Nagumo's strike force bore down on Pearl Harbor, others simultaneously invaded the US's Pacific possessions—the Philippines, Guam, and the Marianas Islands— and landed in Thailand and the British colonies of Hong Kong and Malaya.

The US is counting the cost of the attack. Nineteen warships are out of action, including four battleships sunk; 188 aircraft have been destroyed and a further 159 damaged. American aircraft carriers were elsewhere, and so escaped.

Japan has been trying to conquer China since 1937 and has long wanted to take over all of Southeast Asia. Last year Japan signed an alliance with Germany and Italy. Now the world truly is at war.

▶ *Roosevelt signs declaration of war.*

ENTERTAINMENT

Vera Lynn sings for the boys

APRIL It's official: she's the forces' sweetheart. Men of the British army have consistently voted Vera Lynn, the daughter of a London plumber, their favorite singer. Miss Lynn's gentle voice comforts British servicemen wherever they are, singing sentimental tunes like "Faithful for ever," "We'll meet again," and this year's hit, "White Cliffs of Dover"—a beautiful ballad expressing hope for a peaceful future. Her songs are always on the radio, and she even has her own show, appropriately named *Sincerely Yours.*

▼ *A scene from* Citizen Kane.

Welles' masterpiece

In a debut that has rocked Hollywood, Orson Welles, the 25-year-old maverick of the New York theater, has created what could be an all-time movie masterpiece. *Citizen Kane*—starring Welles and produced, directed, and cowritten by him too—is the tale of a corrupt newspaper mogul who lives in a castle called Xanadu. Kane is loosely based on William R. Hearst, head of the world's largest newspaper empire. Superb acting and stunning cinematography by Gregg Toland lift this movie far above anything yet seen.

▲ *Little remains of the US warships after being bombed in Pearl Harbor by Japanese troops.*

Nazis take Greece and its islands

WAR

1 JUNE German tanks rolled into Athens on 27 April, forcing Allied forces to retreat to the island of Crete. Tonight Royal Navy ships evacuated thousands of Allied troops from Crete—12 days after the skies over the island were filled with German paratroopers. Greece and its islands are now firmly in the hands of the Nazis.

The attack on Crete—the first airborne invasion in history—was conducted with clockwork precision. Allied soldiers inflicted heavy casualties, but could not stop the German tide.

▲ *Backup German mountain troops land in Crete.*

Hitler invades the USSR

WAR

19 SEPTEMBER German armies today marched into Kiev, the capital of the Ukraine, to find it peppered with time bombs and stripped of anything they might find useful. The Soviets have destroyed their own water and electricity supplies rather than allow the invaders to use them.

On 22 June, Hitler went back on his 1939 agreement not to invade the USSR for 10 years. He made the promise so that he would not have to fight enemies to the west and the east at the same time, but after the fall of France this was no longer important. A sworn enemy of Russia's communist system, he ordered the invasion against the advice of his own generals and is commanding operations personally from the "Wolf's Lair"— his special headquarters at Rastenburg, in eastern Prussia.

Russia experiences freezing winters—Napoleon was defeated by the cold in 1812 when he invaded Russia. Hitler is determined to avoid the same fate by reaching Moscow before winter sets in.

▼ *The Germans used tanks as part of their weaponry in the Ukraine.*

Churchill calls up women for war services

WAR

4 DECEMBER Winston Churchill today brought in conscription for women: unmarried women in their twenties are to be called up to serve in the armed forces, police, and fire services, and older women must register to work in factories for the war effort.

Previously women been able to volunteer for military service. Many have joined the Auxiliary Territorial Service (ATS), the Women's Auxiliary Air Force (WAAF), or the Royal Navy (the Wrens). In the ATS, women work as drivers, mechanics, and antiaircraft gunners; WAAFs play key operational roles as bomb plotters, radio operators, and administrators.

▼ The impressive giant granite heads of (left to right) George Washington, Thomas Jefferson, Theodore Roosevelt, and Abraham Lincoln.

1941

NEWS • 1941 • NEWS

11 March • President Roosevelt signs Lend-Lease Bill, allowing US to supply Britain with arms and equipment.

5 April • Erwin Rommel's Afrika Korps attacks Allied troops in North Africa.

10 May • German bombs destroy House of Commons.

3 September • Poison gas, Zyklon B, first used by Nazis to murder inmates of Auschwitz concentration camp.

ART
Unveiled—presidents' heads in stone at Rushmore

1 NOVEMBER A granite monument, 15 years in the making, was unveiled today at Mount Rushmore, in the Black Hills of South Dakota as the 60-foot (18-meter) high heads of Presidents Washington, Jefferson, Lincoln, and Theodore Roosevelt emerged from behind the builders' scaffolding. About 450,000 tons of granite were excavated from the rock using explosives, pneumatic drills, and chisels. The sculptor, Gutzon Borglum, used an enormous pointing machine to transfer his design from scale models made in his studio. The noble heads make a stirringly patriotic quartet as they stare out over the pine forests of the Black Hills. Borglum died this spring, however, so he never saw his finished masterpiece, which was completed by his son Lincoln.

TECHNOLOGY
Codebreakers crack Enigma

30 NOVEMBER Using radar and depth charges, an RAF Whitley bomber today sank an enemy U-boat (submarine) in the Bay of Biscay. The RAF shares the glory with the talented codebreakers of Britain's top secret Code and Cipher school at Bletchley Park, near Bedford—who found out the location of U-boat U206 from an intercepted message.

All German armed forces use a compact cipher machine called Enigma. Two codebooks have fortunately been captured this year, so the Bletchley team have been reading naval Enigma messages for most of the year. As a result, Britain is winning the Battle of the Atlantic.

POLITICS
Jews to wear yellow star

1 SEPTEMBER All Jews in Germany over the age of six must now wear a special symbol on their outer clothing in order to make them stand out in a crowd. The symbol is the traditional six-pointed Star of David, on a yellow background, with the word *Jude* (Jew) in the middle. Jews in occupied Poland and the Baltic States have already been ordered to wear similar badges.

This move is yet another measure toward the "final solution of the Jewish question," ordered by Reichsmarschal Herman Goering in July, and further singles out the Jews.

◀ *The Star of David badge identifies this child as a Jew.*

Rationing is on the increase

NOVEMBER Books of coupons have become a national obsession in Britain. Meat and sugar were rationed last year, but in spring jam and marmalade were restricted, too. Then, in a surprise move on 2 June, clothes were rationed. This month everyone is being urged to eat potatoes and carrots: add them to pastry, or mash them up for a tasty sandwich filling, says the government.

Rudolf Hess—the uninvited guest

10 MAY Rudolf Hess (below), Hitler's deputy, set off on a solo peace mission after astrologers told him that his destiny was to bring Britain and Germany together. Tonight he crashlanded on a hillside near Glasgow. Hess says that Germany will keep off the British Empire if Churchill lets Germany control Europe. Hitler has already disowned Hess—and this uninvited Nazi "ambassador" is now under arrest.

The Atlantic Charter

11 AUGUST Winston Churchill and President Roosevelt today met off Newfoundland, on the British battleship *Prince of Wales*, to sign an Anglo-American declaration of eight common principles. The Atlantic Charter, as it is being called, looks forward to a postwar future in which people live together in harmony and refrain from using force to settle disputes.

By stating his determination to defend democracy and free trade, Roosevelt has brought the US much closer to Britain.

◀ *The* Prince of Wales *where the momentous secret meeting took place.*

Sinking of the *Bismarck*

27 MAY Last week the Royal Navy's biggest battle cruiser, HMS *Hood*, was sunk by Germany's biggest battleship, the *Bismarck*. A shell tore through the *Hood*'s armor and sank it in minutes, killing all but 3 of its 1,416 crew.

Today the Navy had its revenge. The *Bismarck* was spotted by an RAF reconnaissance flight—and planes from the nearby *Ark Royal* crippled its steering gear with torpedoes. British battleships moved in. As the *Bismarck*'s commander prepared to scuttle his ship, HMS *Dorsetshire* sank it. A lurking German U-boat forced the British fleet to leave without rescuing the survivors. More than 2,200 men drowned as a result.

▼ *The German battleship, the* Bismarck, *before the Royal Navy's attack.*

Henry Moore's sheltering sleepers

British artist Henry Moore (right) is well known for his extraordinary sculptures, which portray the human body as an abstract shape pierced by holes. Last year he was appointed one of Britain's official war artists, and has now reached a wider audience with his drawings of sleeping Londoners, sheltering from the Blitz in the Underground. Moore tours the shelters with his sketchbook. There is something profoundly beautiful and moving about his restless, slumbering figures.

1940

1941

1942

1943

1944

1945

1946

1947

1948

1949

Wonder cure hope

Major quantities of penicillin are being produced by the US pharmaceutical company Commercial Solvents Corporation of Indiana. It is hoped that the wonder cure may soon be available for mass miracles on the battlefield. Last year scientists Howard Florey and Ernst Chain used penicillin to cure a policeman of septicemia (blood poisoning).

▲ *Penicillin on the assembly line.*

Wartime love story

Hollywood's *Casablanca* is set in a Nazi-dominated Moroccan city in 1941. In the film, Pearl Harbor has yet to be attacked, but after seeing this stirring tale no one could regret the US's recent entry into the struggle against Nazi tyranny. Humphrey Bogart plays the cynical antihero, Rick, who regains his youthful ideals when he re-encounters the love of his life, played by Swedish star Ingrid Bergman.

▶ Casablanca, *a movie to match the times.*

WAR

De Gaulle renames his Resistance fighters

14 JULY On the anniversary of another great event in French history, the storming of the Bastille prison, Charles de Gaulle has decreed that all of the forces resisting his country's occupation are to be known as "Fighting France." Since the fall of France in 1940, General de Gaulle has led French soldiers who are continuing to fight Germany, but with this declaration he is reaching out to the men and women of the home resistance. De Gaulle is urging them to resist and fight the German occupying forces in the north of France.

Within France, the Resistance operates in conditions of great secrecy and danger. It is thought to be a vast interlocking and overlapping web of networks, with different groups specializing in sabotage, propaganda, or intelligence work. Just recently Armel Guerne, a resistance leader, was arrested when the Gestapo pounded on his door; and his wife, thinking it was a joke, threw it open, leaving him no time to escape. Every resistance worker risks arrest and much worse, but for every person who falls into the hands of the Gestapo, another steps forward to carry on the work.

▲ *A member of the French Resistance with a homemade bomb. Some Resistance groups specialize in sabotage.*

Humphrey BOGART Ingrid BERGMAN Paul HENREID

A HAL B. WALLIS PRODUCTION

Casablanca

CLAUDE RAINS · CONRAD VEIDT · SYDNEY GREENSTREET · PETER LORRE
Directed by Michael Curtiz

▲ *Japanese soldiers celebrate after capturing this American gun in Bataan, in the Philippines.*

Japan attacks Singapore

WAR

15 FEBRUARY Japanese forces are still advancing across the Pacific after attacking Pearl Harbor 10 weeks ago. After days of heavy bombing, the Japanese landed in Singapore six days ago, and this morning, when Lieutenant-General Percival surrendered to the Japanese commander-in-chief, 60,000 Allied troops were captured.

The fall of the great naval fortress of Singapore, the only dry dock between Pearl Harbor and Durban, is a grave blow to the Allies. It seems that nothing can stop the Japanese from taking over all the American, British, and Dutch colonies in the Pacific and Indian oceans.

US revenge on Japan

WAR

7 JUNE Japan is suffering a bitter defeat off the Pacific island of Midway. As soon as US codebreakers figured out that Midway Island was a Japanese target, Admiral Chester Nimitz sent three American aircraft carriers to intercept the Japanese fleet, which had four carriers. While Japanese aircraft attacked shore targets on Midway Island, US aircraft divebombed their carriers.

After three days of fierce fighting in the air and on the sea, Japan's naval power has now been shattered. For the Americans, still smarting after Pearl Harbor, and for all of the Allied forces in the Pacific, the Battle of Midway Island is a heartening victory.

▲ *A US aircraft carrier takes a hit in the Midway Battle.*

Gold disk awarded to big band leader

Glenn Miller's big band is officially the most popular dance band in the world. The big band leader received a golden disk this year, his reward for selling more than one million copies of "Chattanooga choo choo," which was first played in last year's film, *Sun Valley Serenade*. Now Miller is forming an all-star US Army personnel band, guaranteed to put Allied troops "in the mood" for victory.

Heavy losses in Dieppe raid

WAR

19 AUGUST For nine hours Allied forces, including Canadian, British, American, and French troops, held on to the French port of Dieppe, where the Germans have been building up their coastal defenses on the French North Sea and the Atlantic. The Allied forces did "useful" damage to the port's facilities, but the number of casualties on both sides is likely to be large, and over 2,000 prisoners have been taken.

Allied victory at El Alamein

WAR

4 NOVEMBER After weeks of fierce fighting along the 40-mile (65-km) El Alamein front, Germany's Afrika Korps and the Italian army are in retreat. The Allied offensive began 10 days ago, commanded by General Montgomery, who has been building up his forces since last August when he was put in charge of Britain's North African campaign. The Battle of El Alamein has cost the Axis Powers (the alliance of Germany and Italy) 60,000 men, 500 tanks, and 1,000 guns so far.

▶ *British soldiers capture a German tank during the Battle of El Alamein.*

153

THE HOLOCAUST

Adolf Hitler and his followers believed that there was a "pure" Germanic race destined to rule the world. Peoples such as gypsies and eastern European Slavs were considered "inferior." But for Hitler, the Jews were worse than inferior, and he blamed them for all the world's problems. The term "Holocaust" (meaning great destruction or loss) was used to describe the extermination of the Jewish people by the Nazis.

During World War II, Germany occupied many countries that had large Jewish populations, and the Nazis seized the chance to exterminate them systematically. When Germany invaded Russia in 1941, special death squads moved in to round up and kill Jews. This method proved too time consuming and too public, so specialized camps were set up in eastern Europe: secret factories of death, where people were killed with industrial efficiency.

Anne Frank

A German-born Jewish girl called Anne Frank, whose family fled Frankfurt to live in Amsterdam after Hitler came to power, gave the world one of the most haunting memorials of the Holocaust: a small, red-and-white notebook in which she kept a diary of the two years she lived in a secret annex of rooms above her father's office.

During the German occupation of Amsterdam (1942–44), the Franks, together with four others, hid there to escape deportation. Many friends supported them by bringing them food, but eventually, in August 1944, they were betrayed to the Nazis. They formed part of the last trainload of Jews to be sent to the Auschwitz death camp. Just before the end of the war, Anne was transferred to Belsen concentration camp, where she died of typhus. She was 15 years old.

Miep Gies, one of the family's helpers, found Anne's notebook and kept it safe. The diary, published in 1947, has become one of the world's most widely read books.

▼ *The secret doorway to the Franks' hiding place.*

▼ *Anne Frank, the child whose moving account of life in hiding during the Nazi reign of terror, has shown the world the horrors of the Holocaust.*

▶ *Background: A close-up of two pages from Anne Frank's diary.*

Segregation and the ghettos

A few weeks after the invasion of Poland in 1939, the Nazi authorities ordered "the concentration of the Jews from the countryside into the larger cities." Over the next two years, Jews in occupied Europe were separated from everyone else into special ghettos. They were herded into small fenced-off areas in cities such as Vilna, Warsaw, Lublin, and Lodz and were eventually forbidden to leave or to have contact with the outside world. In these overcrowded conditions, denied adequate food or medical care, thousands died. In 1943 most of the ghettos were closed down and their inhabitants sent to concentration camps.

▲ *Jewish children in a segregated classroom.*

▶ *The segregation of the Jews meant they even had to ride on separate trams.*

The "final solution"

The systematic extermination of the Jews began in 1941. At a meeting in Berlin in 1942, the German security organizations agreed to comb Europe for Jews and ship them to camps where they would die.

At the height of the program, which the Nazis called "the final solution" to the "Jewish problem," people were crammed into railroad freight cars and sent hundreds of miles to camps such as Auschwitz, Treblinka, and Sobibor. Without food, water, or heating, many died on the way. On arrival, the young, the old, and the sick went straight to their deaths in specially designed gas chambers. At Auschwitz and a few of the other camps, the healthy were often saved only to be worked to death or used in cruel medical experiments. Victims' hair was sold for profit; glasses, false teeth, and false limbs were sent to Germany for reuse; gold teeth were melted down.

▲ *Child prisoners in a Nazi concentration camp.*

▼ *Jews wait to be deported to a death camp.*

▲ *SS Commander Stroop (center) in the Warsaw ghetto.*

▲ *German patrols dig up bunkers in the Warsaw ghetto as Jewish people look on helplessly.*

Jewish uprising in Warsaw ghetto

POLITICS

19 APRIL Armed with flamethrowers, dynamite, armored cars, and tanks, the Waffen-SS (SS combat troops) led by the infamous General Stroop have moved into Warsaw's Jewish ghetto for a final "clear up." But as they move through the ghetto's smoke-blackened ruins, they are encountering something extraordinary—a Jewish uprising.

Soon after the Germans set up the Warsaw ghetto in 1940, it was holding at least 450,000 Jewish people. With more than seven people to a room and chronic food shortages, many thousands have died of disease and malnutrition; many more have been taken to concentration camps; others have taken their own lives. But in spite of the horrors of the past three years, an estimated 50,000 Jews are still living in the Warsaw ghetto, and about 750 of these survivors have decided to stand up to the Waffen-SS. Under the pretext of building air-raid shelters, they managed to excavate dug-out bunkers which are connected with the sewer network. Led by 24-year-old Mordecai Anielewicz, and with weapons consisting of 9 rifles, 59 pistols, and a few grenades, the escapees have gone underground.

Demonstration of hallucinogenic qualities of LSD

SCIENCE

19 APRIL Swiss chemist Albert Hofmann deliberately dosed himself with LSD (lysergic acid diethylamide) as a self-experiment—he and a colleague first produced LSD in 1938 and experienced strange sensations. The hallucinogenic effects of the drug, which is derived from a parasitic fungus which grows on rye, have long been known to humans, but only by accident. Medieval Europeans knew the symptoms as "St. Vitus's Dance" or "St. Anthony's Fire."

A simple fable for everyone

Antoine de Saint-Exupéry has written as well as illustrated his book *The Little Prince*. Although it is a children's story, the book is aimed at adults, with the underlying message that the simplest things in life are the best. He has dedicated the book to an old friend, because "all grown-ups were once children—although few of them remember."

Sorgfältig fegte er seine Vulkane.

Battle of Stalingrad

31 JANUARY The siege of Stalingrad ended today when Germany's Field Marshal von Paulus and 15 of his generals surrendered to a Soviet lieutenant, knowing that most of their army had been killed or captured.

Stalingrad gets its name from the fact that Stalin led its defense during Russia's Civil War. Before the war it was a major industrial center—now it is devastated. The Russians allowed the Germans to take the city, then surrounded them, so that 300,000 German troops were cut off from supplies. Germany's efforts to supply the troops by air failed, and there was no let up on the Red Army's attacks.

▲ *Members of the Russian Red Army advance on the last troops of the German Sixth Army in Stalingrad.*

Allies launch new weapon

1943 The US airforce's first "Flying Fortress," the Boeing B-17, is currently carrying out daylight bombing raids on German factories and cities. Now the Flying Fortress has a more lethal and versatile brother, the Boeing B-29 Superfortress. The B-29 has a range of 2,800 miles (4,500 kilometers) and can deliver an impressive bombload of 5 tons (5 tonnes). It has been designed specifically for the war in the Pacific. Japan is at present still out of range of any Allied-held airfields. Soon, however, the advancing Americans hope to have seized Pacific islands that will bring Japanese cities within reach.

◀ *The new B-29 Superfortresses will be used to bomb Japan.*

Heartthrob singer launches solo career

Frank Sinatra, the one who drives the girls wild, is set to sing for another four weeks at New York's Paramount Theater. Sinatra quit Harry James' band less than six months ago and decided to be the first singer since Bing Crosby to make it on his own. Sinatra still looks pretty much like he did when he left school at 16 to sing at functions, and his success at the Paramount shows that he has got what it takes to be a solo star.

PEOPLE

Death penalty for anti-Nazi crusaders

22 FEBRUARY Hans and Sophie Scholl, the brother and sister who were arrested by the secret police four days ago, have been sentenced to death for the crime of encouraging anti-Nazi resistance. Hans, who is 24, and Sophie, who is 22, are students at Munich University and have been active for the past year in the White Rose organization, which campaigns against Hitler's government.

They were handing out anti-Nazi leaflets on campus when they were arrested. It is thought that they will be executed today with three other White Rose members.

▲ *Hans and Sophie Scholl.*

TECHNOLOGY

The Dambusters—first use of the bouncing bomb

▼ Wing Commander Guy Gibson and members of 617 Squadron photographed before the raid on the Ruhr.

18 MAY The Royal Air Force scored a major success last night with a devastating raid on the Möhne and Eder dams, which provide power for the German industrial district of the Ruhr. The raid was carried out by the specially trained 617 Squadron, led by Wing Commander Guy Gibson, flying the new Lancaster bombers with their powerful Merlin engines. Both dams were destroyed, causing floods and many civilian casualties, especially in Mulheim and Dortmund. Over 1,000 people are reported killed, and it is likely that the damage will take months to repair.

Success required precision flying against heavy antiaircraft defenses. A special ball-shaped bomb had to be dropped at a precise altitude and a precise distance from the dam. It then bounced along the surface of the water until it reached the dam, where it sank and exploded. The principle of the bouncing bomb was worked out with models on an indoor tank and tested in the Lake District in England.

▶ The Dambusters' bomb was developed by the engineer Barnes Wallis.

TREATIES

Italy in Axis split

8 SEPTEMBER Less than two months after the overthrow of Mussolini on 25 July, the Axis is broken. Italy has signed an armistice and the Nazis have lost their chief ally. It appears that secret negotiations had been going on with the government of Marshal Badoglio since the overthrow. The Germans still remain masters of northern and central Italy.

▼ Soldiers among the ruins of the Italian town of Montecassino, bombed by the Allies.

New York show provides war relief

A new musical, *Oklahoma*, by Richard Rodgers and Oscar Hammerstein has opened to rave reviews in New York. Set in rural Oklahoma where, as one of the songs says, "the corn grows as high as an elephant's eye," it provides a welcome relief from stories of bombed cities. The title song is just one of the exhilarating hit numbers, which include "People Will Say We're in Love" and "The Surrey with the Fringe on Top." This show, say critics, will run and run.

Japanese sub torpedoes an Australian hospital ship

WAR

14 MAY About 300 people are feared dead after an Australian hospital ship was torpedoed without warning by a Japanese submarine in the South Pacific. That the attack was an error is considered unlikely, since the ship was clearly marked and could hardly be mistaken for a warship.

A year ago, a Japanese invasion of Australia seemed possible. Japanese midget submarines even penetrated Sydney Harbour. The Japanese have been on the defensive since the Battle of Midway last June, and this latest atrocity may be a sign of their growing desperation.

NEWS • 1943 • NEWS

9 February • US Pacific forces gain Guadalcanal (largest of the Solomon Islands) after a six-month battle.

8 April • President Roosevelt imposes freeze on prices and wages in US.

12 September • German commandos rescue Mussolini from prison in Italy.

28 November • Churchill, Roosevelt and Stalin meet in Tehran, Iran to plan the defeat of Germany.

◀ A damaged ship in Sydney Harbour after a Japanese midget submarine attack.

"Zoot suit" riots in Los Angeles

CULTURE

30 JUNE In the US the summer is proving a violent one, with serious race riots in several cities. In Los Angeles, white servicemen attacked groups of African- and Spanish-American youths wearing "zoot" suits. This style was begun by fans of swing music. The main item is a very long coat, with an equally long tie and baggy pants nipped in at the ankle. Colors are as bright as possible.

The worst of the riots took place in Detroit on 20–22 June. About 35 people were killed and hundreds injured.

◀ Police round up a suspect in a zoot suit.

Betty Grable: GI's favorite pin-up

Pasted inside many lockers on US military bases throughout the world you will find this poster. The lady is Betty Grable, Hollywood's "blonde bombshell," whose movie company has insured her legs for a quarter of a million dollars. Grable may be glamorous, but in her movies she also seems like the kind of girl you might find bringing your coffee in a diner, if not living in the house next door. Perhaps that is what makes her so popular with American soldiers serving their country thousands of miles from home.

Kidney dialysis machine invented

A dialysis machine, developed by the Dutch doctor, Willem Kolff, brings hope for patients with kidney failure. Dialysis separates substances in liquid form by filtering them through a membrane which some substances cannot penetrate. Dr. Kolff's machine removes poisonous waste substances from the blood, the task normally done by the kidneys.

1940

1941

1942

1943

1944

1945

1946

1947

1948

1949

▶ *Allied troops and tanks landing on the beaches in Normandy.*

Roosevelt wins record 4th election

In November President Roosevelt was elected president for a fourth four-year term. No previous president has served more than two terms. His majority was smaller than last time and his health is poor but, with the country at war, voters were afraid of a change.

D-day landings in Normandy

WAR

6 JUNE At dawn today, Allied paratroopers landed behind enemy lines in Normandy. They were the advance guard of a mighty invasion fleet which landed troops at several places along more than 50 miles (80 km) of the French coast. Operation Overlord, the code name for the invasion, is by far the biggest land, sea, and air operation in military history. It is headed by Allied commander, General Eisenhower. About 5,000 ships are taking part, plus 12,000 aircraft. Bombers have pounded German defenses and communications in France for weeks, while French Resistance saboteurs have blown up railroad lines and bridges.

Although the German defenses are strong, Field Marshal von Rundstedt, the German commander, did not know where the main thrust would come. Except at Omaha Beach, where the Americans were confronted by a top-quality German division, casualties were light. By dark, the Allied forces were on the way to establishing a united front several miles inland.

Dietrich entertains

German Marlene Dietrich, at 43 still the screen's most glamorous star, has been touring army bases bewitching the troops just as she bewitched her movie audiences worldwide. Miss Dietrich has worked in the US since 1930. Hitler tried to order her home, but she refused and is now a naturalized US citizen.

▶ *Russian troops advance toward Leningrad.*

Siege of Leningrad is over

WAR

27 JANUARY The long and terrible siege of Leningrad came to an end today. A Russian attack forced the Germans to withdraw from the Moscow–Leningrad railroad, freeing the city from its 900-day ordeal. The city has been cut off and bombed since the German advance in August 1941. More than 650,000 people have died of starvation. The first winter was the worst. Later, supplies were brought in across Lake Ladoga in the north.

German withdrawal has left the Finns, who have been at war with the Soviet Union since 1941, isolated. They may seek an armistice from the Russians.

London hit by V2 missiles

TECHNOLOGY

9 SEPTEMBER The Germans have produced another terrible weapon. Today London was attacked by a new ballistic missile (rocket-powered weapon). Known as the V2, it carries a 1-ton warhead, travels faster than any aircraft, and cannot be shot down. It is the second of Hitler's secret weapons. The V1s, called doodle-bugs, first hit London on 12 June. They are a pilotless aircraft whose engine cuts out on reaching the target. Last year the British bombed the V1s' and V2s' development site and set back the program by many months. If the V2 had been ready earlier, it might have turned the war in Germany's favor.

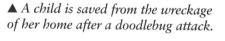

▲ *A child is saved from the wreckage of her home after a doodlebug attack.*

NEWS • 1944 • NEWS

17 February • British government announces plans for a national health service.

3 May • Meat rationing ends in US.

17 June • Iceland becomes a fully independent republic.

9 October • Allied governments announce plans for a United Nations organization.

20 November • London streetlights go on as "blackout" ends.

Assassination of Hitler fails

20 JULY Hitler narrowly escaped death today at the hands of his own officers when a bomb exploded in his eastern HQ, "Wolf's Lair." Several staff officers were killed, but Hitler, though only a few feet from the explosion, was protected by a table and suffered only minor injuries. The bomb, in a briefcase, was planted by Colonel von Stauffenberg, a war hero. Many top generals were sympathetic to the plot and some were directly involved, which shows the extent of opposition to Hitler. However, little is heard of German resistance to the Nazis because all opponents are ruthlessly eliminated.

▲ *General de Gaulle, leader of the Free French since 1940, walks through liberated Paris.*

Warsaw revolt

8 AUGUST The Polish Home Army, which organized resistance to the German occupation, began an open revolt in Warsaw a week ago. The Soviet army, against Polish expectations, has not offered any assistance and is not allowing any supplies from the West into the city. The Poles are having to fight hand-to-hand in the bombed-out streets and sewers. Possibly, Stalin wants the Polish Home Army destroyed before his troops take Warsaw.

Paris is liberated

25 AUGUST A Free French division entered Paris yesterday and ended four bitter years of German occupation. The Allies were fearful that the Germans might obey Hitler's order to burn Paris rather than surrender, but the German commander wisely ignored it. The Resistance rose against the Germans and seized city strongpoints before General Leclerc's tanks led in Allied forces. Amid the celebrations there were also nasty scenes. Collaborators were attacked, and Germans had to be saved from lynch mobs.

THE ATOMIC BOMB

Early in the 20th century, the great physicist Albert Einstein discovered that the smallest particles (atoms) that make up matter could be converted into energy. His theory was confirmed by experiments in the 1930s.

When neutrons (parts of an atom) strike a uranium atom, they cause it to split into smaller atoms. This process releases large amounts of energy. If the new neutrons strike other uranium atoms, a chain reaction occurs, which releases even larger amounts of energy. By 1942, when Enrico Fermi achieved the first controlled chain reaction, other scientists were already working to produce an atomic bomb.

▲ *Oppenheimer (left) and Groves discuss the results of the first atomic-bomb test in the New Mexico desert.*

The Manhattan Project

In 1939 Albert Einstein, on behalf of other top physicists in the US, wrote a letter to President Roosevelt. He explained that, as a result of developments in nuclear physics, it might be possible to make a bomb of huge explosive power. Roosevelt ordered a secret scientific program to produce the bomb. The matter was urgent. World War II had begun in Europe, and German physicists were also trying to make an atomic bomb. So were the British, but when the US entered the war, the British team joined the American program, which later became known by its military code name, the Manhattan Project. The main laboratory was at Oak Ridge, Tennessee, and the chief of the scientific team was J. Robert Oppenheimer. The whole project was under army control, led by General Leslie Groves.

Two types of bomb were produced. The first was a gunlike weapon, in which two pieces of uranium-235 were smashed into each other in a gun barrel, causing an instant explosion. This bomb, "Little Boy," was dropped on the Japanese city of Hiroshima on 6 August 1945. The second bomb, "Fat Man," used plutonium, created by irradiating uranium-238. It was tested in New Mexico on 16 July 1945 and dropped on Nagasaki on 9 August 1945. More than 100,000 people were killed by the two bombs and thousands more injured for life.

Atom bomb facts

"Little Boy" (so-called after Roosevelt's code name) was never tested before it was dropped on Hiroshima.
• An atomic bomb releases a million times more energy than an ordinary, chemical bomb of the same weight.
• In 1945 only the US had atomic weapons.

Human guinea pigs

Spectators watch a nuclear-bomb test in the US in 1955. Their only protection is dark glasses to guard their eyes against the flash. When the atom bombs were dropped on Japan in 1945, scientists did not know how dangerous radiation was.

Nuclear explosions—the three ways in which they kill

Nuclear bombs kill in three ways. The first is by heat: the extreme temperatures cause fatal burns up to 6 miles (10 km) away. The second is the blast or force of the explosion. The third killer, and the most sinister, is nuclear radiation. Direct radiation occurs with the blast and affects everything within the vicinity of the explosion. Then there is fallout, a highly radioactive fine dust, which travels miles away from the site of the explosion. Parts of it are active for only a short time; others are active for centuries, causing long-term and fatal illnesses, such as cancer, in humans.

During the 1950s people feared a nuclear war, and some built bomb shelters in their houses or backyards to protect themselves from an atomic explosion. At the same time, most governments carried out civil-defense nuclear war programs. To be effective, fallout shelters had to be underground, behind thick concrete barriers, and equipped with everything necessary for people to live in them for two weeks.

▲*Children test the escape hatch of a bomb shelter on their property in Bronxville, New York.*

◄ *Schoolchildren practice bomb drill. Ducking under a desk might guard against a firework, but not an atomic bomb.*

The Campaign for Nuclear Disarmament

In the 1950s the two great powers, the US and the Soviet Union, built up their weaponry until they had enough nuclear missiles and bombs to destroy the entire world. All nuclear nations carried out tests. The tests did not kill anyone directly, but they caused radioactive fallout over half the world.

Governments would not give up nuclear weapons as long as possible enemies had them, but many people believed that nuclear weapons should be banned. In Britain, the Campaign for Nuclear Disarmament (CND, founded in 1958) led the opposition. Popular protests took place in most other Western countries as well, but not in the Soviet Union, where they were forbidden. In the 1980s, Britain saw a rise in peaceful protest rallies against nuclear cruise missiles.

The first test ban treaty, which stopped tests above the ground, was agreed in 1963. Other agreements followed. The end of the Cold War in 1989 ended the threat of large-scale nuclear war and led to the removal of nuclear missiles in Europe and North America.

▲ *Demonstrators protesting against French nuclear tests in the Pacific. France was one of the last countries to end nuclear tests, in 1996.*

▶ *The first underwater atom bomb was tested at Bikini atoll on 25 July 1946. The gigantic water column produced by the explosion rose to 5,000 feet (1,500 meters).*

1940

1941

1942

1943

1944

1945

1946

1947

1948

1949

▶ *The crew of the B-29 Super-fortress, the Enola Gay, which dropped the atom bomb on Hiroshima on 6 August.*

▶ *The charred remains of Hiroshima after the bomb.*

Atom bomb facts

Nagasaki was only bombed because the original target was under cloud.

The Americans actually planned to drop three atomic bombs, but after Nagasaki it was obvious that the Japanese were going to surrender, and Truman didn't want to kill any more people.

The *Enola Gay* was named after its captain's mother.

WAR
US drops atomic bombs on Japan

14 AUGUST Japan surrendered unconditionally today after devastating attacks by the US with a new superweapon. Five days ago an atomic bomb destroyed the Japanese city of Nagasaki. It was the second A-bomb (a thousand times more powerful than the largest ordinary bomb) the Americans had dropped in a week. The first wiped out Hiroshima, killing about 78,000 people instantly and injuring many more. Until Nagasaki, in spite of the destruction of almost the entire Japanese Navy and the near starvation of Japanese people, the Japanese would not surrender.

President Truman took the final decision to drop the bomb, and Stalin was informed that the US had a new weapon of "unusual destructive power." Although its explosive capacity was known, the long-term effect of radiation is not yet understood, even by the scientists who developed it.

Pippi Long-stocking

A Swedish children's book, by Astrid Lindgren, *Pippi Langstrump*, is raising a lot of interest. Pippi is a nine-year-old red-headed orphan who lives by herself and believes her dead mother is an angel. Clumsy and untidy, she wears stockings that don't match but has superhuman strength and can pick up a horse. She tells fibs and chatters nonsense most of the time.

▲ *A copy of the German edition of* Pippi Longstocking.

WAR
Red Army liberates Auschwitz

▶ *A prisoner in a liberated concentration camp points an accusing finger at a guard.*

27 JANUARY Advancing Soviet forces today overran the concentration camp at Auschwitz in southern Poland, one of the camps which tried to fulfill the Nazi "Final Solution"—the annihilation of Europe's Jews. Here and at other camps the horrifying scenes of obscene cruelty so enraged the Soviet soldiers that many German guards were shot. Prisoners at Auschwitz had been herded naked into gas chambers and killed with poisonous gas (pellets dropped through the ceiling). The victims' clothing was recycled and valuables given to the SS. Gold fillings in their teeth were melted down. The corpses were burnt in giant furnaces. Estimates of the number killed in Auschwitz vary from 1 to 3 million.

LITERATURE
Orwell publishes *Animal Farm*

17 AUGUST Animal Farm, a new book by the British writer George Orwell, is an animal story, but also a bitter satire on Soviet communism. The animals rebel and create a society in which they are all equal. But the revolution is taken over by the leader of the pigs (Stalin) who declares, "All animals are equal but some animals are more equal than others."

The Big Three in conference

TREATIES

12 FEBRUARY The Allied leaders, Churchill, Roosevelt, and Stalin, have been meeting at Yalta in the Crimea for the past week to decide what will happen when the war ends. It is agreed that Germany will be occupied by Allied forces. The Soviet Union will remain dominant in eastern Europe, and Russia will gain some territory from Poland. Churchill is doubtful about Russian intentions in eastern Europe, despite Stalin's promise of free elections, but Roosevelt, who looks frail, is chiefly anxious to get Soviet help against Japan.

▲ *Churchill, Roosevelt, and Stalin at Yalta.*

Dresden destruction

WAR

14 FEBRUARY The beautiful old German city of Dresden has been destroyed in one of the heaviest bombing raids of the war. British Lancasters blasted the city last night, and American B-17s continued today. Up to half the population— 300,000 people—may have been killed or injured. The Germans seem to have put up very little resistance. The intensity of the bombing, and the right weather conditions, created a firestorm with such high temperatures that everything burst into flames. The need for this destruction has been questioned, especially since Germany's defeat is now certain.

▲ *Dresden in ruins.*

NEWS • 1945 • NEWS

6 March • Tito becomes leader of Yugoslavia with Soviet support.

12 April • President Roosevelt dies.

28 April • Italian partisans capture and kill Mussolini.

5 July • Labour Party wins British general election, defeating Winston Churchill.

23 November • General De Gaulle elected president of French provisional government.

Victory in Europe

WAR

8 MAY The war in Europe is finally over. For the Allies, this is the long-awaited VE (Victory in Europe) Day; for Germans it marks the miserable end of a terrible era. Yesterday, General Jodl, chief of staff of the German army, signed the agreement of unconditional surrender, but in reality, the war has been over for several days. The German forces in Italy surrendered on 29 April. Hitler shot himself in Berlin the following day, and the Red Army took over Berlin two days later. The main German forces in the west surrendered to Field Marshal Montgomery on 4 May.

▼ *Amid the ruins of Berlin, a soldier of the Red Army raises the Soviet flag on the Reichstag (parliament) building.*

The Birth of Bebop

Musicians in the clubs of Harlem, New York's African-American ghetto, have developed a new form of jazz called Bebop, or Bop for short. The name seems to have been suggested by the sound of the music. Some are saying that this is the beginning of modern jazz, as distinct from traditional. A leading figure is the trumpet player Dizzy Gillespie.

▼ *Dizzy Gillespie.*

First Cannes film festival

The international film festival held in Cannes, in the French resort on the Mediterranean, from 20 September is likely to become a popular yearly event. It was originally planned for 1939, but the war arrived. Prize-winning movies were *The Lost Weekend,* an American movie about alcoholism, and René Clément's *La Bataille du Rail,* a documentary about the French Resistance.

▲ *The seafront at Cannes.*

TRANSPORT

Vespa scooters marketed

1 SEPTEMBER You've seen a motorcycle, you've seen a moped, but have you seen a motor scooter yet? You soon will, for the Vespa is selling fast on the Italian market and looks set to hit other world markets. The motor scooter is not a new invention—a few were made in the 1920s but they were not popular then. The new vehicles are different. They come from Italy, from factories that made war supplies but have now turned to civilian production. The pioneer is the 125-cc Vespa, but it is certain to have many competitors soon. The Vespa has much smaller wheels than an ordinary motorcycle, and the engine is placed low, down near the rear wheel. But the chief difference is that the rider of a Vespa sits with his legs inside the machine, as if sitting on a chair, and not astride it. This means that he is shielded from the wind.

◀ *The first Vespa scooter.*

NEWS • 1946 • NEWS

13 June • *King Umberto II of Italy abdicates after referendum favoring a republic.*

4 July • *Philippines gain independence from US.*

19 August • *Thousands dead in Hindu–Muslim riots in Calcutta.*

19 August • *Civil war between nationalists and communists resumes officially in China.*

LAW

Nazis tried at Nuremberg

1 OCTOBER The first verdicts in the trials of Nazi war criminals in the German city of Nuremberg were announced today. The trials began last November, before a military tribunal set up by the Allies. In the main trial, 22 Nazi leaders were charged, including two former deputies of Hitler, Hess and Goering, though some notorious figures were missing, notably Hitler himself. Twelve of the 22 men being tried received death sentences. Although there is little sympathy for the top Nazis, the trials have raised legal doubts. The argument of lesser defendants is that, although they may have committed terrible acts, they were following government orders.

▶ *Nazis in the dock. Goering is on the left, Hess next to him.*

Heath Row Airport opens

TRANSPORT

31 MAY The new London Heath Row Airport, opened today in Hounslow, west London. Direct flights between the UK and the US have already begun. This airport replaces the former London Airport at Croydon, which has been in service since 1928 but is now too small for growing international traffic. The Heath Row site has nearly 3,000 acres (1,200 hectares) available, but another airport for the capital may soon be needed. Gatwick, in Sussex, is a likely future site.

Churchill speaks of "Iron Curtain"

POLITICS

5 MARCH "From...the Baltic to...the Adriatic, an Iron Curtain has descended across the Continent." Winston Churchill, Britain's wartime leader, made this grim remark in a speech today at Fulton, Missouri. He warned that the West is now threatened by a hostile power (the Soviet Union). In the first year of peace, people do not want to think about this.

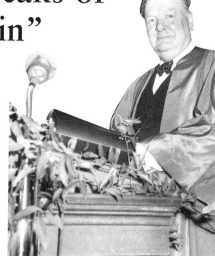

Bikini shocker bares all!

Old-timers strolling on Mediterranean beaches this summer have been shocked, or delighted, by the new two-piece bathing suits, which conceal very little of a woman's body. These skimpy garments are called bikinis. The name comes from the Bikini atoll, a coral island in the South Pacific which is the test site for American nuclear weapons. These bathing suits, it is said, also cause explosions, though less harmful ones!

Perón—president of Argentina

POLITICS

4 JUNE Today Argentina celebrates as General Juan Perón is installed as president. He became enormously popular among the middle class and industrial workers as minister of labor in the previous, military, government, and when he was dismissed his supporters threatened civil war. Strongly nationalistic and hostile to the US, he is influenced by fascist ideas. His glamorous wife, Eva ("Evita"), a former broadcaster, is a far more striking personality than her husband and is one of the chief reasons for his popularity with the masses. As Argentina is enjoying an export boom, rising national prosperity should pay for social reforms, which will also help his government.

US send CARE parcels

PEOPLE

1 JULY Much of Europe is in ruins and there are shortages everywhere. The US, by contrast, is booming. The standard of living is even higher than it was in 1941 and, not for the first time, Europe is depending on American charity. This year the US expects to send over 12 million tons of grain alone. But it is not just a matter of big government aid programs. Ordinary American families are packing up parcels of food and supplies for CARE (Co-operative for American Remittances to Europe). CARE packing cases can be seen throughout wartorn Europe.

▶ *President Juan Perón.*

1940

1941

Ancient remains come of age

1942

1943

American chemistry professor Willard Libby has developed a way to determine the age of ancient remains (such as the fossil above)—by testing them for carbon-14. Living plants and animals contain carbon-14, but after they die, it decays. Scientists know how much carbon-14 there is in each living thing and how quickly carbon-14 decays, so they can work out when it died.

1944

1945

1946

1947

1948

1949

Crew cross Pacific in wooden raft

QUESTS

7 OCTOBER Norwegian scientist Thor Heyerdahl and five crew members have succeeded in crossing the Pacific Ocean on a primitive wooden raft, the *Kon-Tiki*. The men set sail from Callao in Peru on 28 April this year, and on 7 August the *Kon-Tiki* crashed into a reef in the Tuamotu group of Pacific Islands. The sailors have covered 4,300 miles (6,900 km) on the raft, which is just 45 feet (13.7 meters) long.

Heyerdahl wanted to prove his theory that South Americans could have settled on the Pacific Islands thousands of years ago after sailing across the Pacific Ocean. He built the *Kon-Tiki* from logs of balsa wood tied with hemp rope. It had a fixed oar for steering and a large rectangular sail, held up by two masts. A small cabin provided protection from the weather.

Heyerdahl named the *Kon-Tiki* after a sun god worshiped by the Incas, the people who ruled Peru before it was conquered by the Spanish invaders in the 1500s. He has kept detailed records and is planning to write a book about the trip.

◀ *Today, the* Kon-Tiki *crew presented President Truman with the US flag that flew from the raft's mast.*

▲ *Winds and tides propelled the* Kon-Tiki *across the Pacific*

US offers financial aid to Europe

ECONOMICS

13 JULY Western European foreign ministers today agreed on a program for rebuilding their countries after the ravages of World War II.

It was drawn up by Secretary of State George Marshall, who offered help to Europe on 5 June. He said that the hardship being suffered by Europe was a new threat to peace.

Some people think that the offer is partly an attempt to counter Soviet influence in Europe. The Soviet Union and the Soviet-dominated countries of eastern Europe have rejected the Marshall Plan, but other countries have leapt at the chance. British Foreign Secretary Ernest Bevin said "When the Marshall proposals were announced I grabbed them with both hands. Europe can wait no longer." Many Europeans are experiencing hardship as great as that suffered in the war.

▲ *Poverty is a threat to peace.*

▶ *George C. Marshall, the "father of the Marshall Plan."*

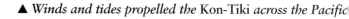

Two countries born out of British Empire

POLITICS

15 AUGUST India won its independence from British rule at midnight last night. It begins its new life as two separate countries, split on religious lines—a smaller India for Hindus and the new Pakistan for Muslims.

The plan to split the country was agreed by Britain's last viceroy in India, Louis, Lord Mountbatten. But many Muslims live in India and many Hindus live in Pakistan. Some will move, but conflict between those who stay behind seems inevitable.

◀ *Jawaharlal Nehru, first prime minister of India.*

▼ *The Bell X-1 shortly after its takeoff as the first supersonic plane.*

Plane breaks sound barrier

TECHNOLOGY

14 OCTOBER American pilot Chuck Yeager became the first man to fly faster than the speed of sound today. In the Bell X-1 research airplane he reached 670 miles per hour (1,072 km per hour) at an altitude of 40,000 feet (12,000 meters).

An airplane flying slower than the speed of sound sends sound waves ahead of it. When it nears the speed of sound, the effect of these waves on the aircraft causes buffeting, which can make it go out of control. The X-1's sleek, bulletlike shape was specially designed to reduce this buffeting. Yeager christened the X-1 *Glamorous Glennis*, in honor of his wife. He was flying today with two broken ribs, after an accident during a party last night.

Discovery of Dead Sea scrolls

ARCHEOLOGY

1947 An Arab Bedouin tribesman has discovered a hoard of ancient Jewish books in a cave near the Dead Sea in Palestine. Archeologists say that the ancient books—written on scrolls of leather and papyrus—belonged to the Essenes, a Jewish religious sect that was based at nearby Qumran from about 150 B.C. to A.D. 68. The scrolls include a set of rules for the Essene community and versions of books from the Old Testament of the Bible.

▶ *The Dead Sea scrolls are carefully examined after their recent discovery.*

New style of painting from Jackson Pollock

American artist Jackson Pollock has put away his easel and instead places his canvas on the floor and drips paint onto it. The images he produces are abstract— they are not recognizable as everyday objects or people. Pollock thinks his method allows him to express unconscious feelings. He says: "The painting has a life of its own. I try to let it come through."

▼ *Jackson Pollock paints in his unique style.*

Bell produces first transistor

TECHNOLOGY

DECEMBER A team at Bell Laboratories in the US has developed a tiny device that can control an electrical current and amplify it. The invention, known as a transistor, uses very little electrical current itself. The transistor can replace much larger valves and should make it possible for electrical circuits and the objects that rely on them—such as radio sets—to be made much smaller. The developers of this first transistor are Walter Brattain and John Bardeen.

1940
1941
1942
1943
1944
1945
1946
1947
1948
1949

1948

Creation of Israel causes conflict in Palestine

14 MAY Jewish leaders in Palestine have declared part of the country to be the new state of Israel. The proclamation was made eight hours before the deadline set for the end of British control in the region, and President Truman has recognized the new government under Prime Minister David Ben-Gurion.

The Jews have the backing of a 1947 United Nations resolution to split Palestine into separate Jewish and Arab areas. But Palestinian Arabs reject the resolution and are willing to fight to protect what they see as their land. Today, as British forces moved out, High Commissioner Sir Alan Cunningham appealed for peace, but forces from Egypt, Transjordan, Syria, and Iraq are arriving in Palestine to support the Arabs. The official Israeli army, the Haganah, is now 30,000 strong and war seems inevitable.

▲ *Jewish people arrive in Haifa, in Israel.*

▼ *Prime Minister Ben-Gurion (center left) watches the last British people leave Haifa.*

Human rights list drawn up

10 DECEMBER The General Assembly of the United Nations today agreed a list of individual rights that it believes should be accepted all over the world. They include the rights to life and freedom, to equal protection under the law, and to own property. The document declares that people should be allowed to meet peacefully with others, to express opinions freely, and to follow a religion. Everyone, it says, has the right to work, to receive equal pay for equal work, and to join trade unions.

The paper, known as the Universal Declaration of Human Rights, was approved by all the countries who voted at today's meeting in Paris. But Saudi Arabia, South Africa, and the eastern European countries dominated by the Soviet Union all abstained from the vote.

◄ *Former First Lady Eleanor Roosevelt helped to draw up the paper.*

Speedy new oven

Life in the kitchen has sped up with production of the first microwave ovens, invented by American Percy LeBaron Spencer. Food inside is bombarded with radiation of a very short wavelength, which penetrates the food and heats it from within, much more quickly than a conventional oven.

National Party elected in South Africa

POLITICS

28 MAY The National Party in South Africa—which backs a policy of "apartheid" under which whites, mixed-race, and black South Africans would be kept separate—has won a surprise victory in the all-white general election.

Nationalist leader Daniël Malan is the new prime minister after the resignation of United Party leader Jan Smuts. The National Party, supported by the Afrikaners (descendants of the Dutch who settled in South Africa from the 17th century) want to maintain white rule.

▲ *The newly-elected National Party cabinet in South Africa.*

POLITICS Gandhi assassinated by Hindu fanatic

30 JANUARY Indian nationalist leader Mahatma Gandhi has been murdered in New Delhi. He was walking with his grandnieces to a prayer meeting when he was shot by Nathuram Godse, a fanatical follower of the Hindu religion. Within half an hour he was dead. Godse was caught by an Indian Air Force sergeant and taken away.

Gandhi secured India's freedom from British rule last year, and had also called for an end to the religious fighting between Hindus and Muslims which has claimed thousands of lives. Recently he gave up eating in an appeal for Hindu-Muslim unity.

New camera takes pictures in a flash

American inventor Edwin Land has created a camera that can develop and print its own photographs—within one minute of taking the picture. The Polaroid Land camera weighs 5 lbs (2.25 kg) and costs $95. Prints are black and white, and coating them with varnish is advised to protect the surface from damage.

▼ *Edwin Land with his own Polaroid picture.*

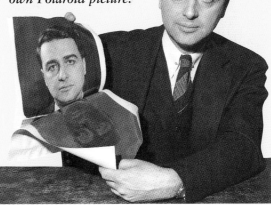

Allies fly in to feed Berlin

POLITICS

26 JUNE American and British aircraft are flying food and materials in for the people of West Berlin, who have had their supplies cut off by the Soviet authorities in the eastern half of the city. Berlin lies deep in the Soviet-controlled eastern part of Germany, but the city's western sector is controlled by the Americans, British, and French.

Two days ago the Soviets cut off all road, rail, and canal routes into West Berlin in an attempt to force the western Allies out of the city. In reply, the RAF and the US Air Force launched Operation Vittles from airfields in western Germany.

▶ *The Allies say they need 2,500 tons of food a day to feed West Berliners.*

Communists take control in eastern Europe

27 FEBRUARY In Czechoslovakia today communist Prime Minister Krement Gottwald announced that 12 right-wing and center government ministers have resigned and have been replaced with communists and left-wing Social Democrats. Czech President Edvard Benes has accepted the changes. If there is any opposition, the Soviet Union is threatening to send the Red Army into Czechoslovakia.

The Soviet Union and its fearsome leader Joseph Stalin now have an iron grip on the countries of eastern Europe. In Bulgaria, a Communist republic was declared in 1946 when King Simeon abdicated. Last year, King Michael of Romania was forced to abdicate, and the country is now a communist republic, and in Hungary, Soviet-backed communists took power in a coup and have proclaimed a new constitution based on that of the Soviet Union. Poland, too, has a Communist government. Yugoslavia, led by former partisan fighter Marshal Tito, has been the only country to resist Stalin. It has been trying to maintain its independence from the USSR.

▲ *Communist Prime Minister Gottwald delivers a speech in Prague.*

Truman beats polls

3 NOVEMBER In one of the biggest upsets in American presidential election history, Democrat Harry S. Truman has proved everyone wrong. Experts and opinion polls predicted a big victory for Truman's Republican opponent, Thomas Dewey. But this morning Truman is still the president, and the Democrats have control of both Houses of Congress. Newspaper editors have been embarrassed by the result. The *Washington Post*'s first edition ran the headline "Mounting Dewey Vote Indicates Victory," while the *Chicago Tribune* was bolder still, printing "Dewey Defeats Truman." Truman first became president when Franklin D. Roosevelt died in office on 12 April 1945.

◄ *President Truman laughs at the early edition of the* Chicago Tribune.

Fanny Blankers-Koen, star of Olympic Games

Dutch athlete Fanny Blankers-Koen outran her rivals at the London Olympic Games in August, winning four gold medals. The 30-year-old triumphed in the 100 meters, the 200 meters, the 100 meters hurdles, and helped the Dutch team win the 4 x 100 meters relay.

▼ *Fanny Blankers-Koen, the "flying housewife."*

Britain introduces free medical service

POLITICS

5 JULY Britain's Labour Government today launched the National Health Service (NHS), which offers free medical treatment for every citizen from birth to death. Drugs prescribed by doctors, dental work, glasses, and even wigs will be provided free under the NHS scheme.

It is the main plank of the new "welfare state," in which the government takes more responsibility for helping the poor, old, or sick. After the hardships of World War II, Labour won the 1945 general election with a promise to provide a better life for the whole population, poor and rich alike.

A new national insurance scheme promising universal financial help for the elderly and the unemployed also begins today.

The government's Health Minister, Aneurin Bevan, faced great opposition to the NHS plans from the British Medical Association and some doctors and dentists. Last night Prime Minister Clement Atlee said that he expected "difficulties" with staff and accommodation, but that these could be overcome "with patience and goodwill."

▲ *An NHS nurse gives advice to British children.*

New long-playing records

The CBS Corporation has unveiled the long-playing record, or "LP." Traditional records have room for only a single song. The new LP, developed by Peter Goldmark, can carry longer pieces because the grooves on the disk are narrower and it plays at 33⅓ revolutions per minute rather than the usual 78 rpm. But music lovers will have to invest in new record players—the existing ones will not play at the new speed.

Bradman retires

SPORT

14 AUGUST Australian cricket captain Don Bradman has made a surprising last appearance for his country. His batting dominated international cricket for 20 years, but today, on only the second ball, he was bowled out for 0 by England's Eric Hollies.

Bradman, a farmer's son from New South Wales, has played in 52 Test matches and scored 100 runs or more 29 times. His Test total is 6,996 runs. Superb concentration and an ability to judge the flight of the ball have made him seem unbeatable. He is also a brilliant fielder and a successful team captain. In his 12 years as Australian captain, his team has not lost a single series of matches. Today's match once again ended in triumph for Australia.

Stylish family car launched in Britain

The Morris Minor was launched in October. It is wider than its rival cars, allowing room for a large, comfortable interior. The extra width also means that the Minor does not rock on corners—the car is more stable because the wheels are farther apart. Designed by Alec Issigonis at the Morris Works, Oxford, England, the Morris has a small 918-cc engine and a top speed of 62 mph (100 km per hour).

▼ *The Morris Minor.*

FASHION FOCUS

The many and rapid changes of the 20th century have been reflected in the clothes people have worn. The result has been a kaleidoscope of styles and colors, from the ruffles of the 1910s to the simple but stylish clothes of the late 1950s.

Fashion became a merry-go-round in the second half of the century, and clothes that went out of style inevitably became trendy again a few decades later. But there has been steady progress toward clothes that are easy on the eye and comfortable to wear. Technology has had an enormous impact: synthetic textiles such as nylon and Lycra; zippers and velcro fasteners; computerized manufacturing; and new dyes all make clothes cheaper and easier to wash and wear.

▶ *Knee-length skirts and loose clothing with influences from Arabia in the 1920s.*

◀ *Long skirts, tiny waists, and an S-shaped profile in the 1900s.*

Top designer Christian Dior introduces the New Look

In the spring of 1947, Christian Dior, a French designer, astonished the fashion world with a collection he called the New Look. At a stroke, he brought an end to the straight lines, square shoulders, and short skirts of the wartime austerity years, when—at least in Europe—clothes were styled for economy and strictly rationed.

The New Look featured soft, unpadded shoulders, a fitted top that showed off the bust, a well-defined narrow waist, and a full, billowing, long skirt. The resulting wide-hipped "hourglass" look, extravagant on fabrics and very feminine, caught on around the world. It was a romantic style that in many ways looked back to the glamour of the previous century. After years of working hard for the war effort, women wanted to be womanly again.

▲ *Background: The 1950s saw a trend toward brightly patterned fabrics, like this piece of cloth. Different colors and shapes were mixed and matched in the designs.*

▲ *A typical New Look outfit. Accessories, such as hats and gloves, were an essential part of this style.*

174

Bathing belles and the birth of the bikini

The first bathing suits covered most of the body—women were even expected to wear black stockings and a dress in the water. In 1909, Annette Kellerman, an Australian swimmer, caused a sensation by stepping onto a California beach in a one-piece knitted bathing suit just like a man's. When she wore it in Boston, she was arrested for indecency. Modest by today's standards, it left too much flesh uncovered and too little to the imagination.

In 1946 the bikini was unveiled by its inventor, a French car designer named Louis Réard. This garment was a new two-piece swimming costume that covered no more than a bra and briefs did.

By the end of the century increasing awareness of the damage done by exposing skin to the sun encouraged many people to start covering up again.

▲ *After the shock of the first tiny bikinis, 1950s two-pieces were much more modest.*

▼ *Bathing belles from the early 20th century display a variety of different bathing suits.*

▶ *Daring miniskirts and thigh-boots in the 1960s.*

◀ *Ponytails, circle-skirts, and bobby socks in the 1950s.*

▶ *Big shoulder pads: power-dressing for the money-conscious 1980s.*

Drawing the line

When nylon stockings came onto the market in 1940, they had a seam running down the back. Nylon became scarce later on in World War II so many women drew a seam on their bare legs.

Hot pants and flared pants are all the rage

Fashion is always changing. Every so often, it enters a really adventurous phase. In the 1960s, people started to dress in their own individual styles. In order to stand out from the crowd, women might wear miniskirts, geometric haircuts, and high plastic boots; men dressed in tight jeans, collarless jackets, and shoes with pointed toes.

In the early 1970s, fashion entered its most bizarre period this century. People were ready for an extreme look, and a generation of inspired designers created clothes which drew elements from many eras and cultures.

Footwear developed platform soles up to 8 inches (20 cm) high, and hospitals dealt with hundreds of ankle injuries as teenagers fell off their clumpy shoes. Young men with big sideburns wore shiny satin jackets with wide lapels; fabrics were enhanced with vivid embroidery; pants were tight, high-waisted, and extravagantly flared, like sailor's bell-bottoms; "tank tops" were skimpy versions of the T-shirt; and hair for both sexes was long and flowing.

▲ *Elton John typified the flamboyant style of 1970s rock stars.*

▼ *Some 1970s women wore "hot pants," tight shorts cut very high to show off their bottoms.*

Timeline (left margin)

POLITICS

Mao's communist victory in China

▶ *Shanghai residents celebrate the founding of the new government.*

1 OCTOBER In Peking today Mao Tse-tung proclaimed China a communist republic. The former nationalist government of Chiang Kai-shek has fled following the defeat of its troops by the communist People's Liberation Army.

China's civil war between the nationalists and communists began in the 1920s. It was put on hold to fight Japan in World War II, but started again after Japan surrendered in 1945. The nationalists were supported by the US, who opposed communism. Although the nationalists far outnumbered the communists, they were poorly led, and the communists won widespread backing in the countryside because they encouraged peasants to seize land from the landowners.

The communists captured several nationalist strongholds this year, including the nationalist capital Nanking on April 24, and China's largest city, Shanghai, on 26 May.

▲ *Mao Tse-tung, chairman of the People's Government.*

Britons sharpen up their image

Britons are looking forward to sharpening up their appearance. Clothes rationing, introduced in 1941 during World War II, finally ended on 15 May. Clothing stores are now holding special sales to celebrate. But the government has warned that it has the power to freeze prices if they go up too sharply.

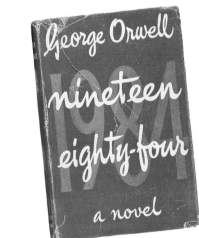

LITERATURE

George Orwell's vision of the future is published

10 JUNE British writer George Orwell's novel *Nineteen Eighty-Four*, published today, describes a future in which every aspect of life is controlled by the government. In his imaginary country everyone must worship "Big Brother," the head of the ruling political party, and history is rewritten to fit in with the present. The book's hero, Winston Smith, tries to resist but is arrested and tortured by the Thought Police. Orwell says that the book is a warning of what might happen if a strong central government was taken to its logical extreme.

▼ *People celebrate the founding of the communist German Democratic Republic.*

POLITICS

Germany divided into East and West

12 OCTOBER The Soviet-controlled eastern part of Germany has become a communist state, the German Democratic Republic. Its first president is Wilhelm Pieck, and Otto Grotewohl is prime minister. On 23 May, British-, American-, and French-held parts of western Germany united to form the democratic state of the Federal Republic of Germany, with its capital in Bonn. The western half of Berlin remains Allied territory, deep in East Germany.

▼ *Konrad Adenauer, the new Chancellor of West Germany.*

176

▲ *The new 2CV has a tiny 375-cc engine.*

Citroën's new 2CV is result of challenge

French car manufacturer Citroën has launched a cheap, tough car aimed mainly at France's peasant farmers. Citroën's managing director challenged designers to design a car that could carry a basket of eggs across a plowed field without any of them breaking. The 2CV's floor is mounted on a spring and attached to the wheels by moving arms, so the car copes easily with the bumpiest surfaces. It is also inexpensive to run, averaging 64 miles (100 km) to a gallon (5 liters) of gas.

New alliance is formed

4 APRIL The US, Britain, Canada, Italy, France, Belgium, and the Netherlands were among 12 countries to sign a defense alliance today in Washington, DC. The countries agree that "an armed attack against one or more of them in Europe or North America shall be considered an attack against them all."

The alliance, called the North Atlantic Treaty Organization (NATO), is a response to the strength of Soviet forces in communist eastern Europe. The US has promised to provide military aid to NATO countries in Europe. Last year Britain, France, Belgium, Luxembourg, and the Netherlands signed the Brussels Treaty, a European defense alliance, but they still needed help against the Soviets.

▲ *The NATO flag and the Eiffel Tower, Paris.*

Soviet Union tests A-bomb

23 SEPTEMBER American and British leaders announced today that the Soviet Union has developed and tested its own atomic bomb. Western politicians knew that the Soviets were working on a bomb, but believed that they were two or three years away from achieving their goal. The explosion recently took place in the remote Soviet republic of Kazakhstan in central Asia. It raises the tension between the Soviet Union and the US and is sure to accelerate the "arms race" to build more powerful weapons.

Fausto Coppi thrills Italian cycling fans

▼ *Coppi has won several championships in cycling.*

JULY This summer Italian racing cyclist Fausto Coppi has won both of Europe's great cycle races— the Tour de France and the Giro d'Italia. In both races he beat his great rival and fellow Italian Gino Bartali into second place. Coppi has taken Bartali's place as the favorite of Italian cycling fans—he is known as the *campionissimo*, the "champion of champions."

The Tour de France and the Giro d'Italia are "stage races"—they consist of several separate sections, or stages. In this year's Giro, Coppi shrugged off Bartali on a grueling stage through the Italian Alps, winning by more than 20 minutes. Coppi has won the Giro twice before, but this is his first victory in the Tour de France.

NEWS • 1949 • NEWS

1 March • American boxer Joe Louis retires, aged 34, after almost 12 years as world heavyweight champion.

18 April • The Republic of Ireland is proclaimed.

27 July • The de Havilland Comet, the world's first jet airliner, flies for the first time.

28 December • The US Air Force reports, after an official inquiry, that "flying saucers" do not exist.

1950

1951

1952

1953

1954

1955

1956

1957

1958

1959

1950

The Cold War between the US and the Soviet Union ran through the 1950s. As the decade began, both countries had atomic bombs and the threat of a devastating nuclear war hung over the world. A race began to outgun the other side with more powerful weapons. Allied soldiers were sent to Korea to fight the forces of communism. The Soviets formed the Warsaw Pact of communist states to oppose the American-led NATO alliance.

But for many people in the US and western Europe, international tension was balanced by home comfort. Particularly after 1955, they enjoyed high wages, large cars, and home comforts like vacuum cleaners and washing machines. Inventions familiar in the modern world made their first appearance.

Cardboard credit

Americans Frank Macnamara and Ralph Schneider have launched a "credit card," which allows users to sign for dinner or drinks on account and then pay at the end of the month. Macnamara had the idea when he was unable to pay a restaurant bill because he had left his wallet at home. Made of cardboard, his "Diners' Club" card can be used in the 28 restaurants listed on the back.

Charlie Brown heads gang in new cartoon strip

2 OCTOBER The new comic strip *Peanuts* made its first appearance today. The daily strip, starring a determined little boy by the name of Charlie Brown, is the creation of American cartoonist Charles Schulz.

Charlie Brown is leader of a group of friends. Lucy is a strong-willed and sometimes bullying girl. Her younger brother, Linus, is low on confidence and drags his "security blanket" around because it makes him feel safe. Then there is Schroeder, a clever boy who spends his life playing pieces by the German composer Beethoven on his toy piano. But Charlie's pet dog Snoopy is perhaps the cleverest of them all.

Peanuts is part of a new wave of cartoons which use humor to examine serious matters. The strip shows how cruel children can be to one another, but also uses their games and quarrels to examine the way adults behave.

Schulz, a freelance cartoonist, had to persevere with his strip—originally called *L'il Folks*—six newspaper syndicates rejected it before he had his break.

◄ *Cartoonist Charles Schulz.*

◄ *From left, Linus, Marcia, Charlie Brown, Peppermint Patty, and Snoopy.*

NEWS • 1950 • NEWS

17 June • US surgeon R.H. Lawler performs the first human kidney transplant.

28 June • Soccer fans are shocked as England lose 0–1 to the US in the World Cup in Brazil.

3 September • In Japan, 250 are killed and 300,000 injured by a typhoon.

26 November • Chinese forces join the North Korean side in the Korean War.

▲ *The invaders build a bridge to help transport supplies and men into Tibet.*

Soccer victory for Uruguay

16 JULY Brazil is in shock tonight. In front of 200,000 fans in the Maracana Stadium in Rio de Janeiro, Brazil's soccer team was unexpectedly beaten 2–1 by Uruguay in the deciding match of the World Cup.

Today's game was not exactly the World Cup Final—it was the last match in a final pool of four teams. Brazil were hot favorites after beating Sweden 7–1 and Spain 6–1 in the other two games in the final pool. But Uruguay, who came from 0–1 behind, won against the odds.

Chinese invade Tibet

WAR

25 DECEMBER The spiritual leader of Tibet, the Dalai Lama, was unable to stop the invasion today of troops from the communist People's Republic of China. The communist forces swept into Tibet, driving back the Tibetan army as they headed for its capital, Lhasa. The Tibetan government appealed to India for help, and there are now fears for the Dalai Lama's safety.

Tibet is an independent state to the southwest of China, which has claimed the right to Tibet for many years. In May, China's Chairman Mao Tse-tung offered Tibet a form of self-government if it became part of China. The Tibetans are now paying the price for not taking up that offer.

Farina wins first Formula One World Motor Racing Championship

Veteran Italian racing driver Giuseppe Farina has won the first World Drivers' Championship at Silverstone in an Alfa Romeo. In the race before this one, the Italian Grand Prix, Farina's Alfa Romeo teammate Juan Fangio was leading the Championship, but had to retire from the race and Farina won.

▲ *Giuseppe Farina chalked up a time of 2 hours and 23.6 seconds at Silverstone.*

◄ *A Black worker pushes garbage past a beach reserved for white people on the Cape coast, in South Africa.*

People to be kept separate by color in South Africa

POLITICS

1950 Under the South African government's policy of apartheid, the white minority of South Africans is to be kept separate from the nonwhites.

The Nationalist government has made apartheid legal. The Population Registration Act splits all South Africans into one of four groups—White, Black (Bantu), Colored (mixed race), or Asian—and each person has to carry a pass that identifies their racial group. The Group Areas Act splits cities into strict separate areas for the different racial groups. For example, Bantus, Coloreds, and Asians may not live in the White area.

Racial segregation existed in South Africa before the Nationalist Party was elected in 1948, but the Nationalists, led by Prime Minister Daniel François Malan, have strengthened the policy.

War in Korea

WAR

31 DECEMBER The tension that has been brewing between the US and the Soviet Union for five years (the Cold War) has exploded into armed conflict in the Korean peninsula. This is the first direct military conflict of the Cold War, in which events seem to be heating up.

In 1945, when a defeated Japan had all its overseas territories taken away, Korea was occupied by Soviet and US forces. For convenience, they divided it into two parts: the Soviets administered the territory north of the "38th parallel"—a line drawn at 38°N latitude—and the south went to the US. Two years ago, the USSR set up a communist administration in the north under Kim Il Sung, while the US backed a pro-Western regime in the south.

On 25 June 1950, North Korea suddenly invaded South Korea. United Nations troops under General MacArthur, and some US troops, rushed to help the South Koreans. By October, MacArthur had driven the communists nearly back up to the Chinese border, when China intervened. This month UN forces pulled out of Pyongyang, the North Korean capital, and as the year ends they are in full retreat. President Truman is now said to be considering using the atomic bomb to stop the war.

▲ *General Douglas MacArthur in Korea.*

◄ *US parachutists in Korea.*

Calf born to virgin cow

SCIENCE

1950 Scientists at the University of Wisconsin have successfully reared a calf born to a cow that has never been mated with a bull. They took a fertilized egg from the womb of one cow and transferred it to another cow, who eventually gave birth to the calf in the normal way.

This technique represents a potentially vital new method for improving herds. Artificial insemination, developed in Russia and Denmark early this century, enables a pedigree bull to sire (father) thousands of calves; now the fertilized ova of a prize dairy cow can fully develop in another cow. This method could also be used on other species, including humans.

▶ *Survivors of the earthquake dig for victims in the rubble of destroyed houses.*

Earthquake devastates Iran

DISASTERS

29 JANUARY Three massive earthquakes have shaken southern Iran. 1,000 people are reported dead and another 1,500 injured.

The damage is widespread. Twenty cities and villages have been destroyed completely, and the capital city of south-central Iran, Shiraz, which is situated on the lowlands within the Zagros Mountains, has also been affected by the devastation. Many ports on the southern Iranian coast have been completely wiped out by tidal waves.

Death of Jolson

ENTERTAINMENT

23 OCTOBER One of the world's favorite entertainers has died, aged 70. Al Jolson—born in Lithuania as Asa Yoelson—emigrated to the US with his family in 1895. With his ebullient personality and strong singing voice, he became a fixture of the vaudeville circuit before winning fame on Broadway and in Hollywood. He became an international star with *The Jazz Singer* in 1927, the first motion picture to use sound. Earlier this year he was still working, entertaining US troops in Korea.

▲ *Al Jolson at Warner's Theatre in New York.*

▼ *From left: Lauren Bacall, Humphrey Bogart, June Havoc, Evelyn Keyes, and Danny Kaye. Many Hollywood stars protested against the anticommunist "witchhunt."*

▼ *McCarthy points out US communist centers.*

McCarthy makes surprise allegations

POLITICS

22 FEBRUARY The Senate's Foreign Relations Committee today opened investigations into the extraordinary allegations made by Wisconsin Senator Joseph R. McCarthy earlier this month. McCarthy calmly announced that he had a list of 205 employees of the State Department who were also card-carrying members of the Communist Party. His implication is that the Secretary of State, Dean Acheson, and by extension President Truman, are turning a blind eye to the subversive activities of red agitators in the corridors of power.

McCarthy has whipped up a storm of anticommunist hysteria in the press. Following so soon after revelations that Soviet spies stole the secrets of the US atomic bomb, McCarthy's stance as the defender of American values has struck a profound chord with the American public.

Ho Chi Minh vs Emperor Bao Dai

POLITICS

7 FEBRUARY Vietnam, the eastern part of the Indochina peninsula and officially a self-governing French colony, was effectively divided into two different countries today. A week after the Soviet Union recognized Ho Chi Minh's communist administration in Hanoi as the government of Vietnam, western nations—led by France, Britain, and the US—today agreed to endorse Vietnam's traditional emperor, Bao Dai, who is based in Saigon. Ho Chi Minh's forces, known as the Viet Minh, are fighting a guerrilla war against French rule, as represented by Bao Dai. Similar stand-offs are taking place in Laos and Cambodia.

▶ *Ho Chi Minh.*

Catholics persecuted in Hungary

RELIGION

30 JUNE Hungary's communist rulers today ordered the closure of all university theology departments. It is another step in the government's policy of persecuting the Roman Catholic church, which plays such a large part in the lives of most Hungarians. Priests have been arrested and churches closed.

Last year Cardinal Joseph Mindszenty, the primate of Hungary, was sentenced to life imprisonment on trumped-up charges of treason and black market currency dealings. The jailed priest has now become a potent symbol of political and religious resistance to communism.

▲ *The Holy Crown of St. Stephen is a symbol of the Catholic Church in Hungary.*

▶ *Cardinal Joseph Mindszenty.*

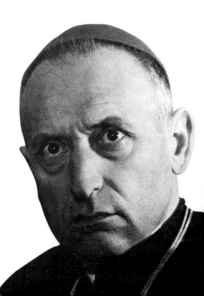

AUTOMOBILES

Car facts

USA: Before World War I there were nearly 2,000 carmakers. By 1976 the number had shrunk to 11.

Britain: Speed limits for cars before 1896 were 4 miles per hour (6.4 km per hour) in the country and 2 miles per hour (3.2 km per hour) in towns.

Germany: The first national freeway (*autobahn*) system in Europe was built in the 1930s.

The car industry is based on the gasoline-driven, internal-combustion engine, invented in the 1880s. Steam engines and electric batteries were also tried, but unsuccessfully.

The first affordable mass-produced car was the American Model T Ford, produced in Detroit since 1908. By 1929 Detroit was making 5 million cars a year. In 1950, the US still produced 65 percent of the world's cars, but since then the industry has become more international. Japan became the world's largest producer of cars in the 1980s.

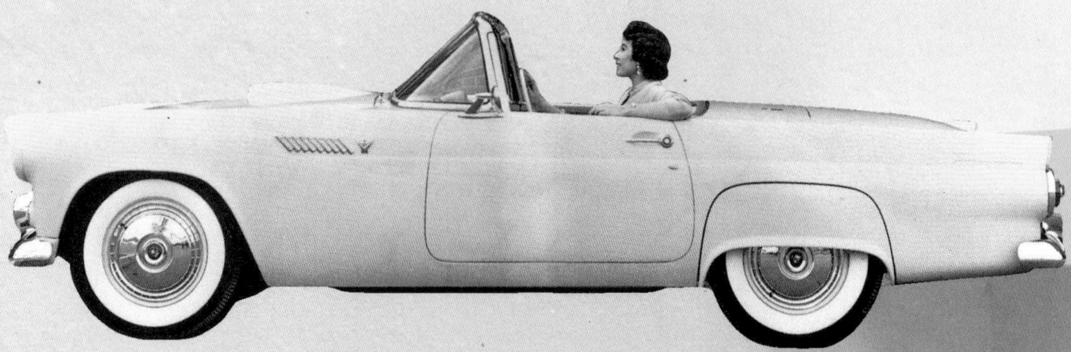

◀ *Ford's Thunderbird sports sedan hit the road exactly 50 years after the "Tin Lizzie" (Model T).*

The age of the car

If there was ever a motorist's paradise, it was North America in the 1950s. Cars were very large and luxurious. Roads were excellent, traffic was light, and gasoline was cheap (less than 10 cents a gallon). No one worried about air pollution. People loved their cars. Styling was exotic, with great fins on the rear wings and huge chrome bumpers. Even in poor parts of town, the streets were lined with cars that were often grander and more comfortable than the houses. In Europe cars were smaller and less showy than American cars, although some European cars cost more to buy. The biggest seller was the German Volkswagen, or people's car, a tough little rear-engined vehicle, nicknamed for its appearance, the Beetle.

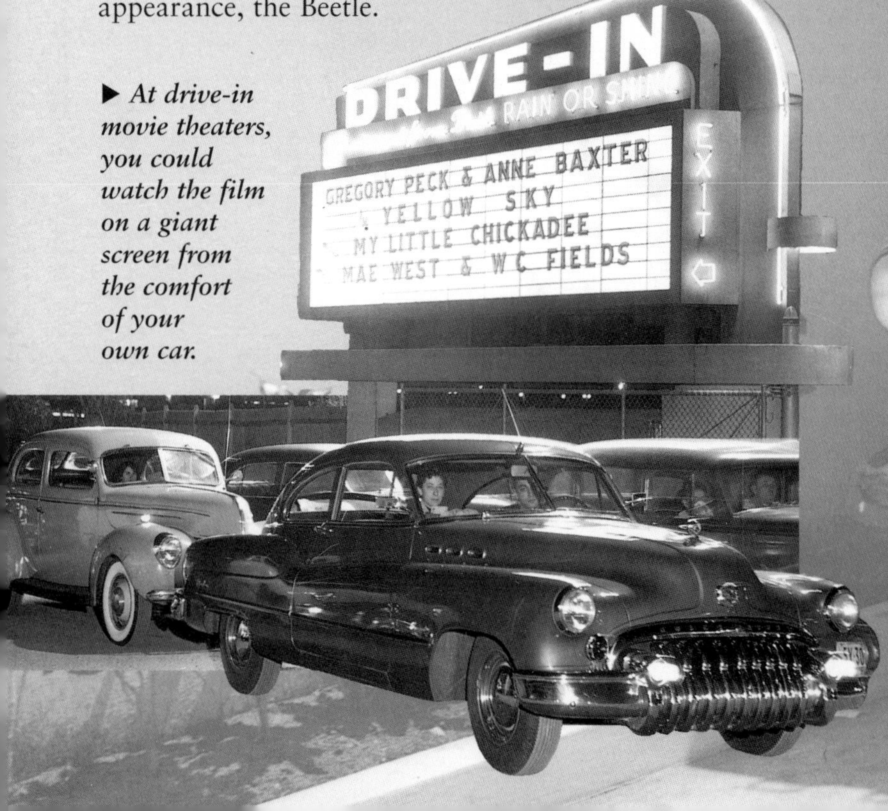

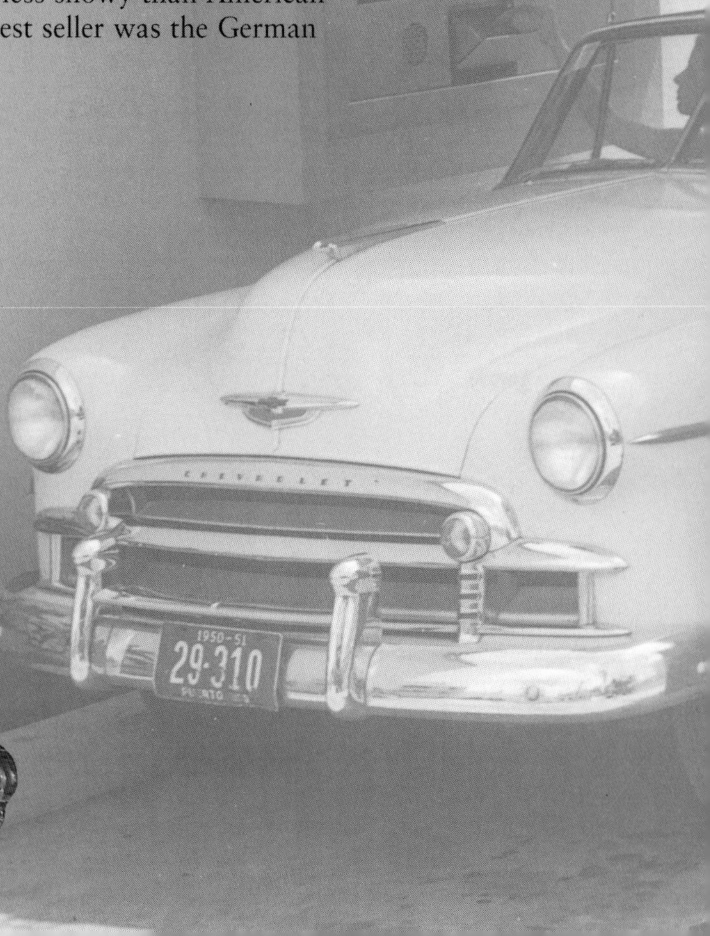

DRIVE-IN
RAIN OR SHINE
GREGORY PECK & ANNE BAXTER
YELLOW SKY
MY LITTLE CHICKADEE
MAE WEST & W C FIELDS
EXIT

▶ *At drive-in movie theaters, you could watch the film on a giant screen from the comfort of your own car.*

29-310

Cars race ahead

The first specially built motor-racing circuit opened for the French Grand Prix in Le Mans in 1906. The American Indianapolis Raceway was first used in 1909, when it was a dirt track. Le Mans and Indianapolis are still famous circuits, but motor racing has grown and branched out into many varieties, such as stock-car racing, with stripped-down, souped-up sedan cars, or drag racing, which takes place on a short, straight course at speeds of up to 250 miles per hour (400 km per hour).

◄ *Alberto Ascari wins at Mar del Plata, Argentina (1950). Like his father, Antonio, the Italian ace was killed aged 36 while testing a car.*

▼ *The Brazilian driver Ayrton Senna, in a Williams-Honda, dominated the world Grand Prix championship in the early 1990s, until a fatal crash in Imola, Italy, in 1994.*

▼ *A customer withdraws cash from the first drive-in bank in Puerto Rico.*

Cars change shape

Cars have come a long way since the early models, called "horseless carriages" because of their shape. In the early 1920s, manufacturers began to make frequent changes in car style to encourage people to buy the latest models, rather than the less expensive used cars.

▼ *Oldsmobile's "Curved Dash" 1901*

◄ *Austin 10 1932*

◄ *Mercedes Benz 1974*

▶ *Rambler Station Wagon 1956*

▶ *Ford "Ka" 1996*

1950
1951
1952
1953
1954
1955
1956
1957
1958
1959

▲ *A nuclear reactor at the testing station in Arco Valley, Idaho.*

TECHNOLOGY

Electricity produced by nuclear reactor

29 DECEMBER The US Atomic Energy Commission today revealed that nuclear energy, so far used as a weapon of war, has now been successfully put to peaceful use. This year the Experimental Breeder Reactor (EBRI) at the Department of Energy's Idaho National Engineering Laboratory (nuclear reactor testing and energy research station) just outside Arco, in Idaho, has produced a steady supply of electricity to power a range of equipment. The station has become the first in the country to produce useful electric power from atomic energy. The EBRI makes more fuel than it needs, and this creates steam to drive turbines which generate electricity in large enough quantities to operate lights and small household equipment.

Nuclear facts

Albert Einstein predicted the power of the atom with his famous equation $E=mc^2$.

•

The first working nuclear power station was a small pressurized water reactor at Obninsk, in Russia, opened in 1954.

POLITICS

MacArthur ordered home by Truman

11 APRIL President Truman today fired General Douglas MacArthur from his command of the US Army in Korea and from all his other posts. The two men have a long history of disagreements, which culminated this week when MacArthur publicly criticized Truman's strategy in Korea—in particular his refusal to declare outright war on China, whose invasion force now has the UN on the run. "We must win," said MacArthur, "There is no substitute for victory."

The President's policy, which aims above all to contain the fighting, will now prevail. "So far we have prevented World War III," he declared, maintaining that his strategy has been successful. MacArthur's replacement in Korea is Lieutenant General Matthew Ridgway.

◀ *General Douglas MacArthur.*

▲ *Ava Gardner (right) in* Show Boat.

MGM's musical Mississippi movie

MGM's movie version of Hammerstein & Kern's musical, *Show Boat*, about entertainers on a Mississippi riverboat, has been given a sparkling treatment. Ava Gardner plays Julie; the role of Joe, sung by Paul Robeson in the last movie version, is taken by William Warfield. His rendition "Ol' Man River" is good— though not on a par with Robeson's.

▲ *A view of The Festival Hall, the Shot Tower, and the Lion and Unicorn Pavilion.*

CULTURE

Festival of Britain gives postwar

4 MAY Britons are giving themselves a pat on the back this summer with a "Festival of Britain" held on the southern bank of the Thames River, in London. Bright colors and exciting displays are intended as an antidote to the long years of war and austerity. Among the attractions are the Dome of Discovery, where you can see 3D movies, and the Skylon, a huge needlelike sculpture.

LITERATURE

J.D. Salinger publishes *The Catcher in the Rye*

JULY This year's literary sensation is a first novel from an unknown author. *The Catcher in the Rye*, by American writer J. D. Salinger, is the tale of a disaffected schoolboy who drifts around New York. It has caught the imagination of young people all over the world. Salinger's hero, 16-year-old Holden Caulfield, doesn't know what he wants, but he knows that he hates the "phonies," people he seems to encounter at every turn. Salinger's novel is a masterful study of a youth on the brink of adulthood.

▲ *J. D. Salinger.*

LAW

The Burgess and Maclean spy scandal

7 JUNE Britain's diplomatic service has been thrown into turmoil by the sudden disappearance of Guy Burgess and Donald Maclean, two senior officials at the British Embassy in Washington. They have not been seen for two weeks. A special search is being conducted along the borders of Germany, Austria, and Finland, which adjoin the Soviet bloc. There is speculation that the men could have been spying for the Soviet Union, and that they have now somehow found their way to Moscow. But so far there is no news of their whereabouts.

ROYALTY

Baudouin crowned king of the Belgians

16 JULY Belgium's long agony came to an end today when Leopold III, the king who surrendered to the German invaders in 1940, abdicated and let his son Baudouin (right) take over. The king has been living in exile since the end of World War II, and until last month he resisted all calls to abdicate. The issue has torn Belgium apart. Many have never forgiven Leopold for giving up after only brief resistance and for staying in Belgium to cooperate with the Nazi authorities.

1950

1951

1952

1953

1954

1955

1956

1957

1958

1959

US tests first H-bomb

TECHNOLOGY

1 NOVEMBER The peaceful waters of Eniwetok Atoll in the Pacific were shattered today when the US military detonated the most powerful bomb ever made. The fearsome addition to the US's nuclear armory was the world's first thermonuclear, or hydrogen, bomb —an even deadlier cousin of the atom bombs exploded over Hiroshima and Nagasaki in 1945.

A bright, silent flash marked the moment of detonation; hundredths of a second later, cameras caught an electrical storm, induced by the sudden shockwave, playing around a massive fireball. Within seconds the entire island of Eniwetok was wiped off the face of the earth by a blast equivalent to 10.4 million tons of TNT—700 times more powerful than the Hiroshima bomb. Five minutes later, a rolling bubble of white-hot radioactive gas rose into the air, followed by the familiar mushroom cloud of vaporized debris. The bomb released huge quantities of radioactive material into the upper atmosphere, which will fall to earth over several years.

It has taken US scientists, led by Edward Teller, nearly three years to devise the hydrogen bomb. Where the atom bomb derives its power from the splitting (fission) of the atom, the hydrogen bomb works by fusion—combining nuclei from two different isotopes of hydrogen. In order to achieve the very high temperatures needed for fusion, the hydrogen bomb is itself detonated by an atom bomb in its casing.

▲ *Hydrogen bomb explosion in the Pacific.*

"Rock and roll" hits the air waves

There's a new sound in the air— a mixture of folk, blues, and country, played fast. Thanks to Alan Freed, a disk jockey in Cleveland, Ohio, it is becoming very popular in the US, even among people who might not listen to other kinds of popular music. The rhythm makes you want to rock your body to the beat. People are calling it "rock and roll."

Le Corbusier's Unité d'Habitation in Marseilles is finally completed

ARCHITECHTURE

1952 Le Corbusier, the innovative Swiss-born architect, has completed his latest remarkable project, the Unité d'Habitation, in Marseilles. The first part of what he hopes will be a much larger development, his prototype "vertical city" combines 340 apartments, stores, a sculpture park, and running track in a single building. The structure is self-contained and serviced by a network of internal streets. The development reflects the two main strands of his thinking: first, that "the house is a machine for living in"—housing should be functional and practical— and second, that people should live in strong communities, like the monasteries and rural settlements he so admires. His trenchant views and stark forms have been dubbed architecture's "new Brutalism."

◀ *Le Corbusier with a model of his Unité d'Habitation.*

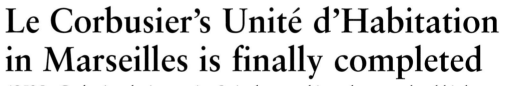

ROYALTY

"Playboy King" Farouk of Egypt abdicates

26 JULY King Farouk of Egypt, known as the Playboy king, abdicated today. His abdication comes three days after General Neguib seized power in a coup, and in the aftermath of a scandal involving secret arms deals conducted by his courtiers. Farouk said bitterly: "There will soon be only five kings left—England, Diamonds, Hearts, Clubs, and Spades."

◀ *Ex-king Farouk of Egypt poses in his hotel suite in Paris. The dethroned monarch is in exile.*

SCIENCE

Man to woman—world's first sex-change operation

15 DECEMBER The secret of Christine Jorgensen, a slim and attractive woman in her twenties, is out. She used to be a man called George, until she left her native US and went to Denmark for a series of operations and hormone injections to change her gender. Hers is the first sex-change operation to have become public knowledge, and it has aroused enormous interest in the more lurid sections of the press.

Christine says that she always felt she should have been a girl—as a little boy she preferred playing with dolls. Even a spell in the US Army did nothing to change her feelings—so she volunteered for the new, experimental procedure. Now, she says, she has become the woman she has always wanted to be.

▶ *Christine Jorgensen, who made medical history.*

Anne Frank's diary published

The diary of Anne Frank, a moving account of a childhood spent hiding from the Nazis, was published in June. She and her family spent two years in a secret annex to her father's office, while German troops raided Amsterdam in search of Jews to deport to their deaths. Mr. Frank, the sole survivor of the family, has published his late daughter's diary as a warning against racial hatred.

▼ *Gene Kelly in the rain scene from* Singin' *in the Rain.*

Gettin' wet singin' in the rain

The smash hit movie of the year is a musical masterpiece. *Singin' in the Rain* is the tale of how a star of silent movies (played by Jean Hagen) tries, and fails, to make it in the Talkies. Debbie Reynolds plays the chorus girl plucked from obscurity by Gene Kelly to dub her silken tones over the squeaky-voiced star. Love, laughs (provided by Donald O'Connor), and brilliant dance sequences abound. Best of all is the song which gives the film its title: Kelly, realizing that he is in love with Reynolds, splashily dances his way through a sudden downpour, getting completely soaked.

▲ *A page from Anne Frank's poignant diary.*

WAR

Mau Mau war of liberation begins in Kenya

25 NOVEMBER British troops today rounded up thousands of Kikuyu tribesmen as the rebellion against British rule in Kenya continues its slide into armed confrontation. The uprising is spearheaded by a secret society, the Mau Mau, who have bullied native Kenyans to join them and promise to drive out the white population. Many have sworn a solemn oath to kill all European farmers, and in the absence of guns, will do so with a spear or knife.

On 20 October a state of emergency was declared after the murder of some 50 White people and Black opponents, including the respected Chief Waruhui. British troops moved in to keep the peace. The Mau Mau's apparently random night attacks have created a sense of fear throughout Kenya, and white settlers are sleeping with loaded revolvers underneath their pillows. Despite the arrest this week of the Mau Mau's suspected leader, Jomo Kenyatta, the killings continue.

◀ *A Kikuyu elder talks to a Kenyan policeman.*

▲ *Heart-lung machine—a type of artificial heart.*

Flood at Lynmouth, Devon

DISASTERS

16 AUGUST A freak flood smashed through the sleepy north Devon village of Lynmouth, England, this morning, demolishing entire streets, killing 36 people, and leaving many others homeless. Tragedy struck after 9 inches (23 cm) of rain fell over Exmoor in a single day, causing several rivers to burst their banks and hills to collapse.

Almost as soon as the waters came, they left, leaving behind tons of rocks, mud, and rubble. The government has declared Lynmouth a disaster area, and the Red Cross has launched a rescue operation to bring food, water, and shelter to the area.

Artificial heart breakthrough

TECHNOLOGY

8 MARCH Heart surgery took a leap forward this year when an artificial (mechanical) heart kept 41-year-old Peter During alive for 80 minutes at the Pennsylvania Hospital. American surgeon John Heynsham Gibbon invented the world's first heart-lung machine last year. The machine takes the place of the heart and lungs, keeping freshly oxygenated blood circulating around the patient's system—enabling doctors to stop the heart for 30 minutes or more to perform complex operations. This medical breakthrough brings hope for future heart operations.

Callas is a knockout

The world of opera has been stunned this November by the dramatic and brilliant performance of the title role in Bellini's *Norma* by a new Greek singer, Maria Callas. The audience at the Royal Opera House at Covent Garden, London, gave Callas a standing ovation, amazed by this versatile soprano.

▼ *Traffic moves slowly as fog descends.*

BOAC launches first passenger jet

TRANSPORT

2 MAY The jet age began today when British Overseas Airways Corporation (BOAC) launched the world's first scheduled passenger flight by jet airliner. The 36-seater de Havilland Comet, with four engines, took off from London Airport for Johannesburg, South Africa. Its cruising speed of 490 miles per hour (789 km per hour) means that it will reach its destination in just under 24 hours.

▲ *Airport staff wave off BOAC's De Havilland Comet on its first flight.*

▲ *Evita, in 1951, with her husband Juan, greeting the people who adored and admired her.*

Death of Evita

PEOPLE

26 JULY Argentina's first lady Eva Perón, died of ovarian cancer today, at the age of 33. Evita, as she was popularly known, was a heroine to her country's millions of poverty-stricken *descamisados* (shirtless ones).

Born Eva Duarte, Evita was already well known as a radio and movie actress before she married Juan Perón—vice-president of the military junta led by President Edelmiro Farrell. When Perón was imprisoned by rivals in the government, Evita rallied the *descamisados*. A week of riots, strikes, and demonstrations persuaded the authorities to let him go. Her political skills, style, and grace became an invaluable asset to Juan after he became Argentina's president in 1946.

She became deeply involved in Argentinian politics, helping to push through policies on health, speeding up the granting of votes to women, and reforming schools. Her particular concern was the welfare of the poor. She wanted to run as vice-president with her husband in 1951, but military opposition and the onset of her final illness forced her to withdraw. Juan Perón, and his government, will be weaker without her.

Husband and wife storm Olympics

SPORT

3 AUGUST This year's Olympic Games in Helsinki will be remembered for the astonishing performance of Czech husband-and-wife team Emil Zátopek and Dana Zátopková. Emil established his prowess as a long-distance runner in the 1948 games, when he won the 10,000 meters race. This year, he dominated the games by winning gold in both the 10,000 meters and the 5,000 meters. He went on to compete in his first marathon, and win it, beating France's Alain Mimoun by 92 seconds. Dana, meanwhile, set a new Olympic record by throwing the javelin 165 feet 6 inches (50.46 meters).

▼ *Emil Zátopek reaches the finishing line.*

"Peasouper" smog leads to 2,000 deaths in London

ENVIRONMENT

31 DECEMBER For 10 days this winter Londoners struggled through the worst smog they had ever known. This "peasouper," caused by water condensing on particles of smoke from coalfires and other pollutants, brought the capital to its knees. Over one weekend, people could not see their own hands held in front of them, and in the Royal Albert Hall, concert audiences were unable to see the orchestra. Antismog masks are being issued, but at least 2,000 people have died of respiratory problems.

1950

1951

1952

1953

1954

1955

1956

1957

1958

1959

1953

QUESTS

Hillary and Norgay reach the top of world's highest point

▼ *Sherpa Tenzing Norgay (left) and New Zealander Edmund Hillary.*

29 MAY At 11:30 this morning, two men set foot on the summit of Mount Everest—at 29,028 feet (8,848 meters) above sea level, the highest point on the planet. New Zealander Edmund Hillary and his Sherpa guide Tenzing Norgay first shook hands politely— then hugged each other with joy. It was Norgay's eighth attempt and Hillary's second.

Hillary's expedition, led by John Hunt, left Kathmandu 10 weeks ago, loaded with nearly eight tons of supplies. Last night Hillary and Norgay spent the night at 28,200 feet (8,595 meters) in a tent underneath the rocky Southeast Ridge which leads up to the summit. The final challenge was a 40-foot (12-meter) high wall of stone across the ridge; Hillary found a narrow crevice and inched up it using the heels of his crampons. He then hauled Norgay up.

The two men spent only 15 minutes on the peak—long enough to plant British, Nepalese, and United Nations flags, munch some mint cake, and take a few photographs. Norgay buried some candy and cookies on the summit as an offering; Hillary pushed a small crucifix into the snow.

▼ *The whole expedition group not far from the summit of Everest.*

LAW

Rosenbergs executed for spy treason

19 JUNE Julius and Ethel Rosenberg today went to the electric chair in New York, becoming the first Americans to be executed during peacetime for espionage. The couple, both communists, were accused of passing the secrets of the atomic bomb— stolen from the top-secret nuclear facility at Los Alamos—to the Russians. Their sons, Michael (aged 10) and Robert (aged 7), are now orphans.

Sympathizers staged a series of protests to demand the death penalty be withdrawn, citing irregularities in the trial and uncertainty about the extent of Ethel's involvement.

▼ *Rally in New York against the executions.*

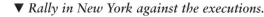

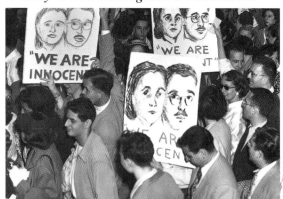

▼ *Norgay on the peak of Everest with British flag.*

Facts about Mount Everest

Everest, which straddles the Nepal-Tibet border, is named after Sir George Everest, a British surveyor who first noted the peak in 1850.

•

Everest's local name is Chomolungma—Nepalese and Tibetan for "Goddess Mother of the World."

•

George Mallory made three failed attempts on the mountain from the Tibetan side in 1921–24.

•

Nepal allowed foreigners to enter in 1947, making the easier southern route possible.

▲ *Stalin lies in state in his coffin.*

Death of Stalin, man of steel

5 MARCH Soviet citizens have been stunned by the news that Joseph Vissarianovich Stalin, their leader for the past 24 years, has died of a stroke. Born Joseph Djugashvili in Georgia 73 years ago, he adopted the name Stalin (man of steel) during the Russian Revolution. Lenin appointed him secretary-general of the Communist party in 1922; seven years later, after Lenin's death, Stalin became Russia's dictator.

He will be remembered for his Five-Year Plans for the Soviet economy, for his bloody purges of the 1930s, and for first allying with, then stubbornly defeating, Germany in World War II.

Churchill wins a Nobel Prize

10 DECEMBER Winston Churchill, Britain's prime minister, has won the Nobel Prize for Literature. Churchill was unable to attend the prize-giving ceremony in Stockholm today since he is at a conference in Bermuda. His wife will attend on his behalf. The prize was awarded for Churchill's historical works—including a four-volume history of World War I, and especially for his work *The Second World War* (6 vol., 1948–53). He has also written a biography of one of his ancestors, the Duke of Marlborough.

Piltdown Man hoax exposed

Kenneth Oakley, a geologist at the British Museum, uncovered the biggest fraud in archeological history this year. His tests on the skull known as Piltdown Man, discovered in Sussex, England, in 1912, prove that it is a fake. For years, paleontologists have said that the skull is evidence of the "missing link" between man and the apes. Far from being half a million years old, it is in fact an orangutan's jaw combined with a 500-year-old human skull.

▶ *Cast of Piltdown Man skull.*

▼ *Jackie and John cut their wedding cake.*

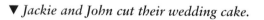

The Kennedy wedding

12 SEPTEMBER The biggest society wedding in the US this year took place today when John Fitzgerald Kennedy wed Jacqueline Lee Bouvier in Newport, Rhode Island. John, the son of former US Ambassador to London, Joseph Kennedy, is a Massachusetts senator; Jackie comes from a wealthy family and has just given up her job as a photographer for the *Washington Times-Herald*.

Kennedy is a handsome young politician from an ambitious Irish-American family. He is the author of *Why England Slept*—a study of prewar politics in Europe. In 1943 he was commander of the US patrol boat PT-109, which was destroyed by a Japanese cruiser in the Pacific; the tale of how he helped to rescue his 11-man crew made him one of the heroes of the war.

1953

Coronation ceremony fit for new queen

2 JUNE Royal representatives from the European kingdoms, as well as heads of government and the common people, witnessed Princess Elizabeth take the coronation oath at Westminster Abbey in London today.

The new queen, Elizabeth II, accompanied by her husband, the Duke of Edinburgh, pledged herself to the service of the people of Britain and the Commonwealth in a moving ceremony full of pageantry. Television meant that, for the first time, a coronation was seen by millions of people all over the world. The queen, who served in World War II, presented an unforgettable sight in her golden carriage, as it was pulled slowly by eight gray horses through the streets of London. Although it was cold and wet, huge crowds gathered along the royal route, cheering and shouting with excitement well into the night. At midnight they were treated to a last glimpse of the queen and the Duke of Edinburgh and a magnificent fireworks display over a moonlit Thames River.

▶ *Queen Elizabeth II's coronation was seen by millions all over the world.*

▼ *A scene from the new movie* The Robe.

First wide-screen film

Twentieth Century Fox has released the first-ever wide-screen movie, *The Robe,* from Lloyd C. Douglas' bestseller. The process, known as Cinemascope, was invented by French physicist Henri Chrétien in the late 1920s. Images are "squeezed" during filming using a special camera lens, and a special projection lens then expands the image on to a wide screen without distorting the proportions.

◀ *Cinemascope produces a projected image two-and-a-half times as wide as it is high.*

German workers in anti-Soviet revolt

17 JUNE Mounting dissatisfaction with the communist regime in East Germany has led to the first popular uprising in the postwar Soviet bloc. Workers went on strike and marched in East Berlin, the seat of government, to protest against increased production quotas.

When, after a couple of hours, the regime had failed to respond, some 100,000 workers took to the streets, setting buildings occupied by Soviet officials on fire, and demanding a change in government. The rebellion quickly spread throughout East Germany and was quelled only when Soviet tanks and troops poured into East Berlin, killing as least 21 people and wounding hundreds of others.

The crowd chanted "Ivan go home" to the Soviet tanks. Martial law was proclaimed by the Soviet commander in East Berlin, who also imposed a dusk-to-dawn curfew. "Provocateurs and Fascists from foreign powers" have been blamed for the uprising.

◀ *Protesters march past the Brandenburg Gate in East Berlin.*

NEWS • 1953 • NEWS

25 June • John Christie is sentenced to death for the murder of four women at 10 Rillington Place, Notting Hill, London. One of the women was his wife. All four were strangled.

13 August • Over 1,000 people are killed by earthquakes and tidal waves in the Greek islands.

24 September • Rocky Marciano knocks out Roland LaStarza to keep the world heavyweight boxing title.

Scientists make genetic breakthrough

▲ *Frances Crick (top) and James Watson.*

25 APRIL American biologist James Watson and English biochemist Frances Crick have worked out the structure of DNA (deoxyribonucleic acid), which contains the blueprint for reproduction in every living cell.

For some time chemists have known that DNA is made up of four different smaller substances, or bases. Now Crick and Watson have come up with an explanation for the way in which these bases are arranged. They did it by examining the patterns that emerge from X-rays when they are beamed at DNA. They have described the patterns as a spiral staircaselike "double helix." They worked very hard to come up with this answer, but the result is a beautiful surprise because it explains a key mystery of life.

▶ *A model of the double helix structure of DNA.*

Little Mo wins Grand Slam

3 JULY Maureen Connolly, nicknamed "Little Mo," is the first woman tennis player to win the Grand Slam—the British, US, Australian, and French championships—in one year.

Connolly began playing tennis at the age of 10 and at 14 became the youngest winner of the National Girls' Tournament. She won her first National Women's title in 1951.

▼ *Tito rebuilt the Communist Party of Yugoslavia in 1937.*

Tito elected first Yugoslav president

14 JANUARY Josip Broz (popularly known as Tito) has been elected the first president of Yugoslavia.

Tito's policy of "non-alignment" with either the Soviet or the Western bloc made him unpopular with both of them. In June 1948, when his relationship with the West was at its worst, he had a falling out with Stalin, who was claiming unofficial control and leadership in the Eastern bloc.

Tito was the first and most powerful communist to break with the USSR, and this made him popular with his people.

Netherlands flood disaster

3 FEBRUARY Today the North Sea broke through the dikes and devastated 775 square miles (2,000 square km) of Zeeland in the southwestern Netherlands. Over 1,000 people have lost their lives. The government has declared it a disaster area.

Zeeland's history has been marked by a permanent struggle against the sea, indicated by its name, meaning "sea land." The coastline of Zeeland is protected by dikes, but floods continue to occur. The government has pledged to set up the Delta Project to look into ways of preventing another flood.

▼ *Boats are used to evacuate people marooned by the flooding in Zeeland.*

POSTCOLONIALISM

After World War II, the European countries that ruled other countries overseas, known as colonies, slowly realized that the era of imperialism was over. People were demanding independence. Beginning with British India, the empires of Britain and France were gradually broken up. Smaller imperial powers followed. The process took many years. In many colonies independence came peacefully; in others, only after long and terrible civil wars.

▼ *A peasant's ox cart makes way for US tanks during the savage Vietnam War, in which the peasants were the chief victims.*

The Vietnam War

French Indochina was conquered by Japan during World War II. After 1945 the French tried unsuccessfully to restore their rule in Vietnam, and in 1954 they were defeated by the Vietnamese (led by the communist Ho Chi Minh) and had to withdraw. Vietnam was divided into the communist-ruled North, supported by the Soviet Union, and the South, supported by the US. French withdrawal left an imbalance of power, and in this unstable set-up civil war soon erupted between communists and their opponents. Even with US intervention, the communist guerrillas (members of an armed force that is against the established forces) in the North could not be defeated. A ceasefire was finally agreed in 1973. Two years later the South Vietnamese capital, Saigon, was captured by the communist forces.

Nonaligned states

The world after 1945 contained two hostile groups, the capitalist US with its allies and the communist Soviet Union with its dependents. A third group, consisting of countries that were not closely tied to either of the great powers, grew steadily larger as more and more colonies became independent. Most of these non-aligned states were not wealthy compared with Russia or the West and were sometimes called the Third World.

▶ *The Arab nationalist leader, Gamal Abdel Nasser (center left), ruler of Egypt from 1956 to 1970, was an outspoken opponent of colonialism.*

▶ *Tito, ruler of Yugoslavia (a nonaligned state) from 1945 to 1980.*

The partition of India

The movement for independence in India went back to the foundation of the Indian National Congress in 1885. Under Mahatma Gandhi the movement gained momentum. He brought heavy pressure to bear on the British authorities by his nonviolent campaign of "passive disobedience." By 1945 the British recognized that, after 160 years of ruling India, it was time to leave.

Despite the promise of independence, religious differences between the Hindus and Muslims stood in the way of Gandhi's dream of a united India. The Muslim League wanted a separate Muslim state in India. The Hindus supported the National Congress and unity. No compromise proved possible, and British India was divided into two countries at independence (15 August 1947). Jawaharlal Nehru became the first prime minister of independent India. Muhammad Ali Jinnah became governor-general of Muslim Pakistan. Pakistan consisted of two separate parts, East and West. In 1971, with India's support, East Pakistan broke away to become the independent state of Bangladesh.

▼ *Hindu refugees fleeing Pakistan in 1947— in the violence that followed partition, 2 million people died, and millions had to leave their homes. Gandhi himself was killed by a Hindu fanatic in January 1948.*

▲ *Jinnah, veteran leader of the Muslim League, was once a supporter of Hindu-Muslim unity but became a determined advocate of a separate Muslim state.*

▶ *Jawaharlal Nehru speaks to the people in New Delhi, capital of independent India. On the right is Lord Mountbatten, last British viceroy.*

1950

1951

1952

1953

1954

1955

1956

1957

1958

1959

Four-minute mile facts

The most men breaking the four-minute mile in a single race is 13. This race took place in Berlin on 8 August 1980.

•

By the 10th anniversary of Roger Bannister's four-minute mile breakthrough, 138 other four-minute mile records had been made by 43 men from 15 different countries.

Polio vaccine trial for children

The National Foundation for Infantile Paralysis in New York has announced that Dr. Jonas E. Salk, who discovered the new polio vaccine, has begun experimental trials of his new vaccine on children. The trial is independently organized and evaluated by Dr. Thomas Francis, Jr., Chairman of the Department of Epidemiology, at the University of Michigan School of Public Health.

▲ *Dr. Salk gives eight-year-old Gail Rosenthal her polio vaccination.*

SPORT

Bannister breaks four-minute mile

▶ *Bannister broke the previous world record by almost two seconds.*

6 MAY History was made today when a British athlete achieved what many have believed impossible. Roger Bannister, a 25-year-old medical student from Oxford University, has become the first man to run the mile in under four minutes.

Bannister achieved his fantastic time of 3 minutes 59.4 seconds at the university track in Oxford in a meeting between the university and the Amateur Athletic Association. Bannister is said to have achieved his speed through scientific training methods and thorough research into the mechanics of running.

Early in the race the pace had been set by fellow students, but Bannister managed to speed up on the last lap by running it in 59 seconds, breaking the nine-year-old record held by Gunder Haegg of Sweden.

TERRORISM

Algerian freedom fighters behind violent attacks

1 NOVEMBER A wave of terrorist violence broke out in Algeria last night in which seven people died and some 14 were wounded. Many properties were also destroyed. The brutal attacks are said to be the work of the National Liberation Front (FLN), an organization whose aim is to oust the ruling French and restore a sovereign Algerian state. Its leader is Ahmed Ben Bella, a former Free French partisan, who distinguished himself in Italy during World War II.

The FLN believes that Algeria has fallen behind the other Arab states because of the strong grip of French colonial rule on the country. It believes this can be remedied by guerrilla warfare at home and diplomatic activity abroad, particularly at the United Nations, where the support of the Arab countries and other states would be sought. The FLN military objective is to undermine French rule by sabotage.

▼ *French soldiers guard a group of Algerian freedom fighters.*

196

Bill Haley heralds in new rock'n'roll era

Bill Haley and the Comets are ready to rock up the charts with their latest record, "Rock Around the Clock," which went on sale today. This exciting new sound with a driving rhythm-and-blues dance beat is already a great hit for the band. Their last record, "Crazy, Man, Crazy" reached number 14 in the music charts.

▼ *Bill Haley (center) and his Comets.*

▼ *The* Nautilus *was christened by Mamie Eisenhower, wife of the president.*

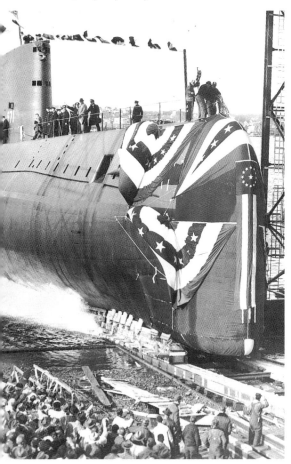

Great conductor retires

MUSIC

4 APRIL Arturo Toscanini, the 87-year-old Italian maestro, one of the great virtuosos, has retired. He gave his farewell concert last night at Carnegie Hall, New York, with the NBC Symphony Orchestra, which was created for him in 1937 after he left Italy because of his dislike of Mussolini.

Toscanini studied at the conservatories of Parma and Milan, intending to become a cellist. At the age of 19, when playing at the opera house at Rio de Janeiro, he was called upon to fill in for the conductor and conducted Verdi's *Aida* from memory. He came into prominence as a conductor in Italy and was appointed musical director of La Scala, Milan, in 1898. He has appeared with orchestras from all over the world.

NEWS • 1954 • NEWS

12 February • *A US study links cancer with smoking.*

1 March • *US explodes its second hydrogen bomb in Bikini atoll in the Pacific.*

2 April • *India: Nehru calls for a halt to the nuclear arms race.*

15 October • *William Golding's* Lord Of The Flies *is published.*

14 December • *Divorce is legalized in Argentina.*

▲ *Arturo Toscanini.*

Launch of world's first nuclear-powered submarine

TECHNOLOGY

21 JANUARY The US Navy launched the world's first nuclear-powered submarine on the Thames River in New London, Connecticut. The *Nautilus* is 319 feet (97 meters) long and weighs 3,180 tons. The nuclear reactor heats water to produce steam to drive the vessel's turbines, making the *Nautilus* the first true submarine, capable of prolonged, instead of temporary, submersion—it can stay submerged for months at a time. It can travel at a speed of more than 20 knots (23 miles/37 km per hour), and is able to maintain such a rate almost indefinitely.

This latest vessel is named after one of the earliest submersible craft, built in 1800 in France under a grant from Napoleon by American engineer Robert Fulton. The *Nautilus* looks set to be a prototype for future submarine vessels with new advanced technologies that will transform navies all over the world.

▼ *Ho Chi Minh, founder and leader of the Viet Minh.*

WAR

France defeated in Indochina

7 MAY The village of Dien Bien Phu was lost by the French today when it was overrun by the Viet Minh nationalist forces. In his last radio message, the French commander reported, "They are a few yards away... they are everywhere." The 16,000 French soldiers in Dien Bien Phu have been under siege for almost two months, cut off from support except by parachute. It seems that the whole force has been killed or captured.

Indochina (Vietnam, Laos, and Cambodia) was occupied by the Japanese during World War II. In 1945 at the end of the war, the French tried unsuccessfully to regain control. Their efforts led to the Indochina War (1945–54). Fighting against the Viet Minh (who had led resistance to the Japanese) flared up when they declared Vietnam an independent republic in 1945, and has continued ever since. The French, supported by the US, deliberately lured the Viet Minh into this decisive battle at Dien Bien Phu.

France recently agreed to discuss Indochina at a conference in Geneva. This defeat makes a full French withdrawal from Indochina more likely.

◀ *During the siege of Dien Bien Phu, the French parachuted in 3,000 more troops. They were not enough.*

First pocket-sized transistor radio

Soon we will be able to carry a radio receiver around in a pocket. Regency, a US company, has developed the first transistor radio (below) this year. What makes miniature radios possible is the development of the transistor, which ends the need for large, fragile valves.

TRANSPORT

First flight of the Boeing 707

15 JULY The US entered the age of the jet airliner today with the first test flight of the prototype Boeing 707 from Seattle, Washington.

The US has lagged behind Britain in developing jet airliners, but since the British Comet went into service in 1952, Boeing has been hurrying to compete. The Boeing 707 has the advantage of the large American market, which includes civil airlines and the armed forces. It is larger than the Comet, and it carries 219 passengers. The wings are swept back, with the four engines mounted in "pods" below them. This is seen as a safety feature—if one engine catches fire, it will not spread as easily.

▼ *The Boeing 707 is not expected to go into airline service for several years yet.*

Jasper Johns first "flag" painting

30 SEPTEMBER The young American painter Jasper Johns has sparked off arguments in New York art circles with his painting *Flag*. It is exactly like an ordinary American flag, except that it is obviously, and rather beautifully, painted, with the brush strokes easily seen. The question that Jasper Johns seems to be asking is: Is this an object or is it a picture of an object?

▲ *Jasper Johns Flag painted in wax colors on canvas.*

▶ *James Stewart, as the photographer, watches the suspect through a zoom lens.*

First shopping mall, in Detroit

1954 The Northland Center near Detroit, Michigan, designed by Victor Gruen's firm, is attracting thousands of enthusiastic shoppers. It is being hailed as an example of a new type of shopping center, or mall. The enclosed, air-conditioned environment contains 200 to 300 shops in arcades on several levels, with music, childcare facilities, restaurants, and plenty of free parking. The hope is that shopping centers will give new life to rundown American cities.

▲ *Aerial view of Northland Center shopping mall, north of Detroit.*

Hitchcock's window thriller

A new movie from director Alfred Hitchcock, *Rear Window*, is attracting the crowds. It is being billed as a movie in which you will "experience delicious terror." A photographer (James Stewart) confined to his apartment by a broken leg, spies on his neighbors with his girlfriend (Grace Kelly). The tension and suspense mount when Stewart witnesses a man murdering his wife. The movie is shocking in its violation of privacy.

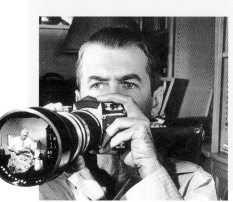

New York Yankee weds movie bombshell

14 JANUARY Two of America's greatest stars, Joe DiMaggio and Marilyn Monroe, tied the knot today. DiMaggio led the New York Yankees to nine baseball World Series titles and hit 361 home runs in 13 seasons. Monroe, a beautiful blonde, is Hollywood's hottest, most glamorous star. But will the quiet DiMaggio be able to accept the fantastic publicity that his wife attracts? Friends see problems ahead.

◀ *Joe DiMaggio and Marilyn Monroe kiss at their wedding.*

Germany win world football title in Berne

4 JULY The fifth football World Cup, held in Switzerland, was won by Germany in an exciting final in Berne. No German team has taken part since the war, and their first-ever win is a surprise. Under Sepp Herberger, manager since 1937, and captained by Fritz Walter, the Germans qualified for the final, playing an electrifying match with Hungary. After being 0-2 down, the Germans finally pulled it off to win 3-2, with their powerful winger Rahn scoring two of the goals.

Timeline:

1950

1951

1952

1953

1954

1955

1956

1957

1958

1959

Denim jeans craze

The new fashion for British teenagers is blue jeans, the tight-fitting, low-slung denim pants which have long been popular in North America. Denim is hard-wearing cotton cloth, which is supposed to have first come from Nîmes in France (hence the name *de Nîmes*, "of Nîmes"). Blue jeans are also called Levis, after the first big manufacturer who used to supply them to cowboys.

▲ *Schoolgirls wearing jeans.*

ENTERTAINMENT

Teen hero dies in crash at 24

30 SEPTEMBER James Dean, the young American movie star, was killed today in a road accident in California. He had just finished filming *Giant* and was driving his Porsche sportscar to Salinas, where he was to take part in a race. He had been stopped at Bakersfield for speeding earlier in the day by an officer who told him that, if he didn't slow down, he would never reach Salinas alive. He collided with another car, driven by a student, at a crossroad. The student escaped with minor injuries and the mechanic traveling with Dean was thrown clear, but Dean's neck was broken. He was only 24. While *Giant* was being filmed, he had promised the director that he would not do any racing.

The moody, rebellious young star is already a hero to the world's youth although only one of his films, *East of Eden*, has been released. With his second film, *Rebel Without a Cause*, due out next month, he is likely to become a cult hero. Already, the news of his death has caused scenes of teenage mass hysteria.

▶ *James Dean's car after the crash.*

▼ *James Dean in the film* Giant.

Warsaw Pact formed

TREATIES

14 MAY The Soviet Union and its communist allies in eastern Europe today signed a military "mutual assistance treaty," likely to be called the Warsaw Pact for short after the city where it was signed. The members are Albania, Bulgaria, Czechoslovakia, East Germany, Hungary, Poland, Romania, and the Soviet Union. The members of the pact have agreed to give immediate assistance to each other if attacked. In practice, it seems likely to give the Soviet Union an excuse to move military forces into the territory of its allies.

The immediate reason for the pact's formation is that, against Soviet protests, West Germany was this year admitted to NATO (North Atlantic Treaty Organization —the alliance of the US, Canada, and the Allies in western Europe, set up in 1949).

◀ *A map showing the countries formally allied under the Warsaw Pact.*

Volkswagen "Beetles" hit the million mark

Workers at the Volkswagen factory in Wolfsburg, Germany, have been celebrating the success of their famous product, the Beetle. One million of Ferdinand Porsche's little rear-engined sedans have been made since it was introduced in 1936, and the Volkswagen is now a familiar sight around the world.

▼ *The factory celebrates a million Beetles.*

1955

NEWS • 1955 • NEWS

10 February • South African police evict thousands from Johannesburg township of Sophiatown.

3 April • UEFA representatives agree to organize first European soccer championship.

5 April • Winston Churchill resigns as British prime minister.

31 October • Princess Margaret calls off her engagement to Group Captain Townsend, a divorced man.

DISASTERS

Catastrophe at Le Mans: 80 dead

12 JUNE About 80 people died in France last night in the worst accident in the history of auto racing. It took place at the famous Le Mans track, the first specially built motor-racing circuit, when several cars collided on a bend at a speed approaching 150 miles per hour (240 km per hour). One car hurtled over the barrier into the crowd. Witnesses spoke of headless bodies, severed arms and legs, and terrible screams. In spite of the disaster, the organizers of the race refused to stop it, a decision that is being strongly criticized. The winning drivers refused to accept their prizes when they learned of the deaths.

◄ *Clearing up after the worst crash in racing history, in which 80 people died and about 100 others were injured.*

▼ *French driver Pierre Levegh died instantly when his Mercedes crashed into the crowd.*

ART

"Family of Man"

1 OCTOBER The photographic exhibition "The Family of Man," shown at the Museum of Modern Art in New York this summer, has been booked by major museums all over the world. It was organized by the museum's director of photography, Edward Steichen, now 76, who has been a major force in photography since the early years of the century. It is based on the idea of the solidarity (unity) of the human race, influenced by the poet Carl Sandburg, Steichen's brother-in-law. Steichen examined more than 2 million prints before selecting 500 for the exhibition, which is proving to be one of the most popular exhibitions of photographs ever shown.

▲ *Photographs being assembled for the exhibition.*

ENTERTAINMENT

Disneyland opens in Los Angeles

18 JULY Niagara Falls, look out! If today's crowds are anything to go by, the Falls may soon lose their position as the North America's greatest tourist attraction to a new amusement park which opened today at Anaheim, near Los Angeles. Disneyland has been created by the movie-producer inventor of Mickey Mouse, Walt Disney. Visitors walk or ride through a series of fantasy worlds, based on Disney movies. Disneyland cost $17 million to build, and there is already talk of expanding it.

POLITICS

USSR establishes relationship with West Germany

13 SEPTEMBER The Soviet Union today officially recognized the Federal Republic of West Germany as an independent state, two days after the arrival in Moscow of West German Chancellor Konrad Adenauer. It signifies Moscow's acceptance that Germany is now divided into two countries.

One reason why German reunification has proved impossible, besides Soviet suspicion, is the pro-Western Adenauer's hostility to communism and his refusal to recognize the German Democratic Republic (East Germany), which is controlled by the Soviet Union.

▼ *Visitors to the new Disneyland are greeted by life-sized Disney characters.*

1950

1951

1952

1953

1954

1955

1956

1957

1958

1959

POLITICS

Bus boycott in Alabama

1 MARCH Alabama is in turmoil today as African-Americans demonstrate against racist segregation laws in the Deep South. In the capital, Montgomery, crowds have been demonstrating against segregation on the city buses. The campaign began last December, when Rosa Parks, a black woman, insisted on sitting in the front of a bus, a section reserved for whites. Most bus passengers in Montgomery are African-Americans, and the front section is often almost empty. She was arrested and jailed, which led to mass protests and a boycott of the buses. Martin Luther King, a local minister is leading the bus boycott.

Yesterday, in a case brought by the NAACP (National Association for the Advancement of Colored People), a Federal court ruled that the University of Alabama must admit Autherine Lucy, a black student. The day after she was admitted, three weeks ago, white students rioted. She was suspended—for her own safety, according to the university—but the court ruling requires the university to provide protection. The US Supreme Court ruled in 1954 that public schools must admit African-American students, but in Southern states the rule has not been applied to universities.

NEWS • 1956 • NEWS

9 March • *Makarios expelled from Cyprus by British governor.*

15 March • My Fair Lady, *a musical based on G.B. Shaw's play* Pygmalion *opens in New York.*

29 June • *Marilyn Monroe weds dramatist Arthur Miller. Her previous marriage to Joe DiMaggio lasted less than a year.*

6 November • *Second term for Eisenhower as president.*

▼ *Rosa Parks sits in the front of a city bus.*

Segregation facts

Despite the Supreme Court's ruling that segregation was unconstitutional in 1954, Alabama's white officials avoided integrating schools until 1963.

●

In September 1956 Governor Faubus of Arkansas used National Guardsmen to prevent nine African-American children from entering the high school in Little Rock.

●

In 1962, Federal troops were called out to get an African-American student, James Meredith, into the University of Mississippi.

POLITICS

European North Africa is shrinking

20 MARCH The French are retreating from their colonial empire. As of today, Tunisia is a sovereign state, independent of France, under a government led by Habib Bourgiba. A few weeks ago, French and Spanish Morocco became an independent kingdom under Sultan Muhammad V, while the Sudan, formerly ruled by Britain and Egypt, has been independent since 1 January. However, the third major French territory in North Africa, Algeria, remains officially part of France, in spite of the Algerian nationalist movement which is fighting for independence. Their resistance to French rule has also taken the form of terrorist campaigns.

TUNISIA

MOROCCO

SUDAN

▶ *This year alone, the African states of Sudan, Morocco, and Tunisia have gained independence.*

The Suez crisis

3 NOVEMBER Under pressure from both the Soviet Union and the US, the British and French today agreed to withdraw their troops from the Suez Canal area. Their agreement is seen as a major defeat, signaling the end of British imperial power in the Near East.

The Suez crisis began on 26 July when the Egyptian leader, Gamal Abdel Nasser, nationalized the Suez Canal in defiance of an agreement that control of the canal should remain with the international Suez Canal Company. Israel invaded Egypt, with the encouragement of Britain and France, whose forces later invaded the Canal Zone, stating that their intention was to stop the fighting. In fact, it is clear that their aim was to defeat Nasser, while Israel hoped to strengthen its position in the Middle East.

▶ *President Nasser with the jubilant Egyptian crowd in Port Said.*

Knockout "Rocky" retires undefeated

Rocco ("Rocky") Francis Marciano has retired from boxing at the age of 33. Just under 5 feet 11 inches (1.8 m) tall and weighing about 185 pounds (84 kg), he won 43 of his 49 professional bouts by knockout. He gained the world heavyweight title in 1952 and defended it successfully six times, five times by a knockout and once on points.

Royal opening for nuclear power plant

17 OCTOBER The atomic power station at Calder Hall, on the coast of Cumbria, England, was opened today by Queen Elizabeth. Part of a complex that includes the Windscale Atomic Research Centre, it was built by the Atomic Energy Authority. Calder Hall has a gas-cooled magnox reactor with a capacity of about 200 megawatts electrical output and is the first nuclear station in the world designed to generate electricity on a commercial basis. More British stations are planned.

▶ *Calder Hall in Cumbria, northwestern England.*

New phone lines cross Atlantic

Europeans can now talk on the telephone to friends in North America almost as easily as they can to friends in the next town. The first transoceanic telephone cable was completed this year. Unlike the earlier telegraph cables, there are two cables, one in each direction. They extend between Newfoundland and Oban in Scotland.

Sailer skis to three gold medals at Winter Olympics

6 FEBRUARY The Winter Olympic Games, held this year at Cortina d'Ampezzo in Italy, ended today. Without question, the star of the games was Toni Sailer, who won all three gold medals in skiing: slalom, giant slalom, and downhill. He won the giant slalom by the amazing margin of 6.2 seconds over the silver medalist. Sailer has introduced the Austrian hip-wagging *wedeln* style to international skiing.

◀ *Toni Sailer, the 20-year-old Austrian star of the white slopes.*

▲ *Opening ceremony of the Transatlantic Phone System.*

◄ A monumental Stalin is toppled in Budapest, but Soviet domination of Hungary won't be knocked over so easily.

◄ Nikita Khrushchev, the daring new Soviet leader who has denounced Stalin as a mass murderer.

POLITICS

Khrushchev announces Thaw: de-Stalinization

18 MARCH Details have reached the West of a remarkable speech by Soviet leader Nikita Khrushchev at a secret session of the Communist Party in Moscow last month. The subject of the speech was the crimes of Stalin, the Soviet dictator who died in 1952. Until this speech, no open criticism of Stalin has ever been allowed in the Soviet Union. Now Khrushchev has exposed him as a mass murderer, a power-mad egotist who ruled by terror and betrayed the country and the communist movement. Commentators are hoping that Khrushchev's straight talking will help to open the Iron Curtain between eastern and western Europe.

POLITICS

Hungarian uprising crushed

13 NOVEMBER According to Hungarian refugees, all resistance to the Soviet invasion has now ended. Budapest radio went off the air a week ago, its final broadcast a desperate appeal for help.

The Hungarian rising against Soviet domination began with student demonstrations on 23 October. The protests spread and fighting broke out. Soviet troops were forced to withdraw from Budapest and the pro-Soviet government resigned. Imre Nagy took over as prime minister. He announced that Hungary was withdrawing from the Warsaw Pact and promised greater political freedom. Russian reinforcements then entered Hungary and, early on 4 November, hundreds of tanks moved into the capital. Thousands have died; tens of thousands have fled the country. Nagy and his comrades are feared dead. Despite Khrushchev's anti-Stalin speech earlier this year, it's clear that the USSR will not tolerate democracy in eastern Europe.

Elvis "the Pelvis" divides America

The popular music charts have been dominated this year by the records of a sensational new singing star, Elvis Presley. He combines the tradition of black blues singers and white country-and-western music, with hard, fast, rhythmic backing. His succession of hits, including "Heartbreak House," "Don't Be Cruel," and "Blue Suede Shoes" have sold 7 million copies, and when he appeared on the Ed Sullivan Show, he drew a record viewing audience of 54 million. A poor boy from Memphis, Tennessee, Elvis is a millionaire at 21. He inspires hysterical adoration in his young female fans, but adults are less impressed. They see his raw, sneering sex appeal as an evil influence. "Vulgar and untalented" is the verdict of one music critic.

► Elvis Presley's nickname is inspired by his uninhibited performing style.

Grace Kelly and Prince Rainier wed

19 APRIL A fairytale wedding—the prince and the movie star—took place today on the French Riviera. Prince Rainier's family has ruled the tiny state of Monaco for over 500 years; Grace Kelly was born in Philadelphia to a wealthy family. In fact, the prince looks like a movie star, and the cool and elegant Grace Kelly looks every inch a princess. About 1,200 guests were invited—the rich and the famous—and the jingle of diamonds almost drowned out the choir. In this glittering celebration, there was one sad thought. Now that she is a princess, Grace Kelly will vanish from our movie screens.

▲ *Rainier III and Grace Kelly at their wedding ceremony.*

Fresh air for Britain

5 JULY The Clean Air Act, passed today, should help to improve the quality of air in British cities when it comes into force in two years' time. Dark or dirty smoke is banned, and local councils gain the power to specify "smokeless zones." The banning of coalfires should put an end to London's famous "peasoupers," caused by a mixture of smoke and fog (smog). In winter the long-suffering British capital gets only half as much sunshine as unpolluted country districts. Smog in London and industrial cities is thought to have caused many deaths in recent years. During the Great Smog of 1952, thousands of Londoners died of heart and lung diseases. Since 1953 antismog masks have been available, with a doctor's prescription, on Britain's National Health Service.

◀ *Flares guide a London bus through a smog-ridden intersection.*

Separate Olympics held for horseriding events

30 SEPTEMBER This year's Olympic Games were the longest on record. They began in January with the athletics in Melbourne, Australia. But because of distance and quarantine problems, the equestrian (horseriding) events took place in Stockholm, Sweden. Gold medals went to West Germany, Great Britain, and Sweden, but the star of these Olympics was German rider Hans Gunter Winkler, who won an individual gold medal.

▶ *Equestrian champion Hans Gunter Winkler.*

Don Larsen's perfect World Series game

8 OCTOBER The Baseball World Series between the New York Yankees of the American League and their neighbors, the Brooklyn Dodgers of the National League, ended in victory for the Yankees, four games to three. Yankees pitcher Don Larsen set a record when he pitched not only the first nohitter in a world series but also a perfect game—nine innings without a single striker reaching first base. He has a unique action, with practically no windup before delivery. But Dodgers pitcher Don Newcombe has won the Cy Young award for best pitcher of the season.

1950

1951

1952

Device to curb drunk drivers

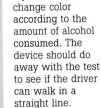

Police in the US are now using the "drunkometer" (above). When they suspect that a driver has drunk too much, he or she is asked to blow into a bag, which is attached to a container holding crystals. These change color according to the amount of alcohol consumed. The device should do away with the test to see if the driver can walk in a straight line.

1953

1954

1955

1956

1957

1958

1959

Soviets winning space race with *Sputnik I* launch

4 OCTOBER The Soviet Union has launched the manmade satellite *Sputnik I* into orbit around the Earth. The satellite weighs 185 pounds (84 kg) and is traveling at an altitude of more than 500 miles (800 km). Each circuit of the Earth, at a speed of 17,400 miles per hour (28,000 km per hour), takes 96.17 minutes.

Excitement at the Soviet achievement has swept around the world. Transmitters aboard the satellite are emitting a radio signal, which has been picked up in the US by the RCA broadcasting company and in Britain by the BBC. The Americans have a small 3¼-pound (1.5-kg) satellite almost ready for launch.

▲ *A Russian guide-engineer at a Moscow exhibition displays a replica of the Soviet satellite* Sputnik I.

One giant leap for man's best friend

TECHNOLOGY

3 NOVEMBER Laika, a black and white dog, is orbiting the Earth on board the Soviet Union's satellite *Sputnik II*, which was launched today. She is the first living being to leave the Earth and make a flight into space.

Laika has food and drink on *Sputnik II* and scientists have installed an oxygen tank to allow her to breathe. Her flight is part of a research program to investigate how conditions in space affect animals. Sensors and electrodes on her body are monitoring Laika's movement, her pulse, and her respiration, or breathing. The information is being sent back by radio transmitters to scientists on Earth. They will use what they learn to plan a human mission in space. Also on board is a "regenerator" to remove the carbon dioxide and water vapor in Laika's exhaled breath from the air.

But Laika has no way of returning to Earth, because the satellite will remain in orbit. The mission planners expect Laika to die after about a week, when the oxygen runs out.

◄ *Laika was sent into orbit in* Sputnik II *to show that living beings can survive in space.*

Common Market set up with new treaty

TREATIES

25 MARCH Government ministers from France, West Germany, Italy, Belgium, Holland, and Luxembourg have agreed to set up a common trading area. The European Economic Community (EEC)—or Common Market— means that in the future money, people, and goods will be able to move freely between member states. Some European countries chose not to take part in the talks that led to the EEC's creation, but are now trying to create a rival free-trade area.

▲ *The Treaty of Rome was signed in Rome today.*

IBM develops first high-level computer language

TECHNOLOGY

APRIL Setting up a computer to perform a complex activity is now easier with the creation of Fortran, a "programing language." Until now, computer languages have been binary—they consisted entirely of the digits 1 and 0 in different combinations. Fortran ("formula translation") uses mathematical symbols. Developed by John Backus and a team at the US company International Business Machines (IBM), it is aimed at scientists.

Fangio delights motor-racing fans a fifth time

Argentinian racing driver Juan Manuel Fangio has won the Formula One World Drivers' Championship for the fifth time. Driving a Maserati 250F, he won the Grand Prix races in Argentina, Monaco, France, and Germany. He finished the season with 40 points, 15 ahead of British driver Stirling Moss, who was driving for Vanwall.

Fangio was also drivers' champion in 1951, 1954, 1955, and 1956. Now 46, he must be nearing the end of his career—but he is still driving superbly. In the German Grand Prix this year he drove his best race ever.

▶ *Many racing fans claim Fangio is the best.*

The voice of the Beat Generation

LITERATURE

▲ *Jack Kerouac.*

DECEMBER American writer Jack Kerouac has hit the literary headlines with his novel *On the Road*, published this year. Kerouac is a member of the Beat Generation, a group of young people who are bored with American values and reject the material comforts of 1950s US. They find fullfilment instead in jazz music, expressive poetry, drugs, and alternative religions—especially Zen Buddhism.

On the Road, written in just three weeks, describes journeys across the US made by Sal Paradise and his friend Dean Moriarty. The book is a freely flowing succession of episodes—Kerouac writes in bursts and does not change what he has written.

President sends in troops to resolve racial conflict

POLITICS

25 SEPTEMBER President Eisenhower sent more than 1,000 Federal troops to enforce school desegregation in Arkansas, meaning that black and white children should be taught together rather than in separate schools. Desegregation in Arkansas was ordered by the Federal District Court on 3 September, but Arkansas state governor Orval Faubus sent troops to keep black children away from Little Rock High School. Today, escorted by the federal troops, nine black children walked into Little Rock High School to begin their lessons alongside white children.

▼ *Federal troops protected the children from white protesters.*

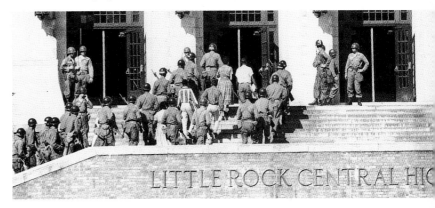

THE CONSUMER AGE

For most of the 20th century, Western countries have been consumer societies—ones in which most people can afford to live in relative comfort. People can (usually) afford to buy more than the bare necessities, and are able to choose from a wide variety of goods and services on offer. In such a competitive world, every business wants people to buy its goods instead of those of its rivals. Companies constantly bring out new improved products and keep prices low. But this is not enough. To sell a product, advertising, marketing, and sophisticated salesmanship have to play ever-larger roles.

◄ *"Heaven for the hostess"—a new idea in compact, multi-purpose rooms, on display at the National Home Furnishings Show in New York in 1952.*

▲ *Entertaining outdoors in the 1950s was made easier with unbreakable, barbeque-friendly trays and platters.*

▼ *Typical 1950s homes in Levittown, Long Island.*

Postwar households

A maid and cook who lived with the family, common features of middle-class homes at the beginning of the century, were virtually unheard of by 1950. The keyword for the postwar home was efficiency, and houses in the Fifties and early Sixties were full of labor-saving machines to make housework easier.

Toasters, blenders, electric irons, washing machines, and vacuum cleaners took over from housemaids. Householders enjoyed centrally-heated homes with running hot water. New furniture styles were bright, inexpensive, light, and easy to move around.

Door-to-door salesmen

There is a ring at the door. A smiling salesman comes in and throws dirt and soot all over your carpet. He then cleans it up with a new vacuum cleaner—and tries to sell you one, payable in small but regular installments. Almost anything could be sold door to door: encyclopedias, cleaning equipment, and cosmetics were particularly successful.

The art of selling

In the second half of the 20th century, everyone had something to sell. In the US—home of the Avon lady, the Fuller brush man, and a host of traveling salesmen—selling became an art form. Manufacturers researched what color and size a product should be, the price people could be persuaded to pay, and the way to sell it.

Advertising toothpaste on television and having it endorsed by dentists or by movie stars could boost sales dramatically. Design and marketing became inseparable—every product had to have "unique selling points" to make it seem better than the competition.

Companies such as McDonald's became rich by franchising their distinctive product—local businessmen bought the right to sell it in a particular area. In the new self-service supermarkets, eye-catching displays boosted sales.

◀ A 1950s toothpaste advertisement.

Consumer age facts

The world's first TV commercial, for Bulova Watches, was shown in New York on 1 July, 1941.

•

By 1947, 94 percent of British women had no hired help at all in the house.

•

Nearly $30 billion worth of McDonald's hamburgers were sold worldwide in 1995.

▶ Laundry detergent is displayed in a supermarket on an attention-grabbing stand.

1950

1951

1952
1953
1954
1955
1956
1957
1958

1959

▲ *Workers holding up posters of Mao.*

China: the "Great Leap Foward"

AUGUST China's Communist leader Mao Tse-tung has launched a campaign to reorganize the country's workforce. He is calling for a Great Leap Forward in economic production, in which agriculture and modern industry in China will be revolutionized.

This month the Communist Party is promoting "people's communes" in the Chinese countryside. Thousands of peasants are being brought together to work on farms and in local industry. Small steel furnaces are being set up in villages, as are communal kitchens, so more of the peasants can join the workforce.

In the 1920s the communists in the Soviet Union invested in industrial machinery at the expense of agriculture. But in China the Soviet way is impossible because all of the farm produce is needed to feed the people, and many people fear that the disruption in agriculture in China could have disastrous effects and may lead to famine.

NEWS • 1958 • NEWS

1 February • The US launches Explorer, *its first satellite, into orbit around the Earth.*

2 March • British explorer Vivian Fuchs completes the first land crossing of Antarctica.

29 June • Brazil win the soccer World Cup Final, beating Sweden 5–2, thanks to 17-year-old striker Pelé.

4 October • British airline BOAC launches the first jet service across the Atlantic Ocean.

Hula hoop fad in full swing

It is not only rock'n'roll fans who are swiveling their hips—all over the US children and adults are twisting their bodies to keep a plastic hoop spinning around their waists. The first hula hoops, based on a bamboo hoop used by Australian children, were marketed by Californians Arthur Melin and Richard Knerr this summer. Around 25 million have already been sold.

◄ *Ten-year-old Mimi Jordan drinks milk during her hula-hooping three-hour world record.*

▼ *About 600 supporters marched all the way.*

CND stages first Aldermaston march

7 APRIL Around 3,000 supporters of the Campaign for Nuclear Disarmament (CND) took part in the final stage of a three-day 50-mile (80-km) protest march from London to Aldermaston, in Berkshire. They joined 12,000 protestors at a rally today outside the British government's Atomic Weapons Research Establishment. The campaign, which is pressing the British government to surrender nuclear weapons, was founded on 17 February.

Manchester United air crash tragedy

DISASTERS

6 FEBRUARY A crash at Munich airport has plunged English soccer into mourning. Seven members of the Manchester United soccer team were killed when their aircraft, trying to take off in icy conditions, smashed into buildings at the end of the runway.

The youthful United team—nicknamed "Busby's Babes"—had landed in Munich on their way home from Yugoslavia, where they tied 3–3 with Red Star Belgrade to go through to the European Cup semifinals.

▲ *Rescuers sift through aircraft wreckage.*

Pasternak declines Nobel prize

LITERATURE

OCTOBER Russian author Boris Pasternak has been awarded the Nobel prize for Literature for his novel *Dr. Zhivago*. It is a love story which examines the failings of the Russian Revolution.

The Soviet authorities refused to publish it and now the Soviet Writers' Union wants Pasternak to be expelled from the country. Pasternak has declined the Nobel prize, and is begging to be allowed to stay.

▲ *Russian author Boris Pasternak.*

Brussels hosts World Exhibition

CULTURE

17 APRIL King Baudouin of Belgium opened the World Exhibition in Brussels, which features displays from 42 countries. The symbol of the fair represents an atom of iron magnified 150 million times; its nine steel spheres each measure almost 60 feet (18 meters) across.

The British pavilion features historical costumes and a Hall of Technology. Among the attractions in the US's pavilion is a creative play center for young children. The Soviet display offers a replica of the *Sputnik II* space satellite.

▼ *The Atomium—symbol of the World Fair—towers over the exhibition site in Brussels.*

First stereo records are a hit on the market

A new world of sound is opening up with stereophonic recording, in which two microphones are used to record music from different positions. Stereo tape recordings have been around for four years, but those who have listened to the new stereo records are very excited—and say there is no going back to the old mono recordings.

▲ *Two speakers are needed to play the new stereo records.*

De Gaulle rises to French leadership

POLITICS

21 DECEMBER General Charles de Gaulle, France's Prime Minister, has been elected the first President of the Fifth Republic.

In World War II De Gaulle was the leader of the Free French, who opposed the French government's cooperation with the Nazis. He was head of a provisional French government at the end of the war but resigned in 1946.

In May this year France reached the edge of civil war over whether it should keep its colony of Algeria in northern Africa. De Gaulle, who is seen as a strong leader, was asked to return as prime minister.

POLITICS

Fidel Castro overthrows Batista

2 JANUARY Fidel Castro has declared a new government in Cuba. For more than two years Castro and his followers have been fighting a guerrilla war against dictator Fulgencio Batista. Yesterday Batista gave up power and fled the country. When news of his flight was confirmed, jubilant Cubans celebrated in the streets. Cuba's new President is to be Dr. Manuel Urrutia, but 32-year-old Fidel Castro, the charismatic leader of the rebellion, is to be commander in chief of the Cuban armed forces.

▶ *Castro, once a Havana lawyer who fought for the poor, now leads revolutionaries.*

Batista, who was president of Cuba from 1940–44, returned to power in an army coup in March 1952 and headed a corrupt regime. Castro, a landowner's son, launched a revolt against the government the following year. He led an attack on an army barracks in Santiago in July, 1953, but the maneuver failed—around 55 rebels were killed and others, including Castro, were jailed. In 1955, when he was released from prison, Castro went to Mexico to plan the revolution in exile. Late in 1956, he secretly returned to Cuba and fought against the Batista dictatorship from a country hideout.

▶ *Batista, who ruled Cuba as a military dictator until his overthrow, has gone into exile in Spain.*

Quiz show scandal

Americans are shocked to discover that the heroes of a favorite TV quiz show are in fact frauds. Apparent geniuses such as Charles Van Doren, who seemed to know all the answers on *Twenty-One*, knew all the questions before the show. Apparently, this kind of cheating is not unusual. Many quiz shows are told by their sponsors which contestants should continue to win.

POLITICS

Alaska and Hawaii become states of the union

21 MARCH Hawaii today became the 50th US state—less than three months after Alaska became the 49th, on 3 January. The new arrivals are the first for over 45 years. The most recent state was Arizona, which was admitted to the union of states in 1912 by President Taft. A new version of the flag, the Stars and Stripes, has been unveiled by President Eisenhower. It now has 50 stars; one for each state.

Alaska covers more than 591,000 square miles (1.5 million square km) in the northwestern corner of North America. A state territory since 1912, it has been pressing for full statehood for over 40 years. Hawaii, an island group in the Pacific, was ruled until 1893 by a native monarchy. Annexed by the US in 1898, it adopted a US state constitution in 1950.

◀ *Van Doren live on* Twenty-One.

▼ *Purchased in 1876 for $7.2 million from Russia, Alaska celebrates full statehood.*

Guggenheim Museum opens

ART

DECEMBER The Guggenheim Museum of Art in New York welcomed its first visitors. But its architect, American Frank Lloyd Wright, was not there. He died, aged 89, last April. The spiral building rises above Fifth Avenue like a vast seashell. Inside, a six-floor winding ramp leads to the top of the building, which is enclosed by a glass dome. Wright's only building in New York, it's a spectacular example of his innovative "open plan" style of interior design.

◄ *Exhibits line the walls of a continuous spiral ramp in the sensational Guggenheim Museum.*

Barbie doll makes US Debut

American girls have a new friend—Barbie— a doll with the appearance of an elegant young woman. Ruth Handler, who founded Mattel Toys with her husband Elliot, watched her daughter Barbara playing and saw that she would love to have a doll who could play roles taken from the adult world. Barbie was launched at the American Toy Fair, held in February in New York.

► *Barbie's fabulous wardrobe includes outfits for a winter bride and for a singer.*

Khrushchev visits the US

POLITICS

27 SEPTEMBER Soviet leader Nikita Khrushchev flew back to Moscow today after a 12-day visit to the US, where he had discussions with President Eisenhower about the German city of Berlin, still divided between the Western powers and the Communists. On his travels he went to a farm in Iowa, visited an IBM factory in San Francisco, and had a tour of Hollywood. But for "security reasons" he was refused permission to go to Disneyland.

▼ *Khrushchev lifts his hat to the US as Eisenhower reads a statement on the runway.*

▼ *The Queen speaks at the ceremony.*

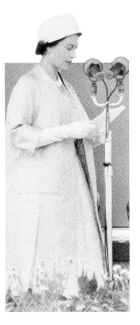

Queen opens St. Lawrence Seaway

TRANSPORT

26 JUNE The St. Lawrence Seaway opened today, enabling ships to sail from the Atlantic Ocean inland through Canada, as far as the Great Lakes on the US/Canada border. Queen Elizabeth, Canadian Prime Minister John Diefenbaker, and President Eisenhower opened the Seaway in a splendid ceremony at St. Lambert Lock in Montreal.

The 2,350-mile (3,780-km) long seaway consists of canals, locks, lakes, and rivers and extends to Duluth, Minnesota, at the western end of Lake Superior. It cost $750 million to complete, with the Canadian government putting up four-fifths of the money.

Dalai Lama escapes from Tibet

RELIGION

20 APRIL An emotional crowd of 7,000 exiled Tibetans today greeted the Dalai Lama, their spiritual leader, in northern India. Disguised as a servant, he made the long trek from Tibet over the Himalayas by yak and arrived safely in Assam yesterday. He fled Tibet at the end of last month after the Chinese, who have been occupying Tibet since 1951, launched a fierce onslaught against Tibetan rebels.

The Dalai Lama then traveled to New Delhi to meet the Indian prime minister, Jawaharlal Nehru. The Indian government does not want to antagonize China and is unlikely to allow the Dalai Lama to campaign against the Chinese presence in Tibet while he is living in India.

▲ *Indian Prime Minister Jawaharlal Nehru (right) exchanges greetings with Tibet's Dalai Lama.*

USSR rocket reveals new Moon view

TECHNOLOGY

14 OCTOBER Scientists had their first look at the dark side of the Moon today. The Soviet spacecraft *Luna III* beamed back photographs of the side of the Moon that faces out into space and so remains invisible from the Earth. It shot pictures of 70 percent of the Moon's unseen part, including one large area that has been called the Moscow Sea. The Soviets' *Luna* program has been a triumphant success. On September 14 *Luna II* was deliberately crashed on the Moon. It sent back valuable information about radiation and the gases and particles of matter that exist in space, proving for the first time that space is not a vacuum.

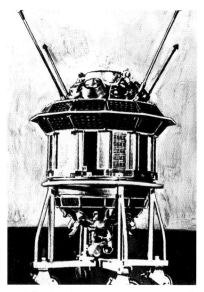

▲ *The Soviet's* Luna III *spacecraft.*

Continent of Antarctica becomes a science reserve

SCIENCE

1 DECEMBER Antarctica, the continent that includes the South Pole, has been set aside for science. Twelve countries—including the US, the Soviet Union, and the United Kingdom—have signed a treaty guaranteeing that they will not claim any part of Antarctica as their own exclusively. The agreement bans nuclear weapons tests, the dumping of nuclear waste, and the creation of military bases in Antarctica. It says that scientists from all countries should be allowed access to carry out peaceful research. The treaty has still to be formally approved, but once in force it will be valid indefinitely. It can only be altered if all the countries that have signed agree to the change. It is the first international treaty of this kind ever to be signed.

▶ *Deputy Soviet Foreign Minister Vasil V. Kuznetsov signs for his country.*

Buddy Holly is dead

MUSIC

3 FEBRUARY Rock'n'roll fans have been stunned by the news that rising star Buddy Holly and two other singers died tonight in an airplane crash in Iowa. Holly, Ritchie Valens, and "Big Bopper" Richardson were on tour with several other bands in the Midwest. Most of the musicians traveled by bus, but Holly hired a four-seater Beechcraft airplane to fly from Clear Lake, Iowa, to the next venue in Fargo, North Dakota.

Fans will particularly miss Holly and Valens, but all three stars had hit records. Valens, a 17-year-old Mexican-American whose real name was Ricardo Valenzuela, had a big-selling hit with "Donna," while 24-year-old Richardson had enjoyed success with "Chantilly Lace." Holly, aged 22, hit the heights with his band The Crickets, playing "That'll Be The Day" and "Rave On."

▲ *Buddy Holly.*

Ben-Hur triumphs

Ben-Hur, an epic tale of ancient Rome, sold more tickets than any other film in the US this year. Charlton Heston stars as Ben-Hur, a Judean prince who gains revenge over his Roman enemy, Messala, played by Stephen Boyd. The film used 300 sets and cost $15 million to make. It includes a breathtaking 40-minute chariot race between Ben-Hur and Messala.

▼ *Still from the film Ben-Hur.*

Mini likely to be major British success

The new Mini, launched this summer by the British Motor Corporation, is proving that big is not necessarily best, even in the motoring world. Designer Alec Issigonis has created a surprisingly spacious four-seater car on a small frame. The Mini's engine, mounted sideways at the front, is also small—with a capacity of 850 cc—but it can power the lightweight car to a top speed of 70 miles per hour (112 km per hour). Drivers eager to try it can choose between the Austin Seven and the Morris Mini Minor. The only difference between them is in the design of the front.

▶ *British Motor Corporation's Mini Minor.*

▲ *The referee stops the bout in the third round; Johansson stands over Patterson.*

Johansson wins world heavyweight championship

SPORT

26 JUNE Swedish boxer Ingemar Johansson stunned the raucous fans at Yankee Stadium in New York tonight. Johansson easily defeated the defending champion, American Floyd Patterson, and knocked him down seven times in the third round.

Johansson won the European heavyweight championship in 1956 and last year brushed aside American heavyweight Eddie Machen, knocking him out in the very first round. Today's win makes Johansson the first Swedish world heavyweight champion. The Patterson and Johansson camps are certain to set up a rematch.

Escalation of the "Cod War"

ECONOMICS

30 APRIL A dispute is raging between Britain and Iceland over the right to fish for cod in waters off the Icelandic coast. The "Cod War" has been running for nine months but is heating up—today an Icelandic gunboat fired live ammunition at the British trawler *Arctic Viking*, missing it by a few yards.

The Cod War began last summer when the Icelandic government in Reykjavik announced a 12-mile (19-km) limit around the Icelandic coast, in which British trawlers could not fish. This was to replace an existing 4-mile (6.5-km) limit. But British fishermen refused to recognize the new limit, and British trawlers, supported by Royal Navy boats, continued to fish in the waters as far in as the 4-mile (6.5-km) limit.

THE GENERATION GAP

In the 1950s, adolescents—people between childhood and adulthood—developed their own distinctive opinions. They had their own heroes, their own music, their own way of dressing, and spent heavily on leisure—clothes, records, and going out.

The word "teenager" was coined to embrace everyone between the ages of 13 and 19. The teenage world had its own standards—nothing should be too sensible. For better or worse, teenagers were here to stay, and so was the "generation gap" between older and young adults.

Teenager facts

150 million pairs of blue jeans were sold in the US in 1957.
•
British teenagers' spending power in 1959 was £830 million.
•
In 1960, the average 15-year-old had $5 spending money a week.

▼ *Teenagers "hanging out" and listening to the jukebox in a 1950s malt shop diner.*

Hula-Hoop Craze!

Australian children were already familiar with the Hula-Hoop by the time it exploded onto the US market in 1958. Whirling bamboo rings around their waists was a regular activity at school. But it took California's Wham-O company to create a hoop frenzy. Soon they were selling hundreds of millions of hoops a year—and a teenage fad was born.

Teenage bandwagon

Journalists, marketing experts, and advertising agencies jumped on the "teenage bandwagon," by exploiting the standards and identities that teenagers had invented for themselves. Companies energetically sought ways to get young people—the so-called youth market— to spend their hard-earned wealth. Magazines, cosmetics, and even cars and motorbikes were all designed to appeal to young people's taste and their desire to fit in and express themselves. Coffee bars, with their jukeboxes, became places where young people liked to meet and "hang out."

For teenagers, rock and pop stars like Elvis Presley and movie stars like James Dean were important role models, whose lives seemed to reflect their own. Their songs and movies were all about growing up. The teenagers eagerly followed their idols' public lives, went to their movies, bought their records, concert tickets, and magazines by the million. This eagerness was cultivated by big business.

Rebel teenagers

A scene in the 1954 movie *The Wild One* summed up the attitude of the new teenagers. When asked what he is rebelling against, the leader of a motorcycle gang replies: "What have you got?"

Marlon Brando, who played the biker, was one of a new wave of actors who expressed the brooding spirit of teenage rebellion. The life of James Dean, who died in a car crash in 1955 aged 24, seemed to reflect the troubled, self-destructive character he played in *Rebel Without a Cause*.

Musicians also challenged adult values. The Beatnik scene based in New York's Greenwich Village spawned a new breed of protest singer, like Bob Dylan and Joan Baez. "The times, they are a-changin'," Dylan ominously warned the grown-up world. And one of the main changes was that young people were rejecting the standards and beliefs of their parents.

▶ *James Dean in his car in California. Teenagers identified with his attitude to life.*

▼ *Beatniks in Greenwich Village, New York. Beatniks were members of the Beat Generation that developed in the 1950s. They rejected the political views of the time.*

▲ *Background: Posters and souvenirs of the teenage hero James Dean clutter the bedroom of an adoring young fan.*

'80s and '90s technorave

Young people who want to be different have to keep inventing new ideas. Dance music such as techno, jungle, and acid house became increasingly important in the 1980s and '90s. This music (heard at illegal warehouse raves) was loud, and lyrics were often crude and full of sexual and drug-related innuendos. It combined heavy rhythms with the savagery of punk rock and pioneered new uses of electronic sound.

▼ *Techno Festival— The Love Parade— in Berlin, 1995.*

1960

The 1960s was a decade of rapid scientific and technological progress and huge social change. The Soviet Union and the US took the Cold War into space, indulging in a race through the stars to the Moon.

Back on Planet Earth, in the Western world, the contraceptive pill and amplified music fueled revolutions in relations between generations and between men and women. But the decade of student revolutions and "flower power" also saw an intensification of Cold War conflicts. For one dreadful week in 1962, the capitalist and communist superpowers, the US and Russia, stood on the threshold of nuclear war over the Cuban missile crisis.

Pill for women is cleared for sale

Four years after starting medical trials, the Contraceptive pill, Enovid-10, has been approved by the US Food and Drug Administration. The Pill, as it is already known, alters the balance of the hormones estrogen and progesterone in women, preventing eggs from leaving the ovary. The invention of Dr. Gregory Pincus, the Pill allows women to decide when, or if, to have children.

▲ *The birth control pill is designed to be taken daily, but it will not be widely available to women for several years yet.*

POLITICS

US gets youngest president ever

▶ *JFK and Jackie on the New York leg of the campaign.*

9 NOVEMBER By one of the narrowest margins in American political history, Democratic Party candidate John F. Kennedy has been elected president of the US. Richard Nixon, his Republican Party opponent, conceded defeat just after 1:00 this afternoon. Kennedy's popular majority was just 118,000 out of 68 million votes cast. Kennedy is the first Roman Catholic to take office in the White House, and at 43 years old, he is also the youngest US president ever. His campaign, based on the slogan "Let's get America moving again," struck a chord with Americans tired of the faces and policies of the Truman and Eisenhower era. For the first time, television played a major part in the election, and the rival candidates discussed policy in four televised debates. On television the tall, handsome Kennedy did better than Nixon, who looked haggard under his thick studio makeup, his neck scrawnily poking out of a collar half a size too large.

Kennedy facts

President Kennedy's father, Joseph Kennedy, was a selfmade millionaire and US Ambassador to Britain 1936-40.

•

During World War II Kennedy served in the US Navy, earning a distinction when he saved the lives of fellow crewmen.

•

His brothers Robert and Edward also entered politics.

KENNEDY FOR PRESIDENT

LEADERSHIP FOR THE 60's

▲ *Residents of the Sharpeville township protest at South Africa's restrictive new pass laws.*

A massacre in Sharpeville, South Africa

POLITICS

21 MARCH Police opened fire on demonstrators in the Black township of Sharpeville, near Johannesburg, today, killing 69 Africans and injuring nearly 200. Several protesters were apparently shot in the back; among the casualties were many women and children.

The tragedy marks the first day of a campaign against South Africa's pass laws, which restrict the movement of black South Africans. What is already being dubbed the Sharpeville Massacre happened after the township's police panicked.

New Horror from Hitchcock

▲ *Janet Leigh*

This year's offering from Alfred Hitchcock, the master of suspense, is being hailed as his most chilling movie ever. In *Psycho*, Hitchcock has pushed the thriller into horror. The film's most violent sequence shows an unknown assailant repeatedly stabbing Janet Leigh through a shower curtain; cutaway shots of the drain show her blood staining the water. Anthony Perkins plays Norman Bates, the creepy owner of Bates Motel.

Ceylon has the world's first female prime minister

POLITICS

21 JULY Today Mrs. Sirimavo Bandaranaike took office as premier of Ceylon, becoming the world's first woman prime minister. She entered politics after the assassination of her husband and predecessor, Solomon, last year, swearing to carry on his policies. Bandaranaike, aged 43, is leader of the socialist Sri Lanka Freedom Party, which won half of Ceylon's 150 parliamentary seats. She plans to rule in coalition with the minority Marxist Party.

▲ *Sirimavo Bandaranaike.*

U-2 incident leads to diplomatic crisis

POLITICS

▼ *Until recently the American U-2 spy plane was beyond the reach of intercepting aircraft.*

▼ *American airman Francis Gary Powers is sentenced for espionage.*

19 AUGUST Today's sentencing in Moscow of a US spy to 10 years' detention is a major blow to American foreign policy. Pilot Francis Gary Powers, shot down over Sverdlovsk on 1 May, now faces the prospect of three years in prison and seven years of hard labor. He was flying a mission for the US Central Intelligence Agency (CIA) in a top-secret U-2 spy plane. The U-2 is equipped with high-tech photographic and electronic eavesdropping equipment, and it cruises at 70,000 feet (21,300 meters), thought to be beyond the reach of intercepting aircraft or missiles.

Amid US denials that it was carrying out aerial espionage, Soviet premier Nikita Khrushchev canceled a summit meeting with President Eisenhower in Paris. He then produced Francis Powers, pieces of wreckage, and film footage to prove that the CIA, unable to gather intelligence on the ground, was photographing airfields and missile bases from the sky.

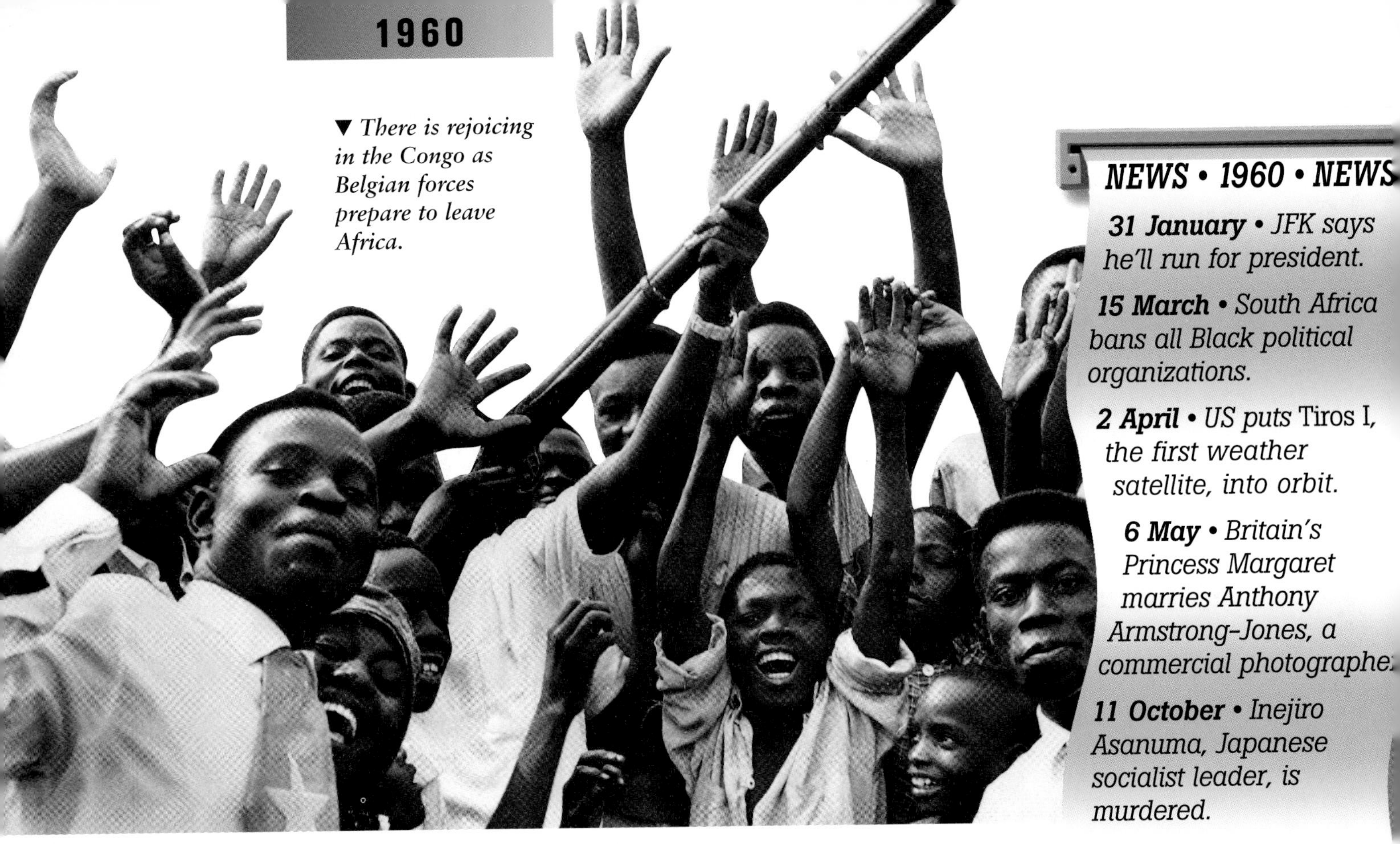

▼ *There is rejoicing in the Congo as Belgian forces prepare to leave Africa.*

Many African states become independent

POLITICS

1 OCTOBER The sun rose over a newly independent Nigeria this morning, and Africa's most populous country joined the growing ranks of the continent's nation-states that no longer belong to European empires. Within a few years, Britain's remaining colonies, which include Uganda, Zambia, and Kenya, should be independent. At the same time, France is relinquishing its cluster of colonies in western and central Africa: Mauritania, Mali, Senegal, Ivory Coast, Upper Volta, Niger, Chad, Togo, Cameroon, Gabon, and the Central African Republic.

The political map of Africa is changing so quickly, it's hard to believe that, just 40 years ago, seven western European countries controlled about 700 million people in overseas colonies. Some commentators fear that, once independence has been achieved, older, precolonial disputes and divisions will come to the surface. For a prosperous, stable future, many of the new states need a continuing relationship with the old imperial power. The Belgians are being criticized for leaving the Congo in a state of chaos, in which civil war is likely to erupt. However, former British colonies, such as Nigeria, will be given support by being part of the Commonwealth, a free and equal association of nations.

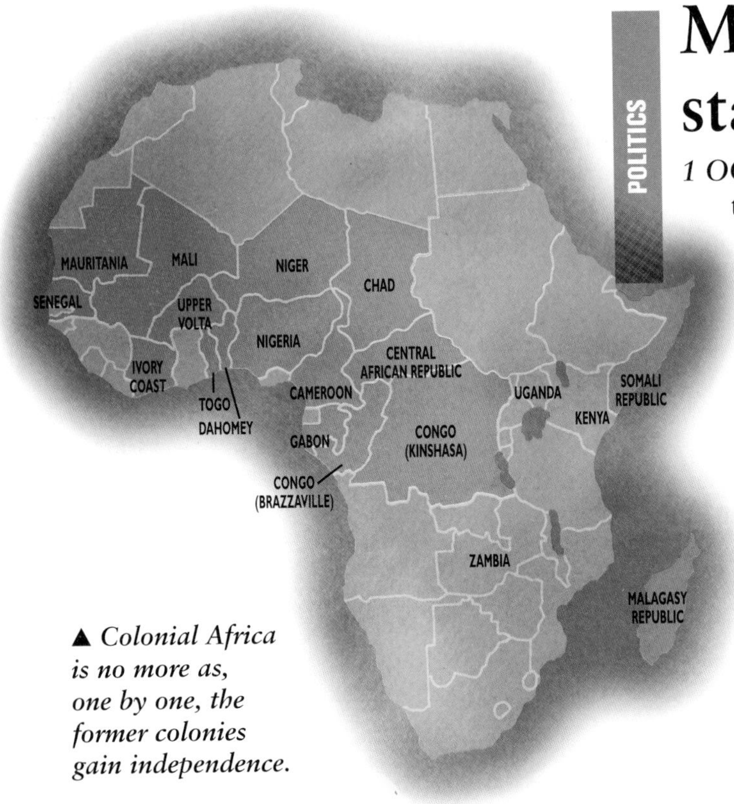

▲ *Colonial Africa is no more as, one by one, the former colonies gain independence.*

Makarios declares independence

POLITICS

16 AUGUST Cyprus became a republic at midnight last night, bringing 81 years of British colonial rule to a close. Makarios III, the Archbishop of Cyprus, is the new republic's first president and a Turkish Cypriot, Dr Kutchuk, is vice-president. Since 1955 Cypriot Greek nationalists have been fighting for *enosis*—union with Greece—but it is hoped that the new government will steer the island toward a peaceful future.

Wilma wins Olympic gold

11 SEPTEMBER An American runner was one of the stars of this year's Olympic Games in Rome. Wilma Rudolph, from Tennessee, sprinted her way to triple gold, winning the 100-meter and 200-meter races and forming part of a triumphant 400-meter relay team. Remarkably, Rudolph suffered from polio as a child and only learned how to walk properly aged eight. Other stars were Abebe Bikila, the barefoot marathon winner from Ethiopia, and an 18-year-old boxer from Kentucky named Cassius Clay.

▼ *Wilma Rudolph in action.*

Piccard dives to ocean's deepest point

On 23 January, Swiss engineer Jacques Piccard and US Navy Lieutenant Don Walsh descended to the bottom of the Pacific Ocean's Marianas Trench—the lowest point on Earth. It took their bathyscaphe, a specialized deep-sea vehicle, 4 hours and 48 minutes to descend the 35,813 feet (10,916 meters) to the bottom.

Macmillan hails "wind of change"

3 FEBRUARY Addressing South Africa's parliament in Cape Town today, British Prime Minister Harold Macmillan warned: "The wind of change is blowing through this continent, and, whether we like it or not, this growth of national consciousness is a political fact." There could be no clearer indication of the British government's determination to accept the end of colonialism in Africa. The future of the world, Macmillan went on to say, depended on whether the newly independent nation-states of Africa and Asia decided to align themselves with the communist empires of China and Soviet Russia or the capitalist West. He also urged South Africa's white politicians to adopt policies of racial equality.

▲ *Real Madrid team.*

Real Madrid win fifth Cup title

18 MAY Real Madrid will keep soccer's European Cup for a record fifth year after beating Eintracht Frankfurt by seven goals to three. A crowd of 135,000 watched at Hampden Park as Madrid fended off Frankfurt's attacks. Stars of the match were Alfredo Di Stefano, who hammered home three of Real Madrid's goals, and Ferenc Puskas, who slammed in the other four.

▲ *The explorer's vehicle, the* Trieste.

Brasilia, Brazil's new capital, is born

21 MARCH Today the capital of Brazil officially moved 625 miles (1,000 km) north, from Rio de Janeiro to Brasilia, a brand new city located in rural Goias state, on Brazil's central plateau. Planner Lucio Costa has laid out Brasilia in the shape of an airplane, reflecting the importance of this remote settlement's air links with the rest of the country: the "wings" are residential areas, and a grand avenue called the Monumental Axis is the fuselage. The chief architect was Oscar Niemeyer. His sensational government buildings are set among grand avenues and artificial lakes.

◄ *Niemeyer's Square of the Three Authorities in Brasilia.*

1960

1961

1962

1963

1964

1965

1966

1967

1968

1969

Berlin's wall of fear rises up

POLITICS

20 AUGUST Although it's only a week since work began, a concrete wall 28 miles (45 km) long, and 5 feet (1.5 meters) high now divides Berlin in two. The wall has been erected by East Berlin's ruling communist authorities to stop the flow of East Germans who have been "voting with their feet" and fleeing to the West. More than 45,000 people had flooded into West Berlin before East German troops unrolled the barbed wire that, within a matter of days, has grown into this grim barrier. Western protests against the violation of Berlin's status as an open city, controlled equally by the four Allied victors of World War II, have been in vain. The protests of Berliners are met by armed force. Meanwhile, as the East German authorities reinforce the Berlin Wall with watchtowers and gun emplacements, the Western powers (France, the US, and Great Britain) are getting ready to place troops along their side of the wall. Although Willy Brandt, mayor of West Berlin, has told East Berliners that they cannot be enslaved forever, for the foreseeable future the Iron Curtain between East and West is a physical reality.

▲ *Made of prefabricated concrete blocks, the wall that snakes between East and West Berlin went up very quickly.*

▶ *As the Berlin Wall rises, an East German soldier takes the chance to escape to freedom.*

Jaguar E-type launched

Jaguar's new sports car, the E-type, caused a stir when it was unveiled at this year's Geneva car show. The main talking point was not its 150 miles (240 km) per hour top speed, nor its powerful 3.4 liter "gold top" XK engine, nor even its stunning looks. No, what amazed viewers was its price: at $3,300 it is about half the cost of its competitors.

▼ *The "E" type Jag, sportscar of the 1960s.*

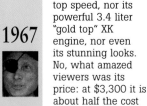

THE JAGUAR "E" TYPE G.T. OPEN TWO-SEATER

UN Secretary General killed in air crash

POLITICS

18 SEPTEMBER Dag Hammarskjöld, Secretary General of the United Nations, died in an air crash early this morning. The DC-6 airliner in which he was traveling to meet Congolese rebel Moise Tshombe fell from the sky near Ndola, in northern Rhodesia.

Swedish diplomat Hammarskjöld, who was 56, had been UN Secretary General since 1953. His interventions in the 1956 Suez crisis and the 1958 Jordan crisis won him a reputation as a peacemaker, but his approval last year of the UN force sent into the Congo to stop Tshombe's Katanga forces from setting up an independent state was attacked by Soviet and Western delegates. Hammarskjöld's diplomacy in dealing with sensitive issues will be sorely missed.

▼ *Hammarskjöld— UN Secretary General.*

222

POLITICS
Bay of Pigs fiasco

19 APRIL Fidel Castro has crushed a US-backed attempt to overthrow his revolutionary government in Cuba. Two days ago, 1,500 Cuban exiles—trained and armed by the Central Intelligence Agency—landed at Cochinos Bay (Bay of Pigs), on Cuba's coast. With neither air support nor the general uprising predicted by the CIA, the rebels were no match for Castro's Russian-made MiG fighters and tanks. The failure of the operation has embarrassed the United States.

◀ *Some of Fidel Castro's victorious troops.*

Happy to be an American hit movie

Stephen Sondheim and Leonard Bernstein's 1957 Broadway musical *West Side Story* has made a triumphant transfer onto celluloid. Based on Shakespeare's *Romeo and Juliet*, and set against a background of gang warfare in modern New York, it stars Natalie Wood and Richard Beymer, but George Chakiris and Rita Moreno, in lesser roles, manage to steal the show.

◀ *A dance scene from West Side Story.*

POLITICS
White South Africa goes its own way

31 MAY As of today, following a White referendum, the Union of South Africa is a republic and no longer a member of the British Commonwealth. "It is clear after the lead given by a group of Afro-Asian nations that we will be no longer welcome," was the defiant comment of Prime Minister Hendrik Verwoerd. After this move, it is likely that Black South African political leaders will adopt a policy of armed resistance to the policy of apartheid (racial segregation).

▲ *Patrice Lumumba before his murder.*

WAR
Civil war in the Congo

21 DECEMBER Today's surrender of Moise Tshombe, the leader of the Katanga rebels who want their mineral-rich province to be a separate country, marks the end of a troubled year in the African Congo. In January, the Congo's first prime minister, Patrice Lumumba, was found dead in suspicious circumstances—possibly murdered by the Katangans. But while African opinion is generally in favor of the UN's support for the Congolese army, Western and Soviet powers are saying that UN forces shouldn't have become involved in the conflict.

TECHNOLOGY
Gagarin is the first man in space

12 APRIL Russia has beaten America in the race to put a man into space. Soviet test pilot Yuri Gagarin today orbited the Earth in the spacecraft *Vostok I*. He took off from the Baikonur cosmodrome in Kazakhstan at 9:07 this morning, and landed in his capsule near Saratov, in Russia, 108 minutes later. Today's mission proves that humans can survive the stresses of rapid acceleration and deceleration during takeoff and landing. Gagarin, whose flight capsule was only 8 feet 5 inches (2.58 meters) in diameter, says he felt fine.

▶ *Yuri Gagarin, the first man in space.*

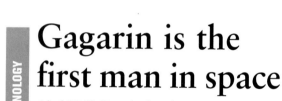

"Freedom riders" meet with violence

14 MAY As they tour the southern states, a group of antiracist campaigners is meeting with violent opposition. The racially mixed group of passengers, the "freedom riders," are traveling on local and interstate bus services in order to test whether Federal orders to integrate public transportation are being obeyed. Some of the ugliest scenes have taken place in the town of Montgomery, capital of Alabama, where white segregationists, who include members of the notorious Ku Klux Klan, have tried to burn and block the path of buses, and attacked freedom riders with clubs.

Attorney-General Robert Kennedy has sent Federal marshals to Montgomery, where a local Baptist preacher, the Rev. Dr. Martin Luther King, has pledged to continue the struggle for equal rights. Dr. King was prominent in the 1955 bus boycott in Alabama, during which 500 African-Americans protesting against segregation on the buses were arrested. Then, as now, the eloquent Dr. King insists that "passive resistance and the weapon of love" are the most effective means of fighting bigotry and racism.

◄ *A freedom rider is seized and searched by a local policeman.*

Asterix the wily Gaul makes his debut

Asterix the Gaul has been a familiar comic character in France since 1957, when he first appeared in the weekly magazine *Pilote*. Now his creators, artist Albert Uderzo and writer René Goscinny, have published their first book featuring the freedom fighter from 50 B.C. and his friends Obelix and Getafix.

▲ *The ancient Gaul's modern creators.*

Amnesty candle is lit

28 MAY When British lawyer Peter Benenson heard that Antonio Salazar's regime in Portugal had jailed two students for seven years, just for drinking a toast to freedom, he resolved to take action. Today he launches a campaign against such abuses of human rights. According to Benenson, thousands of men and women are imprisoned and tortured because they express political or religious views that differ from their government's, yet according to the UN Declaration of Human Rights, everyone is entitled to freedom of speech, belief, thought, and opinion. The "Appeal for Amnesty" will alert the international public to breaches of that UN Declaration. It will try to secure a fair trial and, if possible, freedom for victims of injustice, wherever they are.

▶ *Amnesty's striking symbol, a candle of hope within barbed wire.*

Spotted dogs are Disney's new stars

The latest full-length cartoon from the Walt Disney studios is a beautifully animated version of Dodie Smith's classic children's tale, *101 Dalmatians*.

The adorable spotted dogs of the title and a host of other animals cause havoc in London and the countryside as they try to escape Cruella de Vil, most memorable Disney female villain since the witch in *Snow White*.

ONE GREAT BIG ONEDERFUL MOTION PICTURE

WALT DISNEY'S NEW ALL-CARTOON FEATURE

One Hundred and One Dalmatians

technicolor

▲ The Vasa *was made with 1,000 oak trees.*

LAW Nazi Eichmann to hang

15 DECEMBER Adolf Eichmann, the former SS colonel in charge of transporting millions of Jews and other "undesirables" to death camps during World War II, was sentenced to death in Jerusalem today. His trial, which started in April, followed his abduction from Buenos Aires by Israeli agents last year. The testimony of over a hundred witnesses, including 90 Holocaust survivors, reverberated around the world. Eichmann said he was a minor cog in a big machine, but the judges found that he was a key perpetrator of the century's greatest crime.

▲ *Adolf Eichmann.*

ARCHEOLOGY Sensational finds at Olduvai Gorge

24 FEBRUARY Husband and wife fossilhunters Louis and Mary Leakey believe that the skull and bone fragments recently unearthed in Tanzania's Olduvai Gorge belonged to an ancient human, or hominid. If they're right, human origins, currently thought to date from 1.7 million years ago, will be pushed back by another 1.25 million years.

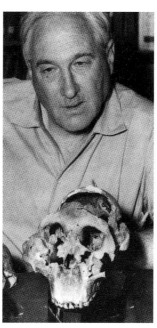
▶ *Louis Leakey with the Olduvai skull.*

ARCHEOLOGY The raising of the *Vasa*

24 APRIL Excited crowds gathered around Stockholm's harbor today to witness the raising of the *Vasa*, the Swedish warship that sank on its maiden voyage more than 300 years ago. In the summer of 1628, when she capsized in full view of the Stockholmers who had come to see her off, the *Vasa* was the largest and most expensive naval vessel ever built in Sweden. No one was punished for the disaster, in which at least 50 people drowned, because it wasn't clear who or what was to blame. Now that it's been salvaged, modern archeologists may be able to explain why she sank. It is planned to turn this spectacular relic of Swedish history into a museum.

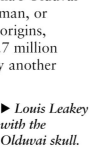

NEWS • 1961 • NEWS

26 April • Coup by French army officers in Algiers collapses.

5 May • Alan B. Shepard is the first American astronaut in space.

4 June • Kennedy and Khrushchev meet at Vienna summit.

23 October • USSR detonates a massive nuclear bomb.

3 November • New Secretary General of UN is Burmese diplomat U Thant.

ENTERTAINMENT Rudolf Nureyev wants to stay in the West

16 JUNE Today, just as he was about to board a plane to London, Rudolf Nureyev made a dramatic bid for freedom. The 23-year-old star of the Kirov Ballet Company rushed up to police at Paris' Le Bourget Airport and demanded their protection.

The French authorities have granted asylum. Soviet officials were allowed to see him, but failed to persuade him to return to Russia. With his striking looks and his virtuoso style, which combines skill with artistry, Rudolf Nureyev is already regarded as the greatest male dancer since Vaslav Nijinsky. There will be no shortage of roles for him in the West.

▶ *Dance virtuoso Rudolf Nureyev.*

225

1960
1961
1962
1963
1964
1965
1966
1967
1968
1969

1962

► *This little girl is a victim of the drug thalidomide, used as an ingredient in the pharmaceuticals in the foreground.*

Tragic babies, thalidomide to blame

SCIENCE

5 NOVEMBER Today a Belgian family and their doctor were found not guilty of the mercy killing of Corinne van de Put, their baby who was born without arms. They used barbiturates to poison the baby soon after her birth. Her deformities were caused by the drug thalidomide. Thalidomide is an ingredient used in medicines as a sedative and prescribed mainly to expectant mothers in the early stages of pregnancy. Recent discoveries point to this being the main cause of deformities such as malformation of limbs or internal organs.

In many cases, babies whose mothers had taken the drug were born with malformations of the ear and stomach. Estimates say that 500 such deformed babies have been born in Great Britain and some 3,000 in Germany. Since it was brought out in 1959, thalidomide has been freely prescribed by doctors in both these countries for minor ailments such as backache, lack of sleep, morning sickness, or general depression. It has been withdrawn immediately from all pharmacies since the terrible discovery that these malformations have a direct link to the drug.

Close-ups of the planet Venus

The US space probe *Mariner 2* (below) has today (14 Dec) sent back the first close-up pictures of Venus. Little was known about this planet due to its dense atmosphere, containing 96% carbon dioxide, 3% nitrogen, and traces of water vapor, argon, and neon. The carbon dioxide traps the heat of the Sun and creates a raging inferno of about 860°F (460°C) on the planet's surface.

NEWS • 1962 • NEWS

8 January • In Holland 93 people are reported dead in a collision between two trams.

20 February • John Glenn is first American to orbit Earth.

23 April • British driver Stirling Moss' injured in 110-mile per hour (177-km per hour) crash.

31 May • Eichmann hanged for his Nazi war crimes.

17 June • Brazil wins World Cup.

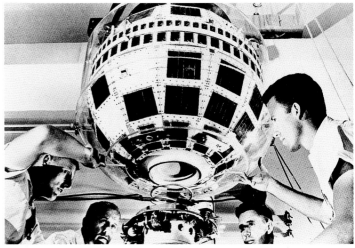

▲ *Technicians working on Telstar before its launch.*

Yves is first "Telstar"

TECHNOLOGY

11 JULY Live worldwide broadcasting was made possible today with the launch of the Telstar communications satellite by the American Telephone and Telegraph Company. The artificial satellite beamed black and white pictures from its transmitter at Andover, Maine, to receiving stations at Goonhilly Downs in Cornwall, in England, and Pleumeur-Boudou in Brittany, in France. While France managed the best picture transmission, sending images of Yves Montand singing to the US, Britain only sent a testcard transmission in its final minute of broadcast. It is believed that this satellite will change the broadcasting of pictures quite dramatically, thus making worldwide television possible for the future.

▲ *Even women were trained during the Chinese-Indian war.*

ENTERTAINMENT

Marilyn takes her own life

5 AUGUST Early this morning the body of Marilyn Monroe was found in her Hollywood apartment. The star of many memorable movies such as *Some Like It Hot* and *Bus Stop* was discovered naked in her bed, clutching a bottle of sleeping pills, and a telephone. Born Norma Jean Baker, she had a troubled childhood, moving from one foster home to another. Married three times, first at 16 years of age, her next, much publicized, marriage to baseball star Joe DiMaggio lasted 9 months. Finally she married Pulitzer prize-winning playwright Arthur Miller, who wrote the screenplay for her last film *The Misfits*.

◀ *Marylin Monroe, sex goddess of stage and screen, who died*

POLITICS

Ceasefire after Bomdila

21 NOVEMBER Following the capture of Bomdila, an Indian border town, Chinese troops have stopped their advance into India. A ceasefire has been agreed, together with further talks to resolve the frontier dispute over territory along the Himalayan border and to end the war. The Chinese advantage has forced India into a very difficult position, and the Indian army has no option but to accept defeat. With one division already cut off from the rest of the troops, they have lost a good part of the mountainous northern border territory.

POLITICS

Algeria for the Algerians

3 JULY After more than a century of French rule, and decades of bitter conflict, Algeria is to be an independent country. Ninety-nine percent of voters in the referendum held two days ago were in favor of breaking all ties with France. The referendum was part of the Evian peace agreement signed between Louis Joxe for France and Benyoussef Ben Kheddah, who was acting as head of the Algerian government. Today, the President of France, Charles de Gaulle, "solemnly recognized" the result of the referendum, and tomorrow Algeria will become a sovereign independent state.

◀ *Ben Bella (below left), who conducted the Evian talks, and a poster urging peace.*

▶ *Campbell's Soup Can by Andy Warhol, an icon of the way-out world of pop art.*

Warhol shocks with soup and soap

Andy Warhol revealed his unique brand of pop art at an exhibition in New York today. Paintings of Campbell's Soup cans, Coca-Cola bottles, and replicas of Brillo Soap Pad boxes went on show to instant acclaim. Born in Pittsburgh, Warhol graduated from the Carnegie Institute of Technology with a degree in pictorial design in 1949. He then went to New York City where he worked as a commercial illustrator, the experience that inspired his art.

Cuban crisis over

POLITICS

28 OCTOBER Today has seen the peaceful resolution of possibly the closest approach to nuclear war ever. The world could only watch in disbelief as President Kennedy and Soviet Premier Nikita Khrushchev waged a battle of nerves.

The seeds of the crisis were sown in May 1960 when the Soviet Premier vowed to defend communist Cuba against US aggression. The Soviets began to install long-range-missile launch sites in Cuba that would have threatened much of the eastern US.

On 29 August this year new military construction and the presence of Soviet technicians had been spotted by US U-2 spy planes. On 16 October photos of launch sites were delivered to President Kennedy. After considering the alternatives, he ordered a naval blockade of Cuba and warned that US armed forces would seize offensive weapons and associated material that Soviet vessels tried to deliver to Cuba.

On 24 October Soviet vessels began turning back but work continued on the sites. Messages were exchanged between Kennedy and Khrushchev with extreme tension on both sides. The crisis was finally settled today with the agreement that the Soviets would dismantle the launch sites in Cuba and return the missiles to the Soviet Union. In return, Kennedy promised never to invade Cuba. The Cuban missile crisis was over.

LAUNCH POSITION

MISSILE-READY TENT

MISSILE ERECTOR

▶ *JFK goes on TV to tell the American people about the blockade of Cuba.*

▲ *An aerial photo of the Soviet missile base in Cuba.*

Maiden flight of British hovercraft

Across the River Dee between Rhyl and Wallasey, 24 passengers made a hovercraft journey this July. This was Britain's first commercial hovercraft service, which carried mail as well as passengers. The hovercraft (above) runs on land or water with its weight supported by the "cushion" of air created between it and the ground or water.

Racists riot as black student enters Deep South college

POLITICS

30 SEPTEMBER James Meredith (right) has today become the first African-American student to enroll at the University of Mississippi. His admission to the university was agreed upon by the University Board of Trustees in compliance with the new desegregation law. Meredith's entrance was blocked by state troopers, who were sent in by Governor Ross Barnett. President Kennedy, however, ordered Federal marshals to escort Meredith to class. Three people were killed and 50 others were injured as angry whites, enraged by Barnett's actions, stormed the university in protest against Meredith's admission.

Pan Am reaches for the sky

ARCHITECHTURE

1962 A landmark building was inaugurated today in New York City. The Pan Am Building, the flagship building of the airline giant, Pan American Airways, has been designed by Emery Roth & Sons, Pietro Belluschi, and Walter Gropius. Dominating Park Avenue at 59 storys high, it stands between the New York Central Building and Grand Central Terminal. The sheer height and width draw the eye away from its neighboring buildings. The sweeping curve of this giant concrete monster represents the introduction of modern architecture into one of New York's grandest streets.

▶ *Aerial view of the new Pan Am Building.*

Saint-Laurent launches his own label

CULTURE

15 JANUARY Christian Dior's protégé, Yves Saint-Laurent, has opened his own fashion house in Paris. Born in Algeria in 1936, Saint-Laurent was only 21 when he was given the top job at Dior. Christian Dior achieved worldwide fame with his full-skirted "New Look" and was a tough act for any young couturier to follow. At the outset of his stint at Dior, Saint-Laurent was criticized for being too flamboyant with his use of vibrant colors. This tendency may have been a legacy of his early days as a theatrical costume designer, but under his new YSL label he can give free rein to those extravagant instincts. For the time being he has abandoned the short skirts for which he was so heavily criticized and is promoting slacks for women. Saint-Laurent's current image is one of elegance and sophistication, with equal attention to city and country wear, and there is great interest in his "A line" dresses (which flare slightly from the shoulder) in delicate fabrics.

▼ *Saint-Laurent surrounded by some of his models at a fashion show.*

True Brit Bond has international appeal

"007," the suave superhero of Ian Fleming's thrillers, made his screen debut today. Sean Connery and Ursula Andress, seen below, costar in the movie version of *Dr. No*, which is delighting movie audiences. Bond's creator, British novelist Ian Fleming, has written 12 Bond novels, and plans are already under way to film the next two stories, *From Russia With Love* and *Goldfinger*.

Fear of smallpox in Britain

SCIENCE

14 JANUARY Following the outbreak of smallpox in Britain, six people have died and six more are still dangerously ill. Doctors are doing all they can to prevent a major epidemic. One of the victims is a pathologist who contracted the virus after conducting a post-mortem on a child who died of the disease. A group of foreign visitors who arrived at London Airport were detained for observation because they were suspected smallpox sufferers, but were found to have a severe case of travel sickness. Some British politicians are now calling for compulsory vaccination for everyone.

SECRETS AND SPIES

What is a spy—a James Bond hero, or a woman sending Morse signals across a frontier? In reality there are many types of spy, from trained agents, who adopt false identities and live "normal" lives until called into action, to amateurs, lured into working for another country.

Spies may work for money or out of personal belief, for example, the communist sympathizers in the West who gave defense secrets to the Soviet Union. They may act alone or they may be part of a network, such as that run by Richard Sorge, a German agent working in Japan in 1941.

Cold War secret agents

◄ From the top: Famous Cold War spies— Maclean, Philby, Fuchs, Blunt, and Penkovsky.

The conflict between the Communist bloc and the West between 1945 and 1989 may have been "cold" (without fighting), but the spy war was often violent.

The Russians recruited many Westerners sympathetic to communism as double agents. Donald Maclean kept the Russians informed of US and British secrets while he was a high official in the British Embassy in Washington. "Kim" Philby, another double agent spy, reached a high rank in the British Secret Service (MI6) while working for the Soviets. Klaus Fuchs was a brilliant German physicist who fled the Nazis in 1933 and settled in Britain. He took part in the top secret development of the atom bomb, during which time he passed technical details to a Russian agent. Anthony Blunt, a famous British art historian, passed information to the Russians while he was with British Intelligence during World War II. As a Cambridge lecturer, he recruited agents for the Soviet secret service.

The West also found sympathizers in the Soviet Union. Oleg Penkovsky was a colonel in Soviet military intelligence (GRU) who offered to work for the British in 1961. He passed over 5,000 photos of secret documents before he was arrested, tried, and executed for treason in 1963 in the Soviet Union.

▼ Julius and Ethel Rosenberg, American "atomic spies" (like Fuchs), were executed in 1953.

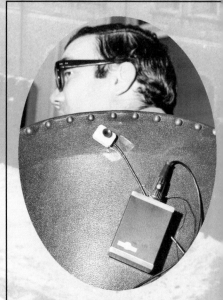

▲ A bugging device that can be installed on the back of a chair.

Spy facts

Russia: During the Cold War, a complete "American" town was built in Russia to train spies for service in the US.

•

Britain: During World War II every German spy in Britain was caught.

•

Germany: German spy chiefs perfected the microdot, a miniaturized message that can be concealed underneath a period in a printed document.

Femme fatale spies

One of the first female agents was Delilah in the Bible, who discovered the secret of Samson's strength and passed it on to the enemy, the Philistines. Some of the best secret agents in history have been women— although one of the most famous, Mata Hari, was not a successful spy. Like Delilah, her secret weapon was sex. Mata Hari was the stage name of Dutch-born Margarete Gertrud Zelle. A dancer, well known in the nightclubs of Europe, she relied on sex appeal rather than talent for her success, and she had many lovers. During World War I Mata Hari traveled around Europe, dancing and having affairs with important officials on both sides of the war. She had friends in the German secret service, and she received money from them for giving away Allied secrets. She was arrested by the French in 1917, accused of passing information to the Germans. After a seemingly unfair trial in a military court, she was convicted and shot.

▲ A view of the formidable "fortressed" Moscow Kremlin (1947), the center of Russian government.

▶ The seductive Mata Hari performs an exotic Eastern dance.

Tools of the trade

The main job of a spy is to obtain and transmit information in secret— often making use of the latest advances in communication technology. The days are long gone when a spy set out equipped with a bottle of invisible ink and a false mustache. Agents in the Resistance during World War II contacted London with a cumbersome radio carried in a large suitcase, but 30 years later, spies had radio transmitters small enough to fit into a matchbox. During the Vietnam War, one agent was caught when his own clothes were bugged by his servant (an agent for the other side). One of his tunic buttons was a microphone.

▶ The camera in a hat was a novelty item, not for serious spies!

ADAMS & CO.'S "HAT" DETECTIVE CAMERA.

ADAMS & Cº

ADAMS & Cº

THIS folds inside the same as an ordinary opera hat, and the lens can be removed in a moment, it simply fitting in with a bayonet joint. It takes pictures 4¼ × 3½, and is fitted with a best quality Rectilinear Lens, working at f/11. The shutter works in the diaphragm slot and time as well as instantaneous exposures may be given. A focussing screen is also supplied. This is really a good instrument, and is not to be classed with the small postage stamp so-called cameras, like the scarf, purse, and button-hole. By taking 4¼ × 3½ it becomes a useful instrument. They are sent out all ready for fitting, or we fit them free of expense if hat is sent. **Price £3 3s. net, with two Slides. Extra Slides, 4/- each.**

▲ A secret message hidden in a shoelace.

▶ The lady's wallet is really a camera. That watch looks suspicious, too!

Timeline

1960

1961

1962

1963

1964

1965

1966

1967

1968

1969

1963

POLITICS

Luther King speaks at civil rights march

28 AUGUST More than 250,000 people walked through the streets of Washington today and gathered at the Lincoln Memorial in the biggest civil rights march to date. The Rev. Dr. Martin Luther King, Jr., gave a speech to the gathering, which included the likes of Judy Garland, Marlon Brando, Burt Lancaster, and Bob Dylan. King said: "I have a dream. It is a dream chiefly rooted in the American dream. I have a dream that one day this nation will rise up and live out the true meaning of its creed: we hold these truths to be self-evident that all men are created equal. I have a dream that the sons of former slaves and the sons of former slave owners will sit together at the table of brotherhood." President Kennedy said that his actions and the actions of other activists had speeded up the "cause of 20 million negroes" and would have an impact on all of our lives.

East–West "hotline" set up

Today saw the opening of a "hotline" between the White House and the Kremlin. This direct link has been designed to defuse any sudden East–West tensions. This will lessen the risk of accidental war, and enable a more secure, faster exchange of information. The test communication, which was in code, has been deemed a complete success.

▲ *Civil rights leader the Rev. Dr. Martin Luther King, Jr., addresses a gathering of 250,000 at the Lincoln Memorial in Washington. Here he delivered his speach, "I have a dream."*

TREATIES

Elysee Treaty signed

22 JANUARY After bitter enmity for 100 years, France and West Germany today signed a treaty of cooperation in Paris, France. Known as the Elysee Treaty, it marks a turning point for Europe, as France and West Germany agree to be friends. President Charles De Gaulle of France and the German leader, Konrad Adenauer, decided that the heads of states and Ministers for Foreign Affairs, Defense, and Education from both countries are to meet several times a year to coordinate their policies. Their aim is to find common ground on any problems affecting NATO, the Common Market, communism, and the underdeveloped world. French is to be taught in German schools and vice versa, and French and German students are to be exchanged.

◀ *The Beatles—John, Paul, Ringo, and George.*

Beatlemania!

The Beatles hit "She Loves You" has been at No. 1 in Britain, for four weeks, selling over a million copies and creating Beatlemania. The "Fab Four" held up traffic when thousands of screaming fans mobbed the London Palladium, where the band was featured in a TV show, and even delayed the prime minister's car due to the traffic congestion.

The Great Train Robbery

LAW

8 AUGUST The biggest robbery in British history occurred today, when a Royal Mail train was stopped by a train signal that had been sabotaged. The 15 robbers, armed and wearing masks, jumped on board the train and stole £2.6 million mainly in used bills, which were on their way to be destroyed.
The gang escaped in a getaway car to their country hideaway to divide the loot. The robbers captured the fireman who went to investigate the signal and severely injured the driver, who was battered repeatedly on the back of the head during the raid.

▶ *Two men, held in connection with the Great Train Robbery, on their way to court.*

Nuclear Test Ban Treaty

ENVIRONMENT

5 AUGUST A Nuclear Test Ban Treaty, signed today in Moscow by the US, the UK, and the USSR, was described as a "great occasion for us all" by British foreign secretary, Lord Home. Mr. Khrushchev of the USSR said "a nuclear test ban does not mean disarmament and does not mean the end of the arms race." What it does mean is a ban on weapons testing in the atmosphere, outer space, and under water, making the world safer for future generations.

▼ *J.F. Kennedy and wife Jackie photographed in a motorcade driving through Dallas, Texas, shortly before his assassination.*

NEWS • 1963 • NEWS

5 June • John Profumo, British secretary of state for war, resigns after lying about his affair with Christine Keeler, which may have breached government security.

16 June • Russia puts first woman, Lieutenant Valentina Tereshkova, into space in a Vostok spaceship.

24 November • Lee Harvey Oswald, the man charged with the assassination of Kennedy, is murdered.

Kennedy assassinated

POLITICS

22 NOVEMBER John F. Kennedy, the 35th president of the United States of America, is dead. An assassin fired at Kennedy while he was riding in a motorcade through the streets of Dallas, Texas, also killing a local policeman. John Connally, the governor of Texas, who was riding in Kennedy's car was seriously wounded. Glorious weather had brought hundreds of people out to see their president. Kennedy received several shots to the head and fell into the arms of his wife, Jackie, who was next to him in the convertible. The stunned First Lady cradled her husband's severely bleeding head as the car and its motorcycle entourage rushed him to nearby Parkland Hospital. Surgeons fought in vain to save him, but he died 25 minutes later. Lee Harvey Oswald, a former Marine, has been arrested for the assassination.

UNESCO to save Abu Simbel temples

ARCHEOLOGY

1964 A project has been started today to save the temples of Abu Simbel, spectacular examples of ancient Egyptian art, from water damage from the reservoir behind the new Aswan Dam. The work is being undertaken by the United Nations Educational, Scientific, and Cultural Organization (UNESCO) and is partly sponsored by the Egyptian government. The reservoir, which has a depth of 300 feet (91 meters) and a width of 14 miles (22.5 km), supports a fishing industry and provides navigational links. The complex engineering work is being carried out by an international team of engineers and scientists backed by funds from more than 50 countries. The project is expected to last for more than two years. The aim is to move the four statues in front of the main temple, then dig away the top of the cliff and completely disassemble both temples, reconstructing them on high ground 200 feet (60 meters) above the riverbed and well away from potential damage by the floodwaters.

▲ *Face to face with antiquity, an archeologist works on the head of one of the statues.*

Abu Simbel facts

The two monuments were cut into 1,050 pieces, the heaviest weighing about 33 tons (33 tonnes). The face of Ramses II alone weighed 21 tons (21 tonnes).

•

The four statues of Rameses II are more than 67 feet (20 meters) high.

•

The cost of relocating the Temple was originally estimated at $36 million and was not due to be completed until 1967.

▲ *Abu Simbel was built for Ramses II in the 13th century* B.C.

PLO is founded in Palestine

POLITICS

1964 The Palestine Liberation Organization has been created to represent the world's estimated 4.45 million Palestinians who found themselves dispersed among the Arab countries after the breakup of Palestine and the creation of the state of Israel in its place. The purpose of the PLO is to unify the various Palestinian factions which previously had to operate as secret resistance groups. Ideals within the PLO are varied, ranging from a willingness to negotiate with Israel for a Palestinian state to the desire to destroy Israel and replace it with a state in which Muslims, Jews, and Christians could live as equals.

Nikita Khrushchev deposed in the Soviet Union

POLITICS

14 OCTOBER Nikita Khrushchev, the 70-year-old Soviet leader, has been ousted in a sinister plot by members of his own Communist Party. He was called back to Moscow from a vacation by the Politburo, for what he thought was a meeting. It was a trap, and he was arrested and charged with 15 offenses, ranging from making bad decisions to being undiplomatic to foreign dignitaries. Some of these criticisms were true. He was swiftly replaced by Leonid Brezhnev as Communist Party leader and Alexei Kosygin as prime minister.

▲ *Turkish-Cypriots evacuating their village after a battle against Greek fighters.*

Greek-Turkish Cypriot war begins

WAR

12 FEBRUARY Fighting has erupted in independent Cyprus today between Greek and Turkish Cypriots. The hostilities have so far left 20 Turks and one Greek Cypriot dead. British troops are still in Cyprus, since Britain maintained sovereignty over its two military bases when it granted the island independence four years ago. But attempts by the British to arrange a ceasefire have so far failed. The Prime Minister of Turkey, Ismet Inonu, has appealed for a UN peacekeeping force to be sent to Cyprus to protect the rights of the Turkish minority—Greek and Turkish Cypriots are supposed to share power on the island.

Japan's new high speed train

A high-speed rail link has been built between Tokyo and Osaka in Japan. The track, known locally as the New Tokaido Line, is 320 miles (515 km) long. Bullet trains are run on the line and can reach speeds in excess of 130 mph (200 km/h), thanks to new innovations such as prestressed concrete ties and welded sections of track that are a mile (1.6 km) long.

▶ *Japan's new Shinkansen bullet train.*

Pandit Nehru dies

POLITICS

27 MAY Jawaharlal Nehru, the first Prime Minister of independent India, died of a heart attack in New Delhi today, aged 74. A brilliant leader, who established India's parliamentary government and achieved acclaim for his "neutralist" foreign affairs policies, he will be deeply missed in India and the world over. Nehru is to be cremated, following the Hindu custom, on 29 May on the banks of the Jumna River in the presence of heads of state from around the world.

◀ *Jawaharlal Nehru.*

Sidney Poitier wins Academy Award

ENTERTAINMENT

13 APRIL The Academy Award for Best Actor has gone to Sidney Poitier for his role as the handyman who helps a group of nuns build a chapel in the Arizona desert in *Lilies Of The Field*. Written by James Poe and directed by Ralph Nelson, the movie promotes racial harmony and Christian unity, which relies on the light handling of comedy, so ably displayed by Poitier. At a time when the major studios have tried to outspend each other for success, it is refreshing to see a small budget movie make a box-office killing.

▶ *Oscar winner, actor Sidney Poitier.*

Mary Quant gives skirts a rise

Ingenious British designer Mary Quant has come up trumps with another fashion sensation, the miniskirt. The creative force behind the Chelsea boutique, Bazaar, Quant has broken free of the dictates of Paris fashion, which she describes as "out-of-date," and has come up with a version of the miniskirt that is simple but daring, with its high-above-the-knee length. A former art student, Quant has had to go into mass production to meet the demand for her fashion both here and in the US, and it looks as if this miniskirt is destined to be a success, too.

▶ *Quant wears her version of the miniskirt.*

TECHNOLOGY

The first close-up photographs of the Moon

31 JULY Detailed photographs of the Moon have been sent back to Earth from *Ranger 7*, one of a series of unmanned probes sent to the Moon by NASA (National Aeronautics and Space Administration), the first of which was launched in 1961. *Ranger 7* has just become the first American spacecraft to reach the Moon and crashlanded on its surface as planned. The photographs, which were taken using remote-controlled cameras, have unraveled many mysteries about the Moon, such as its age, the characteristics of its soil and climate, and its general history.

▲ *A photograph sent back by* Ranger 7.

▲ *Nelson Mandela pictured in the early 1960s before he was sentenced to life imprisonment.*

NEWS • 1964 • NEWS

14 March • *Jack Ruby is found guilty of the murder of Lee Harvey Oswald (the man accused of Kennedy's assassination).*

27 March • *Ten of the Great Train robbers are found guilty.*

16 October • *Harold Wilson becomes British prime minister, heading the first Labour government in 13 years.*

24 October • *Rev. Dr. Martin Luther King is awarded the Nobel Peace Prize in Oslo.*

POLITICS

Life sentence for Nelson Mandela

14 JUNE Nelson Mandela, organizer of the banned African National Congress, was sentenced to life imprisonment today, along with eight other ANC members, on charges of sabotage, treason, violent conspiracy, and plotting to overthrow the racist white South African government. Mandela was sent away to Robben Island, an inescapable prison surrounded by freezing waters. Many people are angered at the outcome of the trial, and a crowd of Africans was seen saluting and chanting "we have the strength" as their leader was taken away.

Rolling Stones in US

The Rolling Stones opened their first American tour this evening in San Bernardino, California. The Stones—Mick Jagger on vocals, guitarists Brian Jones and Keith Richards, drummer Charlie Watts, and Bill Wyman on bass—have attracted enormous attention since the release of their first single "Come On" and their first TV appearance in June 1963. Like The Beatles, they have captured the imagination of music fans and receive an hysterical response at every appearance.

▼ *The sensational Rolling Stones in concert.*

Tonkin Bay resolution

POLITICS

7 AUGUST The Tonkin Bay Resolution, which gives President L. B. Johnson vast authority over matters and decisions about the war in Vietnam, has been passed today by Congress with votes of 88 for and 2 against. This follows attacks on US destroyers by North Vietnamese patrolboats. Though the ships were undamaged, President Johnson, who has been given free license by Congress to use retaliatory armed forces to defend the Allied forces fighting in Vietnam, ordered US warplanes to retaliate by bombing Vietnamese bases for torpedo boats. The Tonkin Bay resolution amounts to a "blank check" for presidential warmaking in Southeast Asia.

▲ *US helicopters in battle in Vietnam.*

Civil Rights Act signed

POLITICS

2 JULY President L.B. Johnson, determined to carry on the civil rights work of President Kennedy, has today signed the Civil Rights Act of 1964, the most radical civil rights law in US history. The Act prohibits racial discrimination in employment, public facilities, places of public accommodation, union membership, and federally funded programs. Johnson has worked hard to make sure Congress did not alter or dilute the law in any way.

▲ *President Johnson shakes hands with Rev. Dr. Martin Luther King.*

Cassius Clay wins heavyweight title

SPORT

25 FEBRUARY The unknown Cassius Clay stepped into the ring today and before the end of the seventh round was proclaimed world heavyweight boxing champion. He defeated the legendary Sonny Liston, world heavyweight champion for the last two years. Liston, suffering from an injured shoulder, failed to finish the fight and forfeited his title. The eccentric Clay had the Miami audience stunned with his speedy footwork and his double-quick counter-punching, a technique which seemed to confuse his opponent but delight the crowd.

CULTURE

Mods and Rockers battle on Brighton beach

18 MAY England's southern coast was hit by gang riots this weekend. The worst was at Brighton, where more than 600 youths had to be controlled and 76 were arrested. The violence, which included fist fights, bottle- and stone-throwing, and vandalism, terrified vacationers as they were engulfed by the chaos. The tension between the gangs of fashionably dressed Mods and leather jacket-wearing Rockers had been brewing for some time, but nobody envisaged this scale of violence, along with such widespread injury.

◀ *Mods and Rockers congregate on a beach in Brighton before rioting.*

237

1960

1961

1962

1963

1964

1965

1966

1967

1968

1969

UNICEF wins a Nobel

PEOPLE

10 DECEMBER The Nobel Peace Prize was awarded to UNICEF, the United Nations Children's Fund, in Oslo tonight. It is not the first time a UN agency has won the prize. In 1954 it was awarded to the UN High Commissioner for Refugees. UNICEF was set up in 1946 at the first General Assembly of the UN as a temporary organization (it did not become permanent until 1953), and was called the United Nations International Children's Emergency Fund, hence the acronym by which it is known. Its purpose was to help those children, mainly in European countries, whose lives had been devastated by World War II, providing money, clothes, medicine, food, and daily milk. Since the early 1950s, UNICEF's program has concentrated on the developing nations of Africa, Asia, and South America. It helps governments create programs that will provide children with proper nutrition and decent healthcare. In emergencies, such as famine or war, it supplies food and medicine.

▲ *The UNICEF logo.*

UNICEF's headquarters is in New York. Funds come from voluntary contributions by United Nations member countries and gifts from charities or rich people. It also makes money itself, for example, by selling greeting cards. UNICEF's first greeting card was drawn by a Czech girl who sent it in 1949 to say thank you for the milk that the organization had provided for deprived children in postwar Czechoslovakia. UNICEF now has a huge warehouse for its emergency supplies.

▶ *The Nobel Peace Prize is presented in Oslo to Henry Labouisse (left), Executive Director of UNICEF, by Gunnar Jahn of the Norwegian parliament's Nobel Committee.*

Malcolm X gunned down

POLITICS

21 FEBRUARY American black nationalist leader Malcolm X was shot dead at a rally of the OAAU (Organization for Afro-American Unity) in New York City. The gunmen, one of whom was caught, are believed to be connected with the Black Muslims, the sect in which Malcolm X was formerly a leading figure.

Malcolm X converted to the Black Muslim (Nation of Islam) religion when he was in prison for burglary. Like other Black Muslims, he changed his name to "X" because he regarded his family surname as a legacy of slavery. Founded by Elijah Muhammad, the Black Muslims proclaim the supremacy of blacks and the evil of whites, and Malcolm X, a brilliant speaker and journalist, was their most effective organizer. A year ago, however, after making a pilgrimage to Mecca, he decided that Elijah Muhammad's version of Islam was mistaken and broke with the Black Muslims. His new organization, the OAAU, campaigns for justice for black Americans, but it believes in the possibility of future multiracial harmony.

▼ *Malcolm X, the eloquent OAAU leader, has been murdered.*

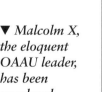

NEWS • 1965 • NEWS

18 March • Soviet cosmonaut Alexei Leonov makes first space "walk" outside his spaceship.

13 May • Israel and West Germany set up diplomatic relations.

16 July • Mont Blanc tunnel linking France and Italy opens.

27 July • Edward Heath becomes British Conservative Party leader.

9 August • Singapore gains independence. from Malaysia.

Blackout in NYC

TECHNOLOGY

10 NOVEMBER The biggest power outage in history hit some northeastern states and parts of eastern Canada last night. About 30 million people found themselves in the dark. In New York, theaters and restaurants were dark, though some managed to keep going with the aid of gas and candlelight. Hundreds of people were stranded in elevators. The trouble began in the power station at Niagara Falls and spread from there as transmission lines became overloaded.

◄ *No spotlit skyscrapers on the night of the big blackout, only car headlights.*

UDI declared in Southern Rhodesia

POLITICS

11 NOVEMBER Ian Smith, prime minister of Southern Rhodesia, a British colony, has declared independence without Britain's agreement. Mr. Smith heads the Rhodesia Front, which believes in keeping power in the hands of the white population, as is the case in South Africa. Commonwealth leaders are urging Britain to take strong action against the white Rhodesians' illegal declaration, but economic sanctions are more likely than war.

The world's alive with the sound of Julie

This year's hit musical is *The Sound of Music*, based on the true story of an Austrian family. Julie Andrews, who won an Oscar earlier this year for *Mary Poppins*, stars as the governess of the seven Von Trapp children, who flee their home in the Austrian Alps when the Nazis take over. The songs such as "Do Re Mi" are memorable.

▼ *Julie Andrews in a scene from* The Sound of Music, *which was filmed in Salzburg, Austria.*

Dylan shocks folk fans

MUSIC

25 JULY The stars of this year's folk music festival at Newport, Rhode Island, are again Joan Baez and Bob Dylan, who have made folk music the voice of protest for American youth. But there is a change in Dylan's style, which did not go down well with folk purists. He has gone over to "folk rock" and appeared on stage in flashy clothes with an electric guitar and backed by a rock band. Dylan ignored the boos as he pounded out "Like a Rolling Stone."

▲ *Bob Dylan and Joan Baez, king and queen of the Newport Folk Festival.*

World's final farewell to Winston Churchill

POLITICS

30 JANUARY Sir Winston Churchill, Britain's great wartime prime minister who died last week, aged 90, was buried today in a churchyard near his birthplace, Blenheim Palace. The 3,000 mourners from 110 countries who attended his funeral in St. Paul's Cathedral, London, were led by Queen Elizabeth. It is the first time a monarch has attended the funeral of a subject. About 350 million people worldwide watched the service live on TV.

▲ *Winston Churchill.*

1960

1961

1962

1963

1964

1965

1966

1967

1968

1969

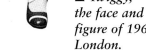

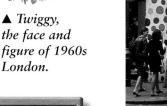

▲ Twiggy, the face and figure of 1960s London.

Swinging London is where it's at

CULTURE

11 JUNE Britain's Queen Elizabeth has honored Mary Quant, which means that the daring young fashion designer is now a member of the Order of the British Empire. Miss Quant, OBE, has been a key figure in the rise of "Swinging London," which in recent years has become the mecca of international youth culture. In the boutiques of Carnaby Street and the King's Road, young people buy pop records, posters, and "way-out" gear. While the "dolly birds" are wearing miniskirts and panty hose, the boys are letting their hair grow long. Pop groups like The Beatles and The Who are these teenagers' heroes. "I don't know what will go first," says Beatle John Lennon, "rock 'n' roll or Christianity." Today's young people have more money, more power, and more freedom than their parents did, but as some of the old class barriers tumble down, a new generation gap is opening up.

◀ Tourists from all over the world are coming to Swinging London for shopping weekends. They throng the boutiques of Carnaby Street (left) and Chelsea.

NEWS • 1966 • NEWS

13 January • Robert C. Weaver is first black member of US cabinet.

19 January • Menzies resigns after 17 years as Australian premier.

11 March • General Suharto gains power in Indonesia.

6 September • H.F. Verwoerd, South African premier, is assassinated.

28 October • Britain and France agree plans for a channel tunnel.

China's "Cultural Revolution"

POLITICS

15 AUGUST China is being torn apart by a crusade the veteran communist leader Mao Tse-tung has described as a Cultural Revolution. The crusade is designed to wipe out the "four olds"— old ideas, old culture, old customs, and old habits—and the crusaders are Red Guards, fanatical young supporters of Chairman Mao, and readers of his published thoughts, *The Little Red Book*. For its victims, this campaign is no cultural matter. All over China, senior party officials, intellectuals, and artists suspected of having pro-Western or pre-revolutionary ideas are being denounced and driven from their jobs to work in the fields.

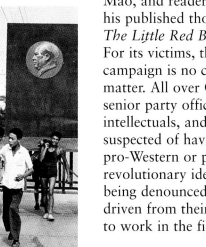

▶ Red Guards, mostly students and soldiers, proclaim China's Cultural Revolution.

Tragedy at Aberfan in Wales

21 OCTOBER In one of the worst peacetime disasters in modern British history, 144 people, including 116 children, were killed yesterday when a slag heap above the Welsh mining village of Aberfan engulfed the village school and several houses. The slag heap, waste from a coal mine, had been soaked by heavy rain, which made it unstable. Yesterday morning, without warning, it began to slide toward the village. Within seconds, the school was engulfed. Rescue work went on all night. The principal was rescued alive; the body of the vice-principal was found with his arms around five children. The government has promised an inquiry. It will want to know why the heap was in such a dangerous position, why its dangerous condition was not recognized, and what is the current state of hundreds of similar heaps in South Wales.

▲ *A mass grave has been built on the side of a mountain above the Welsh village of Aberfan to accommodate the many victims of the landslide that engulfed a school and several homes.*

Ghana's Nkrumah is deposed by army

24 FEBRUARY President Kwame Nkrumah of Ghana (left), on a state visit to China, today learned that he has been overthrown by the army. Once a national hero, he led opposition to British colonial rule and became prime minister on the independence of Ghana in 1957. Recently, economic failures, corruption in government, and Nkrumah's abuse of power, which included imprisoning people without trial and spending enormous sums on himself, turned most of the people against him.

Pickles finds World Cup

The missing soccer World Cup, which was stolen earlier this month, was found yesterday. Great police work? Well, no. The trophy, seen here with a senior detective, was found by Pickles, a dog. Pickles' owner, a London docker, saw him sniffing a bundle of newspaper and picked it up to find the famous gold trophy inside. So far, one man has been arrested in connection with the cup's theft.

Missing H-bomb

7 APRIL A crisis in the Pentagon (the US Defense Department) ended today. Three months ago a US bomber collided in midair with another aircraft off the coast of Spain, killing eight men. The Pentagon admitted that the B-52 had been carrying nuclear weapons, and that one H-bomb was missing, presumably at the bottom of the ocean. After a huge search, the bomb was found, completely intact, by a midget submarine.

▼ *American B-52 bombers are used to carry nuclear weapons.*

POLITICS

Panthers proclaim "Black Power"

30 OCTOBER Two years ago, in his "I have a dream" speech, Martin Luther King, Jr., imagined a United States where people are judged by "the content of their character, rather than by the color of their skin." Rather than wait for that dream to come true, some African-Americans are seeking new solutions to continuing injustice and poverty. In Oakland, California, Huey Newton and Bobby Seale have founded a new political organization, the Black Panther Party for Self-defense. For now the Panthers aim to protect the ghetto community from racist police, but they also hope to organize clinics, community centers, and free breakfast schemes. Their violent language has disturbed many of the older campaigners for civil rights, but it reflects a new attitude among young African-Americans. The Black Panthers are part of the growing Black Power movement. Instead of trying hard to be accepted by white American society, Black Power supporters want revolutionary change. The fashion for natural "afro" hairstyles is an indication of the popularity of the new militancy.

◄ *Stokely Carmichael, the leader who coined the phrase Black Power.*

▶ *A child in Harlem learns the black-power salute.*

Victory for England in the World Cup

The soccer World Cup ended in Wembley today with a first-time victory for the red-shirted host nation, England, who won 4–2. The German team, led by Franz Beckenbauer, slight favorites, took an early lead. After 90 minutes the score was 2–2. Early in overtime, England scored a goal, when the ball bounced off the German crossbar on to or, as the referee decided, over the line. In the final minute, England striker Geoff Hurst scored his third, and the winning, goal.

◄ *England captain Bobby Moore.*

ART

Florence floods damage art treasures

9 NOVEMBER
Devastating floods in northern Italy have caused nearly $1.5 billion of damage, most of it to artworks in the Renaissance city of Florence. At least 600 paintings and over 1,000 old manuscripts and books have been severely damaged. Some masterpieces, such as a 13th-century Crucifixion scene by Cimabue, have been totally ruined. Art restorers from all over Italy are already hard at work, and an international appeal for help in the restoration work is being launched.

▲ *The floodwaters of the Arno River hurled a car against an ancient memorial.*

242

ENTERTAINMENT | Walt Disney dies

15 DECEMBER Walt Disney, pioneer of animated movies, died today in Hollywood. The unique cartoon style of Disney and his partner, Ub Iwerk, began in the days of silent movies. In the 1920s he introduced Mickey Mouse, Donald Duck, and Goofy to movie audiences, and his classic feature-length cartoons, including *Snow White*, *Pinocchio*, and *Fantasia*, followed.

▲ *Claus von Amsberg and Princess Beatrix.*

ROYALTY | Princess Beatrix marries

10 MARCH Princess Beatrix of the Netherlands today married an aristocratic German diplomat, Claus von Amsberg, in Amsterdam. They first met on a skiing vacation little more than a year ago. The princess, who is 28 and has a doctorate in law, is heir to the Dutch throne. The match is not popular in the Netherlands, and the occasion was marred by protests. A smokebomb was thrown at the wedding coach as it rolled through the streets. The trouble is that the bridegroom, who is 11 years older, is German, and the Dutch remember all too well the cruel years of the last war when their country was occupied by the Germans.

POLITICS | Grand coalition in West Germany

1 DECEMBER Kurt-Georg Kiesinger was sworn in as West German chancellor, or prime minister, today. He succeeds Ludwig Erhard, forced from power by his own party, the Christian Democrats. Kiesinger heads the first coalition government between West Germany's two main parties, the Christian Democrats (CDU, moderate conservative), in office since 1949, and the Social Democrats (SPD, moderate socialist). The SPD leader is Willy Brandt, former mayor of West Berlin, who becomes vice-chancellor and foreign minister.

The starship boldly sets out

A new science-fiction television series seems set for a long run. In *Star Trek*, William Shatner plays the captain of the starship *Enterprise,* whose mission is "to boldly go" (the split infinitive has provoked some mockery) where no man has gone before. The crew includes pointy-eared Mr. Spock, who comes from another galaxy. He is unable to feel emotion, which calls for a rather wooden performance from actor Leonard Nimoy.

▶ *Shatner, DeForest Kelley (ship's doctor), and Nimoy of* Star Trek.

POLITICS | Indira Gandhi is India's new leader

19 JANUARY India's ruling Congress Party has elected Mrs. Indira Gandhi as leader, and therefore prime minister, succeeding Lal Bahadur Shastri, who died suddenly last week. A widow aged 48, Mrs. Gandhi was a minister in the last government. Although she is a skilled politician, her selection as India's new leader also owes something to her background. She is the only child of Jarwaharlal Nehru, India's first prime minister, but no relation to Mahatma Gandhi.

▶ *Mrs. Indira Gandhi, the first woman to become India's prime minister.*

1960

1961

1962

1963

1964

1965

1966

1967

1968

1969

1967

SCIENCE

Dr. Barnard performs first heart transplant

▼ *Louis Washkansky after his heart transplant.*

3 DECEMBER The South African heart surgeon, Dr. Christiaan Barnard, today carried out the world's first human heart transplant operation at Groote Schuur Hospital in Cape Town. The patient is Louis Washkansky, 53, a storeowner who was suffering from heart failure. He agreed to have the operation as the only chance of saving his life.

The father of a young bank clerk, Denise Darvall, who was fatally injured in a car accident, agreed to the use of his daughter's heart. Dr. Barnard led a team of 30 people in an operation that took six hours. When the heart was in place, it was restarted with a tiny electric shock. Doctors have known for some years that the transplant of human organs is theoretically possible. The most successful human organ transplants are kidneys, because a kidney patient (unlike a patient with heart failure) can be kept in good health until a kidney becomes available. As Dr. Barnard said, the heart transplant itself was "not really a problem." The greatest danger is that the body may reject the new heart.

▶ *Dr. Barnard (left) discusses technique with top international heart specialists Michael de Bakey and Adirn Kantrowitz.*

Transplant facts

Washkansky died as a result of lung complications after 18 days. His new heart continued beating right until the end.

•

Six months later, the first human heart transplant ever in the UK was carried out.

Blake cover for latest Beatles album

The cover of the Beatles' new album, *Sergeant Pepper's Lonely Hearts Club Band,* is the work of Peter Blake, one of Britain's foremost pop artists. This arty collage suits the collection of new-style songs with psychedelic lyrics, which are tipped to be the Beatles' most successful.

WAR

Civil war in Nigeria

30 MAY The Ibo leader Colonel Ojukwu today declared the independence of Nigeria's Eastern Region as the Republic of Biafra. The move follows 18 months of violence in Nigeria, of which Ibo people living in other regions have been the chief victims. Ojukwu is now convinced that a separate state is the only safe way forward for the Ibo, a minority within Nigeria. However, his declaration means civil war, and the breakaway Biafran state will find it hard to survive. Britain (the former colonial power) and most other countries are likely to back the Nigerian federal government.

▶ *Young Ibo men prepare to fight for an independent Republic of Biafra.*

"Six-day" Middle East war ends

WAR

10 JUNE Today, after just six days, the war between Israel and its Arab neighbors ended, when Israel agreed to a hurriedly arranged UN ceasefire. Israel has captured extensive territory from Egypt, Jordan, and Syria, including all of Jerusalem, the West Bank, the Gaza Strip, and the Golan Heights. Although the fighting has stopped for now, the war has increased tension in the Middle East and there now seems to be little chance of a lasting peace settlement.

▲ *The defense minister during the Six Day War, Moshe Dayan (center), planned the Israelis' lightning campaign.*

NEWS • 1967 • NEWS

15 January • *Winners of NFL and AFL play each other for first time. Green Bay Packers beat Kansas City 35–10.*

27 January • *Three US astronauts burn to death in Apollo spacecraft during training.*

30 July • *40 people die in Detroit in race riots.*

17 December • *Australian prime minister Harold Holt is presumed drowned. He disappeared while swimming in the sea.*

Torrey Canyon oil disaster

DISASTERS

31 MARCH Divers are now inspecting the wreck of the *Torrey Canyon*, the giant oil tanker that went aground two weeks ago. In Britain's worst pollution disaster, 30,000 tons of oil escaped after the tanker broke in half during salvage attempts. Bombs and napalm were dropped to sink the ship and burn off the oil. The slick spread over 270 square miles (700 square km) of sea, affecting 93 miles (150 km) of Cornwall's coast, in southwestern England.

▲ *Che (right) with Castro.*

Che Guevara dies in Bolivia

PEOPLE

9 OCTOBER The Latin American revolutionary hero, Ernesto Guevara, was reported killed today by Bolivian troops. He was Fidel Castro's righthand man in the Cuban revolution and got his nickname from his habit of saying "che!" An Argentinian by birth and a doctor by training, in 1965 he went "underground" to help revolutionary guerrillas in South America.

Antiwar demo turns violent at the Pentagon

POLITICS

21 OCTOBER Smoke and tear gas hung around the Pentagon, the US Defense Department in Washington, this evening, after a demonstration against the Vietnam War turned violent. Tens of thousands of people, mostly young, besieged the building in the climax to a week of protests about US policy in Indochina. Hundreds of protesters have been arrested. The Vietnam War, in which more than 500,000 US troops will soon be engaged, has divided the American nation more sharply than any issue since last century's Civil War.

▶ *Antiwar protesters confront military police outside the Pentagon.*

POP MUSIC

At the beginning of the 20th century, opera was one of the popular forms of music. With the new gramophone record, music reached mass markets worldwide, and the first million-selling record was made in 1902 by the legendary Italian tenor, Enrico Caruso.

In the southern states at this time, African and European music styles were converging, which created a new type of popular music—jazz. Black people moved to the industrial northern states during World War II for work, and jazz was reborn as rhythm-and-blues. This became the basis for pop music in the latter half of the 20th century, such as soul, rock'n'roll, disco, punk, heavy metal, grunge, techno, and rap.

▲ *Chuck Berry began his career as a blues guitarist in local clubs.*

▼ *Elvis Presley, the "king" of rock'n'roll.*

► *The Beatles, from Liverpool, were the first pop supergroup.*

Rock'n'roll years

The rhythm-and-blues music of African-Americans became the first rock'n'roll sound in the 1950s.

Racial barriers between black and white music began to break down, and in 1954, Elvis Presley, a white boy from Mississippi, released his first record. "That's Alright Mama" was his version of a black R & B song, and this new musical fusion of R & B, country music, and gospel music came to be called rock'n'roll.

In the mid-1950s, a black guitarist and songwriter, Chuck Berry, released a string of all-time great hits, such as "Maybelline," "Sweet Little Sixteen," "Johnny B. Goode," and "Back in the USA." He perfected the rhythms and guitar riffs, which were then copied by British groups such as The Beatles and The Rolling Stones in the 1960s.

Music with a message

Rock music was to the 1960s what rock'n'roll had been to the 1950s. It moved from teenagers and coffee bars to political protests and rock festivals. In the swinging sixties there was a revival of interest in the folk and blues roots of rock. Virtuoso guitarists such as Jimi Hendrix and Eric Clapton experimented with extended solos and utilized the new electronic gadgets that were available in increasingly sophisticated recording studios. Bob Dylan began writing folk songs with a political message, protesting against racism and the spread of nuclear weapons. He was a major influence on other recording artists, including The Beatles.

▲ Madonna, a star of the '80s and '90s, shocked the world with the sexuality of her stage and video performances and lyrics.

Pop music facts

The Velvet Underground, one of the most influential rock groups of all time, never made it into the Top 100 of the album charts while they were together.

•

The expressions "See you later, alligator" and "In a while, crocodile" derive from a hit of Bill Haley and the Comets in the 1950s.

Blues, pop, gospel: Motown

Most African-American music stars, such as Aretha Franklin and Marvin Gaye, began their careers by singing in gospel choirs. During the 1960s, gospel singers began to sing about personal relationships and social problems. This new style of music became known as soul.

Motown, the most successful African-American record label, was started by Berry Gordy in Detroit ("Mo[tor] Town"). From 1961 to 1971 Motown had 110 Top Ten hits. Motown artists include Stevie Wonder, Diana Ross, and the Jackson Five.

▶ The Supremes—from left, Florence Ballard, Diana Ross, and Mary Wilson.

1960

1961

1962

1963

1964

1965

1966

1967

1968

1969

▶ *During the New Year, or "Tet" offensive, Vietcong forces have been active in Saigon, pictured here.*

The Tet offensive

WAR

24 FEBRUARY It's three weeks now since Vietnam's communist forces (Vietcong) unfurled their Tet offensive, a sudden but coordinated cluster of attacks on more than 100 cities and military bases in South Vietnam. The operation has shattered the ceasefire that was declared for "Tet," the Vietnamese New Year. The world has been amazed by media images of a Third World peasant army inflicting grave damage on the American war machine. Now the Americans and the South Vietnamese are hitting back, and today they recaptured the port of Hue, but US commander General Westmoreland is calling for 206,000 reinforcements. As this war continues to cost so many lives, and it becomes clear that there is no easy victory just around the corner, more and more Americans are questioning their country's continuing role in Vietnam.

French students revolt

REVOLUTION

30 MAY French President Charles De Gaulle today tried to turn back the tide of revolution sweeping France. In a radio broadcast he said he would not resign and called a general election for next month. These "May Days" began in Paris when police broke up a student protest at the Sorbonne University. The students set up barricades in the streets and fought the police with cobblestones and homemade bombs. Across the country workers, angry at low wages and poor conditions, joined the Paris students' struggle, and by last week around 10 million workers were on strike.

▶ *French students tussle police.*

NEWS • 1968 • NEWS

10 May • Peace talks to end the Vietnam War begin in Paris.

29 May • Manchester United wins soccer's European Cup, beating Benfica 4–1.

1-2 September • Earthquakes in Iran kill 11,000 people.

6 November • Richard Nixon elected as president.

31 December • First flight by first supersonic airliner, the Soviet Tupolev Tu-144.

Bobby Kennedy shot dead

POLITICS

6 JUNE Senator Robert Kennedy, the late President Kennedy's brother, was fatally wounded by a gunman at a Los Angeles hotel early yesterday morning. He had just won the California primary election to be the Democrats' presidential candidate. A 24-year-old Palestinian, Sirhan Sirhan, shot Kennedy shouting: "I did it for my country!" It is the first anniversary of the Arab-Israeli Six Day War.

▶ *Bobby greets supporters.*

POLITICS

The "Prague Spring" is over

22 AUGUST Soviet tanks rolled into Prague today to remove the liberal communist government of Alexander Dubcek. In March Dubcek reduced press censorship and arrested the former head of the notorious secret police. His government has been called the Prague Spring, but as the USSR's grip on Czechoslovakia tightens it seems that the "winter" of hardline communism is back. The Russians are afraid that Dubcek's democratic reforms might lead to a weakening of communism in other eastern European (Warsaw Pact) countries. Dubcek and five of his government colleagues have been seized and taken to Moscow.

◄ *After the invasion, Czech students confront Soviet tanks in Prague.*

POLITICS

Chicago police attack demo

29 AUGUST The Democratic Party Convention in Chicago has been clouded by the brutal actions of the local police force. Images of truncheon-wielding Chicago policemen clubbing opponents of the American role in Vietnam have been shown on national TV. One senator has compared their tactics to those of the Nazi Gestapo. At least two Democratic delegates were dragged out of the convention in the Hilton Hotel, and around 700 demonstrators have been hurt.

POLITICS

Riots follow the slaying of Martin Luther King

5 APRIL All over the US African-Americans are taking to the streets to express their grief and rage at the assassination of Martin Luther King, Jr. Yesterday, the revered civil rights leader was shot dead in Memphis, Tennessee, by a white rifleman who escaped. Dr. King, who was a Baptist minister, led the 1950s Alabama campaign against racist segregation laws and stood for nonviolent protest, but his death has provoked riots in 167 cities and on innumerable campuses.

► *Riots have followed news of Dr. King's murder.*

Kubrick in space

American director Stanley Kubrick's epic *2001: A Space Odyssey* is a troubling yet poetic vision of the future, showing the beauty and bleakness of life in space. On a mission to find the source of a baffling signal, the onboard computer HAL 9000 tries to kill the astronauts. One of them, David Bowman (Keir Dullea), must disable HAL. In a final fantasy sequence, Bowman seems to go past space and time forever.

▲ *A scene from Kubrick's space epic.*

SPORT

Black Power at Olympics

16 OCTOBER Black American athletes Tommie Smith and John Carlos today used the Olympic Games in Mexico City to protest about racism in the US. As they received their medals for the 200-meter sprint, gold-winner Smith and bronze-winner Carlos raised their black-gloved clenched fists high above their heads in a salute identified with Black Power, a militant black movement in the US. Furious American officials are considering how to punish the athletes—they may be sent home.

▼ *Tommie Smith gives Black Power salute.*

1960
1961
1962
1963
1964
1965
1966
1967
1968
1969

TECHNOLOGY

First man on the Moon

21 JULY Millions of people crowded around TV sets early today to see the astonishing sight of two men walking on the Moon. *Apollo 11* orbited the Moon while Neil Armstrong and Edwin Aldrin, equipped with a camera, descended to the surface in the lunar landing module *Eagle*. After gingerly climbing out of the *Eagle*, Armstrong said: "That's one small step for a man, one giant leap for mankind."

The mission began last week when a *Saturn V* rocket launched *Apollo 11* from Cape Kennedy, Florida. After a trouble-free, four-day voyage to the Moon, the third mission member, Michael Collins, stayed at the controls in the main capsule in orbit while Armstrong and Aldrin made their descent. The two astronauts spent 13 hours on the surface, gathering Moon rock and setting up experiments, before returning to Collins and starting the long voyage back to Earth.

▶ *Leaving a footprint on the lunar surface.*

▶ *The astronauts planted the US flag, the Stars and Stripes, on the surface of the Moon.*

Moon landing facts

Apollo 11's Saturn V rocket burned ½ gallon (2.3 liters) of fuel in the first two and a half minutes of the flight.

•

Armstrong had to switch from automatic to fuel-saving manual control as the *Eagle* descended because boulders on the Moon's surface forced him to fly farther than planned.

•

On their return, the astronauts were kept isolated for 17 days in case they had picked up an unknown infection in space.

POLITICS

Death of Ho Chi Minh

3 SEPTEMBER Ho Chi Minh, the political leader of communist Vietnam since 1954, has died of a heart attack, aged 79. For almost 30 years he led resistance to foreign power in Indochina. Before World War II Vietnam was a French colony. Ho, who had worked as a teacher and a ship's cook in his youth, declared Vietnam independent in 1945. Wars against the French followed but the peace settlement divided the country into North and South Vietnam. For his people, he symbolized the struggle to reunite Vietnam.

◀ *Ho Chi Minh. His adopted name means "he who enlightens."*

LAW

Manson "family" murder trial begins

24 DECEMBER In Los Angeles today, ex-convict Charles Manson and four members of his hippie commune were charged with the murder of movie actress Sharon Tate and six other people. Manson, 35, called himself "Jesus Christ" and dominated the teenage girls in his commune, which was known as The Family. Prosecutors say that drug-crazed members of Manson's family invaded Tate's Hollywood house and slaughtered the pregnant actress, three of her friends, and a passerby. They smeared the walls with blood and the following night killed two more people.

▲ *Charles Manson after his arrest.*

POLITICS

Stonewall riot starts gay rights movement

28 JUNE NYC police have just had a shock. They regularly raid the bars where homosexual men and women meet, but last night at the Stonewall Bar in Greenwich Village, they met with resistance. It began with catcalls, but later stones were thrown to drive police back. Already, this act of defiance is being talked of as the beginning of something bigger, a "Gay Liberation Front."

Rock on the road

A new hit movie is sweeping the US. *Easy Rider* stars Peter Fonda and Dennis Hopper as a pair of hippies who hit the road on their motorbikes. They ride from Los Angeles to New Orleans and meet up with a disillusioned lawyer played by Jack Nicholson. The movie's rock soundtrack includes songs by The Byrds and Jimi Hendrix.

POLITICS

Irish "Troubles" continue

16 AUGUST British troops have arrived in the cities of Northern Ireland to keep the peace between Catholics and Protestants. This summer, many Catholic districts became "no-go" areas to the local police force, the Royal Ulster Constabulary, but the British troops are welcomed because they are seen as impartial peacekeepers. Five people have already died this week, and hundreds have been injured.

▶ *A British soldier on duty in Belfast.*

POLITICS

Israel elects Golda Meir as Prime Minister

17 MARCH Veteran politician Golda Meir today became prime minister of Israel, a state she helped to found. Born in Kiev, Ukraine, Meir was raised in the US and emigrated to Palestine from Milwaukee in 1921. She was known as Goldie Myerson when she was first elected to the Knesset (Israeli parliament), but took the Hebrew version of her name when she became Israel's foreign affairs minister in 1956.

Mrs. Meir is keen to settle Israel's disagreements with its Arab neighbors by diplomatic rather than military means.

▶ *Golda Meir, Israel's new leader.*

251

▼ The festival is over, and thousands of young people leave Woodstock.

CULTURE | # Woodstock Festival

17 AUGUST Rock fans are traveling home from the Woodstock Festival in New York state tonight, convinced that a new era of peace and love has finally arrived. For three days a crowd of 400,000 has lived happily together—despite thick mud and bursts of torrential rain—on farmland close to the village of Woodstock. They'd gathered for a rock festival featuring Jimi Hendrix, The Who, Janis Joplin, The Band, and Jefferson Airplane. As they shared drugs, cheered, and exchanged peace signals, they felt a tide of positivity flow around them.

Woodstock is the biggest of a wave of outdoor rock festivals this summer. Over 100,000 fans attended the Atlanta Pop in July—the day after the Newport Jazz festival had pulled in 80,000 with a bill that included Led Zeppelin, B.B. King, and Jethro Tull. The hippies' counterculture of peace and love, born in San Francisco four years ago, is sweeping across the US and Europe. The hippies see the flower as a symbol of their peaceful values and use the phrase "flower power" to suggest that love can overcome aggression. As the protest movement against the Vietnam War grows, these values are taking root in young people from many backgrounds.

▼ The festival is over, and thousands of young people leave Woodstock.

North Sea oil drilled

The icy waters of the North Sea may be hiding a fortune. Top-quality crude oil has been discovered in the seabed. It is far from the shore and beneath very deep waters. Oil companies are investigating whether the deposits are valuable enough to cover the high costs of drilling for them.

POLITICS | # Yassir Arafat is new PLO leader

3 FEBRUARY Yassir Arafat is the new chairman of the Palestine Liberation Organization (PLO). The PLO represents Arabs who lived in Palestine and who lost their homeland when the state of Israel was established there in 1948. More than half a million Palestinians left their homes that year, but another 200,000 to 400,000 more left during the 1967 war. Most are now living in UN refugee camps, and the PLO aims to establish a new Palestinian state for them on land it wants to regain from Israel. Arafat was born in Jerusalem, but studied in Cairo and joined the Egyptian Army, serving in the Suez campaign. In 1963, while he was working as an engineer in Kuwait, he became head of the al-Fatah, the main military group coming under the PLO umbrella.

▶ Yassir Arafat, the new chairman of the Palestine Liberation Organization.

NEWS • 1969 • NEWS

10 March • James Earl Ray, Martin Luther King's killer, is jailed for 99 years.

1 April • Lin Piao is elected to succeed Mao Tse-tung when he retires as Chinese Communist Party Chairman.

23 April • Sirhan Sirhan, Robert Kennedy's killer, is sentenced to death.

5 July • The Rolling Stones give free concert in Hyde Park, London.

Gaddafi seizes power in Libya

POLITICS

1 SEPTEMBER Army officers led by Captain Moamer al Khaddhafi (known in the West by the name of Gaddafi) declared a republic in Libya today. The army took power while 70-year-old King Idris was away in Turkey. Crown Prince Hassan Rida says he supports the new government.

Khaddhafi is the son of a Bedouin tribesman. Although he is just 27, he has been plotting the coup for years with army colleagues. His new regime says that it stands for "freedom, socialism, and unity."

◀ *Captain Khaddhafi, Libya's new leader.*

Willy Brandt elected Chancellor

POLITICS

31 OCTOBER The German Social Democratic Party is in power in West Germany for the first time. Today the Social Democrat leader, Willy Brandt, was elected as chancellor, or prime minister, with the support of a coalition of his party and the Free Democrats.

A young man when the Nazi Party came to power in 1933, Brandt spent World War II in Norway and Sweden, and was elected to the West German parliament in 1949. From 1957 to 1966 he was mayor of West Berlin. He is keen to limit the proliferation (spread) of nuclear weapons.

Nigeria bans aid flights to Biafra

POLITICS

16 JUNE The Nigerian government has shocked relief workers by banning Red Cross night flights carrying food and medicines to Biafra, an area in eastern Nigeria that has declared independence and is at war with the bulk of the country. Outnumbered and outgunned, the Biafrans are suffering heavy losses. Thousands are in desperate need and face starving to death. The Nigerian government claims that the rebels are using the flights to deliver weapons. The Biafran conflict grew out of violence between the Ibo and Hausa peoples. In September 1966 as many as 30,000 Ibos were slaughtered by Hausas in northern Nigeria, and around a million Ibos fled to the eastern region, which is dominated by their people. In 1967 civil war followed Colonel Ojukwu's declaration of an independent Biafra.

▶ *Children in the breakaway Biafran state rely on international aid during the conflict with Nigeria.*

Meet Kermit & company

American preschool children are learning letters and numbers from a zany new breed of fluffy teachers. *Sesame Street*, a new children's TV show, features a cast of lovable "muppets," such as Big Bird, Cookie Monster, and Kermit the Frog. The show has adult presenters and uses fast cutting and comical cartoons.

◀ *Big Bird, a resident of Sesame Street.*

PEOPLE

Czechs mourn student martyr Jan Palach

27 JANUARY Thousands of young Czechs are marching through central Prague shouting "Russians go home!" In the recently renamed Red Army Square, they are putting up signs reading Jan Palach Square, in memory of the student who set fire to himself in protest against the Soviet occupation of Czechoslovakia. Yesterday, 21-year-old Jan Palach died in hospital. Before dying he said: "My deed has fulfilled its purpose, but let nobody else do it."

▲ *Mourners for Jan Palach.*

TUNE IN TO TELEVISION

▲ *In 1962, color pictures were transmitted across the Atlantic by Telstar satellite. This BBC picture was seen in New York.*

The world has been transformed by television in the second half of the 20th century. News, sports, and drama are beamed via satellites in space from one side of the globe to the other. Advertisers have come to rely largely on television to sell their products, making it a billion-dollar industry.

But at the end of the century, the television with which we are familiar is changing fast. There are hundreds of channels we can now tune in to. Lighter, cheaper camera and recording equipment has made it easier to make more programs. The experience of watching television is getting better, too, with larger, wider sets, improved sound quality, and sharper pictures.

Entertainment in your living room

After World War II, the television set began to replace the radio as the main entertainment form in North American and British homes. Its popularity grew, and by 1949 there were one million sets in the US, and by 1959, 50 million. In 1990, 98 percent of homes in the "developed world"—the richer countries in Europe and North America—had at least one television.

At its best, television offers a stream of highly varied and enjoyable programs, including game shows, music programs, live sports, and soap opera. The television links the family home with the outside world. News pictures from around the world can have a major effect on viewers. In the 1980s, images of people starving in Africa because of famine caused great concern and led to rock and pop stars' fundraising triumphs in Band Aid and Live Aid.

▼ *Far more than a box in a corner, television is usually the centerpiece of the living room.*

Television facts

The first live outdoor broadcast was the British Broadcasting Corporation's relay of King George VI's coronation procession in November 1937.

•

John F. Kennedy's TV performances helped him beat Richard Nixon in the Presidential election in 1960.

•

In July 1969, more than 100 million people around the world watched the first men walk on the Moon on TV.

Small-screen entertainment for kids

When *Sesame Street* first appeared in the US in 1969, it was unlike any other children's television program. Bright colors and fast cutting—swapping from one image to another—grabbed children's attention. It starred a gallery of zany puppets—including Kermit the Frog, Big Bird, and Snuffluppagus—specially designed by Jim Henson. Created by Joan Ganz Cooney and the Children's Television Workshop, *Sesame Street* became a hit all over the world. By the mid-1990s it was showing in 78 countries.

◀ Sesame Street *residents include Big Bird, Oscar, Sherlock, Ernie, and Bert.*

▼ *John Logie Baird during a television demonstration in 1926.*

▶ *Once the rooftop aerial was the only way to pick up TV broadcasts. In the 1990s more and more people received their television pictures via a satellite dish or by underground cable. The television aerials pictured here were designed by Radio Corporation of America engineers.*

Television pioneer

Scottish inventor John Logie Baird was the first person to demonstrate a working television in public. Using a special camera and receiver, he sent a picture from one studio to another in London on 27 January, 1926. Although the BBC tested his system in 1929 and an improved one in 1936, they chose to use another. In 1944, Baird invented a way of transmitting color pictures.

1970

1971

1972

1973

1974

1975

1976

1977

1978

1979

1970

The 1970s saw an ebbing of confidence in the developed world. The sudden rise of oil prices in 1973 disrupted international trade and brought about the return of widespread unemployment.

But it was also a decade of progress. The US and the USSR agreed on nuclear weapons reductions. The Space Shuttle, a reusable spacecraft, was built; and the first "test-tube baby," grown from an egg that was fertilized outside the mother's body, was born.

Pakistan mourns its dead

DISASTERS

20 NOVEMBER Today is a day of national mourning in Pakistan, where 150,000 people were killed after a tidal wave ravaged East Pakistan last week. The wall of water—30 feet (9 meters) high— killed cattle, ruined crops in fields, and destroyed entire villages. It came in the wake of a typhoon with winds of 125 miles (200 km) an hour.

American and British helicopters are being used to survey the area. But at ground level it will be difficult to move supplies because roads have been swept away. Bodies of the dead are floating in the water or being left on the land as the floods go down, and relief agencies are worried about the risk of disease. Survivors are stunned. One said: "Only Allah knows why this has happened to us."

▲ *Above left, a ship tossed into a field. Above, a survivor mourns the loss of his family.*

Floppy disk invented in US by IBM

The US firm IBM has made a breakthrough in the storage and retrieval of computer information.
The new IBM 3740 system can be used with a "floppy disk" —a thin, flexible plastic disk that is 8 inches (20 centimeters) across, covered with magnetic iron oxide. The "floppy" (below) is inserted into a slot in the computer, which can copy data onto it or take information from it. It is far faster than the reel-to-reel magnetic tapes used by older systems.

VietnamWar spreads to Cambodia

WAR

30 APRIL President Richard Nixon today stated that US and South Vietnamese troops have been sent into Cambodia to destroy communist Vietnamese troop bases and supply lines. In spite of this latest move, Nixon is still hoping to "Vietnamize" the war by gradually removing American troops from Indochina and leaving the South Vietnamese to continue fighting on their own.

In the meantime, in China, Cambodia's exiled leader, Prince Sihanouk, has joined forces with his old opponents, the communist Khmer Rouge (Red Cambodia) movement.

▶ *US troops in Cambodia. President Nixon says they'll withdraw within 3 to 7 weeks.*

"Black September" in Jordan ends

30 SEPTEMBER After a month of fighting, an uneasy peace has returned to the Kingdom of Jordan. Fighting between Jordanian government troops and Palestinian guerrillas began after Palestinian terrorists blew up three hijacked Western airliners in the Jordanian desert and took 56 passengers hostage. The Jordanians defeated the Palestinians and drove back a Syrian invasion in support of the guerrillas. It has now been three days since a ceasefire agreement was signed in Cairo, the Egyptian capital, by Jordan's King Hussein and Yassir Arafat, chairman of the Palestine Liberation Organization (PLO). The conflict is over, but the Palestinians have been evicted from their strongholds in Jordan. For them, this past month has been a Black September.

▲ *Jordanian troops move against Palestinians.*

Gomulka goes after Gdansk riots

20 DECEMBER After weeks of anti-government unrest Wladyslaw Gomulka, Poland's Communist Party boss has resigned in favor of examiner Edward Gierek. The unrest started in Gdansk, where dockers' protests over food prices led to looting and rioting and an attack on the local Communist Party headquarters. Some sources say that 300 people have died in the clashes.

▲ *Kent State University, where an antiwar demonstration ended with the shooting of four students.*

Love and tears

There isn't a dry eye in the movie theater after Arthur Hiller's *Love Story*. Ryan O'Neal plays Oliver, a student who wins the heart of Jenny (Ali MacGraw) in spite of snobbish family objections—but then loses her when she dies of leukemia. O'Neal, a former stunt man, won the part after top actors including Michael Douglas and Jon Voight rejected it.

▼ *Young lovers: Ryan O'Neal and Ali MacGraw.*

Tragedy at Kent State

4 MAY Today, at Kent State University in Ohio, a protest against the US invasion of Cambodia ended in the death of four unarmed students. Ohio's governor ordered national guardsmen onto the campus after a few days of disorder and some damage. At lunchtime the guardsmen tried to break up a banned student rally, firing teargas when the protesters would not move on. The students fought back with rocks, and the nervous guardsmen opened fire, killing 4 and injuring 11 others. The students say that the dead, two of whom were girls, were just bystanders, and that one, William Schroeder, actually belonged to a military volunteer force. But President Nixon insists that the killings "should remind us all once again that when dissent turns to violence it invites tragedy." Two students have also been killed at Jackson State University in Mississippi.

Apollo 13 returns safely to Earth

TECHNOLOGY

17 APRIL Three US astronauts splashed down into the Pacific Ocean today after a brush with death on their mission to the Moon. Five days ago, James Lovell, John Swigert, and Fred Haise left the Earth on board the *Apollo 13* spacecraft. The plan was to put the command capsule, *Odyssey*, into orbit around the Moon and descend to the surface in the smaller lunar module, *Aquarius*. But when an oxygen tank on board *Odyssey* overheated and exploded, the astronauts had to transfer to *Aquarius*, which was attached to *Odyssey*. Unable to turn back, they nursed the damaged spacecraft around the Moon and back to Earth. Just before reentering the Earth's atmosphere, they moved back into the main capsule.

Since the triumphant first Moon landing of *Apollo 11* last July, there has been a second successful mission. In November, *Apollo 12* astronauts Charles Conrad and Alan Bean walked on the Moon. *Apollo 13* will be remembered as a near-disaster, but it has brought back some lunar photographic evidence.

◀ *The* Apollo13 *command module after its return to Earth.*

Tommy performed at the Met

Rock music arrived in the splendid surroundings of New York's Metropolitan Opera House this June. British group, The Who (below), began a season performing their rock opera *Tommy*, about a boy—struck deaf, dumb, and blind when he witnesses a murder—who has a gift for playing pinball machines. The *Tommy* double album is already a hit.

▲ *The World Cup final, Brazil versus Italy.*

Brazil wins World Cup

SPORT

21 JUNE Brazil's soccer stars swept Italy aside today in front of 107,000 fans in Mexico City to win the World Cup with a score of 4–1. Their free-flowing attacking game featured Pelé, Tostao, Jairzinho, and Rivelino in electric form throughout. Today's triumph follows earlier successes in 1958 and 1962. Because it is their third victory, Brazil will keep the Cup, known as the Jules Rimet trophy, and a new one will be made for the next tournament in 1974.

France mourns De Gaulle

PEOPLE

12 NOVEMBER Charles de Gaulle, the veteran French war leader and statesman who died three days ago, has been buried close to his home in the village of Colombey-les-Deux-Eglises. Thousands crowded the streets to see the simple ceremony. De Gaulle, who was a World War I hero, led the Free French forces in World War II and became president of France in 1958. He settled the crisis over Algerian independence and began the Fifth French Republic, which remains the constitution of France. A fervent patriot, de Gaulle stood for a strong France at the heart of a "European Europe," as opposed to a Europe dominated by the US.

▶ *General Charles de Gaulle, a major player in the story of modern France.*

Merckx wins Tour de France

SPORT

JULY Eddie Merckx of Belgium has won the Tour de France cycle race for the second year in a row. At the end of the long race, which has many stages, or sections, he was 17.54 seconds ahead of Frenchman Roger Pingeon. Merckx is very strong—at 6 foot 4 inches (1.9 meters), he is one of the tallest cyclists in the sport. Merckx began cycling at 14 and became world amateur champion when he was 18. He also won this year's Giro d'Italia. His determination to win every cycling trophy has earned him the nickname "the cannibal."

▲ *Eddie Merckx, the Belgian cycling champion, races to another victory.*

Tony Jacklin wins the US Open golf

British golfer Tony Jacklin kept cool in the Minnesota sun to win the US Open golf tournament in June. He led from the first round and ended seven strokes ahead of the US's Dave Hill in second place. Jacklin leapt to fame in 1967 when he became the first man to shoot a hole-in-one in front of television cameras, during the Dunlop Masters competition. Last July he became the first Briton to win the British Open golf championship since Max Faulkner in 1951.

◄ *Tony Jacklin in action at the US Open golf tournament.*

◄ *Germaine Greer, "second wave" feminist.*

Germaine Greer introduces *The Female Eunuch*

CULTURE

DECEMBER Germaine Greer, an Australian academic working in Britain, is the author of a brilliant new polemic about the role of women in the modern world. In *The Female Eunuch*, she argues that traditional marriage is just a legalized form of slavery for women. Dr. Greer says books like hers are part of a "second wave" of feminism. The first feminists, the suffragettes, struggled to win political rights for women. Today's feminists, many of whom belong to Women's Liberation groups, are campaigning for sexual and economic freedom and equality.

▲ *The Statue of Liberty on Liberty Island, NY, adorned with a feminist slogan.*

EXPLORING SPACE

For thousands of years humans have dreamed of exploring the heavens. Advances in the 20th century made it possible for humans to walk on the Moon by 1969. Since then, both the Soviet Union and the US have launched space stations in which astronauts can study space.

Unmanned vehicles have explored much of the solar system. The American probes *Viking* in the 1970s and *Pathfinder* in 1997 sent back data from Mars. *Voyagers 1* and *2* sent back pictures of Jupiter, Saturn, Uranus, and Neptune and are now heading out of the solar system. They carry messages from the Earth in case other living beings find them.

The space race

In the 1950s and '60s, the US and the Soviet Union raced each other to be first into space. The Soviet Union won. On 4 October, 1957, the Soviets launched *Sputnik I*, the first spacecraft to circle the world in space orbit. Then on 12 April, 1961, Soviet astronaut Yuri Gagarin became the first man to fly in space. In his craft *Vostok* ("East") he completed one orbit of the Earth in a flight lasting 108 minutes.

But the Americans were not far behind. Less than a month later, on 5 May, Alan Shepard became the first American in space, aboard *Liberty Bell 7*. The following year, on 20 February, 1962, John Glenn, aboard *Friendship 7*, became the first American to match Gagarin's feat of flying in orbit around the Earth. Then, on 21 July, 1969, US astronauts Neil Armstrong and Edwin "Buzz" Aldrin became the first people on the Moon. President Richard Nixon claimed the time as "the greatest in the history of the world since Creation."

Space Exploration facts

The *Saturn V* rocket used in the American missions to the Moon delivered 9 million pounds (4 million kg) of thrust, the power of 50 jumbo jets.

•

The first space station was *Salyut 1*, launched by the Soviet Union on 19 April, 1971. The first American space station was *Skylab*, launched on 15 May, 1973.

•

A dog named Laika was the first animal in space. She flew in a Soviet *Sputnik* satellite launched on 2 November, 1957, and died after a week in space.

▼ News headlines reflect the sense of awe people felt at the Soviets' launch of Sputnik, *the first satellite, in 1957.*

▶ Yuri Gagarin, the first man in space, reached a height of 195 miles (315 km) above the Earth.

News Chronicle
RUSSIA WINS SPACE RACE

'NEW MOON' SPO

Daily Mirror
UP GOES A MAN-MADE MOON

THE STAR
RED 'MOON' OVER LONDON

Daily
RUSSIA LAUNCH

DAILY HERALD
IA WINS THE RACE TO OUTER SPACE

The Evening N

RUSSIA LAUNCHES EARTH SATELLITE

The Dai

The best view of the Earth

Soviet cosmonaut Alexei Leonov left his *Voskhod 2* spacecraft and walked through space in his orange spacesuit on 18 March, 1965, attached to his craft by a cord. While his colleague Pavel Belyaev watched from inside the *Voskhod 2*, Leonov tested tools, took pictures, and turned a somersault. His excursion— the first "space walk"—lasted 10 minutes.

On 3 June, 1965, US astronaut Edward White became the first American to take a space walk. He stayed outside *Gemini 4* for 20 minutes, tied to it by a nylon line. While outside, White traveled 6,000 miles (9,600 km) at a speed of 17,500 miles per hour (28,000 km per hour). White did not want it to end—when he reentered the spacecraft, he said it was the saddest moment of his life.

▶ *Ed White had a jet-gas gun to propel himself as he floated 100 miles (160 km) above Earth.*

▲ *Valentina Tereshkova*

Women join men in space missions

Soviet cosmonaut Valentina Tereshkova became the first woman to travel into space on 16 June, 1963. She made 49 orbits of the Earth in the *Vostok 6* spacecraft before landing in the Soviet republic of Kazakhstan. During her flight she spoke to Soviet premier Nikita Khrushchev. Before Tereshkova was selected for the space program, she was already an experienced parachute jumper.

The first American woman in space was physicist Sally Ride, who flew on board the *Challenger* space shuttle on 18 June, 1983.

Rendezvous in space

Astronauts in space need to be able to maneuver their craft with great precision. The US *Gemini* program was launched in 1965–66 to practice this. On 15 December, 1965, Wally Schirra and Thomas Stafford in *Gemini 6* steered to within one foot of *Gemini 7*, piloted by Frank Bormann and James Lovell. The first docking of vehicles in space was between *Gemini 8* and an Agena rocket on 17 March, 1966.

▼ Gemini 6 *chased* Gemini 7 *for 100,000 miles (160,000 km).*

1970

1971

1972

1973

1974

1975

1976

1977

1978

1979

1971

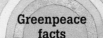

Greenpeace facts

After the Amchitka campaign Greenpeace grew into an international organization.

•

Greenpeace was instrumental in having Antarctica declared a World Park in 1991.

•

In 1996, when nuclear weapons testing ended, Greenpeace ended its longest-running campaign.

▲ *The first Greenpeace protesters at Amchitka.*

ENVIRONMENT

Greenpeace nuclear protests

30 SEPTEMBER US coastguards today prevented members of a new Canadian environmental pressure group, Greenpeace, from sailing across the Aleutian archipelago off the coast of Alaska. The eight campaigners, along with two reporters and a small crew, had planned to reach the island of Amchitka, the site of an imminent US nuclear test. Their fishing boat, *Phyllis Cormack*, has been renamed *Greenpeace* for the voyage.

In spite of this setback, the campaigners are drawing world attention to the possible consequences of the test. Amchitka is in a sensitive area, which is prone to earthquakes. Local people fear that a massive underground blast could trigger new tremors and disturb the region's ecological balance.

Bangladesh in turmoil

POLITICS

31 MAY Millions of Bengalis have fled to India and hundreds of thousands more have died since Sheikh Mujibur Rahman proclaimed the independence of Bangladesh, formerly East Pakistan, from its distant masters in West Pakistan. Now troops loyal to Pakistan's dictator, Muhammed Yahya Khan, are trying to root out the pro-Bangladeshi rebels, and they don't distinguish between fighters and ordinary civilians. India has allowed Bangladesh to set up a government-in-exile in Calcutta, but in the teeming refugee camps, aid workers are worrying about cholera.

▼ *Indian soldiers celebrate the birth of Bangladesh.*

New Testament musical

Offended Christians are picketing a London theater every night in protest at Andrew Lloyd Webber and Tim Rice's new hit musical *Jesus Christ Superstar*, which they feel is irreverent and inappropriate. The show tells the story of the life of Christ in rock music, songs, and dance. Webber and Rice surely agree that the Bible is the greatest story ever told, having drawn their previous smash hit, *Joseph and His Amazing Technicolor Dreamcoat*, from the Old Testament.

▼ *The writer Tim Rice (left) and composer Andrew Lloyd Webber.*

◀ *Switzerland's modern-day suffragettes on campaign.*

At last, votes for women in Switzerland

POLITICS

7 FEBRUARY Another bastion of sex discrimination crumbled today when Swiss women won the right to vote. A referendum, in which only men voted, resulted in 621,403 in favor of women's suffrage and 323,596 against. But some cantons, mainly in the rural areas of Uri, Schwyz, Appenzel, St. Gallen, and Thuringia, are resisting the principle. Still, this October's parliamentary election will be the first in which Swiss women can make their voices heard. And since women outnumber men by 250,000 in Switzerland, the result will be worth watching.

Idi Amin takes power in Uganda

POLITICS

20 FEBRUARY Major-General Idi Amin, who last month ousted Uganda's elected president Milton Obote, has declared himself president and promoted himself to the rank of general. A former army boxing champion, Amin has banned all political opposition but freed political prisoners held by the Obote regime and promised to hold free elections in five years' time.

▲ *Idi Amin.*

Walt Disney World opens in Florida

The town of Orlando in Florida has a new landmark—Sleeping Beauty's Castle —and a host of new residents, including Mickey Mouse, Goofy, and Pluto. In January the Walt Disney company opened its second theme park here. Over the next year at least 10 million people are expected to pass through the gates of the $400 million complex.

NEWS • 1971 • NEWS

3 May • Thousands of antiwar protesters march on Washington.

25 July • Vote is granted to 18-year-old Americans.

31 July • Apollo 15 astronauts go for a drive on the Moon.

3 December • India and Pakistan go to war over Bangladesh.

25 December • Kansas City and Miami Dolphins play the longest game in NFL history.

New London Bridge open

ARCHITECTURE

10 OCTOBER The world's largest antique was officially opened today when officials of Lake Havasu City in Arizona dedicated the old London Bridge. It has been rebuilt in their city as a tourist attraction. Today's operation is a dream fulfilled for Lake Havasu City's founder, Robert McCulloch, Sr. He paid $2.46 million for the bridge in 1962, and arranged for it to be carefully dismantled, before it was shipped and trucked to its new life in Arizona. Built in 1824 by John Rennie to reach across the Thames River, it is now being replaced in London by a more modern bridge.

▲ *Mickey Mouse and gang lead the parade at the new Walt Disney World in Florida.*

◄ *From left: Romano, Zabari, and their coach, Weinberg.*

גד צברי מתאבק
GAD ZABARI
Wrestler

יוסף רומנו משקולאי
JOSEPH ROMANO
Weightlifter

משה ויינברג מאמן האבקות
MOSHE WEINBERG
Wrestling Coach

▲ *A masked Black September gunman at the Israeli athletes' compound in Munich.*

Bobby Fischer is new world chess champion

This September 29-year-old Bobby Fischer became the US's first world chess champion, beating the Russian titleholder Boris Spassky in Reykjavik by 12½ games to 8½. Temperamental Fischer at one point refused to play until the organizer upped the prize money, but impressed all with his inspired game.

Fischer:black

69th move

Spassky:white

▲ *The 69th move (1072, Rook to E-1+) of the widely publicized Spassky versus Fisher match held in Iceland.*

SPORT | Black September strikes at Israel's Olympic athletes

5 SEPTEMBER Carnage broke out today at the Olympic Games in Munich, starting with a tense siege and ending in a bloody gun battle. Palestinian terrorists, members of the Black September group, stormed into the Israeli athletes' compound just after 5 o'clock this morning, killing coach Moshe Weinberg and weightlifter Joseph Romano. Fifteen athletes escaped, including Gad Zabari who broke free of his captors' clutches, dodging bullets as he made a dramatic dash for freedom. Holding nine athletes at gunpoint, the terrorists demanded the release of 200 Palestinians from Israeli jails. Israel's premier, Golda Meir, refused, and West German Chancellor Willy Brandt flew in to take charge of the operation. The gunmen were promised safe passage to Cairo, and this evening they and their hostages were all flown to a nearby military airfield. However, as they left their helicopter to walk across the apron to a waiting Boeing 727, the airport lights were turned off and police snipers opened fire. All of the hostages, five Palestinians, and a German policeman were killed. The rest of the Israeli team is to fly home immediately. Controversially, the Olympic Committee says that the games will carry on.

POLITICS | Bloody Sunday in the Bogside

30 JANUARY British troops breaking up a banned civil rights march in the Catholic Bogside district of Londonderry, in Northern Ireland, have shot dead 13 civilians. The incident, which is being dubbed Bloody Sunday, will do nothing to improve the already strained relations between the British security forces, which arrived last summer, and the nationalist community. While British army chief, Major-General Robert Ford, insists that men of the Parachute Battalion opened fire only after they had been fired on, other witnesses say that none of the marchers were armed with anything more than stones.

◄ *Paratroopers vault over the barricade at Free Derry Corner during the "Battle of Bogside."*

▲ *A friendly atmosphere prevailed throughout the meetings between Nixon (right) and Chou En-lai.*

Mark Spitz wins unprecedented seven Olympic gold medals

After winning a record seven gold medals in this year's Munich games, US swimming champion Mark Spitz has become an Olympic legend. The 22-year-old can now add his new trophies—individual medals for butterfly and freestyle, and three as part of the US relay team—to the two golds he won at the Mexico City Olympics four years ago.

▶ *Mark Spitz on his way to a seventh gold medal during the butterfly leg of the 4 x 100 meters medley.*

POLITICS

Nixon's Chinese visit ends in new accord

28 FEBRUARY President Nixon's historic state visit to China ended today. He went there with Secretary of State Henry Kissinger at the invitation of the Chinese communst government, and held talks with party head Mao Tse-tung and Premier Chou En-lai. Until now relations between China and the US have been strained because the Americans recognize the nationalist Chinese government of Taiwan. But after these "serious and frank talks," the American and Chinese leaders have committed themselves to "a long march together" for world peace. The new relationship was sealed by an exchange of gifts: giant pandas from China and musk oxen from the US.

DISASTERS

Hutus and Tutsis at war in Burundi

6 MAY Thousands of people are reported to have been massacred in the past week in the landlocked East African republic of Burundi. The mass killings took place after an attempt by rebels of the Hutu tribe, backed by Congolese mercenaries, to overthrow the minority Tutsi government of President Michel Micombero. According to the refugees now in Tanzania, Micombero's troops staged genocidal attacks on Hutu villages in reprisal. At the same time, gangs of Hutu outlaws are roaming the countryside, killing anyone in their way.

▼ *Uniformed troops belonging to Burundi's Tutsi people, the ruling minority tribe, guard captured members of the Hutu tribe.*

NEWS • 1972 • NEWS

25 January • *World's first kidney and pancreatic tissue transplant takes place in London.*

24 February • *North Vietnamese leave Paris peace talks in protest at US bombing raids.*

5 May • *115 die in Alitalia DC-8 crash.*

30 May • *Japanese Red Army terrorists kill 26 people at Lod Airport, Tel Aviv.*

LAW

14-year-old drug-dealer jailed

1 MARCH A Turkish court today sentenced Timothy Davey, a 14-year-old English schoolboy, to six years and three months in jail for conspiring to sell 56 pounds (25 kg) of cannabis resin. Davey, who was taken away in handcuffs to Istanbul's Sagmalcilar prison, admitted to the court "I did know I was committing a crime...we were hungry...I accepted to sell the hashish and now I am here." The harsh sentence has outraged British public opinion, and a series of appeals looks inevitable.

MUSIC

Young pop bands woo the "teenyboppers"

14 OCTOBER Back in the 1960s, pop fans were teenage girls, now they're "teenyboppers," girls who are too young to have boyfriends and whose idols aren't much older than themselves. Fourteen-year-old Michael Jackson, the youngest of The Jackson Five brothers, is number one in the US charts with "Ben." It is the theme song for an animal rights movie about a boy and his rodent pals. Another teenybopper idol is David Cassidy, Keith in television's *The Partridge Family.* The strictly Mormon Osmond brothers also score high in teenybop popularity stakes. After their joint smash hit, "Crazy Horses," heartthrob Donny recorded the hit "Puppy Love," and Little Jimmy—aged nine— triumphed with "Long-Haired Lover from Liverpool."

▼ *Below: The Jackson Five. Their name was a neighbor's suggestion. Below right: the Osmond brothers (left to right) Alan, Wayne, Merrill, Jay, and Donny.*

▲ *Singer and actor David Cassidy, a teenybop idol.*

First home video recorder marketed

Dutch electronics group Philips, inventors of the compact cassette, are now marketing the video recorder (below). Called the N-1500, this machine can record and play back TV movies using a special tape cassette that records TV signals. A timer allows operators to record programs in advance.

DISASTERS

10,000 feared dead after massive earthquake in Managua

24 DECEMBER The capital of Nicaragua, Managua, has been shaken to rubble by a severe earthquake. Up to 10,000 people are believed dead after tremors reaching up to 6.5 on the Richter scale hit the city late last night. The tremors continued into the early hours of this morning. The Nicaraguan government has ordered a total evacuation of the city and a mass exodus is now under way.

Among the survivors is the reclusive American billionaire, Howard Hughes, who was staying at the Intercontinental Hotel when the earthquake took place; he took shelter in the hotel parking lot. Nicaragua's President, General Anastasio Somoza—whose palace was ruined in the quake—said "We shall never know Managua again as it used to be. We shall have to rebuild it."

▶ *The city of Managua, devastated by a severe earthquake.*

Andes air crash: cannibal survivors

DISASTERS

29 DECEMBER Sixteen people who survived an airplane crash in the Andes ate the flesh of those who had died in the accident, it was learned today. The survivors, members of a Uruguayan rugby team, were stranded on a remote peak for 10 weeks. After three weeks, having eaten all the available food, their leader, who is a medical student, convinced them that they wouldn't survive unless they obtained protein from the bodies of the dead. Before butchering the first corpse, the men appealed for divine forgiveness by making a gigantic cross in the snow.

▶ *Their 10-week ordeal over, survivors stand beside the wreckage of their plane as a rescue helicopter approaches.*

Vietnam horror

WAR

9 JUNE Last night, American planes, intending to hit Viet Cong military targets, bombed a Vietnamese village. This morning the world's newspapers splashed Huynh Cong Ut's photographs of the aftermath: children running, one of them a girl, Phan Thi Kim Phuc, who has torn all her clothes off to escape burning napalm jelly. Moments before this harrowing scene, she was happily playing. Now she represents the continuing horror of the war in Vietnam.

▼ *Vietnamese children run in terror from their burning village.*

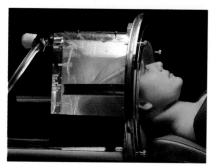

▲ *A CAT (Computerized Axial Tomography) scanner.*

CAT brain scanner used for first time

TECHNOLOGY

MARCH Thanks to an amazing new device, it's now possible to see inside the skull without surgery. A CAT scanner uses a computer to create detailed cross-sectional X-ray images, like a series of "slices," of the head. Invented by British engineer Godfrey Hounsfield and South African physicist Allan Cormack, it works by rotating an X-ray beam and detector around the head. The computer creates an image from data supplied by the detector, which picks up the variations in the signal caused by different tissue densities.

Historic summit in Moscow

TREATIES

1 JUNE President Nixon today agreed with Soviet leader Leonid Brezhnev to curb the nuclear arms race. After the first US-USSR summit meeting ever in Moscow, the two leaders signed two accords, known as SALT (Strategic Arms Limitation Talks). The superpowers have agreed to limit the number of ballistic missiles and not to develop antimissile weapons. In his television speech to the Soviet people, President Nixon said: "Let our goal now be a world without fear..."

▶*Nixon (far right) and Brezhnev (center right) celebrate their summit.*

OUR EARTH IN DANGER

In the final 30 years of the 20th century, people are facing up to the fact that they have to change the way they treat the Earth, before it is too late. Accidents like oil spills kill countless birds and fish. Rivers and seas are dirtied by chemical fertilizers from farms, industrial waste, and even sewage.

Campaigning groups, individuals, and governments are, however, trying to create a new beginning for our planet. Recycling and environmental projects are the first steps in a long journey that lies ahead of us all.

Crusade for peace

The protest group Greenpeace was founded in Canada in 1971 by people worried about damage to the environment. Their first mission was to disrupt nuclear tests planned by the US government on Amchitka Island, Alaska. They succeeded—and Greenpeace quickly grew to become an international body, funded by its members, with headquarters in Amsterdam, Holland.

As well as fighting pollution, Greenpeace tries to stop nuclear weapons testing and to save species of animals and plants that are in danger of dying out. Greenpeace activists do not use violence, but they often take drastic action to stop governments or industries who are damaging the environment.

Environmental facts

Scientists estimate there are 8 million animal and plant species in the world, but they have only named 1.5 million.

•

Three-quarters of the world's animal and plant species live in tropical forests.

•

5,929 animal species are in danger of dying out.

•

More than 50,000 tigers existed in India in 1905, but by 1972 their numbers were down to 1,827. Thanks to environmental programs, by 1986 there were more than 4,000 tigers.

▲ *Greenpeace members hang from a bridge across the Rhine, Europe, to block ship traffic in protest against pollution of the river.*

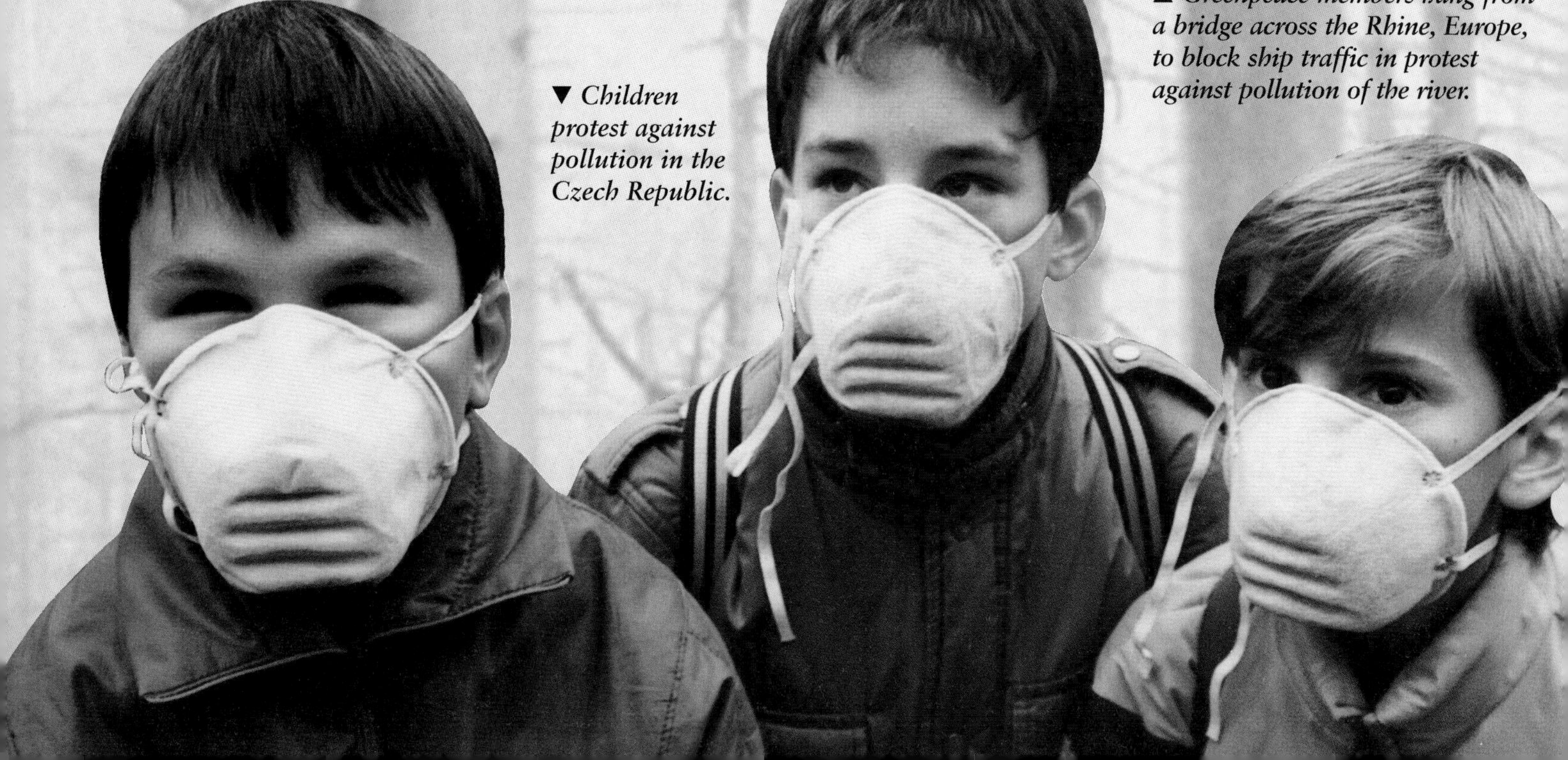

▼ *Children protest against pollution in the Czech Republic.*

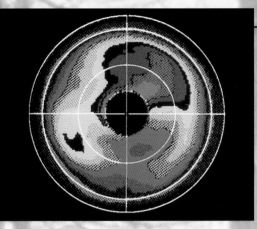

Hole in ozone layer

In the mid-1980s, a drop in ozone gas was discovered over parts of Antarctica. Found in the Earth's atmosphere, ozone absorbs dangerous ultraviolet radiation from the Sun. Too much ultraviolet radiation will damage plants and can cause skin cancer. The hole in the ozone layer has been partly caused by pollution.

Effects of pollution

▼ *Trees have been destroyed by acid rain.*

The Earth's atmosphere is being poisoned by pollution. "Acid rain," which devastates trees and plants, is caused by the sulfur dioxide and nitrogen oxide found in the fumes released by car exhausts and from power stations that burn oil or coal. The gases mix with water vapor in clouds, forming sulfuric and nitric acids, which pollute the rain.

The "greenhouse effect" also poses a long-term threat. Certain gases in the Earth's atmosphere stop some of the Sun's heat from escaping back into space, similar to the way that glass keeps warm air inside a greenhouse. But increasing amounts of carbon dioxide, released when humans burn oil and coal, is leading to more and more of the Sun's heat being trapped. Scientists believe that if this continues, the ice at the North and South poles will melt, causing sea levels to rise—which would lead to widespread flooding—and weather patterns to change.

▲ *Garbage is another form of pollution. In the 1990s there have been efforts to reduce packaging on products. Municipal authorities have also launched recycling schemes.*

▲ *Oil spills are detrimental to sealife. In 1991 Iraqis deliberately released oil into the Persian Gulf after invading Kuwait, causing terrible damage.*

▶ *Ivory is destroyed in Kenya, where trade in ivory is banned.*

Endangered species

It is a law of nature that animal species that are unable to adapt to their environment do not survive. But many species are now facing extinction because of humans, mainly through the destruction of landscapes in which the animals live. Trade in animal parts is also a problem. Elephants are killed for their ivory tusks, and the number of elephants in Africa has fallen from 2 million in 1970 to 500,000 in the late 1990s. Trade in ivory is partially banned in African countries.

1970

1971

1972

1973

1974

1975

1976

1977

1978

1979

▼ *One of Pinochet's troops guards pro-Allende prisoners in Santiago's sports stadium.*

POLITICS

Allende dies during Chile coup

11 SEPTEMBER Tension is running high in Chile tonight following the overthrow of President Salvador Allende. A coup led by General Augusto Pinochet started early today. As the streets of Santiago, Chile's capital, filled with troops loyal to Pinochet, Allende barricaded himself into the presidential palace.

Chilean air force planes targeted the building with rockets and bombs, and this evening the president was reported dead. A Pinochet spokesman said that he had killed himself when he realized that he was doomed; Allende's supporters say he died, submachine-gun in hand, defending the palace to the end. The coup marks the end of Chile's democratically elected Marxist government. Allende's policies of nationalization, land redistribution, and raising wages were popular with Chilean workers, but mistrusted by big business. The US Central Intelligence Agency helped to fund opposition groups, who mounted a series of terrorist attacks, and recently the coalition of political parties that backed Allende started to crumble. Now Chile is in the hands of a right-wing military dictator.

▲ *Salvador Allende (wearing glasses) in the presidential palace during the recent coup in Chile.*

NEWS • 1973 • NEWS

23 January • Agreement to end the Vietnam War is reached in Paris.

8 April • Spanish artist Pablo Picasso dies.

14 May • Skylab space station is launched.

17 May • Start of Senate hearings into Watergate affair.

17 October • The OPEC oil-producing states put up prices by over 70 percent in protest at US support for Israel.

Nobel prize for Lorenz

The Austrian animal behaviorist Konrad Lorenz, together with his colleagues Karl von Frisch and Nikolaas Tinbergen, are the winners of this year's Nobel Prize for Physiology and Medicine. Lorenz is the founder of ethology, the science of comparing animal behavior with that of human beings. Lorenz is best known for his work with goslings: by being the first living thing they saw when they hatched, Lorenz was recognized by the goslings as their mother.

ECONOMICS

Denmark, UK, and Eire join the Common Market

1 JANUARY The United Kingdom, Republic of Ireland, and Denmark today became part of the European Economic Community, joining Belgium, France, Italy, Luxembourg, the Netherlands, and West Germany to form the biggest economic bloc in the world. The new members, which mark the Community's first enlargement since it was founded in 1958, mean that the EEC now has a larger population than the US. Britain first applied to join the EEC in 1961, but its application was repeatedly vetoed by France's President de Gaulle. British feelings about being part of the EEC remain mixed.

▼ *Konrad Lorenz with the subjects of his research.*

▲ *Representatives of the nine nations belonging to the European Economic Community.*

Britain's "three-day week"

13 DECEMBER In order to save dwindling coal reserves, Britain's factories are to open only three days a week starting in the new year, it was announced today. The economy has been crippled by a combination of huge increases in the price of oil and united strike action from miners, railroadmen, and power station workers. Drivers have been issued with rationbooks and given a new, fuel-saving speed limit of 50 miles (80 km) an hour. Already, 200 gas stations in England have shut down because of the shortage of fuel. Nighttime television broadcasting will finish an hour earlier, and people are preparing for inevitable power outages by buying candles and gas heaters.

▲ *The opera house is sited on Sydney Harbour.*

Sydney Opera House

At last, 13 years after work started, Sydney has its opera house. A stunning structure created by Swedish architect Jørn Utzon, it resembles a pile of enormous tiled shells. The Opera House holds four theaters, including an auditorium capable of seating 1,500 people. The project's troubled history was forgotten at the opening ceremony as Queen Elizabeth declared it to be one of the wonders of the modern world.

▼ *Israeli soldiers raise their flag on Syrian territory.*

Yom Kippur war in Israel

24 OCTOBER Egypt and Syria launched a joint attack on Israel on 6 October—Yom Kippur, the holiest day in the Jewish calendar. Taking Israel by surprise, the Arab allies recaptured the eastern bank of the Suez Canal and the Golan Heights (both captured by Israel in 1967), before being expelled. Last week, during a vicious tank battle, Israel pushed behind Egyptian lines to seize land on the west bank of the canal. Today a UN ceasefire brought the fighting to an end.

Native Americans occupy Wounded Knee

8 MAY An extraordinary standoff in the Pine Ridge Sioux Reservation, South Dakota, came to an end today as 120 protesters agreed to leave Wounded Knee, the site of the 1890 massacre of 200 Sioux by Federal troops. The 69-day occupation by members of the American Indian Movement began last February. The campaigners accuse the government of breaking treaties and violating their civil rights. They dared the authorities to repeat the massacre and are demanding a Senate investigation into the plight of Native Americans today.

◀ *Native Americans guard the Sacred Heart Catholic Church in Wounded Knee.*

▲ *The royal family on the balcony after the wedding.*

Princess Anne and Mark Phillips wed

14 NOVEMBER Britain, racked by industrial unrest and oil shortages, seized the chance to celebrate the first royal wedding for 10 years. Watched by an estimated worldwide television audience of 500 million, Princess Anne wed equestrian Captain Mark Phillips at Westminster Abbey. The bride wore a high-necked white silk gown; the groom was resplendent in the scarlet, gold, and blue of the Dragoon Guards. They will honeymoon in Barbados.

1970
1971
1972
1973
1974
1975
1976
1977
1978
1979

1974

▲ *Outside the White House on the day of Nixon's resignation, the 2,027th day of his presidency.*

◀ *Nixon is the first US president to resign from office.*

POLITICS

Nixon resigns over Watergate scandal

9 AUGUST "Our long national nightmare is over," stated new president, Gerald Ford, after Richard Nixon's resignation today. The nightmare began in June 1972, when intruders were caught bugging Washington's Watergate building, headquarters of the Democratic Party's national committee. Thanks to investigations by Judge John J. Sirica and the Senate Committee, chaired by Sam Ervin, it emerged that the intruders, several of whom had worked for the CIA, were linked to the Committee to Reelect the President. Two *Washington Post* journalists, Bob Woodward and Carl Bernstein, worked hard to keep the scandal in the news.

It soon became clear that Nixon's senior aides were involved in "dirty tricks" and that the president himself knew of the Watergate break-in. Three days ago, prosecutors obtained a White House audio tape on which Nixon is heard telling his aides to obstruct FBI inquiries into the Watergate break-in. Nixon chose to resign to avoid impeachment.

Queen pioneers the rock "video"

Rock band Queen's (below) "Bohemian Rhapsody," a six-minute work featuring a ballad as well as hard rock and heavy metal musical styles, is a long-running No. 1 hit in Britain. Its popularity may have something to do with the short promotional movie that accompanied its release.

▼ *Clockwise from top: Brian May, Roger Taylor, Freddie Mercury, John Deacon.*

POLITICS

"Carnation" revolution in Portugal

25 APRIL Army officers today brought to an end the right-wing regime that has ruled Portugal since 1933, when Antonio Salazar became premier. In a relatively gentle coup—only three people were killed and 40 wounded—General António Spínola's Armed Forces Movement has deposed Salazar's successor, Marcello Caetano. Spínola has promised democracy for Portugal and independence for Portuguese colonies. People are displaying red and white carnations, symbolizing their hopes for a new socialist future.

▼ *Supporters of the "carnation" revolution in Lisbon.*

WAR

Turkey invades Cyprus

24 JULY Greece's ruling military dictatorship collapsed today, four days after Turkish troops invaded the northern part of Cyprus. The Turks invaded Cyprus after its moderate president, Archbishop Makarios, was overthrown in a coup just over a week ago. Makarios' opponents were militants campaigning for *enosis*—the union of Greece and Cyprus—and they were backed by the colonels who rule Greece. But moves toward *enosis* concern the Turkish government, which takes an interest in the welfare of Cyprus' minority Turkish population. Now, as Turkish troops and arms continue to arrive in northeastern Cyprus, Greek Cypriots are fleeing to the south of the island. Talks aimed at calming the tension are expected to begin shortly at the UN in Geneva. Makarios has flown to London, where there is a large Cypriot community.

◀ *Turkish troops arriving in Famagusta, northern Cyprus.*

NEWS • 1974 • NEWS

22 February • *Pakistan recognizes Bangladesh.*

6 March • *Harold Wilson is UK prime minister again.*

12 September • *Coup topples reign of Emperor Haile Selassie of Ethiopia.*

29 October • *Muhammad Ali regains world heavyweight boxing title.*

26 November • *Japan's premier Tanaka resigns after corruption scandal.*

POLITICS

Arafat makes historic speech to the UN

13 NOVEMBER Yasir Arafat, the leader of the PLO (Palestine Liberation Organization), has addressed the General Assembly of the United Nations in New York. In his 90-minute speech he urged the establishment of a new Palestinian state in which Christians, Muslims, and Jews would live together.

His speech, which opened a major UN debate on the Middle East, is a triumph for Arafat, marking the UN's official recognition of him as the political leader of a dispossessed people. Calling upon Israel to abandon Zionism, he concluded by saying: "I have come bearing an olive branch and a freedom fighter's gun. Do not let the olive branch fall from my hands."

CN tower in Toronto

A new record is being set as a massive concrete tower rises above the Toronto skyline. When it is complete, the Canadian National Tower will be 1,815 feet (553 meters) tall. It is not quite the world's tallest manmade structure but it will be the world's tallest freestanding building. The CN Tower will house an observation platform and a restaurant with a radio mast on the very top.

LITERATURE

The Gulag costs Solzhenitsyn his citizenship

14 FEBRUARY Novelist Alexander Solzhenitsyn, who won the Nobel Prize for Literature four years ago, has been deprived of his Soviet citizenship and was expelled from the Soviet Union. His crime is his new book, a searing account of life in the Soviet prison labor camps of the Gulag Archipelago. He has been sent to Frankfurt. His family is expected to join him in exile.

▶ *Solzhenitsyn (left) with Heinrich Böll.*

1970

1971

1972

1973

1974

1975

1976

1977

1978

1979

1975

China's "terracotta army" is revealed

ARCHEOLOGY

11 JULY Just over a year ago some villagers near Mount Li in northern China were digging a well and came upon some curious pottery sculptures. Archeologists rushed to the scene, and now the extraordinary "terracotta army" of China's first emperor is being uncovered. The life-sized figures are replicas of the soldiers of Ch'in Shih-huang-ti, the emperor from whom the name China derives. Ch'in Shih-huang-ti was a ruthless and extremely efficient tyrant. He began the construction of the Great Wall and work on his spectacular tomb, which is nearby, began during his lifetime. When he died, around 210 B.C., a terracotta replica of his army was ready to guard him for eternity.

Archeologists have now uncovered the soldiers of Pit No. 1, which is 689 feet (210 meters) from east to west, and 197 feet (60 meters) from north to south. There are 3,000 men in this pit, and they are arranged in 11 parallel corridors. All the faces are different, as if they represent real individuals. What's more, this pottery army is equipped with horses, chariots, and weapons. More pits now await the archeologists, but judging by what has been revealed so far, Ch'in Shih-huang-ti's terracotta army will be considered another wonder of the world.

▲ *The terracotta soldiers stand in battle formation. No two faces are the same.*

Computers get personal

TECHNOLOGY

MARCH A microcomputer, the first of its type, which is designed for home use, is now widely available for sale in the US. For the price of $297, the MITS Altair 8800 has 256 bytes of memory and is assembled from a kit. But it is quite complicated to operate—to start it up a series of 25 switches has to be pressed, all in the correct sequence. So, as yet, this pioneering "personal computer" is strictly for computer wizards. However, the manufacturers are starting to work on more "user-friendly" computers.

Franco's death marks the end of an era

POLITICS

22 NOVEMBER The man who has ruled Spain since the end of the Civil War in 1939, Generalissimo Francisco Franco, died two days ago. He will be buried in the Valley of the Fallen, the official military cemetery. Today, Prince Juan Carlos, who will preside over the dead dictator's funeral, was sworn in as Spain's king. In his speech to the Spanish parliament, known as the Cortes, Juan Carlos said he would encourage "far-reaching improvements." Many Spaniards are hoping that the new king's cautious words signal a gradual return to democratic government.

▲ *Unrest in the late 1960s caused Franco to harden his regime.*

Symbolic meeting in space of Soviets and Americans

The Russian *Soyuz* and the American *Apollo* vessels were docked together in space for a historic greeting between the two superpowers. Cosmonaut Alexei Leonov and astronaut Tom Stafford shook hands in space and greeted each other in Russian and English. The astronauts were then able to board each other's vessels to carry out scientific investigations, compare notes on their space experiences, and have a meal together.

◀ *Soviet and American astronauts meet.*

Aerosols damage the ozone layer

From now on all US aerosol hairsprays, antiperspirants, and deodorants will carry an official government health warning. Public concern about aerosols began last year when two American scientists claimed that fluorocarbons released into the atmosphere in large quantities might destroy the protective ozone layer, exposing the Earth to ultraviolet radiation and increasing the risk of skin cancer.

◀ *Members of a Muslim militia in Beirut.*

WAR

Civil war in Lebanon

16 SEPTEMBER The cosmopolitan city of Beirut has become a battleground as Lebanon is torn apart by civil war. It has been nearly five years since "Black September" in Jordan turned Lebanon into the main base of Palestinian guerrillas, making it a major Israeli target. This civil war has started because the continuing struggle between Israel and the Palestinians has upset Lebanon's already fragile balance of power. The Palestinians' actions against Israel are supported by many Lebanese Muslims, but they are resented by Lebanese Christians. Lebanon is a country of 14 different religious denominations, many of which are now represented by armed militias.

WAR

Vietnam is reunited

29 APRIL The forces of the victorious Vietnamese communists are preparing to enter the city of Saigon, the capital of South Vietnam. The city's surrender will mark the true end of the Vietnam War. The peace of 1973 allowed for US withdrawal, but fighting between South Vietnam and the communist Vietnamese has continued until now. For days the US Embassy in Saigon has been surrounded by thousands of people, desperate to get away on the shuttle service of helicopters carrying people to the warships waiting in the South China Sea, before Vietnam's new communist government takes control.

◀ *Saigon after the last bombing offensive. Above: fighting for a place on a US evacuation flight.*

CULTURE

First International Women's Year

31 DECEMBER British women now have the benefit of two newly enacted laws, the Sex Discrimination Act and the Equal Pay Act, which aim to end discrimination against women in the workplace. These laws provide a proper finale to the first "International Women's Year" and a triumph for British feminists, who, like their "sisters" all around the world, are campaigning for women's liberation.

▶ *Protesters leave El Vino's, a London bastion of "male chauvinism" where women customers are not allowed to drink at the bar.*

1970

1971

1972

1973

1974

1975

1976

1977

1978

1979

Sex Pistols lead UK's punks

Young people like to rebel, and in 1976 the young rebels are "punks." New bands like the Sex Pistols, the Clash, and the Buzzcocks have abandoned complex and expensive equipment in favor of loud, raw, and challengingly tasteless sounds. Sex Pistols manager Malcolm McLaren says: "...they're yobs, but they're proud of it."

▼ *The Sex Pistols—proud to be punks.*

1976

◄ *Soweto's turmoil has renewed world concern about apartheid.*

▼ *South African police confront black children.*

POLITICS

Soweto rises up in anger

18 JUNE Thousands of black South Africans have taken to the streets in protest at an order from the Transvaal Education Authority that Afrikaans and English are to be taught side by side in black secondary schools. This has angered the residents of Soweto and other Johannesburg townships, for whom Afrikaans, the language spoken by South Africa's Dutch-descended ruling white minority, is the language of apartheid.

The uprising, which started in Soweto two days ago, became nationwide after police killed 13-year-old Hector Peterson. Hundreds of people are dead, and over 1,000 people have been wounded. To bring about what Prime Minister Vorster called "order at all costs," South Africa's police have been authorized to shoot at crowds without any warning. Newspapers show photographs of black children, still dressed in their school uniforms, who have been shot dead.

NEWS • 1976 • NEWS

12 January • Agatha Christie, doyenne of crime fiction, dies, aged 85.

2 June • Record number of bankruptcies in UK.

29 July • Chinese city of Tangshan is devastated by huge earthquake.

10 September • 176 die in the world's worst midair collision, in Yugoslavia.

2 November • Jimmy Carter is elected US President.

TERRORISM

Israeli raid on Entebbe

4 JULY Three Hercules transport planes landed Israeli commandos at Entebbe airport in Uganda last Saturday night, in an attempt to rescue the 100-odd hostages being held by pro-Palestinian terrorists. The Israeli commandos had the advantage of being totally unexpected, but after they'd successfully stormed the aircraft, 20 of the Ugandan soldiers who had been surrounding the plane were dead, along with all seven of the hijackers, three of the hostages, and one member of the Israeli commando team. The hijackers, allegedly backed by Idi Amin, had been demanding the release of Palestinian political prisoners held in Israel and four other countries.

◄ *After their rescue, the exhausted but relieved Entebbe hostages returned to Israel.*

Chairman Mao's long march is over

PEOPLE

23 OCTOBER At the venerable age of 82, Mao Tse-tung, the great Chinese leader, is dead. Within minutes of the official announcement, hundreds of distraught mourners were pouring into Beijing's (Peking's) Square of Heavenly Peace. But while Chairman Mao is lying in state, his would-be successors are competing for power. His widow, the former actress Chiang Ch'ing, is leading one faction. The more moderate followers of Hua Kuo-feng (who became premier of the People's Republic of China after the death of Mao's deputy, Chou En-lai earlier this year) are opposed to her strictly communist policies.

▲ *Chinese citizens pay their last respects to Mao Tse-tung. He is thought to have died after suffering a series of strokes.*

America celebrates 200 years

ENTERTAINMENT

4 JULY The whole of the United States is celebrating the country's bicentennial. It is two hundred years ago today— 4 July 1776—that America declared its independence from Britain. In Washington, a million people gathered to watch fireworks and a laser display, and in New York 15 tall ships sailed into the harbor. Other fun celebrations included throwing 1,776 frisbees into the sky in Boston.

Army takes power in Argentina

POLITICS

24 MARCH The third wife of Argentina's former president, Juan Perón, was arrested by military leaders early this morning as she returned to her home in Buenos Aires. President Isabel Perón, 45, has been in power since the death of her husband in 1974. Her plane was diverted by the pilots to the city airport where she was arrested on arrival. Mrs. Perón's government has been overthrown because of the dire state of Argentina's economy.

▲ *Argentina's President Isabel Martinez de Perón.*

Nadia Comaneci scores 10 out of 10

Fourteen-year-old Romanian gymnast, Nadia Comaneci, delighted this year's Olympic crowds in Montreal, Canada.
She won three gold medals, a silver, and a bronze. Having been told to reject 10 out of 10 as impossible, the Olympic computer was baffled by her maximum scores.

▶ *Nadia Comaneci captured spectators' hearts at the Montreal Olympics.*

Dioxin leak leads to severe contamination

ENVIRONMENT

▼ *A young gas victim.*

20 JULY A cloud of poison gas, which escaped by accident from a factory near Milan in Italy has killed animals and plants in the surrounding countryside. About 15 people have been treated for burns. According to a factory spokesman, the gas, called trichlorophenol, was the same as the chemical sold to the United States in 1970 to be used as a defoliant during the Vietnam War.

▶ *Protected chemical workers inspect the area.*

1970

1971

1972

1973

1974

1975

1976

1977

1978

1979

Tenerife air crash

DISASTERS

30 MARCH The world's worst aviation disaster ever occurred three days ago when a Pan Am and a KLM jumbo jet collided on the ground at Tenerife airport in the Canary Islands. The American plane was turning into the runway just as the Dutch plane was taking off. All 248 of the KLM jumbo's passengers were killed immediately, but about 70 of the Pan Am jet's 326 passengers did survive and are now being treated in local hospitals.

Many of them are badly burned. Eyewitnesses were horrified by the sight of the two jumbos colliding and bursting into flames.

It is not yet clear what or who caused this catastrophe, which would never have happened if it hadn't been for an earlier bomb explosion at Las Palmas airport. Originally, the Pan Am and KLM jumbos were supposed to land and takeoff at Las Palmas airport, but after the explosion they were rerouted to Tenerife airport, with tragic consequences.

▲ *The control tower looms high in the background as soldiers clear away the wreckage of the Pan Am jumbo jet.*

▶ *An American official checks identities on the coffins of the dead prior to their shipment off the island.*

Centre Pompidou opens

The Centre Pompidou for the arts was opened today in the old Marais district of Paris. With its brightly colored, unashamedly external pipes and ducts, the building is a major cultural achievement in its own right. The Pompidou's joint architects were Renzo Piano and Richard Rogers.

▼ *Paris' Centre Pompidou.*

Czech dissidents launch Charter 77

POLITICS

6 JANUARY A revolutionary document calling for the restoration of human rights in Czechoslovakia has been distributed today among West German newspapers. "Charter 77" has the support of 240 leading Czech intellectuals. They include Dr. Jiri Hajek, who was foreign minister under the liberal communist government of Alexander Dubcek, and the playwright Václav Havel. It's the first active opposition to the communist regime since the Prague Spring of 1968 was crushed. After the Soviet invasion of that year, ex-government ministers and prominent intellectuals had to take menial jobs, police harassment increased, and there was a general mood of despair in Czechoslovakia.

Bhutto ousted by Zia

POLITICS

5 JULY Zulfikar Ali Bhutto, the prime minister of Pakistan, has been arrested by General Zia ul-Haq, the army's chief commander. General Zia's move comes after months of unrest in Pakistan. Hundreds of people have died since Mr. Bhutto's People's Party won a suspiciously large majority in the election last March. In April Mr. Bhutto imposed martial law on the cities of Karachi, Lahore, and Hyderabad, and he appointed General Zia as the army chief of staff. But opposition parties continued to accuse Bhutto's party of rigging elections, and now General Zia has had Bhutto arrested.

▲ *Pakistan's Prime Minister Ali Bhutto at a press conference during a visit to Paris.*

▲ *Fantastic creatures from* Star Wars.

Footloose and fantastic

The science fiction movie *Star Wars* has been a huge success for its writer and director, George Lucas, taking $185 million at the box office. The special effects alone are utterly breathtaking. In contrast, the disco movie *Saturday Night Fever* is also a smash. The sensational dancing of John Travolta and The Bee Gees' catchy soundtrack have set off an international epidemic of disco fever.

◀ *John Travolta's dream comes true in* Saturday Night Fever.

MUSIC
Death of Elvis

16 AUGUST The king of rock 'n' roll, Elvis Presley, was found dead today in the bathroom at Graceland, his palatial home in Memphis, Tennessee. Presley, who was 42, dominated pop music in the late 1950s and early 1960s and released more than 40 albums. In 1968, after almost eight years in seclusion, he returned to live performances with a series of shows in Las Vegas. All over the world millions of fans are mourning his sad and untimely death.

▲ *Elvis Presley sings in Las Vegas.*

TERRORISM
Hans Martin Schleyer

19 OCTOBER The body of Dr. Hans Martin Schleyer, the director of Mercedes Benz in West Germany, was found today in the trunk of a car near Mulhouse in eastern France. Dr. Schleyer was kidnapped by members of the Baader-Meinhof group, a German terrorist organization. They were demanding a huge ransom and the release of 11 of their jailed leaders. The German government refused to give in to their demands, but Schleyer was alive until yesterday, when German antiterrorist commandos stormed a hijacked Lufthansa jet in Somalia. The jet's hijackers were allies of the Baader-Meinhof group. Today, in revenge for the German authorities' success in Somalia, they murdered Schleyer.

◀ *The photograph of the kidnapped German businessman that was sent by his captors to a French newspaper.*

NEWS • 1977 • NEWS

17 January • *80 die in a train crash in Sydney, Australia.*

2 April • *Red Rum is the first horse to win the Grand National for the third time.*

29 May • *Nigel Short qualifies for chess final aged 11.*

15 June • *Spain's first election day for 41 years.*

26 June • *Djibouti, France's last African colony, gains independence.*

POLITICS
Biko inquest

2 DECEMBER Steve Biko, the 30-year-old founder and first president of the South African Students Association, didn't die as a result of police brutality according to the official inquest that ended today. His brain injuries were caused by the "application of force to his head" and while he was in custody he "collided with walls and tables," but even so the policemen who interrogated him for five days cannot be blamed for his death three months ago, according to the inquest. Outside the courthouse, Steve Biko's family and friends protested at the verdict.

▲ *Biko's last journey as his coffin is carried through the 20,000 mourners.*

COUNTERCULTURE

In the 1960s many young people rebelled against their parents' way of life. In the North America and Europe, they rejected traditional family life, the power of money, and conflict between races and between nations. They believed instead in communal living and the power of love.

The young rebels saw themselves in conflict with their parents' views and assumptions—or "culture"—and some called their movement the "counterculture." Other youth rebellions have taken place before and since—young city dwellers in the 1920s chose fun over their parents' formal ways.

▼ *Background image: Hippies dressed in colorful handmade clothes in natural fabrics. Tie-dyed patterns were ideal for this.*

▲ *Cast members of the rock musical* Hair *epitomize the hippie style.* Hair *was a big hit when it was first staged in 1968.*

Love, peace, and drugs

The hippie movement was born in California in the mid-1960s and spread across North America and Europe. Hippies rejected conventional values, preferring free love for all, and they established communes in rural areas in an attempt to separate themselves from society.

Hippies wanted no part in the world as it was, and were determined to change it. Some hippies protested against the war being waged by the US in Vietnam and supported civil rights movements.

They experimented with mind-altering drugs to experience a heightened consciousness and used the word "hippie" to describe themselves, taken from the slang word "hip," meaning in tune with the latest attitudes. Others focused on changing themselves. They explored religions and ideas from eastern countries such as India. They tried yoga and other forms of meditation.

The hippie movement had had its day by the mid-1970s, but it was a great influence on the following decades.

Peace and harmony

Folk singer Joan Baez first appeared at the 1959 folk festival at Newport, Rhode Island, and, with fellow singer Bob Dylan, helped to popularize folk music. Her religious beliefs as a Quaker also made her a committed opponent of war and racial discrimination, and she stood up for her convictions in life as well as in her songs. In 1964 she refused to pay part of her income tax in protest at government spending on weapons. In 1967 she was arrested and jailed for her part in an anti-Vietnam War demonstration.

◄ *Joan Baez performs at a demonstration. Her song "We Shall Overcome" became an anthem for protesters.*

The punk revolution

Punk rock invaded the music scene in Britain in the mid-1970s. It seemed to be a reaction to the peace and love advocated by hippies, and was more about attitude than music—the young musicians in punk bands were outspoken, rebellious, and famous for not being able to play their instruments very well.

The British band that launched punk rock was the Sex Pistols, who released their first single, "Anarchy in the UK," in 1976. In March 1977, the Pistols fired their bass guitar player Glen Matlock, claiming it was because he was too good a guitarist. His replacement was Sid Vicious, who could hardly play at all—but who had plenty of sneering attitude.

Fans reacted to the loud, thrashing punk music by jumping up and down in a dance called the pogo. Performances often ended with fans tearing up seats or fighting. Many city governments banned punk bands, so they played under false names.

British punk did not export well to the US. An American punk scene did develop, but it was more artistic than the deliberately dirty and downmarket British version.

▼ *Punks rebelled against convention—they spiked their hair and tore their clothes. Some even wore garbage bags as shirts.*

▼ *Sex Pistols Sid Vicious (left) and Johnny Rotten assault their fans' eardrums. The band split up during a tour of the US in 1978.*

Counterculture facts

The first hippie rock concert was on 16 October, 1965, in San Francisco. A hippie commune organized the show, which included the bands Jefferson Airplane and the Charlatans.

•

The Sex Pistols' single "God Save the Queen" had an artwork of the Queen wearing a safety pin through her nose on the sleeve. It was banned by many stores and the BBC, but still hit No.2 in the singles charts in May 1977.

•

The hippie phrase "flower power" was coined by American poet Allen Ginsberg at a 1965 rally in Berkeley, California, against the Vietnam War.

281

1970

1971

1972

1973

1974

1975

1976

1977

1978

1979

1978

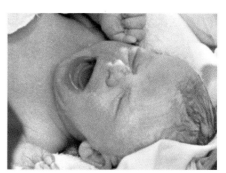

"Boat people" flee Vietnam

POLITICS

17 FEBRUARY As the tension between the Chinese and Vietnamese governments mounts, thousands of people, many of whom are ethnic Chinese, continue to flee what was South Vietnam. According to one estimate, more than a thousand people a month are leaving the country by sea. These "boat people" are so desperate to get away that whole families are taking to the sea in anything that sails. Once out on the open sea—at risk from storms and pirates—their best hope is to be rescued by a larger ship and taken to a new life in the United States, Canada, Australia, or Europe. The plight of these refugees is related to the conflict between Vietnam and China, which hinges around Cambodia, Vietnam's neighbor. China backs Cambodia's Khmer Rouge regime, which is hostile to the pro-Soviet government of postwar Vietnam.

▲ *"Boat people" risk everything to leave postwar Vietnam.*

NEWS • 1978 • NEWS

29 January • *Sweden bans ozone-damaging aerosol sprays.*

25 June • *Argentina wins the soccer World Cup.*

11 July • *Explosion in Spanish campsite kills 200.*

30 September • *Pope John Paul dies after a 33-day reign.*

10 December • *Begin (Israel) and Sadat (Egypt) share the Nobel Prize for Peace.*

First test-tube baby born

SCIENCE

26 JULY Around midnight last night, in a hospital in Manchester, England, Mrs. Brown's baby girl was delivered by cesarian section. Little Louise Brown is like any other healthy baby, but her life began in a test tube, where one of her mother's eggs was fertilized by her father's sperm. Mrs. Brown was formerly sterile and the birth is a tribute to the pioneering research of Patrick Steptoe and Dr. Robert Edwards.

▶ *Baby Louise, a 20th-century miracle.*

▶ *Anwar Sadat and Menachem Begin embrace after the breakthrough at Camp David, Washington. The talks are a triumph for President Carter.*

Begin and Sadat reach Camp David Accord

TREATIES

18 SEPTEMBER President Carter has succeeded in bringing together Israel's premier, Menachem Begin, and Egypt's president, Anwar Sadat. At Camp David, the presidential retreat, Israel's leader has agreed to a gradual withdrawal from the Egyptian Sinai and to "recognize the legitimate rights of the Palestinians." In return, Egypt's leader has agreed to begin more normal diplomatic relations with Israel. Next year, this Camp David Accord may become a full-scale peace treaty.

▲ *Atlantic waves batter the supertanker* Amoco Cadiz *off the coast of northwestern France.*

Aldo Moro found dead

TERRORISM

9 MAY The senior Italian statesman Aldo Moro who served twice as his country's prime minister, has been found dead in the back of a car in central Rome. It has been two months since Moro was kidnapped by members of the Red Brigades, an Italian terrorist group who were demanding the release of other terrorist prisoners. While he was in captivity, Moro wrote pleading letters to all his influential government friends, but they refused to negotiate with his captors, who then shot him. His family are bitter about the government's refusal, which cost Aldo Moro his life.

▲ *The memorial service for Aldo Moro, terrorist murder victim.*

Disastrous oil spillage off Brittany

ENVIRONMENT

24 MARCH Much of Brittany's coastline is polluted with black slime after the stricken supertanker *Amoco Cadiz* finally split in two, spilling the last of its 220,000 tons of crude oil. Because of fears that the oil slick is moving toward the beaches of the Channel Islands, a fleet of British ships is spraying chemicals into the water to disperse the oil. According to the French authorities, the disaster seems to have arisen from a dispute about pay between the captain of the oil tanker and the captain of the boat that had been called to tow it, which caused the tow rope to break and left the tanker adrift. Both captains have been detained by French police pending further inquiry.

▶ *Three balloonists touch down in France.*

The big balloon that crossed the ocean

A three-man American crew landed today in France, exhausted after their historic, and eventful, transatlantic flight in a helium-filled balloon. The *Double Eagle II*'s crew, Ben Abruzzo, Maxie Anderson, and Larry Newman, touched down in a field some 55 miles (88 km) west of Paris. They described their six-day journey, in which they battled with icy winds and freezing rain, and lived on hot dogs and canned sardines, as "the most exciting thing we have ever done." Next week they'll be meeting President Jimmy Carter to relate the full story of their amazing journey. The trio, who are all from Maine, are already planning their next flight.

New pope is Polish

The first non-Italian pope for 400 years has been elected. Formerly Poland's Cardinal Wojtla, he has taken the name John Paul II. Instead of addressing the wellwishers who gathered in St. Peter's Square in Latin, as is traditional, the 58-year-old pope spoke Italian. A dynamic, uncompromising personality, he also speaks English, French, and German.

▲ *Pope John Paul II, the youngest pontiff this century.*

Mass suicide in Guyana

RELIGION

19 NOVEMBER The bodies of nearly a thousand members of an American religious cult have been found dead at their village in Guyana. Two years ago, cult leader Jim Jones started the Guyana commune, but rumors of his cruelty prompted an investigation by Congressman Leo Ryan. The murdered body of Ryan and five other investigators have been found near the bodies of the dead cult members. Survivors, who hid in the jungle, claim that Jones, who seems to have shot himself, persuaded 913 members of his cult to drink a deadly poison.

1970

1971

1972

1973

1974

1975

1976

1977

1978

1979

▲ *Shah Mohammed Reza Pahlavi and his wife Empress Farah on their way to the Boeing jet that flew them to Aswan, Egypt.*

The shah leaves, Khomeini is due

POLITICS

16 JANUARY The streets of Tehran and other Iranian cities are packed with jubilant crowds. Their hated ruler, the shah, has left. The shah's family made oil-rich Iran into a strong, wealthy state, but at the cost of waste, inflation, and corruption. Wages remained low and opponents were crushed by the brutal SAVAK secret police. The shah was especially unpopular with religious leaders, who are opposed to the westernization of Iran. Last month, when demonstrations against a new military government brought Iran to a standstill, the shah was forced to appoint an opposition leader, Shahpur Bakhtiar, as premier. Bakhtiar took the job on condition the shah himself left.

The most powerful leader in the new Iran will be an elderly religious leader, the Ayatollah Ruhollah Khomeini, who led the opposition from his own exile in France. He is expected in Tehran within days.

▼ *Tory leader Margaret Thatcher gives a victory wave after winning the general election in Britain.*

Thatcher is Britain's first female premier

POLITICS

4 MAY The Conservative Party's electoral victory yesterday means that Britain has its first woman prime minister. Margaret Thatcher, 53, is on the right of her party. Outside 10 Downing Street she said, "Where there is discord may we bring harmony...where there is despair may we bring hope," but in view of her staunch antisocialist principles and her uncompromising, forthright personality, future battles are likely.

Bokassa is overthrown

POLITICS

20 SEPTEMBER The ruthless dictator and emperor of the Central African Empire, Jean-Bédel Bokassa, has been removed from power by his nephew, former president, David Dacko. It has been nearly three years since Bokassa, who is said to have eaten his enemies, declared himself emperor for life. Now his troubled country is once again a republic.

Rap is the new fad

The Sugar Hill Gang, a Bronx group, has scored a major success with "Rapper's Delight." Rapping, sometimes called hiphop, is rapidly chanted, rhythmical "street poetry," originally improvised, with a musical backing. The style started among African-American and Hispanic teenagers of New York City's outer boroughs and derives from the patter of disk jockeys linking records.

Sandinista victory sends Somoza into exile

WAR

17 JULY After months of savage civil war, the Nicaraguan dictator General Anastasio Somoza Debayle has fled the country, conceding victory to the rebel National Liberation Front, the Sandinistas.

Nicaragua's new rulers take their name from Augusto César Sandino, a popular leader who was shot in 1934 by order of police chief Anastasio Somoza García, father of the deposed dictator. It is hoped that they will bring peace and honest government to Nicaragua. Much depends on the country's business leaders and the US government, which for so long supported the Somoza family's regime.

◀ *Celebrations in Nicaragua after the victory of the Sandinistas.*

NEWS • 1979 • NEWS

7 January • *Pol Pot regime in Cambodia overthrown by Vietnamese invaders.*

26 March • *Egypt's President Sadat and Israel's Prime Minister Begin sign peace treaty.*

4 April • *Zulfikar Ali Bhutto, Pakistan's ex-premier, is executed.*

15 August • *Britain's Seb Coe is first athlete to hold world indoor records for 800 meters, 1,500 meters, and the mile simultaneously.*

Three Mile Island: nearly a nuclear disaster

ENVIRONMENT

30 MARCH Yesterday a major accident occurred at the Three Mile Island nuclear power station in Pennsylvania. A leaking coolant led to overheating, but the signals were wrongly interpreted by staff, who temporarily shut off the emergency coolant designed to prevent just such an incident. Experts say little radioactivity has escaped into the environment, but 10,000 people are being moved out of the area, and it may take years to decontaminate the plant.

▶ *A faulty valve started the atomic leak at Three Mile Island.*

Smoking causes cancer

Cigarette smoking causes cancer, that's the indisputable conclusion of the US surgeon-general's newly published report. In 1,200 pages the report details the dangerous consequences of addiction to nicotine. As well as causing cancer, smoking is connected with numerous other diseases.

USSR invades Afghanistan

WAR

27 DECEMBER The Soviet Union has invaded Afghanistan. Three days ago, Soviet commandos seized Kabul airport. As a massive airlift of supplies and troops got under way, military convoys began to roll across the USSR-Afghanistan border. This invasion is an attempt to stop a civil war and protect Soviet interests. Afghanistan's pro-Soviet ruler is alleged to have requested Russian help. Already, it is being suggested that the Russians in Afghanistan are making the same mistake as the Americans in Vietnam—entering a war they cannot win.

▶ *The Soviet convoy of troops and military supplies enters Afghanistan.*

TERRORISM

Terrorism is an attempt to win a political objective by committing acts of violence that undermine governments and create fear among ordinary people. It is adopted by people who cannot get what they want by legal methods. They usually form a group which, to create terror and gain publicity, employs the most extreme violence, including mass murder. Besides radical political ideas, their most common motive is some form of nationalism or religious fanaticism.

◄ *The papers published the Red Brigade's messages, including a photograph of Moro and his desperate letters to friends and colleagues.*

► *The photograph of Aldo Moro in captivity taken by his kidnappers, with a daily newspaper to prove it was not an old photograph.*

Aldo Moro and the Red Brigades

The *Brigate Rosse* (Red Brigades) was an extreme left-wing Italian group. Founded in 1970, the group used serious terror tactics throughout the decade, kidnapping and killing a number of judges and politicians. Their most famous victim was Aldo Moro, a former prime minister who angered them by persuading the Italian Communist Party to join with the ruling Christian Democrats. Moro was kidnapped in Rome on 16 March 1978. The kidnappers threatened to kill him unless certain conditions were met, including the release of their associates from prison. The government refused to negotiate. Moro's body was found abandoned in Rome eight weeks later. Since then, the Red Brigades' activities have slowly diminished, in part due to better antiterrorist measures.

ETA's fight for Basque independence

One of the oldest terrorist groups in Europe is ETA (*Euzkadi ta Azkatasuna*—Basque Territory and Freedom), founded in 1959. Its aim is independence for the Basque Country, northern Spain. ETA's political wing is a nonviolent front called *Herri Batasuna* (Popular Unity). Since 1968, ETA has assassinated over 800 people. The demands of moderate Basque nationalists were granted by the Spanish government in 1979. Despite these government concessions, ETA continues in its acts of terrorism and its fight for independence.

► *The funeral of an ETA terrorist in the Basque Country.*

286

Palestine Liberation Organization

The Palestine Liberation Organization (PLO) was set up in 1964 to unite the various Palestinian Arab groups opposed to the Israeli presence in Palestine. The more extreme groups, such as al-Fatah, waged international terrorism against Israel and its supporters in an attempt to achieve the PLO's aim of a democratic Palestinian state. Many Arab countries didn't agree with the PLO's methods and expelled it. The continuing violence and splits within the party forced Yassir Arafat (leader of the PLO since 1969) to adopt a more realistic search for a solution to peace with Israel. A fragile settlement agreement is undermined by those who see compromise as a betrayal.

▶ *Freed hostages leave a plane hijacked by PLO terrorists in Mogadishu, Somalia.*

▲ *The PLO raised an army from Palestinian refugees in Lebanon.*

◀ *Mug shots of some of the alleged Red Brigades terrorists.*

Terrorism facts

US: Right-wing fanatics blew up a government building in Oklahoma City (19 April 1995).

Lebanon: Palestinian suicide-bombers killed 360, mainly US soldiers, in Beirut and Tyre (4 November 1983).

England: IRA bombs in Guildford and Birmingham pubs killed 26 (October–November 1974).

The IRA's campaign

The history of the Irish Republican Army (IRA) goes back to 1919, when Sinn Fein (the party for an independent Ireland) recognized it as the army of the Irish Republic. In 1936 the IRA was outlawed by the Irish government. By 1969 it had become active again, initially trying to support Roman Catholics against the Protestant Unionist majority. Hardline members of the IRA broke away from the main group and its nonviolent political wing, Sinn Fein, to form the Provisional IRA, when the IRA granted recognition of the Dublin and London parliaments. The Provisionals embarked on a campaign of terrorism with bombs and assassinations to drive out the British and unite Ireland. In 1994 a ceasefire was called, but by February 1996, the Provisional IRA resumed its acts of terrorism. The Irish and British governments negotiated another peace settlement with the IRA in 1997.

◀ *A modern office building in Canary Wharf, London, wrecked by a huge IRA truck bomb.*

▶ *IRA men carry the coffin of a comrade who died in a hunger strike to demand rights as a political prisoner.*

287

1980

The 1980s saw the collapse of the Iron Curtain and the end of the Cold War. In 1985 Mikhail Gorbachev became the leader of the Soviet Union, and within six years the Soviet empire had ceased to exist.

But while European communism was dissolving and people in the West were becoming richer, drought, famine, and civil wars intensified distress in the Third World. After the nuclear disaster at Chernobyl and the discovery of a hole in the Earth's ozone layer, environmental issues aroused global anxiety, and the beginning of action.

1980
1981
1982
1983
1984
1985
1986
1987
1988
1989

▲ *Lech Walesa, the Gdansk shipyard worker who leads Poland's new union, Solidarity.*

Rubik Cube fever

The puzzle invented by Hungarian Erno Rubik is driving people nuts. It is a handheld cube, made up of interlocking smaller cubes, exposing nine squares, marked in different colors on each face. The object is to manipulate the small cubes to get nine identical squares on each face. Some people do the Rubik Cube in a few minutes, but most people can't do it at all.

POLITICS

Solidarity for workers in Poland

17 SEPTEMBER Just a few weeks after winning the right to organize free trade unions, Poland's workers have launched Solidarity, an independent national union. Its leader is charismatic shipyard worker Lech Walesa, who helped the strikers achieve their aim. Solidarity's public, legal existence confirms the victories won by the Polish workers against the communist government.

Poland's summer strikes were about political freedom as well as rising prices and food shortages. After consulting the Soviet Union, the Polish government agreed to many of the strikers' demands, including increased wages, pensions, and vacations, promotion on merit rather than communist party membership, less censorship, broadcasting of religious services, and the right to organize in free trade unions. Solidarity is, in effect, a political opposition party in a one-party state.

TERRORISM

Bologna bomb blast

2 AUGUST Eighty-four people are dead, hundreds more injured, after the horrific explosion that tore apart the central railroad station in the northern Italian city of Bologna. The explosion, which has left a huge crater, was caused by a massive bomb, 100 pounds (45 kg) of explosives packed in a suitcase and left in a waiting room.

An extreme rightwing terrorist group has claimed responsibility for the outrage. It appears to have been an act of revenge by supporters of the eight fascists who were charged with causing another explosion on a train at Bologna in 1974. Bologna is a largely communist city, with an elected communist city government, which makes it a target for fascists.

▼ *The scene at Bologna's station after the explosion.*

Conservation a matter of urgency says "Global 2000"

MARCH To the dismay of environmentalists, the report of the UN's World Conservation Strategy, the result of three years' international research, suggests that one million plants and animals face extinction because humans, by clearing the rain forests and polluting the environment, are destroying vital sources of food. The forest fires also contribute to global warming, which threatens the whole planet. If present trends continue, the report says that environmental damage will be irreversible in 20 years' time. It asks every country to make conservation plans. The US already has a plan, which was initiated by President Carter in 1977.

▲ *Guatemalan rain forest, destroyed by "slash and burn" clearance techniques.*

John Lennon assassinated

9 DECEMBER John Lennon, the former Beatle, was shot dead last night outside the Dakota, the New York apartment building where he lived with his wife, Yoko Ono. His killer, Mark Chapman, had recently flown in from Hawaii, where he bought the revolver with which he shot Lennon five times at point-blank range. He had been stalking Lennon for several days and was photographed earlier in the day while getting the star's autograph. So far, his motive is a mystery.

Tito is dead

4 MAY Marshal Tito, the founding father of modern Yugoslavia has died at the age of 87. Born Josip Broz, Tito led anti-Nazi partisans in the region during World War II and established a communist state in 1945. His independent policies later caused a break with the Soviet Union, and in the 1950s he became a leader of the nonaligned group (not aligned with the US or USSR) in the United Nations. A Croat himself, Tito united the different peoples of the six republics that together make up Yugoslavia. Now that he is dead, there is a danger that old ethnic and religious hostilities will resurface.

Zimbabwe wins independence

18 APRIL Today the British colony of Rhodesia died and the African republic of Zimbabwe was born. In 1965 Prime Minister Ian Smith declared Rhodesia's independence in order to preserve white minority power. Britain refused to accept his regime, and armed resistance by black African groups, plus an international economic boycott, brought Smith to the negotiating table. Democratic elections were won by the Zimbabwe African National Union, led by Robert Mugabe.

▶ *Robert Mugabe, prime minister of independent Zimbabwe.*

Brody's new look magazine

Within days of publication of its first issue, a new British magazine is arousing international media interest. *The Face* is another magazine devoted to art, design, music, and fashion, but it doesn't look like any other style magazine. Radical graphic designer Neville Brody has introduced a new approach to fashion photography in which atmosphere, attitude, and lifestyle are the focus. The brainchild of publisher Nick Logan, *The Face* is unashamedly London-based and set to become the most influential magazine of the decade.

▶ *The first cover of The Face.*

War breaks out between Iran and Iraq

WAR

22 SEPTEMBER Iraqi forces today struck across the border into Iran, destroying the oil refinery at Abadan and advancing several miles at different points. The months-long border conflict is now a full-scale war. Iraq's objective is to gain control of the Shatt-al-Arab waterway, which divides the two countries and commands the Persian Gulf. It has been under joint Iraqi-Iranian control since 1975.

Iraq's ruler, Saddam Hussein, is clearly hoping to take advantage of the unsettled state of Iran. Since the Shah of Iran was overthrown last January, the aged religious leader, the Ayatollah Khomeini, has presided over a fundamentalist Islamic state. He introduced a new constitution based on Islamic law and intends to destroy all Western influence. Thousands of people, including many military leaders, were executed or fled, and Iran is currently ruled by religious gangs rather than a central government.

There are other divisions between these two historic rivals. In particular, Saddam and his ruling clique, who are Sunnites, fear the influence of Khomeini's Islamic revolution on the Shi'ites (another branch of Islam) in Iraq. Officially, the major powers are not taking sides in the dispute, but the Persian Gulf is a sensitive area: a large proportion of the world's oil supplies passes through it.

◀ *Iraqis signal victory in front of a bullet-peppered poster of Khomeini.*

"Personal" stereos for public listening

The days of the "ghettoblaster" and the "boom box" may be numbered. The Japanese electronics firm Sony is now marketing its "Walkman," a new type of portable, shockproof, stereophonic radio-cassette player. It is small enough to be carried in a pocket and the sound is listened to through tiny earphones.

◀ *Sony's pocket-sized Walkman, the latest radio-cassette machine.*

NEWS • 1980 • NEWS

27 March • 124 killed when North Sea oil rig off the coast of Norway collapses.

5 May • Hostages freed after SAS raid on terrorist-occupied Iranian Embassy in London.

19 May • Huge eruption of Mount St. Helen's volcano in Washington State.

30 June • Deaths from famine in East Africa are estimated at more than 10 million.

Western boycott of Moscow Olympics

SPORT

3 AUGUST The international spirit of this year's Olympic Games in Moscow was flawed by the absence of 65 countries, including the US, West Germany, and Kenya. The boycott was a protest against the Soviet invasion of Afghanistan. However, 36 records were broken, and in all likelihood none of the absentees would have beaten Britain's champions, Sebastian Coe (1,500 meters) and Steve Ovett (800 meters). Otherwise, athletics events were dominated by the Soviet Union and East Germany. East Germans took 29 medals out of a possible 42 in women's swimming events.

"Old" Reagan to be new president

POLITICS

4 NOVEMBER Challenger knocks out Champion! Ronald Reagan has defeated President Jimmy Carter in the presidential election by a landslide. He won 44 out of the 50 states, though the popular vote was closer—44 million to 35 million. Ronald Reagan was a well-known movie actor before entering politics in the 1960s. Although he is a conservative Republican with hawkish anticommunist views, he proved to be a practical politician, ready to compromise if necessary, when he was California's governor. At the campaign's outset Reagan was considered too old, at 69, to become America's 40th president, but his relaxed manner, especially on television, won over many voters.

Bjorn Borg wins fifth Wimbledon title

Swedish tennis star Bjorn Borg entered the sports record books on 5 July when he won his fifth successive Wimbledon men's tennis championship. In a marathon match lasting four hours, he defeated American John McEnroe in five sets. Tennis commentators are hailing Borg as the greatest player of all time.

▲ *Borg hoists the Wimbledon cup for the fifth time. McEnroe, beaten by a whisker, wonders when the Swede will let it go.*

◄ *Ronald Reagan, with his wife Nancy, acknowledges the cheers of Republican voters after Jimmy Carter conceded defeat in the presidential election.*

WHO puts smallpox in the past

SCIENCE

8 MAY According to the World Health Organization (WHO), the disease of smallpox has been destroyed forever. The virus no longer exists anywhere on Earth, and if nobody has it, nobody can catch it. It was once one of the world's worst killers. Those who did survive infection were left with pockmarked skin, and some were blinded. In 1796 the English surgeon Edward Jenner discovered a vaccine against it, but if you were not vaccinated and caught the disease, there was no cure. The WHO has been conducting a campaign against smallpox since 1967. It was thought that the disease was extinct in 1977, but one year later the smallpox virus escaped from a laboratory in Birmingham, England, causing several deaths.

Japan builds more cars than US

TRANSPORT

31 DECEMBER Japan is now the world's biggest car maker. This year the Japanese produced 12.7 million vehicles, out of a world total of 48 million, knocking US car manufacturers into second place. What's more, one in four of the cars sold in the US is Japanese.

The US car industry is in serious trouble. The Chrysler Corporation was saved from bankruptcy this year by a $1.5 billion government-guaranteed loan. Ford and General Motors are also deep in debt. Last year's oil crisis, causing sharp rises in fuel prices, encouraged people to buy smaller cars. American manufacturers were unprepared, so Nissan, Toyota, and Honda grabbed a large share of the market.

1980

1981

1982

1983

1984

1985

1986

1987

1988

1989

PEOPLE

Charles and Diana tie the knot

29 JULY Not just the wedding of the year, it was the wedding of the decade! Today, Charles, Prince of Wales, heir to the British throne, married Lady Diana Spencer, a kindergarten assistant, in St. Paul's Cathedral, London. Besides the happy crowds who lined the streets, a worldwide audience of about 700 million, probably the biggest in history, watched on

Charles and Diana facts

Diana and Charles met in a muddy plowed field, when Charles, a friend of Diana's eldest sister, went on a hunting expedition.

•

Charles is the first royal heir to the throne since 1659 to have an English wife.

•

Both Diana and Charles can trace their ancestors back to James I.

▲ *After the ceremony the royal newlyweds kiss.*

TV as the shy 19-year-old bride, spectacularly beautiful in an unusual cream-colored wedding dress, arrived at the cathedral in a horsedrawn carriage, just one minute late. Twelve years younger than Charles, the new princess is a daughter of the Eighth Earl Spencer, and at one time her elder sister was one of the many young ladies suggested as a possible bride for Prince Charles. Diana already has royal connections—her illustrious ancestors include the Stuart kings Charles II and his brother James II.

▲ *François Mitterrand casts his own vote.*

POLITICS

Mitterrand is the new President of France

30 MARCH For the first time since the 1930s France has a socialist president. François Mitterrand, the veteran socialist leader, won the presidency on his third try, defeating the Gaullist candidate Giscard d'Estaing. His decisive victory is due to his success in uniting leftwing parties, including communists, behind his campaign. He promises nationalization of banks, higher taxes for the rich, and full employment. Rightwingers hold the majority in the National Assembly now, but after taking office Mitterrand is likely to call a general election, which will probably result in a socialist victory.

POLITICS

Ronald Reagan shot by would-be assassin

30 MARCH The horror of Dallas in November 1963, when President Kennedy was assassinated, was almost repeated in Washington today. Ronald Reagan, president for only three months, was shot by John Hinckley II, a 25-year-old drop-out, as he walked from a hotel to his car. A bullet was later removed from his chest, but doctors say that he should make a complete recovery. Three other men, a presidential assistant, a body-guard, and a policeman, were also wounded as the Hinckley fired six shots from close range. The weapon was a small .22 pistol. A larger gun would probably have been fatal.

▲ *The gunman is seized by security officers as President Reagan's car rushes him to the hospital.*

A summer of riots in Britain's inner cities

12 JULY Areas of Britain's cities are out of control as crowds of youths continue to run riot, burning, smashing, and looting property. Last year the St. Paul's district of Bristol erupted, and earlier this year there were riots on the streets of Brixton in south London. This week the worst disturbances were in Toxteth, in Liverpool, where mobs forced police to withdraw. Unemployment and poor housing are contributory factors.

▲ *Chiang Ch'ing speaking at the trial.*

LAW China: the trial of the Gang of Four

25 JANUARY The widow of Mao Tse-tung, Chiang Ch'ing, was today given a suspended death sentence for crimes against the state. She is one of the Gang of Four, who were arrested in 1976 when they tried to seize power after Mao's death. They are blamed for the Cultural Revolution, which had a such a traumatic effect on China starting in 1966. The trial began last November. Of the other three accused, one was sentenced to death, the others to life imprisonment.

Lloyd Webber's felines sing and dance

One of the biggest successes in the theater this year is the musical *Cats* by Andrew Lloyd Webber. Inspired by verses about cats by the great poet T. S. Eliot, the show features spectacular dance scenes as well as memorable songs. The makeup, costumes, and dance routines performed by the cast are sensationally feline. Critics are already predicting a long run for the show.

▲ *Slinky felines from the new hit musical.*

▲ *Sadat, ringed, shortly before his assassination.*

Sadat assassinated in Egypt

6 OCTOBER Anwar Sadat, president of Egypt, is dead, shot by his own soldiers while reviewing a military parade in Cairo. The assassins drove up to the reviewing stand in a jeep and opened fire while everyone's eyes were on the sky watching an air force fly-past. Five others were also killed.

Sadat succeeded President Nasser in 1970. In the past 10 years his dramatic changes in foreign policy made him many enemies: his peace agreement with Israel in 1978 was condemned by most other Arab governments. The assassins are thought to be members of the extremist Muslim Brotherhood group, but some suspect that Colonel Gaddafi's government in Libya may have been involved.

NEWS • 1981 • NEWS

3 February • Gro Harlem Brundtland becomes Norway's first woman prime minister.

23 February • Army officers attempt coup in Spain.

20 March • Former Argentinian president, Isabel Perón, is jailed.

7 June • Israeli planes destroy nuclear plant in Iraq.

3 October • Hunger strike in Belfast's Maze prison is called off after 10 deaths.

Iran releases American hostages after 444 days

21 JANUARY The American hostages who were seized in Iran in November 1979 arrived safely in Algiers today, the first step on their journey home. Fifteen months ago, armed men representing the Islamic fundamentalist regime of the Ayatollah Khomeini invaded the US Embassy in Tehran, overcoming the guards and capturing nearly 100 US citizens. Most of the women and all of the African-American hostages were soon released, and a few more escaped later using Canadian passports. When UN mediation failed to gain the release of the remainder, the US launched an airborne rescue attempt in April 1980. It ended in disaster when two of the aircraft collided while refueling in the Iranian desert south of Tehran. The failed rescue attempt further soured relations between the Iranians and the government of President Carter. The release of the remaining 52 hostages was deliberately delayed by the Ayatollah Khomeini until just yesterday, when Ronald Reagan was sworn in as the new president.

▲ *Warm greetings for the American hostages released after a long ordeal.*

▲ *An anti-IRA slogan in a predominantly Loyalist area of Belfast.*

Bobby Sands dies after 65 days on hunger strike

5 MAY More violence broke out in Belfast today as the death was announced of IRA hunger striker Bobby Sands in the Maze prison. Sands and several other Republican prisoners began their fast two months ago in an effort to persuade the British authorities to acknowledge and treat them as political prisoners instead of criminals. The plight of the hunger strikers has aroused international concern, and last month, when he was on the verge of dying, Bobby Sands was elected as a member of the British parliament. He led an earlier hunger strike at the prison, which was called off after 13 weeks last December. British prime minister, Mrs. Thatcher, is still refusing the prisoners' demands.

Denver clans do battle in new TV show

The success of the TV soap opera *Dallas* probably explains *Dynasty*, another lengthy series about rich Americans behaving badly, and also set in a southwestern city. It was livened up with the arrival of scheming Alexis, played by sultry British actress Joan Collins.

▲ *Joan Collins as* Dynasty's *villain.*

Death of Bob Marley

11 MAY The apostle of reggae is dead. Bob Marley died of cancer today in a Miami hospital, aged 36. Reggae, which is related to American soul music, sprang from the slums of Kingston, Jamaica, where Marley was born. With his group The Wailers, he brought it to world attention in the 1970s. His songs expressed his Rastafarian beliefs, and his basic message was moral. He wanted an end to political discrimination and a movement to an Africa-centered Christianity.

▶ *Bob Marley, the charismatic star of reggae.*

General Jaruzelski imposes martial law on Poland

3 DECEMBER The Polish "strong man," General Jaruzelski, today imposed martial law on the country. Borders are closed and government troops are breaking up strikes and protests. Last year, the trade union movement known as Solidarity gained unheard-of concessions from the Communist government, but Poland's disastrous economic situation, with huge foreign debts and high inflation, provoked more political unrest. There remained also the danger that the Soviet Union might intervene using force. The Russians are relying on Jaruzelski, who became premier in February, to restore order. Today's move comes after his visit to Moscow.

▲ *The world's fastest train, ready to leave the Gare de Lyons.*

TGV train service launched in France

Railroad travelers in France can now go from Paris to Lyons in 2 hours 40 minutes, half the old time for the rail journey. The electric-powered TGV (*train à grande vitesse*, or High-Speed Train) runs on special track at up to 106 miles per hour (170 km per hour). Eventually, the line will be continued to Avignon and Marseilles. Breakfast in Paris, lunch on the Mediterranean?

▶ *Polish Americans in New York City demonstrate in support of the Solidarity movement's campaign for democracy and freedom from Soviet interference in Poland.*

Space shuttle's maiden voyage

NASA's new spacecraft, the shuttle, was launched this April. The shuttle is a reusable craft, which is launched into space with the aid of booster rockets but returns under its own power and lands like an airplane. It can carry cargo of up to nearly 66,000 pounds (30,000 kg), such as the space satellites that can be placed in orbit from its hold.

◀ *The space shuttle* Columbia *blasts off.*

Pope survives assassination attempt

13 MAY Pope John Paul II is recovering in a hospital tonight after being shot four times. He was traveling in his white "popemobile," blessing the crowd in St. Peter's Square, Rome, when a man opened fire. Two bystanders were also wounded, and the gunman had to be protected from the outraged crowd by Vatican police. He is believed to be Mehmet Ali Agca, aged 23, who recently escaped from a Turkish prison where he was being held for the murder of a newspaper editor. Turkish police say that they warned Interpol of Agca's dangerous intentions. But so far there is no evidence of an assassination conspiracy.

▶ *John Paul II collapses in his vehicle after being shot.*

1980

1981

1982

1983

1984

1985

1986

1987

1988

1989

▲ *The Union Jack flag flies over Port Howard, West Falkland, for the first time in more than two months.*

▲ *British paratroopers carry out emergency medical treatment of the injured at Mount Longdon in the Falkland Islands.*

Compact disks spell extinction for vinyl

The compact disks being launched by Philips and Sony are lightweight plastic disks just 4¾ inches (12 cm) in diameter, compared to 12 inches (30 cm) for an LP. Music is recorded on a disk in a series of metallic pits. The "CD" player rotates the disk and a laser beams "reads" and converts these pits into sound.

WAR

The high price of war in the Falklands

14 JUNE British troops today recaptured Port Stanley, capital of the Falkland Islands, after its Argentine garrison surrendered. This ends 10 weeks of war over the tiny Falklands, or Malvinas, which lie 300 miles (480 km) east of Argentina in the South Atlantic. The islands have been a British colony since 1833 but Argentina also claims them. After years of failed negotiations, the Argentine military government invaded them in April. Three days later, a British task force set sail to retake the islands, steaming 8,000 miles (13,000 km) to the war zone. Fierce air-sea battles took place before British troops landed on East Falkland at the end of May. After an important victory at Goose Green, they surrounded Port Stanley. Around 700 Argentines and 250 Britons were killed in the conflict.

WAR

Israel strikes at PLO in Lebanon

31 AUGUST Israel has invaded Lebanon and forced the Palestine Liberation Organization to abandon its power base in the Lebanese capital, Beirut. The PLO is dedicated to creating a Palestinian state in the Middle East—something Israel refuses to accept. Israel invaded Lebanon on 6 June, two days after the Israeli ambassador to London was shot by Palestinian terrorists. Yesterday, as he was forced to leave war-shattered Beirut, PLO leader Yassir Arafat vowed that the struggle will continue.

▶ *Burning suburbs of Beirut after an Israeli attack.*

NEWS • 1982 • NEWS

13 January • 78 people die when an Air Florida jet attempting to take off in Washington, D.C., crashes into the frozen Potomac River.

28 May • Argentinian Diego Maradona becomes the world's most expensive soccer player when Spanish club Barcelona buy him for £5 million.

21 June • Diana, Princess of Wales, gives birth to her first child, Prince William Arthur Philip.

Italy scores third soccer World Cup

Italy has won the soccer World Cup for the third time, beating West Germany 3–1 in front of 90,000 fans in Madrid. Victory ends a 44-year wait for Italian fans—their first two World Cup wins were in 1934 and 1938. The crucial first goal in the July final came from virtuoso scorer Paolo Rossi. Earlier, in the semi-finals, Italy beat Poland 2–0 while West Germany tied 3–3 with France and then won the deciding penalty shoot-out.

▲ *Italian Oraili tackled by West German Forster in the final.*

▲ *Antarctica, protected for science.*

ENVIRONMENT

Antarctica gets protection

7 APRIL An international agreement that comes into effect today will protect the environment in Antarctica, the southern continent centered on the South Pole. For the first time since it was set aside as a reserve for science under the terms of the 1959 Antarctic Treaty, Antarctica is under threat. Although Britain and Argentina signed that treaty, the conflict over the Falkland Islands is affecting Antarctic science bases, some of which have been shelled and abandoned.

Spielberg's alien is a box office smash

Steven Spielberg (below) is smiling again. His latest movie, *E.T. The Extraterrestrial*, is breaking all box office records. It's the tale of a wide-eyed, enchanting alien accidentally left behind on Earth by a spaceship. E.T. is protected from adults, who want to treat it as a scientific specimen, by a California boy.

ENTERTAINMENT

Princess Grace of Monaco dies in car crash

14 SEPTEMBER Princess Grace of Monaco died tonight after the car she was driving crashed off a mountain road and fell 120 feet (37 meters). Her youngest daughter, Princess Stephanie, who was beside her in the car, survived the accident. Twenty-five years ago, Princess Grace was known as Grace Kelly, a Hollywood star. In spite of leading roles in movies like *Rear Window* and *High Society*, she gave up her acting career when she married Prince Rainier of Monaco in 1956.

▶ *Grace Kelly on her way to Monaco to marry Prince Rainier.*

POLITICS

Kohl is West Germany's new leader

1 OCTOBER West German premier Helmut Schmidt today lost a vote of no confidence in parliament and was replaced as chancellor, or premier, by another Helmut, Helmut Kohl, who has been leader of the Christian Democratic Union (CDU) party for nine years. Schmidt, leader of the Social Democrats, was heading a coalition government—one that depends on the support of two or more parties. He lost his grip on power when the Free Democratic Party withdrew its backing because he refused to cut social services spending. Today Schmidt criticized the rules that allow a chancellor to be removed without a general election. Chancellor Kohl says he will target unemployment.

SPECIAL EFFECTS

The earliest moviemakers knew that one advantage of the cinema over the stage was that they could play tricks on the audience and make them see something that was not really happening. The simplest tricks depend on the fact that what the audience is watching is not really a moving picture—although it looks like it—but a series of "still" photographs taken, and projected, in quick succession. To make someone disappear by "magic," the camera is stopped, the actor steps off the set, and the camera is restarted. Hundreds of different effects can be made by cutting or "editing" the actual film.

▲ The breathtakingly realistic dinosaurs from Jurassic Park (1993) won an Oscar for best visual effects.

Amazing tricks of the trade

There are two main types of special effects: trick photography, which involves making changes on the film or on magnetic tape; and the use of specially made props, such as puppets or models of real objects.

The most amazing special effects are done for science fiction pictures, such as *Star Wars* (1977) and its sequels, which used both trick photography and models. The director of *Star Wars*, George Lucas, founded a company, Industrial Light and Magic, to create the effects for his movie. Other specialized companies have been formed since.

The "king" of special effects is the director Steven Spielberg, whose films include *Close Encounters of the Third Kind*, *ET*, and *Jurassic Park*. The "hero" of *ET* is a creature from another planet (ET stands for "extraterrestrial"), who gets stranded on Earth and is befriended by some children. ET was a model, or puppet. Its movements were controlled by computer (before computers, puppets had to be moved by hand after every frame: it took hours to film a few seconds).

The computer has caused a revolution in special effects. Computer technology allows any filmed image, when converted to digital form, to be altered in countless ways—things can be added or taken away.

◀ The lovable, though not very pretty, extraterrestrial watches, with a human friend, the approaching spaceship that will take him home.

The making of special effects

Special-effects studios make use of models, especially when filming objects such as spaceships or other large machines. Movements of both camera and object are controlled by computer, and one sequence may be shot several times, with different details from other pieces of film being added each time. Sometimes models and real objects are combined. In a scene from *Back to the Future*, a car flies through the air and lands in a street, where the people get out. The flying car is a model, one-fifth real size, and the people inside are puppets. As it lands, it passes behind a street lamp. The car that comes out the other side of the street lamp is a real car and, when it stops, real actors get out.

▲ *Setting up models for a shot in* The Empire Strikes Back *(1980), the sequel to* Star Wars. *The background mountains show the scale.*

◀ *Background: With clever computer animation in* Star Wars, *George Lucas created a new generation of sci-fi movies.*

Movie facts

Trick photography was discovered by accident in 1896 when Georges Méliès was filming Paris crowds. His camera jammed while filming, and people vanished and reappeared on the film.

In *Superman*, Superman "flies" on wires, which are later edited out by computer.
•
In *Forrest Gump*, actor Tom Hanks appears with long-dead presidents and pop stars.

Audiences enjoy effects with 3D specs!

Competition from TV in the 1950s made moviemakers search for new, exciting processes. One of these was 3D, which creates an illusion of three dimensions. The audience had to wear special glasses with cellophane lenses, one green, one red. The process was not a success, perhaps partly since most 3D movies were simply not very good. At first, people screamed and ducked when speeding trains, baseballs, and other objects hurtled toward them, but the effect wore off. Since then, 3D movies have been made more realistic by the use of special effects and specially designed cinemas that heighten the 3D illusion.

Roger Rabbit stars with famous Hollywood actor

A few movies have been made combining animation (cartoons) with live action. The best example so far is *Who Framed Roger Rabbit* (1988). An army of animators, helped by Industrial Light and Magic, gave the cartoon characters a 3D effect by skillful camera movement and lighting. The live action was filmed first, and the main actor, Bob Hoskins, had to act with thin air. The animation was added later.

▼ *Bob Hoskins "talks" to a cartoon image.*

1980

1981

1982

1983

1984

1985

1986

1987

1988

1989

Swatch is one to watch

Swiss watch company Asuag-SSIH has scored a hit with its low-price Swatch line of brightly colored watches. Ernst Thomke and Nicolas Hayek developed the thin, hard-wearing plastic watches to compete with cheap watches from Japan and Hong Kong. Marketing man Max Imgruth masterminded the innovative strategy that has established the Swatch line of watches as fashion items that are sold alongside clothes.

ENVIRONMENT

Thousands protest against nuclear weapons

22 OCTOBER More than 250,000 people attended a protest rally against nuclear weapons in central London today. Addressing the crowd, Neil Kinnock, leader of the British Labour Party, called the protest a "movement for life." The rally was organized by the Campaign for Nuclear Disarmament (CND), which was founded in 1958 but has not been a significant force since the early 1960s. Similar protests have been taking place in the Netherlands, Belgium, West Germany, and France, and last year more than half a million people joined a demonstration in New York, the biggest antinuclear march in American history.

Since the election of tough-talking Ronald Reagan as president, American spending on arms has increased, and many Europeans are concerned about US nuclear missiles sited in Europe, which can reach Soviet targets in a matter of minutes. In Britain, the antinuclear movement is worried about plans to site 96 cruise missiles at Royal Air Force bases. Women camped at Greenham Common, one of the proposed bases, have been waging a peaceful protest around the clock since last September. The campaigners, who often oppose nuclear energy as well as nuclear arms, are part of the growing ecological, or "green," movement.

▲ *Protesters stage a symbolic "die-in" at a demo in Neu-Ulm West Germany, as part of the European peace movement's autumn 1983 campaign.*

◄ *CND leader Bruce Kent addresses the rally in London's Hyde Park.*

POLITICS

Korean Airlines Jumbo shot down over USSR

1 SEPTEMBER A Korean Airlines passenger jet was tonight shot down by a Soviet fighter jet. All 269 on board the Boeing 747 were killed. The Soviet Union claims that the aircraft was spying. It had left the usual flightpath on route from New York to the South Korean city of Seoul, and shortly before it was shot down, it flew over the Soviet military base at Sakhalin Island, off the coast of Siberia. In the US and Korea there is outrage at the attack. A Soviet spokesman today expressed the USSR's regret over the death of innocent people. Among the victims were 81 South Koreans and 61 Americans.

◄ *A news poster in Korea listing the names of the victims of the air disaster.*

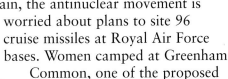

NEWS • 1983 • NEWS

23 March • President Reagan proposes a space-based laser weapons system, the Strategic Defense Initiative (popularly named Star Wars).

9 June • Margaret Thatcher reelected as British prime minister.

5 October • Lech Walesa, Polish trade unionist, wins Nobel Peace Prize.

30 October • Earthquake in eastern Turkey kills 2,000.

300

POLITICS
Riots in Sri Lanka

27 JULY More than 100 people have died as a result of racial violence between Sri Lanka's Sinhalese and Tamil communities. There are more Sinhalese than Tamils in Sri Lanka, an island off the southern tip of the Indian subcontinent. Tamil extremists, called the Tamil Tigers, are demanding a separate state of Tamil Eelam within Sri Lanka.

◄ *Riot-torn street in Sri Lanka.*

SPORT
Australia II takes the America's Cup

26 SEPTEMBER For 132 years American yachts have defeated all comers in the prestigious America's Cup. Today, however, *Australia II*, skippered by John Bertrand, won its stunning victory over the American yacht, *Liberty* (skippered by Dennis Conner), and the trophy is in Australian hands. The winning yacht, which is owned by businessman Alan Bond, came from 1–3 behind in the exciting seven-race contest to win 4–3.

LITERATURE
Hitler diaries are fakes

14 MAY A few weeks ago, Germany's *Stern* magazine and Britain's *Sunday Times* published extracts of diaries supposedly written by Hitler. Today, as the man who forged them, Konrad Kujau, gave himself up to police, the sensational diaries have been proved to be fakes.

▶ *Gerd Heidemann, the journalist who "discovered" the fake Hitler diaries.*

Madonna makes it as a rock star

A feisty 25-year-old named Madonna (full name Madonna Louise Vernon Ciccione) has burst onto the US pop charts with "Holiday." She worked in a New York doughnut outlet before winning the dance scholarship that eventually led to her success as a performer.

▲ *US patrols in St. Georges, Grenada.*

WAR
Grenada seized by US forces

25 OCTOBER The tiny eastern Caribbean island nation of Grenada was invaded today by US forces, sent by President Reagan to depose a military government set up after a leftwing coup. Besides 800 US Marines, the invasion forces includes token numbers of soldiers from Barbados, Jamaica, and other Caribbean states, but the United Nations Security Council has criticized the US's sudden invasion of an independent country as a violation of international law. Even Mrs. Thatcher, normally a staunch ally of President Reagan, is reportedly unhappy.

TECHNOLOGY
Ride is first US woman in space

24 JUNE Sally Ride (right), the first American female astronaut, landed at Edwards Air Force Base in California today aboard the *Challenger* space shuttle. Ride's flight took off on 16 June, 20 years after the first female space rider, Soviet cosmonaut Valentina Tereshkova, took off in *Vostok 6*.

Timeline

1980

1981

1982
OL

1983

1984

1985

1986

1987

1988

1989

AIDS facts

In 12 months, from April 1984 to mid-1985, recorded cases of AIDS in the US more than doubled.

•

In the 1990s the AIDS virus was named HIV (Human Immunodeficiency Virus).

•

By December 1997 AIDS had killed 2.3 million people.

SCIENCE

US and French scientists identify deadly AIDS virus

23 APRIL Research scientists have discovered the microorganisms that cause AIDS, the terrible new disease. Margaret Heckler, the US Health and Human Services Secretary, announced the discovery today. Most people are equipped to resist infections—their immune system fights infection. But AIDS, or Acquired Immune Deficiency Syndrome, damages the immune system, leaving sufferers unable to resist infectious diseases such as pneumonia and tuberculosis. The disease was first isolated in 1981. Since then, there have been 3,775 cases, including 1,642 deaths, in the US, and 40 cases, including 22 deaths, in Britain. Methods of testing blood for the virus are being investigated, but at the moment there is no cure for AIDS.

The virus was discovered at the Pasteur Institute in France and at the US National Cancer Institute. It seems to be passed on in body fluids, for example, during sex and via blood. Last October, World Health Organization officials stated "there is no risk of contracting AIDS as a result of casual or social contact with AIDS patients," but some people are already talking of a plague that may take millions of lives before the year 2000.

◀ *Close-up of the AIDS virus, which attacks and destroys the white blood cells in human blood that fight infection.*

Death of James Fixx while jogging

The man who proclaimed the health benefits of jogging died of a heart attack while he was out on a run in Vermont. James J. Fixx, who wrote the bestselling *Complete Guide to Running*, began jogging himself because heart disease was common in his family. He was 52.

DISASTERS

Poison gas disaster at Bhopal in India

10 DECEMBER Poisonous gas leaking from a chemical factory has killed more than 2,000 people in Bhopal, India. As many as 200,000 others have been blinded or are suffering kidney or liver failure following last week's accident. The factory made pesticides, used to protect crops from insects. It is owned by the US company Union Carbide, which has promised to compensate Indian workers as well as it would US workers. Some reports suggest that the factory was poorly maintained and that smaller leaks have happened before. The Indian government has appealed for help from other countries.

▶ *Union Carbide's pesticide factory in Bhopal, India, now a disaster area.*

ENVIRONMENT

"Greenhouse Effect" warning

OCTOBER Global warming is on the increase, according to American scientists. This is probably because in recent decades, as more and more fossil fuels like coal and gasoline are burned, more and more "greenhouse" gases like carbon dioxide are being released into the Earth's atmosphere. As a result, many scientists expect the Earth's climate to change over the next century.

Itaipu's waters send power to Sao Paolo

OCTOBER Brazil's new hydroelectric power station, Itaipu on the Paraná River near the border with Paraguay, is up and running. The station, which is the largest of its kind in the world, can generate 12,600 megawatts of electricity and sends power directly to the city of Sao Paolo.

An earth-and-rock dam 620 feet (189 meters) tall blocks the flow of the Paraná River, and the diverted water rushes through turbines, or wheels, to generate electricity. Itaipu uses a special form of power transmission known as high-voltage direct current, the best way of transmitting electricity over long distances.

TECHNOLOGY

▲ *The phenomenal new power station in Itaipu, in Brazil.*

Springsteen strikes international chords

Bruce Springsteen's *Born In the USA.* has been the bestselling album of the year in both Britain and the US. The New Jersey-born singer and songwriter's down-to-earth ballads of working-class American life and powerful live shows have made him one of the biggest rock stars in the world. Despite his success, he likes to stay in touch with local bands in Asbury Park, his hometown.

Indira Gandhi assassinated

POLITICS

31 OCTOBER The Indian prime minister Indira Gandhi has been killed by two of her own bodyguards. The guards, both members of the Sikh religion, were taking revenge for the Indian army's storming of the holiest Sikh shrine, the Golden Temple at Amritsar, last June. The Sikhs, based in the Punjab area, are pressing for more independence. When armed Sikhs occupied the Golden Temple, the Indian authorities retook it after a ferocious four-day operation that cost the lives of 90 soldiers and 712 Sikhs. Tonight, Mrs. Gandhi's son Rajiv will be sworn in as prime minister.

▶ *Indira Gandhi and her son Rajiv.*

NEWS • 1984 • NEWS

13 February • *Chernenko becomes Soviet leader after death of Yuri Andropov (leader since 1983).*

14 February • *British ice-skating duo Jane Torvill and Christopher Dean win Olympic gold medal.*

1 April • *American soul singer Marvin Gaye is shot dead by his father after an argument.*

19 November • *A gas plant in Mexico City explodes and 260 people are killed.*

Carl Lewis wins four Olympic golds in Los Angeles

SPORT

8 AUGUST American sprinter Carl Lewis is the star of the Los Angeles Olympics, winning four gold medals, and matching Jesse Owens' 1936 feat in Berlin. Romanian gymnast Ecaterina Szabo also won four golds, and one silver. Just as the US and many of its allies boycotted the 1980 Moscow games, the LA games were boycotted by the Soviet Union and many of its allies.

1980
1981
1982
1983
1984
1985
1986
1987
1988
1989

MUSIC

Live Aid: music as the food of love

13 JULY Sixty of the world's top rock stars raised the roof along with $60 million for the starving people of Africa today. The charity Band Aid arranged two massive concerts—one in Wembley Stadium, London, and the other in JFK Stadium, Philadelphia. More than 160,000 fans watched the shows live, and around 1.5 billion viewers tuned in on TV. The stars played for free, and viewers were asked to phone in pledges of money. Each band was allowed 17 minutes in the limelight. Madonna, Tina Turner, U2, Dire Straits, and Queen were among the acts. Bob Geldof and Midge Ure started Band Aid last year and arranged the recording of "Do They Know It's Christmas?," a huge hit that earned millions for famine victims in Ethiopia. Geldof, an energetic Dubliner, then had the idea of organizing today's extravaganza—Live Aid.

Live Aid facts

Live Aid was shown in 160 countries and raised $60 million for famine relief.

• The Who, Led Zeppelin, Black Sabbath, and Status Quo reunited for Live Aid.

• Traveling by supersonic Concorde, Phil Collins managed to perform in both shows.

▲ *Bob Geldof at Live Aid.*

Amadeus wins eight Oscars

Amadeus, the film of Peter Schaffer's play about the rivalry between 18th-century composers Wolfgang Amadeus Mozart and Antonio Salieri, won eight Oscars at this year's Academy Awards ceremony. The Oscars included Best Film, Best Director (the Czech, Milos Forman), and Best Actor (F. Murray Abraham as Salieri).

▼ *Amadeus' creators after receiving their Oscars.*

NEWS • 1985 • NEWS

11 March • *Mikhail Gorbachev is named as new Soviet leader.*

25 May • *Cyclone kills 10,000 in Bangladesh.*

30 June • *After 16 days 39 US hostages from hijacked jet are freed.*

4 July • *Girl genius, Ruth Lawrence, aged 13, finishes Oxford University degree.*

15 September • *Europe wins golf Ryder Cup.*

9 November • *Gary Kasparov, 22, becomes world chess champion.*

▶ *A child is pulled from the mud in Colombia.*

DISASTERS

Nevado del Ruiz erupts, bringing death to 25,000

13 NOVEMBER Last night, for the first time in 140 years, Colombia's Nevado del Ruiz volcano erupted. While people in four nearby towns were asleep, it spewed out searing torrents of rock, mud, ash, and water. Today, at least 25,000 are feared dead, and the town of Armero, once home to 50,000 people, lies buried under a blanket of burning mud.

The Nevado del Ruiz volcano, which lies 80 miles (130 km) west of the Colombian capital Bogotá, hasn't erupted since 1845. Ash and smoke from this latest eruption is being carried for hundreds of miles, and 70 square miles (180 square km) of the surrounding area has been officially declared a disaster area.

Hinault is first, for the fifth time

30 JUNE Frenchman Bernard Hinault has won the Tour de France, the world's premier cycling event, for a fifth time, in spite of a crash at the St. Etienne stage of the race that left him with blood pouring from his head.

At the end of the Tour, which was first contested in 1903 and is raced over a three-week period, Hinault was just one minute and 42 seconds ahead of American cyclist Greg LeMond.

▲ *Bernard Hinault.*

Football massacre at Heysel Stadium

29 MAY British soccer fans rioted tonight at the Heysel Stadium in Brussels, Belgium, and went on a rampage that left 41 Italian and Belgian supporters dead and several hundred injured. The violence came before the European Cup Final, between Liverpool and the Italian team, Juventus. The game was allowed to proceed, however, and Juventus won 1–0. The tragedy comes less than three weeks after 40 fans died in a fire at a stadium in Bradford, England.

French admit bombing

22 SEPTEMBER The French government today admitted that its agents bombed *Rainbow Warrior*, a ship belonging to the environmental action group Greenpeace. Last July the ship was in Auckland harbor, New Zealand, preparing to sail in a protest against French nuclear weapons testing at the Mururoa Atoll in the Pacific, when it was ripped apart in two explosions. Nine of the Greenpeace activists on board escaped the explosion, but Fernando Pereira, a photographer from Portugal, was killed. The attack provoked an international outcry, and French sabotage was suspected. That suspicion has now been confirmed.

▲ Rainbow Warrior *after it was bombed.*

Becker wins Wimbledon

7 JULY Boris Becker, the 17-year-old West German tennis star, today became the youngest player ever to win the men's singles at Wimbledon. Strong and fast, Becker overpowered the South African Kevin Curren by three sets to one.

Each year at Wimbledon, the top players are seeded—they have special places in the draw for the knockout rounds—so that they don't have to play each other until the final stages of the tournament. Becker wasn't rated among the seeds, so he is the first unseeded player, as well as the first German, to become a Wimbledon champion.

◄ *Boris Becker, youngest winner of the Wimbledon men's singles championship.*

Christo's bridge-wrap

Bulgarian artist Christo brought his monumental art to Paris this September, using 40,000 yards (36,600 meters) of canvas to "wrap" the Pont Neuf over the Seine River. Christo Javacheff specializes in covering large objects and natural features. In 1983 he wrapped 11 islands off of the coast of Florida in pink fabric.

◄ *The Pont Neuf all wrapped up.*

1980

1980

1981

1982

▶ *An aerial view shows the Chernobyl nuclear plant near Kiev after the disastrous accident.*

1983

Halley's Comet returns

1984

Once every 76 years' the ball of ice and rock dust called Halley's Comet returns to the center of the solar system. When it flew past Earth early this year, a fleet of spaceships including two *Vega* craft from the Soviet Union and the European *Giotto* vessel made tests and took pictures. The comet is named after the English astronomer, Edmund Halley, who worked out its orbit in 1705.

1985

1986

1987

▲ *Halley's Comet in 1986.*

1988

1989

ENVIRONMENT

Nuclear disaster in USSR

6 MAY Soviet authorities today released details of the worst accident in the history of nuclear power, the explosion at the Chernobyl nuclear power station last month, which released dangerous levels of radioactivity into the atmosphere. The contamination has been carried far across Europe by the wind—reaching Sweden, Finland, the northern part of Britain, and even France and Italy. The accident happened early on 26 April when scientists were trying to install a safety system. A series of explosions created a ball of fire and blew the concrete lid off of the nuclear reactor. Two people are reported dead.

The station, which is less than 10 years old, is at Pripyat, 60 miles (100 km) north of the city of Kiev in Ukraine. Around 30,000 locals have been evacuated, but in Kiev people seem to be living as normal.

Marcos finally goes

POLITICS

25 FEBRUARY Ferdinand Marcos, president of the Philippines for the past 20 years, fled the country today. Opposition leader Corazon Aquino, who stood against him in the recent elections, has been sworn in as the new president. Marcos' corrupt regime was backed by the US. Mrs. Aquino is the widow of Benigno Aquino, who was killed by Marcos troops in 1983. After her swearing-in ceremony, she said that the Philippines' "long agony was over."

▶ *Standing in front of a statue of Marcos, Mrs. Aquino celebrates victory.*

NEWS • 1986 • NEWS

1 January • Spain and Portugal join the European Community.

4 April • Hollywood actor Clint Eastwood is elected mayor of Carmel, California.

15 April • US aircraft bomb Tripoli in Libya.

29 June • Argentina win the soccer World Cup in Mexico, beating West Germany 3–2.

19 October • President Machel of Mozambique and 28 officials die in air crash.

Challenger catastrophe

DISASTERS

28 JANUARY The US space shuttle *Challenger* blew up 73 seconds after its liftoff today, killing all seven crew members. The shuttle was climbing at 2,000 miles per hour (3,200 km per hour) when a failure in one of the booster rockets started a fire. On board, fuel tanks exploded in a vast ball of flames. One of the crew was schoolteacher Christa McAuliffe, who had been chosen in a special NASA scheme to allow ordinary people to go into space. Her family was at the Kennedy Space Center in Florida to see her off. Some scientists are suggesting that the unusually cold weather may have contributed to the booster rocket's failure. Whatever its cause, the tragedy is a major setback to the space shuttle program.

▶ *Only seconds after takeoff, Challenger explodes, killing all on board.*

Young Tyson is a heavyweight champ

Mike Tyson, a 20-year-old American with a sledgehammer punch, defeated Canadian fighter Trevor Berbick in two rounds on 22 November to become the youngest world heavyweight boxing champion ever.

"Baby Doc" flees Haiti

POLITICS

7 FEBRUARY The people of Haiti in the West Indies are rejoicing at the news that their hated president, Jean-Claude Duvalier, has fled to France. Known as Baby Doc, the 34-year-old Duvalier was even more unpopular than his father, Papa Doc, whom he succeeded as Haiti's dictator, or "president for life." For 28 years the Duvaliers have ruled Haiti, backed by Tontons Macoutes, a brutal secret police.

▶ *"Baby Doc" prepares to leave Haiti.*

▼ *Olof Palme, Sweden's premier.*

Sweden's Olof Palme is killed

POLITICS

28 FEBRUARY A lone gunman fatally wounded Swedish prime minister Olof Palme on a Stockholm street tonight. Palme died shortly afterward in hospital. Leader of the Social Democratic Party, Palme was premier from 1969 to 1976 and again from 1982 to the present. He was a critic of the US's role in the Vietnam War. Before his reelection in 1982 he acted as the UN's special envoy in the attempt to settle the Iran-Iraq conflict.

Waldheim wins despite war record

POLITICS

8 JUNE Kurt Waldheim has been elected Austrian president after a campaign in which his war-time career as a member of a German army unit that committed atrocities in Yugoslavia was exposed. Waldheim, a former UN Secretary General, admits that he didn't tell the truth about his past, but says he's not to blame for wartime crimes.

1980
1981
1982
1983
1984
1985
1986
1987
1988
1989

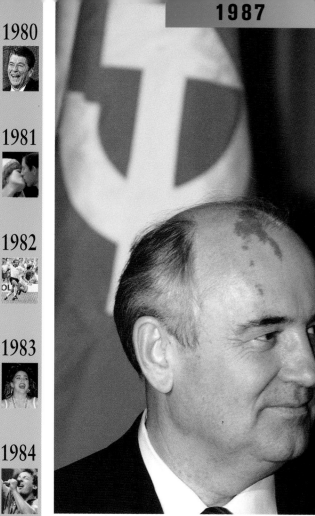

▲ *Mikhail Gorbachev, the reforming USSR leader.*

POLITICS

Gorbachev calls for *perestroika* and *glasnost*

29 JANUARY Soviet leader Mikhail Gorbachev said today that the Communist Party needs to be more open and that voters should have a choice of candidates in elections. Ever since he was elected leader in March 1985, he has made no secret of his commitment to change and reform in the Soviet Union. His policies are known as *perestroika* (restructuring in Russian), meaning the reform of the economy and the government, and *glasnost* (Russian for openness), meaning freedom of information and movement.

Soviet people are used to strict government control over their lives, but Gorbachev is reducing censorship, so that newspapers, broadcasters, and individuals are free to criticize the ruling Communist Party. *Glasnost* was at work last December when Andrei Sakharov, an outspoken campaigner for democracy and human rights in the USSR, was freed from the city of Gorky, where he had been forced to live in a kind of open imprisonment for almost seven years. Gorbachev is also keen to reduce the threat of nuclear war. He has had two summit meetings with President Reagan to discuss cuts in nuclear weapons.

DISASTERS

30 dead after King's Cross Station Inferno

▼ *A policeman lays flowers at the blackened entrance of King's Cross.*

19 NOVEMBER Thirty people died, and many more were injured, in last night's storm of flames at King's Cross subway station in London. The fire began on a wooden escalator and flared into the ticket hall. Smoke billowed through the underground complex and onto the platforms, while trains continued to unload passengers. Some people are blaming the transportation authority for reducing cleaning and safety checks. The station had no water sprinklers, even though they were recommended by a safety report three years ago.

◀ *A fire inspector examines the main ticket hall of King's Cross subway station.*

NEWS • 1987 • NEWS

11 June • Margaret Thatcher is elected for a third term as British prime minister.

22 June • Hollywood legend Fred Astaire dies, aged 88.

26 July • Irish cyclist Stephen Roche wins the Tour de France.

19 October • Stock markets around the world crash on "Black Monday."

8 December • INF missile treaty agreed by US and USSR.

Van Gogh's vibrant flowers beat all records

Early this year, when *Sunflowers,* by 19th-century Dutch artist Vincent Van Gogh fetched around $38 million at Christie's auctioneers in London, it beat all records for the sale of paintings. But later this year, when Christie's in New York sold *Irises,* another Van Gogh flower painting, for $45 million, that record was broken. *Sunflowers* (right) went to the Yasuda Fire and Marine Insurance Company, Tokyo. The *Irises* buyer was not identified.

"Techno" triumphs over soul

As the price of synthesizers and sequencers drops, electronic music holds sway at raves and clubs. "Techno's" creators prefer tomorrow's technology to yesterday's heroes. The percussive style, known as acid house, harks back to the disco craze of the 1970s, and first emerged in Detroit. It is played at influential clubs such as Chicago's Powerplant, and at Hacienda. in Manchester, in northern England.

▼ *Rust's Cessna plane in front of St. Basil's Cathedral in Red Square.*

200 die in *Herald* ferry disaster

DISASTERS

7 MARCH As many as 200 people died in the icy waters of the English Channel last night when a car ferry capsized. The *Herald of Free Enterprise* had just left Zeebrugge in Belgium for Dover in southern England when it rolled over. There were doors at both ends of the hull, so that cars and trucks could drive on at the start of the trip and drive off at the end without reversing. Last night, one set of doors was left open—allowing water to pour into the car deck. The huge ferry started to sink so suddenly that many people had died before rescue services reached the scene.

▼ *The* Herald of Free Enterprise *after the disaster.*

Action on the ozone layer

ENVIRONMENT

16 SEPTEMBER An international agreement to protect the Earth's atmosphere has been signed in Montreal, Canada. Twenty-seven countries, including the US and most European nations, agreed not to increase their use of chlorofluorocarbons (CFCs), chemicals that damage the ozone layer, which are used in aerosol cans and refrigerators. They also pledged to halve the use of CFCs by 1999. The layer of ozone in the Earth's atmosphere offers protection from the Sun's radiation, which can be damaging to crops and human skin. There is concern that the ozone layer is thinning over parts of Antarctica.

Rust's plane lands in Red Square

POLITICS

29 MAY A 19-year-old West German pilot today found a hole in one of the world's most impressive air-defense systems. Matthias Rust flew his four-seater Cessna 172 aircraft right into the heart of Moscow, outwitting Soviet radar by flying at rooftop height. He winged low over the Kremlin, circled around the towers of St. Basil's Cathedral, and landed in Red Square. Rust qualified as a pilot last year. He flew first to Finland, taking off for Moscow from Helsinki.

1980

1981

1982

1983

1984

1985

1986

1987

1988

1989

▲ *Investigators examine the wreckage of the jumbo that exploded over Lockerbie.*

DISASTERS

Pan Am jumbo crashes at Lockerbie

22 DECEMBER In the worst air disaster in Britain since aviation began, an American jumbo jet exploded this evening over the Scottish town of Lockerbie, a few miles north of the border with England. A reported 270 people, everyone on the plane plus 11 on the ground, are dead. Pan American flight 103 started in Frankfurt and was bound for New York after a short stop at London's Heathrow Airport. Many of the passengers were US citizens returning home for the Christmas vacation. According to eyewitnesses, the cruising plane was suddenly engulfed by a huge fireball. Probably everyone was killed instantly; the pilot had no time to broadcast a distress signal. The plane crashed to the ground in burning fragments, starting dozens of fires, destroying more than 30 houses, and blasting a crater 50 feet (15 meters) deep. Bodies, some unrecognizable, and wreckage were scattered over a wide area. Although the reason for the explosion has not yet been established, there is little doubt that it was caused by a bomb. Warnings of a terrorist attack on Pan American have been circulating in US embassies.

NEWS • 1988 • NEWS

8 February • Gorbachev announces timetable for Soviet withdrawal from Afghanistan.

30 June • Stockholm conference estimates that 5 million people carry the HIV virus.

3 July • 290 killed when US warship in Gulf shoots down Iranian civil airliner.

5 October • Referendum in Chile rejects continuation of General Pinochet's military regime.

TERRORISM

Gibraltar IRA Three buried

16 MARCH Mayhem erupted as the three IRA members, Sean Savage, Daniel McCann, and Mairead Farrell, who were killed in Gibraltar 10 days ago, were buried in Belfast today. A loyalist gunman hurled grenades and fired into the crowd of mourners at the gravesides. Three people were killed and 50 injured. This attack has raised tensions, which were already high after the killings in Gibraltar.

Controversy surrounds the sequence of events in which the three IRA members died. They were under surveillance by British security forces, probably the SAS, and were believed to be plotting an explosion in Gibraltar—two days after the shootings, the rented car of the three activists was found containing 140 pounds (64 kg) of explosives. According to the official version, when challenged, they responded in such a way that the officers believed their own lives were threatened, and they opened fire immediately at short range.

▼ *The Gibraltar Three's funeral on 16 March*

▲ *Bangladesh after the deluge. In many areas victims can only be reached by helicopter.*

INF treaty signed by US and USSR

TREATIES

1 JUNE The Intermediate Nuclear Forces treaty has at last been signed today by the President Reagan and Soviet premier, Mikhail Gorbachev. It is the first major agreement to reduce nuclear weapons and reflects Gorbachev's desire for better relations with the West and for reduced military costs at home. The US will remove its medium-range Pershing and Cruise missiles from bases in western Europe. The USSR will remove its equivalent missiles in eastern Europe. Arrangements have been agreed for inspection teams to check that the terms of the treaty are being put into effect.

Millions in peril after Bangladesh floods

DISASTERS

5 SEPTEMBER Bangladesh, one of the world's poorest countries, is facing its worst flood disaster in recent times. Nearly two-thirds of Bangladesh, including the capital, Dhaka, are under water, and more than 20 million people are homeless. Food and fodder crops have been destroyed, along with roads and dikes. The airport is out of action, and even the railroads, which were built by British engineers on causeways 3 feet (1 meter) above the expected high-water mark, are submerged. Deaths are estimated at 300 or 400, but this figure is bound to rise as polluted water supplies spread disease. The government has appealed for international aid, but the state of Bangladeshi communications after the flood means that the delivery of assistance will be an problem. The crisis comes within weeks of another international disaster, the floods in the Sudan.

▲ *A demonstrator waves the Palestinian flag.*

Intifada protest

POLITICS

4 NOVEMBER Palestinians in Jerusalem today published their declaration of independence. The timing was perhaps influenced by the victory of the rightwing Likud Party in the Israeli elections two days ago, which the PLO described as a fatal blow for peace.

The Intifada, a campaign of civil disobedience and protest against Israeli rule in the Occupied Territories, began last December. It is proving more effective than terrorism. The expense of maintaining the occupation has forced Israel to take Palestinian independence more seriously and has highlighted the frustration of the Palestinians, who have seen little progress toward solving their problems through diplomacy. A secretly filmed episode shown worldwide on television, in which Israeli soldiers beat stone-throwing Palestinian youths with rocks and batons, aroused international indignation.

Ben Johnson loses his Seoul Olympics medal

Less than a week after winning the Olympic 100-meter final in the world-record time of 9.79 seconds, the Canadian sprinter Ben Johnson has been stripped of his gold medal and banned from representing his country. Urine tests revealed the presence of an anabolic steroid, a drug which artificially increases strength.

▲ *Ben Johnson, the disgraced champion.*

Earthquake in Armenia

DISASTERS

8 DECEMBER The enormous earthquake that devastated parts of Armenia yesterday has killed more than 100,000 people and left at least 10 times that number homeless. The cities of Leninakan and Spitak, where coffins are being piled in the sports stadium, are in ruins. Poorly built modern buildings have collapsed like matchwood, burying alive the people who lived in them, and the cold weather is aggravating the situation. The tremor, which measured 6.9 on the Richter scale, happened near Armenia's border with Turkey. As survivors search desperately with their bare hands or improvised tools for relatives, a massive international effort is being organized. Mikhail Gorbachev, president of the Soviet Union, has cancelled his visit to the US so that he can visit Armenia today. The natural disaster follows a year of unrest and ethnic violence in the region, stemming from the refusal of Azerbaijan to return Nagorno-Karabakh, a mainly Armenian district that has been part of Azerbaijan since 1921.

▲ *Survivors and rescuers walk among the ruins of the Armenian city of Leninakan.*

Shroud of Turin is declared a fake

Scientific tests, sponsored by the Vatican have cast doubt on one of Christianity's most famous relics. The Turin shroud, kept in Turin Cathedral, is an ancient piece of linen which bears the image of a man. Traditionally it was believed to be the shroud in which Jesus Christ was buried, although its history could be traced only to the 14th century. The tests suggest that the cloth itself was made no earlier than 1260.

▲ *The Turin shroud, still a mystery, but no longer sacred.*

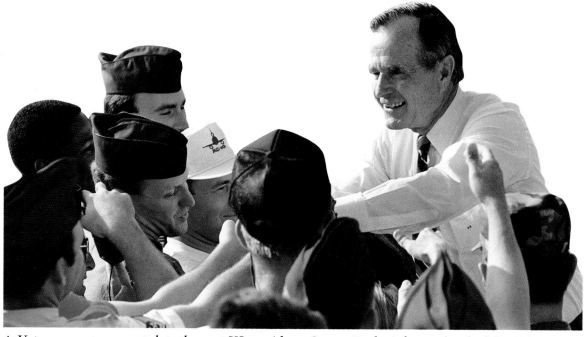

▲ *Voters eager to congratulate the next US president, George Bush. A former head of the CIA, the tall Texan was always the favorite in spite of his weak running mate, Dan Quayle.*

George Bush is elected new US president

POLITICS

11 NOVEMBER As expected, the US presidential election has been easily won by the Republican candidate, George Bush, who is vice president under the retiring President Reagan. He took 40 of the 50 states, and 54 percent of the popular vote nationwide.

Although he waged a surprisingly aggressive campaign, annoying some Republican rivals as well as Democrats, Bush never looked likely to lose to the Democrat candidate, Michael Dukakis, the liberal governor of Massachusetts.

With the Democrats holding a majority in both houses of Congress, Bush may find it difficult to fulfill campaign pledges such as his promise to keep taxes low. However, no major changes are expected from the policies of the Reagan administration.

Iran-Iraq war ends

WAR

8 AUGUST After eight years in which about one million people have died, and unknown numbers have been wounded, a ceasefire in the Iran-Iraq war was announced today by UN Secretary General Perez de Cuellar. The ceasefire becomes effective from 20 August, and talks on a permanent peace agreement will then be held in Geneva under the supervision of the UN. Although both Iran and Iraq are claiming victory, the ceasefire does not represent a clear victory for either side.

▼ *Crowds in Tehran rejoice at news of the ceasefire.*

Australia: bicentennial celebrations

Australians all around the world have been celebrating the 200th birthday of their country. On 26 January, 1788, the First Fleet of British settlers dropped anchor in Botany Bay, near the site of modern Sydney. Aborigine campaigners have objected to the celebration of Australia's settlement by Europeans.

▲ *Tall ships in Sydney Harbour reenact the arrival of the First Fleet.*

Benazir Bhutto is prime minister of Pakistan

POLITICS

17 NOVEMBER The first democratic election in Pakistan for 11 years has been won by the Pakistan People's Party (PPP), whose leader, Benazir Bhutto, becomes the first woman prime minister ever of a Muslim country. The victory is a triumph for Cambridge-educated Benazir Bhutto, whose father, Zulfikar Ali Bhutto, a former prime minister, was overthrown in 1977 and executed by General Zia ul-Haq in 1979. She spent most of the 1980s under house arrest or in exile, but Zia's death in a plane explosion in August opened the way for a return to democratic government.

▲ *Pakistan's new leader, Benazir Bhutto, campaigning among city crowds.*

Europe's seals hit by deadly virus

ENVIRONMENT

12 AUGUST Sick seal pups are now being found in growing numbers along Britain's coasts, suggesting that a deadly virus, which has already killed thousands of seals around the northwestern coast of continental Europe, is spreading. Marine scientists are meeting in London to discuss the epidemic and its causes.

Piper Alpha oil rig disaster

DISASTERS

6 JULY Tonight, after a series of explosions, Occidental Petroleum's Piper Alpha oil rig in the North Sea is a raging inferno. Flames are leaping more than 330 feet (100 meters) into the air, and the intense heat can be felt 1 mile (2 km) away, hampering rescue efforts. About 170 men, three-quarters of the rig's workforce, are feared dead. Many, asleep at the time of the first explosion, were trapped in the self-contained accommodation block, now submerged. Others escaped by leaping into the scalding, blazing sea, where they were rescued by high-speed dinghies. Only eight days ago the rig passed a regulation safety check.

▶ *The Piper Alpha, still ablaze hours after the first explosions.*

COMPUTERS

In the late nineties, computers have become a major part of everyday life. This book was created and printed using computers, and was probably ordered by the store and paid for by computer. Computers help us to learn and relax.

They help to create the special effects we see at the movies and the sounds we hear on a CD. They make shopping and banking easier and more efficient, as well as managing the vast networks that bring water and electricity to our homes.

Almost everything we do today involves the use of an electronic computer, yet the first true computers were only built in the mid-1940s. The progress of the computer is undoubtedly one of the most important technological stories of the century.

Computer facts

- A Pentium Pro microchip contains the equivalent of 5.5 million transistors.
- Computers of the 1990s are more than 1.5 million times faster than those of the 1950s.
- All computers work on the binary system which reduces all information to 0s and 1s.
- The Internet started as a military communications network and is designed to function even under the conditions of war.

◀ ENIAC's control center room at the University of Pennsylvania.

The silicon chip

The computer revolution was made possible by microchips—microscopically minute components etched into strips of the element silicon. These were first made in the 1960s. Now they are present everywhere—from toasters to toys, and from car engines to ovens.

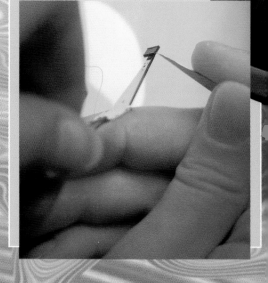

COLOSSUS to UNIVAC, the computer race begins

The computer age began in December 1943, when the world's first programmable electronic computer, a machine called Colossus, went into operation at Bletchley Park—the code-cracking headquarters in Britain. Its 1,500 electronic valves were able to calculate the settings of a German code machine much faster than its mechanical predecessors.

Later versions were more powerful, but were dwarfed by ENIAC (Electronic Numerical Integrator and Computer), built by scientists at the University of Pennsylvania in 1945—just too late to be used in the war. This giant speeded up processing times, but it weighed 30 tons (30 tonnes), contained 17,500 valves, and filled a large room.

Soon computers such as UNIVAC (Universal Automatic Computer), with a console the size of an airplane cockpit and a room full of spinning reels of magnetic tape, entered the world of commerce. People began to realize the potential of this new invention in 1951, when UNIVAC was used to predict the outcome of the US presidential election.

Computers get personal

In 1981, the electronics giant IBM (International Business Machines Corporation) launched its Personal Computer, or PC. IBM asked Intel to produce the all-important microchip, and the software house Microsoft to write the machine's MS-DOS software. IBM's name on the PC, instead of that of its smaller rivals Altair and Apple, gave buyers confidence in the PC's ability to meet their needs. It was also the first time that computers were affordable for home and personal use—computers became accessible to everyone.

The PC became a bestseller. In 1984, IBM was selling more than 3 million PCs a year. Then Apple launched a rival machine—the Macintosh, radically different from the PC. A "mouse" pointing device made the machine easier to use, and files were represented on the screen as little objects (icons) instead of long lists of words.

Microsoft responded by creating Windows, which had a similar look and feel. The 1990s saw strong rivalry between Microsoft and Macintosh.

▲ *Microsoft's multi-millionaire founder, Bill Gates, promotes a new software system.*

▲ *John Scully, Steve Jobs, and Steve Wozniak, cofounders of Apple Computer, pictured with an Apple IIc, in 1984.*

◀ *Inset (on chip): "Red Planet," a 3D virtual reality game set on Mars.*

Computer games

Atari's "Pong" was a console with two control knobs, designed to be plugged into an ordinary TV set. Each knob moved a paddle up or down the screen, so that each player could intercept a moving "ball" and send it back to his opponent. This simple computer game, like tennis without the net, was the world's first—released in 1972.

Computer games have become even more sophisticated. Among the most popular are flight simulators; driving games; sports games, which bring the atmosphere of big competitions to the screen (complete with sports commentary); war games such as "Mortal Kombat" and "Wolfenstein"; and adventure games like "Myst." In addition, the computer games scene has spawned its own superstars—among them Lara Croft, Sonic the Hedgehog, and Super Mario.

◀ *Close-up of a computer chip, held over a computer-generated pattern.*

315

1980

1981

1982

1983

1984

1985

1986

1987

1988

1989

▲*Berliners, East and West, mingle freely opposite the Brandenburg Gate.*

The fall of the Berlin Wall

POLITICS

10 NOVEMBER Just after 11 o'clock last night, the Brandenburg Gate in the Berlin Wall was thrown open by the guards. To the sound of cheering, church bells, and honking horns, thousands of people who had been waiting for this moment poured through. Others climbed onto or over the wall. Some attacked it, knocking pieces off with hammers. Others are just happy to celebrate the end of the Cold War, of which the wall is the most potent symbol.

The 28-mile (45-km) concrete wall that runs across central Berlin, the capital of prewar Germany, was built in 1961 to stop the westward migration that had drained communist East Germany of 2.5 million—mostly young—people since 1949. Since then nearly 100 people have been killed trying to escape to the west. In recent weeks refugees in their thousands have been flooding into West Germany via Czechoslovakia and Hungary, where controls have already been lifted. The East German government, realizing that it could not stop the flow, decided to throw open the border, allowing anyone to enter the West without special permission. The fall of the wall raises the possibility of a reunited Germany.

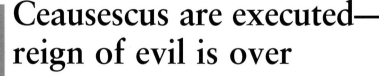

▲ *The Ceausescus were arrested as they tried to escape.*

Ceausescus are executed— reign of evil is over

POLITICS

25 DECEMBER The Romanian dictator, Nicolae Ceausescu, and his wife were executed today after a hasty trial. The old Stalinist empire in eastern Europe has collapsed in a few months. Since June, Poland, Hungary, and Czechoslovakia have thrown out the Communists and gained democatic government. Last month the veteran Bulgarian dictator Todor Zhikov was ejected, and the Communist government of East Germany resigned earlier this month. Romania's communist dictator, Ceausescu is almost the last to go. Since he came to power in 1965 he has pursued policies that were critical of the USSR, which meant that he was well received by many western European governments and politicians. At home, however, Ceausescu was a brutal dictator. He organized schemes, including a repressive family planning policy, that demoralized and further impoverished Romania and promoted and rewarded members of his own family, including his wife, Elena.

Islamic fatwa against Rushdie

15 FEBRUARY The religious leader of Iran, the Ayatollah Khomeini, today declared that it is the duty of Muslims to kill the Indian-born British author Salman Rushdie. His novel *The Satanic Verses*, published to literary acclaim last year, plays on verses left out of the Qur'an by the Prophet Mohammed because he thought they had been inspired by Satan. As a result of the fatwa (legal decree), Mr. Rushdie's life is in danger.

▲ *Khomeini (on poster) calls on all Muslims to honor the fatwa.*

Tiananmen Square massacre

4 JUNE The rulers of communist China have reacted suddenly and with incredible savagery against the students and young people demanding democratic reforms who were peacefully occupying Tiananmen ("Gate of Heavenly Peace") Square in Beijing (Peking). The Chinese army invaded the square and cleared it by force, firing indiscriminately. Makeshift ambulances are trying to reach the hospitals, which are already packed with the dead and dying.

Batman and Robin are movie heroes now

The biggest movie of the year is based on the cartoon *Batman*, which has taken more than $200 million at the US box office. Some of the special effects are remarkable. The outstanding character is not Michael Keaton's caped hero but the grotesquely grinning villain, Jack Nicholson's "Joker."

▲ *Jack Nicholson as the Joker.*

◄ *One individual calmly defies the tanks in Tiananmen Square.*

Panama: US troops topple Noriega

21 DECEMBER In response to President Noriega's declaration of war on the US and the killing of a US soldier, American forces today invaded Panama. Their object is to capture Noriega, a former ally who is now regarded as a criminal. Nearly 300 people, mostly civilians, are reported killed. Noriega, who gained power in May after a blatantly "fixed" election, has taken refuge in a foreign embassy. Opposition leaders were beaten up and prodemocracy demonstrators were attacked by Noriega's strongmen. A recent attempted coup against him, backed by the US, failed.

▼ *A US Marine takes aim in Panama City.*

49ers win Super Bowl

22 JANUARY In the most dramatic finish in the history of the competition, the San Francisco 49ers have won Super Bowl XXIII with a 20–16 victory over Cincinnati thanks to another outstanding performance by quarterback Joe Montana. The 49ers were trailing 16–13 with only seconds remaining when "Joe Cool" drilled a pass to John Taylor in the end zone.

Exxon Valdez accident

24 MARCH 12 million gallons (55 million liters) of crude oil are flowing out of the grounded supertanker, *Exxon Valdez*, in Prince William Sound, Alaska. One of the worst environmental disasters ever in North American waters, it will cause enormous damage. The ship ran aground while commanded by a junior officer. The captain was resting in his cabin.

▶ *A salvage boat assists the supertanker.*

1990

1991

1992

1993

1994

1995

1996

1997

1998

1999

NEW DECADE

1990

The world seemed to be a safer place as the 1990s began. Repressive hardline communism collapsed in 1990 in eastern Europe, and the racially divisive apartheid system was dismantled in South Africa. The Soviet Union and the US declared that the Cold War between them was over.

But new threats to peace emerged. A terrible conflict erupted in Yugoslavia, fueled by ancient hatreds. In the Middle East Iraqi President Saddam Hussein provoked the Gulf War of 1991. Terrorists continued to prey on innocent citizens around the world.

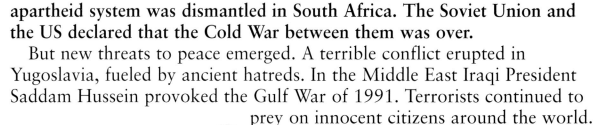

▼ *Mandela and his wife Winnie give the ANC salute.*

POLITICS

Mandela walks to freedom at last

11 FEBRUARY Nelson Mandela, the black political leader who has been imprisoned for 27 years by the South African government, was freed today from Victor Verster Prison near Cape Town. For people around the world his imprisonment was a symbol of the injustice of white rule in South Africa and the apartheid system, which denies political rights to black South Africans. After his release, a crowd of 50,000 gave him an emotional reception in Cape Town. Mandela joined the African National Congress (ANC), a black political organization, in 1944.

In 1960 the government banned the ANC, and the following year Mandela went into hiding and became leader of the organization's military wing Umkhonto we Sizwe (Spear of the Nation). He launched a campaign of sabotage against the government. In 1962 he was jailed for five years, and while in captivity he was tried for sabotage and sentenced to life imprisonment. But the times are changing in South Africa. Nine days ago President F.W. de Klerk lifted the ban on the ANC and other antiapartheid organizations.

World population passes five billion

Pressure on the world's limited resources continues to grow. There are now more than five billion people on the planet (see world population chart below). Figures collected since 1985 show that the average woman in Rwanda, Africa, has about eight children, compared to one child for the average Italian woman. But people in richer countries use many more of the world's resources.

Mandela facts

Nelson Mandela is a lawyer and in the early 1950s with Oliver Tambo – another ANC leader – he set up South Africa's first black legal firm.

•

For 18 years from 1964 to 1982 Mandela was kept in the maximum security Robben Island prison 7 miles (11 km) off the coast of Cape Town.

POLITICS

Thatcher resigns

22 NOVEMBER Britain's first woman prime minister, Margaret Thatcher, has resigned after 11 years in office. Yesterday she failed to win enough votes in the Conservative Party leadership contest to avoid a second round against Michael Heseltine, and last night her advisers told her that she would not win a second vote. Mrs. Thatcher is opposed to joining EMU (economic and monetary union), and disagreements over Europe have split her party. It is only days since deputy prime minister Sir Geoffrey Howe resigned, after telling MPs that Mrs. Thatcher's attitudes to Europe presented "serious risks for the future of our nation."

▶ *A determinedly cheerful Mrs. Thatcher outside 10 Downing Street.*

(Chart: billions — 6, 5, 4, 3, 2, 1, 0 / years 1960, 1970, 1980, 1990)

Navratilova wins her ninth Wimbledon

At the age of 33, Martina Navratilova (left) won the Wimbledon women's tennis singles for a record ninth time. She beat Zina Garrison of the US in two sets, 6–4, 6–1. Born in Czechoslovakia, Navratilova now lives in the US. She won her first Wimbledon championship in 1976.

▲ *Jubilant supporters of Namibia's liberation struggle display the flag of their newly independent country.*

Germany is a single country again

3 OCTOBER At midnight last night West and East Germany were reunited as a single country, 45 years after defeat in World War II. In the streets of Berlin people cried for joy and cheered until they were hoarse. Reunification has happened more quickly than many of them ever dared to hope. Less than a year ago, the Berlin Wall, symbol of Germany's division, was patroled by armed guards. Its fall last year paved the way for the reunification talks launched in March, between East and West German leaders.

Namibia's independence is recognized at last

21 MARCH The Republic of Namibia was born today in southern Africa after a long struggle for independence. South African President F.W. de Klerk formally handed power to the new president Sam Nujoma, leader of the South West Africa People's Organization (SWAPO). In 1966, when Namibia was known as South West Africa, the United Nations declared that it should be granted independence, but South Africa refused to give it up. At about the same time, SWAPO was formed as a guerrilla organization to fight for independence. In 1988, after years of negotiations, South Africa agreed to grant Namibia its independence and last year a SWAPO government was elected.

NEWS • 1990 • NEWS

15 April • Swedish movie actress Greta Garbo dies, aged 84.

14 May • Van Gogh's portrait of Dr. Gachet is the world's most expensive painting after Japanese businessman buys it for $75 million.

23 August • Irish hostage Brian Keenan is released by terrorists after more than four years in Lebanon.

12 November • Japan's new emperor, Akihito, is enthroned.

Walesa is Poland's new president

9 DECEMBER The former shipyard worker Lech Walesa won a landslide victory in the Polish presidential election today. He is the first freely elected president of Poland for 50 years. As leader of the trade union Solidarity in the early 1980s, the charismatic Walesa was a hero of the struggle against the communist government. As a Solidarity activist, he was imprisoned at the end of 1981 until November 1982. In 1989, after being banned for more than seven years, Solidarity was made legal and quickly emerged as the political party that swept to power in free elections.

▶ *Walesa after his historic victory.*

Iraq invades Kuwait

WAR

8 AUGUST Iraqi President Saddam Hussein today declared that Iraq has annexed (absorbed) Kuwait, its neighbor on the Persian Gulf. Six days ago Iraq shocked the world by invading Kuwait, a tiny state which is very rich in oil. Kuwait produces 1.6 million barrels of oil a day, more than half the daily number produced in the whole of Iraq. World leaders including President Bush condemned the invasion at once.

Two days ago, the United Nations imposed an economic blockade on Iraq—under which it cannot export any oil or import any goods. Arab states including Egypt and Saudi Arabia also demanded that Iraq withdraw from Kuwait, but Saddam refused to give in. He has moved Iraqi troops to the border with Saudi Arabia, another neighbor with vast oil supplies. Yesterday President Bush sent US soldiers to Saudi Arabia to defend the country.

Bush said that the Americans had drawn a "line in the sand" and that if Saddam sent his men across it there would be certain war. Other countries, including Britain, have declared that they will send troops in support of the US.

▲ *Saddam paraded hostages from western nations on Iraqi television. This is Stuart Lockwood, a British boy.*

▼ *A corn circle in Hampshire. The work of aliens, freak weather conditions, or New Age jokers?*

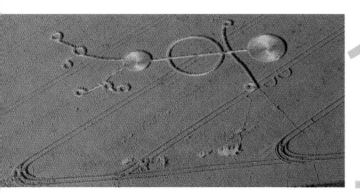

Mysterious corn circles

CULTURE

30 JULY Practical jokers have made fools of the scientists who gathered to investigate "corn circles" in Wiltshire, southern England. Corn circles are strange circular patterns that have been appearing in British cornfields. Overnight, areas of corn are squashed—but with unbroken stems—creating a pattern of perfect circles. Some experts have suggested that small-scale whirlwinds create the effect. Others argue that alien spaceships are responsible. The Wiltshire scientists saw orange flashing lights in the night and, next morning, there were fresh circles. But these circle creators left behind a ouija board, evidence of their teasing purpose.

Germany wins third soccer World Cup

West Germany (below) beat the defending champions Argentina 1–0 in the World Cup final in Rome in July and so won the trophy for the third time. In all, it was a disappointing tournament, spoiled by negative tactics. England, however, surprised everyone by reaching the semifinals. They were edged out by the Germans in a penalty shootout.

Gorbachev wins the Nobel Peace Prize

POLITICS

15 OCTOBER Soviet leader Mikhail Gorbachev has been awarded the Nobel Prize for Peace for his work to improve international relations. Since he became leader in 1985, the Soviet Union's relationship with the US has vastly improved. Moreover, Gorbachev has not tried to block the tide of change sweeping through eastern Europe, accepting the collapse of communist governments in Czechoslovakia and East Germany, and even approving the recent reunification of Germany.

▶ *Mikhail Gorbachev.*

London: anti-poll tax demo ends in rioting

31 MARCH A march in London to protest against the community charge tax ended in rioting and looting today. The rally was supposed to march down Whitehall and end in Trafalgar Square with speeches. When mounted police moved in, however, some of the demonstrators fought back with sticks and missiles. Store windows were smashed, and cars and buildings were set ablaze. Scores of people were hurt, and 341 were arrested.

The community charge, or "poll tax," was introduced last April in Scotland and is due to be launched tomorrow in England and Wales. The old local taxes (rates) were set according to the value of a home, based on size. But under the poll tax each adult must pay a fixed amount set by the local government. A large family in a small home will therefore pay much more under the poll tax than before. It has already proved highly unpopular, and many Scots are refusing to pay.

▶ *Demonstrators brandishing their placards on the march, before the violence erupted. The "poll tax," introduced by Margaret Thatcher, is very unpopular.*

▲ *A bungee jumper takes the plunge.*

Bungee jumping mania

Lovers of excitement are putting their lives on the line. The new youth cult is bungee jumping—leaping from a great height, off a bridge or tower, at the end of an elastic line. The line stops jumpers from smashing to their death, bouncing them back up instead. When people sense danger, their hearts beat faster and sugar surges into their blood. Bungee freaks are seeking this "rush," which is caused by the hormone epinephrine.

The first female president of Ireland

9 NOVEMBER Voters in the Republic of Ireland have produced a major surprise by electing Mary Robinson as president, the first woman to be elected to that office. Robinson, a 46-year-old lawyer, stood as an independent candidate, and she is the first head of state since the end of World War II not to be connected with the Fianna Fáil party (she beat their candidate by 86,566 votes).

Although the Irish presidency is not an executive political role, Mrs. Robinson's known liberalism on such issues as divorce, homosexuality, and family planning were no disadvantage for her election campaign. A Catholic herself, she has criticized the "male-dominated presence of the Catholic Church." As president of the country, she says she will try to represent Irish people of all persuasions.

◀ *Ireland's President Mary Robinson during a trip to France.*

THE END OF COMMUNISM

Two superpowers dominated the globe after World War II: the capitalist US and the communist USSR. By the 1980s, the world economy was becoming a single organism, and it was no longer possible for any one state to develop separately from the whole. In 1985 Soviet leader Mikhail Gorbachev started economic and government reforms. Within a few years the Union of Soviet Socialist Republics had disintegrated, and the communist regimes of eastern Europe were history.

Relations between the superpowers

The postwar conflict between the US and the Soviet Union was known as the Cold War. For 30 years, peace was based on Mutual Assured Destruction or MAD, a strategy that meant that no power could really win a nuclear war.

▲ Two superpower leaders: US President Ronald Reagan and Soviet President Mikhail Gorbachev.

The 1970s saw the beginning of détente—relaxation of Cold War tension—when the US and the Soviet Union agreed to limit their nuclear weapons through SALT—the Strategic Arms Limitation Treaty. A renewed arms race in the 1980s ended with a new agreement—the Intermediate-Range Nuclear Forces (INF) Treaty of 1987, by which Reagan and Gorbachev agreed to scrap certain Soviet and American nuclear missiles. This treaty led to even more far-reaching nuclear disarmament agreements and marked the end of the Cold War.

Campaigners for political freedom

▶ Vaclav Havel, a writer, became president of Czechoslovakia.

Some political leaders in eastern Europe began their careers as opponents of communist regimes. Before Lech Walesa was elected president of democratic Poland in 1990, he was the leader of the free trade union Solidarity, which grew into the democratic reform movement of communist Poland.

In Czechoslovakia, the communist regime which had been in force since 1948 was overthrown in November 1989. Soon afterward, the writer Vaclav Havel was elected as the newly liberated Czechoslovakia's first president. Havel had been prominent in the Charter 77 movement for human rights.

▲ Lech Walesa was a trade unionist.

Fall of the Iron Curtain

When the countries of eastern Europe came under Soviet control after World War II, British statesman Winston Churchill said an Iron Curtain had come down between democratic and communist Europe. This division was epitomized by the Berlin Wall, which was built by the communist authorities in 1961 to stop people from leaving East Germany for West Germany.

In the late 1980s, Gorbachev's *glasnost* (openness) reform encouraged democratic movements in eastern Europe. The Berlin Wall was demolished on 9 November, 1989; border controls slackened in eastern Europe; and the communist governments of East Germany, Romania, Czechoslovakia, and Hungary lost power. But with the removal of communist controls, some nationalist and ethnic tensions resurfaced—for example, war broke out among the states that had belonged to the former communist Yugoslavia.

► *Hungarian soldiers cut the barbed wire that hemmed in communist Hungary's citizens.*

◄ *Background: The hammer and sickle, the symbol of the former USSR.*

► *Pizza Hut, a fast-food restaurant symbolizing American affluence, opened in Moscow in 1990.*

▲ *West and East Berliners celebrate the fall of the concrete Berlin Wall that had divided their city since 1961.*

Soviet dissidents

In Soviet Russia outspoken critics of the political system were regarded as traitors. Soviet human rights campaigners, such as these pictured, attracted world admiration for their courage. Alexander Solzhenitsyn won a Nobel prize for literature in 1970 but was expelled from Russia for his account of life in Soviet prison camps. Andrei Sakharov, the leading Soviet physicist, protested against the testing of nuclear weapons in 1958 and went on to campaign for civil rights. He was awarded the 1975 Nobel Peace Prize.

▲ *Soviet physicist Andrei Sakharov was a pioneer of glasnost.*

◄ *Yelena Bonner, Sakharov's wife, is a human rights campaigner.*

▲ *Alexander Solzhenitsyn, the dissident Russian writer.*

1990

1991

1992

1993

1994

1995

1996

1997

1998

1999

1991

Gulf War ends

WAR

27 FEBRUARY President Bush today declared the end of the war for the liberation of Kuwait. The conflict described by Iraqi President Saddam Hussein as "the mother of all battles" has ended in a devastating defeat for Iraq. Saddam sent troops into Kuwait last August, and on 30 November last year the United Nations passed a resolution threatening war unless Iraq withdrew by 15 January 1991. Saddam refused to move, and on 16 January the US and its allies, led by Norman Schwarzkopf, launched an air war, Operation Desert Storm, bombing strategic Iraqi troops and targets. The air attacks alone were not enough to stop Saddam, and so on 24 February the US and allies sent tanks into Iraq and Kuwait. Much of the Iraqi army fled. The war on the ground lasted only 100 hours.

▲ *An Egyptian soldier talks with Iraqi prisoners of war after they surrender following a battle in Kuwait.*

▲ *General Schwarzkopf (right) and Colin Powell, head of armed services.*

Biosphere II experiment

Eight scientists locked themselves in a 3.15-acre (1.25-hectare) sealed greenhouse in the Arizona desert on 26 September at the start of a two-year environmental study. The greenhouse holds the different ecosystems found on Earth—ocean, desert, savanna, rain forest, and marsh. The scientists will study and maintain these systems. Lessons they learn could be put to use building an artificial environment on another planet or on a spaceship.

▲ *The eight scientists who will seal themselves for two years in Biosphere II.*

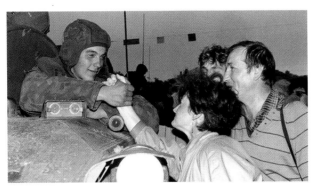

▲ *Soviet soldiers united with ordinary Russians to oppose the August coup.*

USSR dissolves

POLITICS

25 DECEMBER Mikhail Gorbachev today resigned as Soviet executive president because the Soviet Union has ceased to exist. Gorbachev survived an attempted coup launched against him on 19 August by leading Communists, but only thanks to Boris Yeltsin, President of the Russian Republic, who called citizens onto the streets to resist the coup.

Within days, several Soviet republics had opted for independence from the USSR, joining the three Baltic States. On 8 December Russia, Ukraine, and Belarus announced they wanted to set up a Commonwealth of Independent States (CIS), and on 21 December the CIS was founded, backed by most of the former USSR members.

Hostages released

TERRORISM

4 DECEMBER The last American held hostage by terrorists in Beirut, Terry Anderson, was freed today after six and a half years in captivity. Secret negotiations between western governments and terrorist groups have won the release of a wave of hostages over the last 18 months—since Americans Frank Reed and Robert Polhill were set free in April 1990. The Irishman Brian Keenan was freed on 23 August 1990, and almost a year later, on 8 August 1991, British journalist John McCarthy was released. Terry Waite, the special envoy of the British Archbishop of Canterbury, who was kidnapped in January 1987, was freed on 18 November.

▶ *Former hostage Terry Waite waves as he steps from the plane on his arrival in Britain after enduring 1,763 days in captivity.*

Albanians flee to Italy

8 AUGUST Thousands of Albanians are fleeing the political chaos of their country and seeking refuge in Italy. Boatloads of Albanians today came ashore in the port of Bari, southern Italy, after making the short voyage across the Adriatic Sea. They claimed that people in Albania were starving, forced to survive on meager rations of bread and water. Even police and army deserters were among the refugees, who swarmed through the town and onto the beaches but were later rounded up by the Italian authorities. The exodus began months ago—in March 25,000 Albanians landed in Brindisi, a smaller port, south of Bari. Elections were held in Albania in April, but there were allegations of fraud. The country's new Communist government collapsed on 4 June after a general strike of almost three weeks.

▼ *Albanian refugees sail into Brindisi, Italy.*

NEWS • 1991 • NEWS

14 March • The "Birmingham Six," jailed for a terrorist pub bombing in England in 1974, are freed after their conviction is overturned.

25 June • The Yugoslav republics of Croatia and Slovenia declare independence, sparking conflict.

31 July • Soviet leader Mikhail Gorbachev and President Bush sign the Strategic Arms Reduction Treaty, to cut nuclear weapons by one third.

"Glacier Man" discovered in Alps

26 SEPTEMBER The preserved body of a 5,000-year-old man, "deep frozen" by the ice of a mountain glacier, has been discovered in the Austrian Alps. A German couple found the body on 19 September while climbing at an altitude of around 10,500 feet (3,200 meters). In the week since then, the Austrian authorities have arranged for the body to be brought down and scientists at Innsbruck University have studied it. Otzi—as he has been nicknamed—was alive in around 3350 B.C. He stood just over 5 feet (1.5 meters) tall. "Glacier man" was found buried in the ice with a bow and arrow slung over his shoulder. It is believed that he fell asleep in a snowstorm and died, and his body was frozen.

▼ *The mummified body of Otzi, the glacier man.*

Mike Powell's huge jump to success

On 30 August in Tokyo, Japan, American athlete Mike Powell shattered one of the longest-standing records in the history of the long jump. He jumped an outstanding 8.95 meters, beating the 8.90-meter mark set by fellow American Bob Beamon 23 years ago—at the Mexico City Olympics in 1968.

▶ *Mike Powell of the US makes his sixth and final jump.*

Robert Maxwell drowns

5 NOVEMBER The body of millionaire newspaper tycoon Robert Maxwell was today found floating in the Atlantic Ocean south of the Canary Islands. The Czech-born British publisher had disappeared from his yacht *Lady Ghislaine* early this morning. His death is surrounded by mystery. His publishing empire is in financial trouble, and speculation is mounting that Maxwell may have committed suicide or even been murdered. The Spanish authorities have launched an inquiry.

▼ *A woman weeps at the grave of one of her two sons, killed in the fighting.*

▲ *The tall parliament building burns after being hit with an artillery shell fired from Serb positions in the hills surrounding Sarajevo in Bosnia.*

War in Bosnia

WAR

30 AUGUST The former communist state of Yugoslavia in southern Europe has been engulfed by a brutal war. Different national, racial, and religious groups are fighting, as the six republics that once formed Yugoslavia—Bosnia-Hercegovina, Croatia, Macedonia, Montenegro, Serbia, and Slovenia—maneuver for independence. Last year Serbs and Croatians fought bitterly in Croatia after the republic declared independence on 25 June. This year fighting flared in Bosnia after Bosnian voters opted for independence in a referendum on 1 March. The Yugoslav army is controlled by Serbia, and it backed Serbs based in Bosnia in clashes with Bosnian Croats and Muslims. The wider world has witnessed scenes of appalling violence in television coverage of the war, but cannot stop the bloodshed. United Nations troops sent to keep the peace have been caught up in the fighting.

Europe gets its own Disneyland

Mickey Mouse and Donald Duck went to Europe when the Euro Disney amusement park opened near Paris, on 12 April. The 1,483-acre (600-hectare) park, based on the US attractions Disneyland and Walt Disney World, includes six hotels and a golf course, as well as all the rides.

Partition of Czechoslovakia

POLITICS

26 AUGUST Czech and Slovak leaders formally agreed today that Czechoslovakia will become two new countries from 1 January 1993. In elections last June voters in Slovak regions wanted Slovakian independence and state control of industry, while voters in Czech regions wanted a union of Czechoslovakia and a free-market (without state control) economy. Negotiations to split the country began almost at once.

Earth Summit in Rio

ENVIRONMENT

14 JUNE Delegates from 178 countries attended the United Nations conference on the environment that ended today in Rio de Janeiro, Brazil. They agreed a Declaration of 27 Principles to limit damage to the natural world. Delegates want to limit emissions of "greenhouse gases" that harm the atmosphere, as well.

▶ *A child and a delegate plant a tree for the future.*

326

War and famine in Somalia

14 SEPTEMBER United Nations peacekeeping troops today arrived in the east African republic of Somalia on a mission to stem the flood of deaths caused by famine and civil war. Fighting between President Ali Mahdi Muhammad and rebel leader Muhammad Farah Aideed—fueled by ancient clan rivalries—has reduced the country to a state of anarchy. Warlords seize food supplied by international aid agencies. Some aid workers say that more than three-quarters of the 4.5 million population are facing starvation.

▲ *A young Somali child runs past a crouched soldier in wartorn Somalia.*

▲ *Video showing police beating King.*

▼ *Bill Clinton and Al Gore celebrate.*

Race riots in LA

3 MAY Thousands have been hurt and 58 killed in three nights and days of rioting on the streets of Los Angeles. The violence was fueled by racial tension between black and white Americans. On 29 April four white police officers were acquitted of criminal wrongdoing despite videotape evidence that they had beaten black motorist Rodney King in March 1991. Crowds chanting "We want justice!" took to the streets. On 1 May, as Los Angeles began to look like a war zone, President Bush sent in 4,500 troops, and order has slowly been restored.

Clinton becomes President of the United States

3 NOVEMBER Democratic Party candidate William J. Clinton today swept to power in the presidential election. He ran an energetic campaign to defeat his Republican opponent—President George Bush—and Ross Perot, an independent. Clinton is the first Democrat President since Jimmy Carter was defeated by Ronald Reagan in 1980. Clinton has promised to launch an era of renewal in American politics.

Angolan elections

30 SEPTEMBER After years of civil war, a fragile peace is holding in Angola—and the country has held its first free elections. The government of the Popular Movement for the Liberation of Angola (MPLA) has been fighting the National Union for the Total Independence of Angola (UNITA) since the country won independence in 1975. The MPLA won 129 seats in parliament while UNITA won 70. But there are fears that UNITA will reject the result, and restart the war.

▶ *President dos Santos, leader of the MPLA, votes.*

1990
1991
1992
1993
1994
1995
1996
1997
1998
1999

1993

1993

TREATIES

Peace agreement signed between Israel and PLO

13 SEPTEMBER A historic handshake in Washington today between Israeli Prime Minister Yitzhak Rabin and PLO leader Yassir Arafat sealed the fragile peace agreement between the Israelis and the Palestinians. This Washington agreement was reached after long, secret negotiations in Norway and represents the first stage toward Palestinian self-rule. The Israeli government has taken the big step of recognizing the PLO, which it formerly regarded as a terrorist organization, as the legitimate representative of the Palestinian people. The PLO has taken the equally big step of recognizing the rightful existence of the state of Israel. The Palestinians will receive limited self-rule in the Occupied Territories (the West Bank and the Gaza Strip). Israeli forces will eventually withdraw and the territories will be administered by a Palestinian council.

▲ *An unexpected sight, Israeli and Palestinian flags flying side by side.*

◀ *As President Clinton looks on, Arafat and Rabin shake hands.*

The "net" takes off

More and more people are "on the net," a computer network that links other networks, and has the potential to reach anyone in the world. It dates back to a US Defense Department project, ARPANET, designed to link researchers with distant computerized data sources. Its success encouraged other links, which have grown into a complex of many thousands of networks, used by millions of people.

TERRORISM

IRA atrocity in Warrington

20 MARCH With the streets on Saturday full of families buying gifts for Mother's Day, Warrington was a busy British town until a double explosion killed two children, aged 3 and 12, and left over 50 people injured. The two explosions, one minute apart, were caused by bombs planted by IRA terrorists in steel garbage cans, which disintegrated in a shower of metal fragments. Although there was a telephone warning, the site of the explosion was given as an area of Liverpool, many miles from Warrington.

LAW

Aborigines win rights to land

22 DECEMBER The Aborigines of Australia are celebrating the passing of the Native Title Act by the federal parliament. The new act recognizes that Aborigines have rights to territory taken from them by early European colonists. It was strongly opposed by mining interests and landholding companies, and backed by environmental groups. According to some estimates, as much as 10 percent of the land in Australia may be affected by the Native Title Act.

▲ *Aborigines celebrate the Native Title Act.*

Yeltsin crushes Parliament

POLITICS

4 OCTOBER The threat of civil war in Russia has passed. Army comandos stormed Moscow's white slablike parliament building. There were several casualties before the rebellious members of the Congress of Deputies surrendered. Their leaders, Vice President Alexander Rutskoi and Speaker Ruslan Khasbulatov, were taken off to prison. The Russian parliament was dominated by conservative opponents of President Yeltsin. When Yeltsin ordered parliament's dissolution they refused to obey and the siege of the "White House" began. The army, however, remained loyal to Yeltsin.

▲ *Moscow's "White House" after the siege.*

Spielberg's moving Holocaust epic

Steven Spielberg's acclaimed new movie about the Holocaust, called *Schindler's List,* is based on the true story of a German factory boss, Oskar Schindler, and his Jewish workers. Liam Neeson (below left) stars as Schindler, Ben Kingsley (below right) as his accountant, and Ralph Fiennes plays a demented Nazi labor camp commander.

A single Europe

TREATIES

1 NOVEMBER The Maastricht Treaty, agreed late in 1991 by leaders of countries belonging to the European Community, comes into effect today. From now on, the European Community is the European Union (EU). It's a big step, which ran into strong opposition in several member countries before gaining approval. Britain's parliament was the last to ratify it.

▶ *The EU flag: 12 stars, one for each member nation, on a blue background.*

NEWS • 1993 • NEWS

26 February • Bomb shakes New York's World Trade Center.

24 April • IRA bomb hits London's financial district.

2 August • Severe flooding in American Midwest.

8 October • International economic sanctions against South Africa end.

13 October • US scientist reports successful cloning of human embryos.

Waco siege ends in carnage

RELIGION

19 APRIL The siege of Waco, Texas, ended today in terrible slaughter. Only a handful of the 120 members of the Branch Davidian religious cult have survived. The dead include 17 children. The sect was dominated by David Koresh, who saw himself as a messiah. In February Federal agents raided the ranch to arrest him and seize weapons. That raid went wrong, six men died, and the siege began. Today, after officers opened fire, the building exploded into flames, and Koresh died with most of his followers.

▶ *Waco survivors under arrest.*

329

GENETICS

Genetics is a branch of biology that is concerned with the study of the process by which characteristics of living things are handed down from one generation to another—the reason why, for example, red-headed people are likely to have red-headed children.

Genetics as a science began over 100 years ago when an Austrian monk, Gregor Mendel, showed how heredity works by his experiments in crossbreeding sweet peas. His "laws" of heredity, which weren't really noticed in his own lifetime, were based on the existence of "particles" or units that we now call genes.

◀ Crick and Watson's ingenious model of the structure of a DNA molecule. It takes the form of a twin spiral, or "double helix."

▶ Dolly, the world-famous sheep cloned in 1996 at the Roslin Institute in Scotland.

▼ A broken virus particle, greatly magnified, from which DNA has been extracted.

Cloning experiments and Dolly the sheep

A clone is a living creature that has been reproduced, or copied, from a single individual without sex taking place. Genetically, a clone is exactly the same as the individual from which it was derived. Cloning does happen in nature. Since ancient times, gardeners have taken cuttings of valued plants in order to grow more of the same. In humans, identical twins grow when the egg cell splits after fertilization and separates into two separate embryos, whose genes are identical. By imitating this process, scientists can produce cloned animals in a laboratory. Scotland's most famous sheep, Dolly, was produced by extracting DNA from a single cell of an adult ewe, of which Dolly is a perfect copy. The experiment's success has enormous implications for the future of medicine and agriculture but also raises moral issues.

330

DNA

Every human being starts as a single cell packed with an enormous quantity of chemical information. As the cell divides, giving rise to thousands and thousands of new cells, exact copies of that information are passed on. In most cells, genetic data is carried on several separate deoxyribonucleic acid, or DNA, molecules, which are housed in the cell's nucleus. When a cell is about to divide, these DNA molecules thicken and shorten and can be examined under a microscope. A single DNA molecule consists of two strands twisted together to form a double helix. Scientists may soon succeed in making a list, or map, of the 3 billion different "letters" in human DNA. Such a map would identify the genes responsible for hereditary diseases. Cystic fibrosis, for example, the most common gene defect in the North America and western Europe, was tracked down in 1990. Once a particular gene has been mapped, gene therapy may be possible. A "bad" gene can be altered, or prevented from dividing.

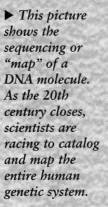

▶ This picture shows the sequencing or "map" of a DNA molecule. As the 20th century closes, scientists are racing to catalog and map the entire human genetic system.

▼ James Watson (below). In 1953 he and Francis Crick saw DNA's double-helix structure.

Genetics facts

Nobody knows exactly how many genes there are. An individual human might have 100,000, most of which are the same.

●

More than 98 percent of a chimpanzee's genes are the same as a human's genes.

●

For experimental purposes, geneticists often use the humble fruit fly, *Drosophila melanogaster*. This tiny creature breeds very often, about every two weeks, so changes from one generation to the next can be seen quickly.

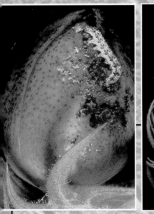

◀ The cotton boll on the right has been genetically "improved" to resist pests. The one on the left has not.

Genetic engineering

Biochemists can alter the genes of a living organism to change its characteristics. Seedless grapes, sweeter apples, and bigger potatoes are some of the food plants that have been "engineered" by gene technology. More crucially, genetic engineering can help to combat diseases such as hemophilia and diabetes. For example, genes controlling the production of insulin can be inserted into bacteria. These bacteria then act as factories for the manufacture of insulin that can be "harvested" and used to treat people with diabetes.

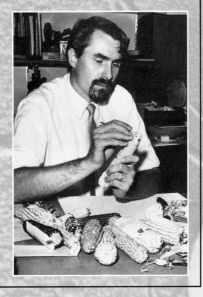

▶ A biochemist studies genetically engineered corn cobs.

▼ Background: A picture of chains of DNA molecules magnified 100,000 times.

331

1990

1991

1992

1993

1994

1995

1996

1997

1998

1999

1994

POLITICS

Nelson Mandela becomes president of South Africa

10 MAY President Nelson Mandela was inaugurated today as the first black leader of South Africa after his African national Congress (ANC) party swept to victory in April in the first "free and fair" election held in South Africa. Whites, blacks, and "coloreds" joined in joyful celebration. In his speech, he gave generous praise to F.W. de Klerk, the last white president, who abandoned apartheid and released Mandela and other political prisoners so that the "rainbow nation" could take its place among free and democratic states.

Channel Tunnel opened

A 35-minute train journey now carries travelers between Britain and France. Serious construction started in the 1980s, and two tunnels, one from Calais in France and one from Folkestone in England, met under the sea in 1990. The Channel Tunnel was officially opened by Britain's Queen Elizabeth and President Mitterrand of France in May, but a regular car sevice only began in the last days of December.

▲ *Mandela casts his vote in April.*

▲ *President Mandela joins hands with ex-President de Klerk.*

▲ *French and British Eurostar trains at the Tunnel opening.*

TERRORISM

The IRA declares a ceasefire

31 AUGUST After 25 years of violence, the IRA today officially declared an end to all its "military operations." The announcement was greeted with joy in nationalist areas of Northern Ireland. But there are problems ahead. The British government insists that Sinn Fein, the political party allied to the IRA, may join only discussions on the future of Northern Ireland if the ceasefire is unconditionally permanent. International observers of the situation feel that this may be an unrealistic demand.

Genocide in Rwanda

DISASTERS

4 JULY The Tutsi Rwandan Patriotic Front (RPF) now have control of the capital of Rwanda in central Africa. The massacres that have made Rwanda a living hell were sparked off earlier this year by the death of the Hutu president in a plane crash—probably sabotage. Estimates suggest that a million people have been killed, mainly by the predominantly Hutu militia. The victims were their traditional enemies, the Tutsi, and moderate Hutu. The RPF's success has since made vast numbers of Hutu flee into neighboring countries, chiefly Zaire. Starvation and disease are rampant in the refugee camps.

▶ *Aid workers struggle to help victims of the Rwandan war.*

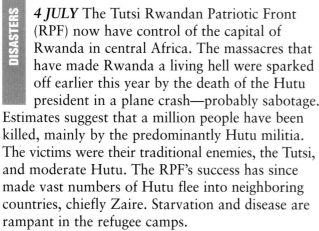

US send troops into Haiti

POLITICS

19 SEPTEMBER US troops landed in Haiti today to restore legal government. There was no shooting. In a last-minute agreement, General Raoul Cédras, whose three-year military rule has ruined Haiti, promised cooperation. He will surrender power next month, when democratically elected President Jean-Bertrand Aristide, in exile in the US, returns. In recent months thousands of Haitians trying to escape by sea to Florida have been rescued by the US Coast Guard.

▲ *US soldiers in Haiti: their invasion was approved by the UN.*

Senna dies in Formula 1 crash

SPORT

1 MAY Ayrton Senna, the Brazilian racing driver, was killed today in the Grand Prix in Imola, in San Marino. His Williams car crashed into a concrete wall at 150 miles per hour (240 km per hour). The winner of 41 Grand Prix races, Senna was generally regarded as the finest racing driver of his day. The cause of the crash is uncertain.

NEWS • 1994 • NEWS

5 February • *68 killed in mortar attack on Sarajevo market.*

24 June • *European Airbus, world's biggest aircraft, Beluga, unveiled in Toulouse, France.*

17 July • *Brazil wins soccer World Cup after penalty shoot-out with Italy.*

31 August • *World chess champ Kasparov defeated by computer.*

19 October • *21 killed by suicide bomber in Tel Aviv.*

Earthquake in Los Angeles

DISASTERS

17 JANUARY An earthquake in the San Fernando valley shattered the predawn peace of Los Angeles, California, today, killing over 30 people, destroying buildings, and bringing down part of an elevated highway. Broken water mains and electric cables caused floods and fires. The quake's force was similar to the Armenia earthquake (1988), which killed 100 times more people. California suffered less because most buildings are designed to withstand shocks.

◄ *Ruined houses in Los Angeles.*

Estonia tragedy

DISASTERS

28 SEPTEMBER About 900 people are reported drowned in the Baltic Sea after the roll-on roll-off ferry *Estonia* capsized and sank. The giant bow doors appear to have given way under the stress of a stormy sea, and the ship, bound for Finland, went down within minutes. The temperature of the water in the Baltic is low, and only 141 survivors are reported out of a total of over 1,000.

The disaster recalls the *Herald of Free Enterprise*, which sank off Zeebrugge in 1987, and casts more doubt on the safety of roll-on roll-off car ferries.

▲ *A salvaged part of the* Estonia.

1990
1991
1992
1993
1994
1995
1996
1997
1998
1999

1995

▲ *The televised chase of O.J.*

▲ *O.J. goes on record with his criminal mugshot.*

O.J. Simpson walks free

LAW

3 OCTOBER Former football star and actor O.J. Simpson was today found not guilty of murdering his ex-wife Nicole Brown Simpson and her friend Ronald Goldman last summer. Live television coverage of "the O.J. trial" has gripped Americans for months. There have been moments of high drama, as when—on 15 June 1995—Simpson tried on a pair of bloodstained gloves, a key piece of prosecution evidence. They seemed to be too small—the prosecution argued that they had shrunk, while the defense said that since they did not fit they could not be his. Simpson's arrest in June last year was also, bizarrely, covered on television. After charging him with the murders, police could not locate Simpson and declared him a fugitive. He was then spotted driving a friend's car on a Los Angeles freeway and was followed. Once he'd driven back to his mansion, Simpson gave himself up.

O.J. Simpson facts

The American sportsman belongs to the professional football Hall of Fame.

•

O.J. Simpson starred in two hit movies, *Capricorn One* (1978) and *The Naked Gun* (1988), and their sequels.

•

There were 100 witnesses and 1,100 exhibits in O.J.'s murder trial.

Rabin's search for peace in Middle East is cut short

POLITICS

8 NOVEMBER Israel's Prime Minister Yitzhak Rabin was fatally shot on 4 November as he walked to his car after a rally for peace between Israelis and Palestinians. He was killed because of his commitment to a peaceful resolution of the conflict in the Middle East. An Israeli student, Yigal Amir, has been arrested, having confessed to killing Rabin because he wanted "to give our country to the Arabs." Foreign Minister Shimon Peres, who has been named as prime minister, promises to continue Rabin's search for a peaceful solution to the Israeli-Palestinian conflict.

▲ *Yitzhak Rabin (left). His funeral was delayed for a day so that world leaders could attend.*

Oklahoma horror

TERRORISM

21 APRIL Terror struck in the heartland of the US two days ago when a bomb ripped apart the Alfred P. Murrah Federal Building in Oklahoma City, Oklahoma. The bomb exploded at 9:03 A.M. inside a truck parked outside the Federal government building. Bodies are still being carried out of the rubble, but so far the number of dead stands at 78. Timothy McVeigh, a US Army veteran, was today charged with the bombing and his friend Terry Nichols, wanted for questioning, gave himself up in Kansas. Some people are suggesting that the attackers left the bomb as revenge for the Waco siege.

▲ *Oklahoma's Federal government building after the blast.*

Earthquake hits Kobe in Japan

DISASTERS

17 JANUARY The Japanese port of Kobe, 280 miles (450 km) west of Tokyo, has been devastated by an earthquake measuring 7.2 on the Richter scale. Movement of the Nojima Fault beneath the Sea of Japan caused the quake, which struck for 20 seconds at 5:46 am. Rescue services are struggling to cope with the carnage, and the death toll may exceed 5,000. More than 50,000 buildings are rubble, and the quake-resistant freeway lies in a tangled mess over the crushed remains of vehicles.

▼ *Kobe's freeway after the quake.*

Rosemary West on trial

LAW

22 NOVEMBER Britain's worst female serial killer, Rosemary West, was today sentenced to life imprisonment 10 times over. A jury found her guilty of murdering 10 young women and girls, including her daughter Heather and stepdaughter Charmaine, between April 1973 and June 1987. She committed the murders with her husband, Frederick, and they buried some of the remains beneath their house in Gloucester, in western England. Frederick West escaped trial by hanging himself in his prison cell in January.

◀ *Greenpeace protesters at Brent Spar.*

Windows 95 is here

A global publicity campaign launched Windows 95, the new computer operating system from the American corporation Microsoft in August. In New York computer stores gave out free pizza to eager crowds as it went on sale. In London, Microsoft paid for *The Times* to be printed and distributed free.

Greenpeace say no to sinking of oil rig

ENVIRONMENT

20 JUNE Activists from the environmental group, Greenpeace, have won a surprise victory over the oil company Shell UK. Earlier this year Shell announced that it was going to sink a disused oil storage platform, Brent Spar, in the Atlantic Ocean. Now, as a result of public support for Greenpeace's campaign, Shell says it will dismantle Brent Spar instead of dumping it.

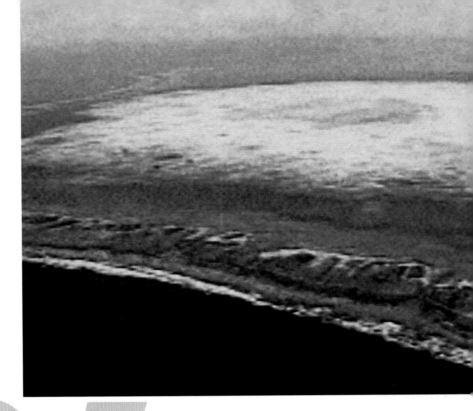

World protest against French nuclear testing

ENVIRONMENT

28 DECEMBER An explosion of international anger and condemnation has greeted France's underground testing of nuclear weapons at the Mururoa Atoll in the southern Pacific Ocean. Yesterday France carried out its fifth underground nuclear test in the French Polynesian islands since September. It used the equivalent of 30 kilotons of explosive, less than in earlier tests in the program, but one and a half times the size of the bomb dropped on Hiroshima in 1945. In November there were violent demonstrations in Tahiti, and protests have come from the governments of Japan, New Zealand, and Australia. Last month 95 countries on the United Nations Disarmament Committee voted for an immediate ban on nuclear testing. France promises to sign a test ban treaty next year, but says it needs to carry out these tests to improve a computer simulation program that it will use in future.

▲ *The Mururoa Atoll in the southern Pacific Ocean.*

Dayton peace agreement

TREATIES

14 DECEMBER The bitter three-year war in former Yugoslavia may finally be at an end. Today in Paris the leaders of the war's Serb, Croat, and Muslim factions signed a peace treaty based on an agreement made in talks at Dayton, Ohio, last month. Franjo Tudjman, Croatia's president, Bosnian Muslim leader Alija Izetbegovic, and Slobodan Milosevic, Serbia's president, shook hands after signing. The war has left 200,000 people dead or missing.

▶ *Signatories to the peace treaty shake hands.*

Barings Bank scandal

LAW

2 DECEMBER Nick Leeson, the 28-year-old financial dealer whose unsupervised, disastrous trading led to the collapse of the distinguished British merchant bank, Barings, was jailed today for six and a half years. Leeson (near left), who worked in Singapore, gambled with the bank's money on the Far East financial markets. He lost more than £800 million, which led to Barings' collapse in late February.

The sheep-pig star

Babe, a big-hearted talking pig who tries his hand at being a sheepdog, is the most unusual screen hero for years. *Babe*, directed by Chris Noonan, uses live animals—including sheep and two collie dogs as well as the pig—for much of the action. The pig in question starts shepherding to avoid being made into Christmas dinner, but is so good at it that he and his owner win the National Sheepdog Trials.

Diana opens her heart on television

ROYALTY

21 NOVEMBER Princess Diana, the estranged wife of Britain's royal heir Prince Charles, has given a sensationally frank interview to the BBC television program *Panorama*. In the interview, broadcast last night, she talked of her unhappy marriage, her love affair with a cavalry officer, and her hopes for the future. Although she thinks it unlikely that she will ever be queen of England, she would like to be regarded as "queen of people's hearts."

▲ *Diana, Princess of Wales, during her television interview.*

NEWS • 1995 • NEWS

4 May • Workers searching the ruins of the bombed Federal building in Oklahoma City, Oklahoma, abandon their search for bodies; the final death toll is 168.

15 June • A rebellion by Iraqi troops against President Saddam Hussein is defeated by loyal soldiers.

22 June • Japanese police free 365 passengers held on a hijacked airliner at Hakodate, Japan.

Terrorist gas attack in Tokyo

TERRORISM

20 MARCH Members of a Japanese religious cult released poison gas into a station on the Tokyo subway today, killing 12 people and making 5,000 severely ill. The *Aum Shinrikyo* (Supreme Truth) cult has 2,000 full members and around 30,000 casual followers. Members hold a mixture of Buddhist and Hindu religious beliefs, and follow the orders of their 40-year-old leader Shoko Asahara. Fearing police raids on his headquarters, he instructed cult members to make the deadly gas, sarin, developed by the Nazis during World War II, and use it against commuters.

▶ *Rescueworkers at the scene of the gas attack.*

US *Atlantis* docks with Russian *Mir*

TECHNOLOGY

7 JULY The US space shuttle *Atlantis* landed safely today at the Kennedy Space Center, Florida, after a triumphant 11-day mission during which it docked, or linked up, in Earth orbit with the Russian space station *Mir*. *Atlantis*, whose liftoff on 27 June was the 100th manned launch of the US space program, delivered Russian cosmonauts Anatoly Solovyev and Nikolai Budarin to *Mir* and took US astronaut Norman Thagard on board to return him to Earth. The two spacecraft docked on 29 June and remained connected to each other for five days while the men carried out life sciences experiments.

▶ Atlantis *(bottom) links up with* Mir *in space.*

1990

1991

1992

1993

1994

1995

1996

1997

1998

1999

1996

SCIENCE | British beef ban in BSE scare

22 MARCH British beef farmers are facing ruin. The market for their meat is collapsing because of fears that beef from animals with "mad cow disease," or BSE, can cause Creuzfeldt-Jakob Disease (CJD) in humans. Yesterday Belgium, France, the Netherlands, Portugal, and Sweden banned imports of British beef, and today a wave of other countries followed. There have been several panics over BSE since it first appeared in 1986. Scientific advisers believe it is likely that the rising numbers of CJD cases are "linked to BSE."

▲ *New safety measures in abattoirs and meat processing plants have failed to calm the BSE furore.*

BSE facts

BSE (bovine spongiform encephalopathy) causes spongy holes in the animal's brain. Researchers think the disease was caused by giving cows fodder that included sheep offal—or inner organs.

•

In 1988 British farmers were ordered to slaughter cattle suspected of having BSE. In 1989 the British government banned the use of all beef offal in food. But fears persisted—consumption of British beef fell 12 percent between 1992 and 1996.

▶ *A French scientist examines the brain of a cow diagnosed with BSE.*

"Buzz Lightyear" furor

Buzz Lightyear, one of the heroes of the hit film *Toy Story*, caused a sensation in British stores this Christmas. He was in such demand that Disney had to set up a rush shipment of 17,000 Buzz dolls. *Toy Story* is a computer-generated animation. Buzz and a toy cowboy named Woody fight for their owner Andy's affections.

ROYALTY | Charles and Diana divorce decreed

28 AUGUST The British royal family's troubles continue. Prince Charles' unhappy marriage to Princess Diana ended this morning in London with a final divorce decree. The couple's separation was announced in December 1992, and Diana said that she did not want a divorce for the sake of their sons William and Harry. But she finally agreed to divorce in February this year. Some reports say she received £17 million in the settlement. She remains a member of the royal family and will share caring for the children with Prince Charles.

TERRORISM | Bombing at 100th Olympics, Atlanta

27 JULY A bomb exploded in Centennial Park, Atlanta, early this morning despite tight security in the city, which is playing host to the Olympic Games. A woman was killed and more than 100 people were hurt. Police and Federal Bureau of Investigation (FBI) officers are searching for a motive for the attack. No terrorist group has claimed responsibility. The games, which opened on 19 July, continued today with flags flying at halfmast.

▲ *Rescuers give first aid to people injured in the explosion at Centennial Park in Atlanta.*

Hubble's amazing pictures

4 SEPTEMBER The Hubble Space Telescope has taken amazing pictures of galaxies—or groupings of stars—as they were beginning to form many millions of years ago. Hubble was launched into orbit around the Earth on 24 April 1990. Its extremely powerful lenses can capture light that has been traveling through space to Earth for billions of years—allowing it to record images of events that occurred billions of years ago. Hubble has made 8,000 space observations so far.

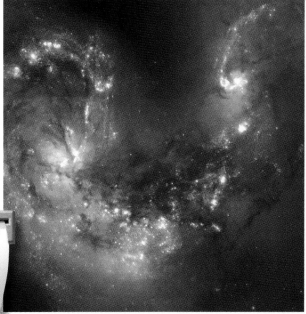

▲ *A fantastic picture of a galaxy taken by Hubble.*

"Magic" moment

Earvin "Magic" Johnson, the 6-foot 9-inch (2.05-meter) tall giant who quit basketball in 1991 because he had the AIDS virus, has made his comeback for the Los Angeles Lakers. This marks a positive step forward in public attitudes to AIDS.

◄ *Magic celebrates an Olympic victory. Knowledge about the risk of infection in contact sports has helped Magic make a comeback.*

TWA flight 800 explodes into sea

18 JULY A passenger jet exploded after takeoff from New York last night, and all 230 people on board were killed. Trans World Airlines (TWA) Flight 800, bound for Paris, took off from John F. Kennedy Airport at 8:19 P.M. but suddenly disappeared from air traffic controllers' radar screens at 8:32 P.M. The cause of the explosion is not known but some people say there was a bomb on board and others that the aircraft was hit by a missile. Divers today began searching for evidence in the Atlantic Ocean. They are hoping to recover the plane's flight recorder.

NEWS • 1996 • NEWS

27 March • *Yigal Amir, assassin of Israel's President Rabin in 1995, is jailed for life.*

24 September • *US, Britain, France, China, and Russia sign a nuclear test ban treaty.*

25–26 September • *Fighting between Palestinians and Israelis in the West Bank and Gaza Strip kills 72.*

27 September • *Former President Najibullah of Afghanistan is executed by militant Islamic rebels.*

Dunblane massacre

14 MARCH A gunman murdered 16 children and one of their teachers in an horrific and unexplained attack on a primary school in the Scottish town of Dunblane yesterday morning. Thomas Hamilton, a 43-year-old former youth leader from the town, walked into the school gymnasium at about 9:30 A.M. and began spraying bullets at the class of five- and six-year-olds. Twelve other children and a second adult were wounded. Hamilton then shot himself.

◄ *Queen Elizabeth II lays a wreath outside Dunblane school.*

▼ *A large section of one of the aircraft's wings floats in the sea after the explosion.*

THE OLYMPICS

▼ Athletes surround the Olympic torch at the opening ceremony of the 1988 Summer Olympics in Seoul.

Every four years, the world's top athletes assemble to compete against each other and the record books in the Olympic Games, the most dramatic of all sports competitions. Years of training and mental preparation must be timed to deliver a peak performance at exactly the right moment.

Founded around 2,000 years ago in ancient Greece, the Olympics were relaunched in 1896 by Frenchman Baron Pierre de Coubertin. In over a hundred years of competition, the games have created an unforgettable gallery of sports heroes and heroines.

▲ Swiss ice skater Denise Biellmann thrilled the crowd but came fourth in the 1980 women's figure-skating contest.

The Winter Olympics

▼ French skier Jean Claude Killy was the star in the 1968 Winter Olympics in Grenoble.

When the Olympics were revived last century, winter sports did not play a big part in the first few games. Although figure skating was one of the sports in 1908 in London, and ice hockey was added in Antwerp in 1920, there was no bobsledding or skiing.

Calls for a separate Olympics for winter sports were opposed by Norway, Finland, and Sweden, who thought that a new competition would overshadow their own Nordic Games. But the International Olympic Committee (IOC)—the body that governs the games—agreed to an International Winter Sports Week in Chamonix, France, in 1924, and it was a triumph. The first Winter Games were held in the Swiss ski resort of St. Moritz in February 1928. Sports included cross-country skiing, ski jumping, figure skating, speed skating, bobsledding, and ice hockey. Norwegian skier Johan Gröttumsbraaten and Finnish speed skater Clas Thunberg were the top achievers, winning two gold medals each.

The Winter Games were held in the same year as the Summer Games until 1992. They were then held in 1994 in Lillehammer, Norway, and in 1998 in Nagano, Japan, and will take place every four years, two years after the Summer Games.

Some Top Winter athletes

- Norwegian cross-country skier Björn Daehlie: 8 gold medals.
- Soviet speed skater Lidia Skoblikova and Russian cross-country skier Lyubov Egorova: 6 gold.
- Speed skaters Clas Thunberg (Finland), Eric Heiden (USA), and Bonnie Blair (USA): 5 gold.
- Cross-country skiers Sixten Jernberg (Sweden) and Raisa Smetanina (USSR): 4 gold.
- German figure skater Katerina Witt (right): 2 gold.

◀ In 1964, Soviet skater Lidia Skoblikova won gold medals in all the women's speed skating competitions.

◄ The 1900 US Olympic team.

The Summer Olympics

In 1896, 211 competitors from 14 countries took part in the first modern games in Athens. In 1992, 9,364 athletes from 169 countries competed in Barcelona. The games were launched as a festival of pure sport. The ruling principles were that competing in the right spirit is far more important than winning and that no professional athletes should be allowed to enter.

The Olympic ideals have come under great pressure, and since 1981, some professionals have been allowed to compete. It has been impossible to keep the games free of politics—official boycotts hit the contest in 1976, 1980, and 1984.

◄ Canadian Ann Montmimy in 1992.

▲ American athlete Bob Beamon set a long jump record of 8.90 meters in 1968. It stood for 23 years.

Perfect gymnastics

Romanian gymnast Nadia Comaneci won three gold medals, one silver, and one bronze at the age of 14 at the 1976 games in Montreal. She was the first Olympic gymnast to score a perfect mark of 10.00, and did it seven times during the games.

Nadia was spotted at the age of seven by top Romanian coach Bela Karolyi and trained intensively for years. She was nicknamed "Little Miss Perfect."

▲ Nadia Comaneci performs on the beam.

Some Top Summer Olympics athletes

- American athlete Ray Ewry: 10 gold medals.
  - Soviet gymnast Larissa Latynina (18 medals in total), Finnish runner Paavo Nurmi (12 in total) and Americans, swimmer Mark Spitz (11 in total) and athlete Carl Lewis (10 in total): 9 gold.
  - American swimmer Matt Biondi (11 in total): 8 gold.
    - Soviet gymnast Nikolai Andrianov (15 in total): 7 gold.
      - Czech gymnast Vera Cáslavská (11 in total): 7 gold.
        - Italian fencer Edoardo Mangiarotti (13 in total): 6 gold.
        - Romanian gymnast Nadia Comaneci: 5 gold.
        - American athlete Jesse Owens: 4 gold.
      - American athlete Florence Griffith Joyner: 3 gold.

▲ Jesse Owens

▼ Florence Griffith Joyner

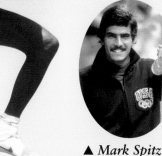

▲ Carl Lewis

▲ Mark Spitz

1990
1991
1992
1993
1994
1995
1996
1997
1998
1999

1997

A nation mourns as the "Queen of Hearts" is laid to rest

6 SEPTEMBER The funeral of Diana, Princess of Wales, was held today in Westminster Abbey. Vast crowds watched the two-hour ceremonial procession as her coffin was taken on a horsedrawn gun-carriage from her west London home, Kensington Palace, to the Abbey. In the six days since she was killed in a car accident, a wave of national mourning has swept Britain.

Diana died on 31 August after the Mercedes limousine in which she was traveling crashed at high speed in a tunnel near the Seine River. She was visiting Paris with her friend Dodi Fayed—son of Mohammed al-Fayed, the Egyptian millionaire and owner of Harrod's department store. Dodi and the car's driver, Henri Paul, also died in the crash.

Within hours of the announcement of her death, crowds began to gather at Kensington Palace. All week they have been flocking there to pay their respects, creating a vast mountain of floral tributes to the Princess who never sat on the British throne but who succeeded in her wish to be "queen of people's hearts."

▲ *Diana, Princess of Wales.*

▼ *Floral tributes for Diana outside Kensington Palace.*

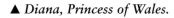

▼ *Diana's sons, second and fourth from left, follow her*

Earthquake in Assisi

27 SEPTEMBER A series of earthquakes struck central Italy yesterday, killing 11 and injuring more than 100 people. They also damaged one of the region's great tourist attractions, the 13th-century basilica of Saint Francis in the hilltop town of Assisi. Parts of the basilica's ceiling fell in, and two 13th-century frescoes, or wall paintings, were destroyed. The tomb of Saint Francis and two frescoes by the great artist Giotto survived. Further tremors were felt today, and Pope John Paul II made a statement expressing sympathy and sorrow. Around 5,000 people have been made homeless by the earthquakes.

▲ *Rescuers carry stones from the roof of the basilica of St. Francis.*

"Candle in the Wind" is biggest-selling single

British rock star Elton John, sang an adapted version of his hit "Candle in the Wind" at Diana's funeral. The song, originally written about Hollywood actress Marilyn Monroe, was released as the single "Candle in the Wind '97," with profits going to a memorial fund for the Princess. On 21 October it was declared the biggest-selling single ever—with 31.8 million sales.

◀ *Elton John sings for England's princess.*

Saintly "Mother" dies

13 SEPTEMBER Mother Teresa (born Agnes Gonxha Bojaxhiu), the Roman Catholic nun who dedicated her life to working with and for the world's poorest people, died on 5 September of a heart attack, aged 87. She named herself Sister Teresa after the Catholic patron saint of missionaries, Saint Teresa of Lisieux. Her adopted home was Calcutta in eastern India where she began her work in the city's slums in 1948.

▶ *Mother Teresa's funeral procession.*

Labour wins landslide victory

2 MAY Yesterday's British general election brought a dramatic end to 18 years of government by the Conservative Party.

The Labour Party, led by Tony Blair, won a stunning majority of 179 seats in the House of Commons. Several senior Conservatives including Defence Secretary Michael Portillo and Foreign Secretary Malcolm Rifkind lost their seats.

Blair, aged 43, fought a cautious election campaign as "New Labour." The Conservatives' image seems to have been tarnished by allegations of corruption.

Land speed record broken in US desert

On 25 September in the Nevada Desert, RAF pilot Andy Green broke the land speed record in the British jet-powered car *Thrust SSC*. He hit 1,149.300 km per hour (714.144 miles per hour). On 15 October he did even better—the car hit 1,232.930 km per hour (766.109 miles per hour), becoming the first land vehicle to break the sound barrier.

Hale-Bopp arrives

Comet Hale-Bopp—named for its discoverers American astronomers Alan Hale and Thomas Bopp—hurtled past the Earth in spring 1997. It is a ball of rock, dust, and ice. The Sun's heat evaporates some of the ice, creating Hale-Bopp's tail. In the northern hemisphere it could be seen without telescopes in April.

▲ *The British jet car,* Thrust SSC, *driven by Andy Green.*

Hong Kong is Chinese again

▼ *Chris Patten, last governor of Hong Kong is handed the Union Jack flag.*

1 JULY At midnight last night, control of Hong Kong, a British colony since 1842, passed back to China under an agreement signed in 1984. Yesterday Britain held splendid farewell ceremonies in the colony. The British national anthem was played as Chris Patten, the 28th and last colonial Governor, left his residence in Government House with his family. He joined Prince Charles, British Prime Minister Tony Blair, and Chinese Premier Jiang Zemin at a farewell banquet.

China's communist leaders have promised not to interfere with Hong Kong's capitalist system, but it is not clear what the future holds.

▲ *A soldier from the Chinese People's Liberation Army stands on a tank as it crosses into the new territory.*

Sumatra in forest fire blaze

15 OCTOBER The skies over Southeast Asia are thick with smoke and soot from forest fires—some of which were started by farmers and lumber merchants to clear land—that have been blazing out of control for months in Indonesia. Last month the authorities in neighboring Malaysia declared a state of emergency because of "hazardous" air pollution. On 24 September more than 1,000 Malaysian firefighters arrived in Sumatra. The Pacific weather pattern El Niño has made matters worse by bringing hot weather instead of the monsoon rains that would help put the fires out.

▼ *From left to right, Sporty, Baby, Scary, Posh, and Ginger Spice.*

▶ *Two Malaysian firemen wearing gas masks battle forest fires in Bayung Lincir, in Sumatra.*

Five girls spice up pop world

"Girlpower" swept all before it in 1997. The Spice Girls—an all-girl British pop band, inspired by the success of all-boy bands such as Take That and Boyzone—had hits all over the world. They also made ads for Pepsi, released a book, and starred in a movie, *Spiceworld*. The five do everything with in an in-your-face style. They are Melanie C (Sporty), Victoria (Posh), Emma (Baby), Melanie B (Scary) and Geri (Ginger).

IRA peace talks

POLITICS

7 OCTOBER The search for peace in the British province of Northern Ireland began a new phase today. Irish nationalists, who believe the province should be part of a united Ireland, and Unionists, who want to keep the link with Britain, joined negotiations with the British and Irish governments. Gerry Adams, leader of Sinn Fèin, the Irish nationalist party with links to the IRA, said today that the party is "committed to democratic and peaceful methods of resolving problems."

◀ *Sinn Fein president Gerry Adams (center).*

NEWS • 1997 • NEWS

19 February • *Chinese leader Deng Xiaoping dies, aged 92.*

13 April • *American golfer Tiger Woods, aged 21, becomes the youngest winner ever of US Masters tournament.*

16 May • *Zairean dictator Mobutu Sese Seko flees. Laurent Kabila prepares for power.*

13 June • *Timothy McVeigh, 29, is sentenced to death for his part in the Oklahoma City bombing of 1995.*

Judge overturns jury's verdict

LAW

10 NOVEMBER An American judge today freed Louise Woodward, the British au pair who was facing life in prison after Matthew Eappen, the baby she was looking after, died of brain injuries. On 31 October a jury found her guilty of second-degree murder, but today Judge Hiller Zobel reduced the conviction to "involuntary manslaughter." He said the 279 days Woodward has already been imprisoned awaiting trial and sentencing were punishment enough.

▲ *Louise Woodward and one of her defense lawyers in court.*

Oldest woman dies at 122

Frenchwoman Jeanne Calment, born in 1875, died on 4 August, aged 122. Since 1993 she had been the world's oldest person. She outlived her daughter, who died in 1934, and her grandson who died in 1963. She said that her sense of humor helped keep her alive.

Planet Mars pictures

TECHNOLOGY

30 SEPTEMBER Scientists lost radio contact three days ago with the *Pathfinder* spacecraft that landed on the planet Mars on 4 July. They suspect that low battery power is the problem. But the project has already been a triumphant success—*Pathfinder* has worked for three times longer than the 30 days that scientists expected. It has sent back to Earth 16,000 pictures of the Red Planet taken from the landing craft and a further 550 taken from the rover *Sojourner*.

▼ *The six-wheeled* Sojourner *has analyzed surface rocks as well as taking pictures.*

1990

1991

1992

1993

1994

1995

1996

1997

1998

1999

DISASTERS

Hurricane hits Central America

4 NOVEMBER The Central American states of Honduras and Nicaragua have been laid waste by the fourth strongest hurricane to sweep the Caribbean this century. Hurricane Mitch brought torrential rains which left vast areas of countryside under water. Whole villages have been buried by landslides of mud and rock. One Honduran woman, Laura Arriola, was rescued by a British frigate today after spending six days drifting in the Caribbean Sea, clinging to floating debris. The death toll is currently estimated at around 10,000, with more than a million people homeless. It will be years before the two countries recover from the devastation.

▲ *The hurricane has created an economic disaster zone, cutting roads and bridges, and destroying valuable banana plantations.*

Hosts France win World Cup

SPORT

12 JULY Thousands of jubilant French people are celebrating on the streets of Paris this evening after their national soccer team won the World Cup for the first time. In front of a home crowd, France beat Brazil, the holders of the trophy, 3–0 thanks to two goals from Zinedine Zidane and another from Emmanuel Petit. Brazil were hampered by the poor form of their top player, Ronaldo, who was seriously ill before the final and almost did not play.

The staging of the tournament in France has generally been judged a success, although some soccer hooligans were involved in violent clashes with police.

▲ *Zidane heads the second of his goals for France. The midfielder was the hero of the French team.*

▼ *Rescue workers search the rubble of an office block destroyed in the bombing.*

TERRORISM

Bombs destroy US embassies in Africa

7 AUGUST At 10.30 this morning, terrorists exploded huge car bombs outside the American embassies in two eastern African cities—Nairobi in Kenya and Dar-es-Salaam in Tanzania. This synchronized double attack is believed to be the work of Islamic extremists. Although the terrorists' target was clearly the United States, most of those killed and maimed by the bombs were Africans. The heaviest casualties occurred in Nairobi, where more than 200 people have died. In all, 12 Americans have lost their lives. A grim President Bill Clinton described the terrorist attacks as "inhuman" and immediately promised "to bring those responsible to justice, no matter what or how long it takes."

Clinton testifies in Lewinsky scandal

21 SEPTEMBER President Bill Clinton risks being driven out of office as a result of an affair with a young admirer, Monica Lewinsky. The affair became public knowledge after a friend of Lewinsky, Linda Tripp, secretly recorded conversations in which Lewinsky spoke of sexual encounters in the White House. The president was obliged to testify to a grand jury about the affair. Today, Americans were glued to their television sets as the videotapes of his testimony were aired. Early indications show that Clinton's reputation does not seem to have been harmed by the broadcast.

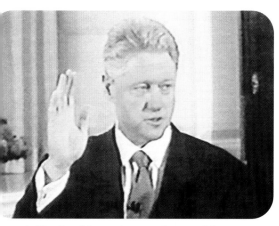
▲ *During his testimony the president seemed composed, although at times he showed impatience with the questioning.*

NEWS • 1998 • NEWS

4 May • *Theodore Kaczynski is found guilty of being the Unabomber.*

15 August • *A car bomb murders 28 people in Omagh, Northern Ireland.*

21 September • *Sprinter Florence Griffith Joyner, winner of three gold medals at the 1988 Olympics, dies aged 38.*

16 December • *The US and Britain bomb Iraq after Saddam Hussein blocks UN weapons inspections.*

John Glenn returns to space

29 OCTOBER Veteran astronaut John Glenn today became the oldest man ever launched into space. The 77-year-old senator is one of the seven-man crew of the space shuttle *Discovery*, which lifted off from Cape Canaveral on a nine-day mission. It is Glenn's second space voyage. In 1962, he was the first American ever to orbit the Earth. Glenn's return to space has excited massive interest. About 250,000 people crowded the area around Cape Canaveral to witness the launch.

▲ *John Glenn (top right) and fellow crew members.*

Disaster movie sweeps the board at the Oscars

The disaster movie *Titanic*, already a monster hit at the box office, triumphed at the Oscars. It took 11 Academy Awards, equaling the record set by *Ben Hur* in 1960. But the Oscar winners did not include the movie's stars, Leonardo DiCaprio and Kate Winslet (below).

McGwire breaks homer record

9 SEPTEMBER Mark McGwire of the St. Louis Cardinals has broken the most revered record in baseball. In front of 50,000 delirious Cardinals fans at Busch Stadium, McGwire hit his 62nd home run of the season, surpassing the record set by Roger Maris of the New York Yankees in 1961. As the president phoned to offer his congratulations on behalf of the nation, McGwire told the press: "People have been saying it is bringing the country together. So be it. I am happy to bring the country together."

Worldwide demand for Viagra

A new wonder pill, Viagra, came on the market this year, promising a cure for sexual impotence, which afflicts one man in ten. The drug has proved popular all over the world and it has become the fastest-selling prescription drug. There are, however, some concerns about the pills' safety.

▼ *Kosovan refugees struggle for a few loaves of bread.*

WAR

Refugees flee Kosovo as NATO takes on Serbs

17 APRIL Reports published today estimate that about 600,000 ethnic Albanians from the Yugoslav province of Kosovo have become refugees since the Yugoslav government launched a full-scale "ethnic cleansing" campaign there last month. Serb-dominated Yugoslav forces are systematically destroying villages and driving out their population, as well as perpetrating massacres and other atrocities. The current crisis began on 19 March, when Yugoslavia's Serbian leader, Slobodan Milosevic, refused to accept a NATO-brokered peace agreement with the Kosovan Liberation Army, which is fighting for independence from Yugoslav rule. As NATO launched air strikes against targets in Yugoslavia, Milosevic ordered ethnic cleansing on a grand scale. NATO leaders have been wrong-footed by Milosevic's aggressive stance. They have stepped up air attacks, targeting Serbian oil supplies, communications, and army command and control centers. But they have been unable to defend the Kosovans against the campaign of atrocities.

◀ *A Serbian government building in flames after a NATO air strike.*

NEWS • 1999 • NEWS

12 February • *The Senate acquits President Clinton over the Lewinsky affair, ending impeachment.*

7 May • *NATO planes mistakenly bomb the Chinese Embassy in Belgrade, Serbia, killing three people.*

25 October • *Ryder Cup golfer Payne Stewart dies in air crash.*

31 December • *The hijacking of an Indian Airlines plane by Islamic militants ends peacefully.*

▼ *Euro coins will come into daily use in Europe in 2002.*

ECONOMICS

Euro currency is introduced

1 JANUARY Eleven member states of the European Union (EU) today launched a single currency, the "euro." The countries taking part in the new monetary union have a combined population of 290 million, comparable to that of the United States. The only EU countries staying outside the "euro zone" were Britain, Denmark, Sweden, and Greece. Old currencies such as the French franc and German mark have not disappeared overnight, however. Euro notes and coins will not replace national currencies in everyday use until 2002.

Funeral of Jordan's respected monarch

POLITICS

8 FEBRUARY King Hussein of Jordan was buried today in the presence of dignitaries from around the world, come to pay their last respects to one of the most admired rulers in the Middle East. Those present included President Bill Clinton and three former US presidents—George Bush, Jimmy Carter, and Gerald Ford. King Hussein, who had ruled Jordan since 1952, died after a long battle against cancer. He is succeeded by his eldest son, the 37-year-old King Abdullah II. Many observers fear that, with the death of Hussein, an important force for peace and moderation in the Middle East has been lost.

▲ *King Hussein's coffin is accompanied by Jordanian soldiers.*

Olympic committee in bribery scandal

SPORT

21 JANUARY The reputation of the Olympic games has been tarnished by a bribery scandal involving members of the International Olympic Committee (IOC). The scandal was a result of the fierce competition between cities wanting to host the 2000 Summer Games and the 2002 Winter Games. The winning cities, Sydney and Salt Lake City, had given cash and favors to win votes in the IOC. There have been calls for the IOC's chairman, Juan Antonio Samaranch, to resign, but he made it plain at a press conference today that he intends to stay.

▼ *Sydney celebrates winning the contest to stage the Olympic Games in 2000.*

School slaying shocks America

DISASTERS

21 APRIL Columbine High School in the quiet suburb of Littleton, Colorado, was yesterday the scene of carnage as two teenagers, Dylan Klebold, 17, and Eric Harris, 18, ran amok, killing 12 students and a teacher before turning their guns on themselves. The boys also injured 28, ten of whom are in a critical condition in hospital. In addition to four firearms, the boys had 30 homemade bombs in their armory. They were obsessed with the Nazis and had timed the massacre to coincide with Hitler's birthday. Police are concerned that further attacks by linked right-wing extremist groups may follow.

Total eclipse of the Sun

The last full solar eclipse of the millennium took place on 11 August, crossing western England, mainland Europe, the Middle East, and South Asia. The next total eclipse of the Sun to be seen from Britain will be in 2090.

Michael Jordan retires

On 12 January, Michael "Air" Jordan, possibly the greatest basketball player of all time, announced his retirement. From 1991 to 1998, Jordan won six NBA championships with the Chicago Bulls. His $35-million salary made him the world's highest-paid sportsman. An inscription on a statue of Jordan in Chicago reads: "Best there ever was, best there ever will be."

◄ *Michael Jordan was the third-highest points scorer in the history of the NBA.*

Major quake devastates Turkish cities

DISASTERS

17 AUGUST In the early hours of this morning, a densely populated area of northwest Turkey was struck by an earthquake registering 7.5 on the Richter scale. Along the Asian shore of the Sea of Marmara from Istanbul to Golcuk, tens of thousands of buildings were destroyed in little more than a minute. A huge tidal wave added to the destruction, hurling boats far inshore. Damage has been recorded as far afield as the Turkish capital, Ankara, more than 180 miles (300 km) from the epicenter of the earthquake. It is already apparent that many thousands must have died. As the desperate search begins for survivors trapped in the rubble of collapsed buildings, popular anger is mounting, directed both at the government, which has been slow to respond to the catastrophe, and at construction companies who are accused of putting up shoddy buildings that collapsed when the first tremor of the earthquake struck.

▲ *A weeping woman stands in front of the rubble of her home in Golcuk, Turkey, after the earthquake.*

UN force goes in to Timor

WAR

19 SEPTEMBER A UN peacekeeping force has arrived in Indonesian-ruled East Timor to put a stop to an orgy of violence that has shocked the world. After four-fifths of East Timorese voted for independence last month, pro-Indonesian militiamen went on the rampage, burning buildings and driving much of the population from their homes. The UN peacekeepers, the majority of whom are Australian, have begun disarming the militias and distributing relief food supplies.

◀ *Australian troops arrest militiamen in East Timor.*

The curse of the Kennedy family strikes down J.F.K., Jr.

PEOPLE

17 JULY The tragic history of the Kennedy family took a new twist today when 38-year-old John F. Kennedy, Jr., son of the president assassinated in 1963, was killed in an air crash. Kennedy was piloting a light aircraft with his wife, Carolyn, and his sister-in-law, Lauren Bessette, on board. They took off from New Jersey airport late last night, heading for a family wedding at Hyannis Port, Massachusetts. The plane was meant to stop off at Martha's Vineyard en route, but disappeared in mist and darkness over the Atlantic Ocean. An air-sea search is in progress, but there are no hopes of finding survivors.

▶ *John F. Kennedy, Jr., and his wife, Carolyn.*

Floyd floods the Carolinas

DISASTERS

17 SEPTEMBER Relieved Americans today saw Hurricane Floyd, one of the most feared weather systems of modern times, drift away northward after spreading panic along the eastern seabord. Whipping up winds estimated at 155 mph (250 kph), Hurricane Floyd provoked what Vice-President Al Gore called "the biggest peacetime evacuation in US history". Over 3 million people quit their homes along the coast, a mass flight resulting in huge traffic jams. The hurricane came to shore at Cape Fear in North Carolina, causing the worst flooding in the state's history. About 1,500 people were rescued from rooftops by helicopter. Travel, power supplies and communications were disrupted along the length of the eastern seabord. However, with a reported death toll in single figures, some are accusing the authorities of overreacting.

Ancient mammoth found

An expedition led by French explorer Bernard Buigues has dug the deep-frozen body of a woolly mammoth out of the Siberian permafrost. It is the first complete specimen of this long-extinct animal to be found. There are hopes that it may be possible to use its genetic material to create a living mammoth clone, using a cow elephant as a surrogate mother.

DISASTERS Paddington rail disaster as commuter trains collide

▼ *The scene after the Paddington crash.*

5 OCTOBER At least 30 people are known to have died in a collision between two commuter trains outside Paddington station in London, England, this morning. An inbound express, believed to be carrying over 500 people, ran head-on into a slower turbo train that had just left Paddington. A fireball engulfed part of the wreckage, inflicting terrible burns on many survivors. The search for bodies is expected to continue for several days. Accident investigators have already established that the turbo train passed through a red light at signal 109.

▲ *Explorer Bernard Buigues observes the tusks of the woolly mammoth in Siberia.*

Cancer survivor wins Tour

SPORT

25 JULY An American cyclist who three years ago almost died of cancer has today triumphed in the Tour de France, one of the world's most gruelling sports events. Lance Armstrong, a 27-year-old from Texas, suffered from testicular cancer that spread to his lungs and brain. He survived only after chemotherapy and extensive surgery. Armstrong attributed today's victory – by a margin of 7 minutes 37 seconds – in part to the experience of fighting disease. He told the press, "What doesn't kill you makes you stronger."

◄ *Cyclist Lance Armstrong celebrates his remarkable victory.*

Another Star Wars hit

The Phantom Menace is the latest of George Lucas's *Star Wars* series of movies – despite being billed as "Episode 1". Boasting some of the best special effects ever seen, this much-hyped prequel took a record $28.5 million on its first day in US cinemas.

▲ *Darth Maul,* Phantom Menace *villain.*

A NEW MILLENNIUM

The end of the 20th century was also the end of the second thousand-year period, or millennium, of the Christian era. The event was marked by worldwide celebrations from midnight on 31 December 1999 – despite some claims that this was a year early, with the new millennium not really due to begin until the end of 2000.

The occasion provided a chance for reflection on the achievements and tragedies of the 20th century, and for the expression of the hopes and fears of the Earth's six billion people as the third millennium dawned. Former South African President Nelson Mandela pointed out that the century was closing with "most people still languishing in poverty". But US President Bill Clinton looked to the future, saying: "The light may be fading on the 20th century, but the sun is still rising on America."

▼ *Time Square, the traditional focus of New Year celebrations in New York, was packed for the millennium eve.*

▼ *As the new year dawned fireworks lit up the Washington Monument in Washington D.C.*

Partying on millennium eve

The celebrations on millennium eve have been described as the biggest party in history. As midnight moved across the globe westward from the international dateline in the Pacific, a wave of festivities moved with it. Highlights included a spectacular firework display in Sydney, Australia, a laser light show at the pyramids outside Cairo, Egypt, and a carnival in Rio de Janeiro, Brazil. Thousands of doves were released at Bethlehem in Palestine, believed by Christians to be the site of Jesus' birth 2,000 years ago. In Rome, some 50,000 pilgrims gathered to hear an address from Pope John Paul II. Paris was recovering from some of the worst storms of the 20th century, which had struck the French capital during the previous week, but still managed to stage an artistic firework display at the Eiffel Tower. In London, England, an estimated three million people lined the Thames, witnessing the opening of the Dome, a 15-minute pyrotechnic display on the river and a laser show focusing on the London Eye, the world's tallest observation wheel, which was built to mark the millennium. In the United States, New Yorkers massed to celebrate in Times Square, while President Clinton ushered in the new millennium in Washington DC at a party on the Mall.

Counting the years to the millennium

Over many centuries, the Christian civilization of Europe came to arrange the dating of years from the estimated birth date of the infant Jesus. This system, which gave the number 2000 to the year in question, has become known in all parts of the world. But many alternative methods of counting the years still exist. For Muslims, for example, "millennium eve" fell during the festival of Ramadan in the year 1420. China claimed to be celebrating the 5,000th year of its civilization.

▲ *The birth of the baby Jesus in Bethlehem, related in the Bible, was taken by Christians as year one of a new era.*

The "bug" that failed to bite

There were dire warnings that a millennium "bug" might cause a widespread breakdown of computer systems at the end of 1999, as many were not programmed to recognize the year 2000 as a possible date. Experts warned that everything from water supplies to power stations and air traffic control networks might fail. There were even fears that nuclear missiles could be launched by faulty computers. In the event, however, only minor problems were reported.

Cults of millennial doom

The approach of the new millennium caused great excitement among some Christian fundamentalists, looking forward to the "second coming" of Christ, and "doomsday" cults, believing in an imminent apocalypse that would end the world as we know it. The arrival of the year 2000 seemed to them a likely moment for such prophecies to be fulfilled. Extremist groups in the United States encouraged people to take to nuclear shelters and stockpile food in preparation for "Y2K". The authorities were worried that cultists, such as the Japanese *Aum Shinrikyo*, might attempt to stage a major terrorist outrage on millennium eve in an effort to make the apocalypse happen.

◀ *Japanese Aum Shinrikyo cult leaders.*

▲ *Fears that the "millennium bug" would lead to catastrophic failures in air traffic control, dependent upon computers, proved groundless.*

Who was first to the millennium?

▼ *Fiji's Turtle Island was one place claiming to be the first to reach 2000.*

Several Pacific islands just west of the international dateline claimed to be the first to enter the new millennium. The Republic of Kiribati renamed one of its islands Millennium Island, claiming to lead the festivities. Fiji, on the other hand, asserted that its Turtle Island had pre-eminence. But the first people to enter the year 2000 may in fact have been the crew of the US submarine Topeka, which was submerged in the Pacific precisely on the dateline.